For
Claire & Allen
from
Paul & Gill
with love

Autumn 1980

The Herb & Spice Book

The Herb & Spice Book

Sarah Garland

Frances Lincoln
Weidenfeld
& Nicolson

Editors: Felicity Luard

Nonie Niesewand

Art editor: Sally Smallwood

Designer: Tim Foster

Picture research: Jackie Burgess

Editorial secretary: Antonia Demetriadi

First published in Great Britain by Frances Lincoln Publishers Limited,
Mortimer House, 37-41 Mortimer Street, London W1N 7RJ
in association with Weidenfeld and Nicolson Limited,
91 Clapham High Street, London SW4 7TA

ISBN: 0-906459-00-1

Filmset in Monophoto Bembo by Keyspools Limited, Golborne, Lancashire
Colour separations by Newsele Litho Limited, Italy
Printed and bound in Italy

Publishers' acknowledgments
The publishers would like to thank Liz Butler and Deborah King for their superb
watercolour drawings in the *Modern herbal;* Christine Hanscomb, Alan Randall
and Rolph Gobits for their special photography for *Cooking with herbs and spices,
Household herbs and spices* and *Cosmetic herbs;* Pamla Toler for her photographs
and Coral Mula for her drawings.

They also gratefully acknowledge Dr Martin Rix and members of staff at the
Royal Horticultural Society, Wisley, for authenticating the botanical names; Bob
Press of the Natural History Museum for his invaluable assistance in verifying
plant descriptions and for his tireless checking of the drawings; and John D.
Hyde, FNIMH, President of the National Institute of Medical Herbalists for his
comments on the chapter *Herbs for health.*

Finally thanks are due to Dinah Morrison for producing many delicious
dishes for the cookery photography; to Jan Palmer and Norma MacMillan for
their help with the American edition; to Vicki Robinson for reading the proofs;
and to Douglas Matthews of the London Library for a clear and comprehensive
index.

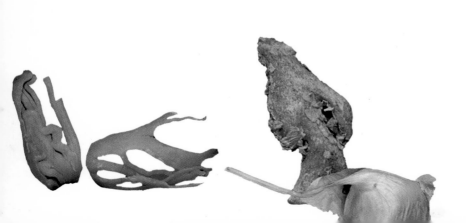

Author's acknowledgments
First I would like to thank Michael Bull for his help and
encouragement. Jane Mann from the Rose Tree Restaurant,
Bourton-on-the-Water, and Prudence Piper have given help and
ideas for new recipes and John Stephen from the Cotswold
Perfumery Ltd, Bourton-on-the-Water has given advice on the
extraction of herb oils. Marianne Monaco has experimented with
many cosmetic oils and ointments and my sister Bryony Hough
has helped me with candle making. Vanessa Roberts from
Dartington, Devonshire has given much help with the dyeing
section. I have been given quantities of unusual herb plants,
especially thyme species, by Tumbler's Bottom Herb Farm,
Kilmersdon, Somerset, and also by Mrs Rosemary Verey from
Barnsley House in Gloucestershire. Finally I must acknowledge
with many thanks the London Library, whose Trustees have given
me a grant during the last three years.

Contents

A modern herbal

The herb garden

Cooking with herbs and spices

Household herbs and spices

Cosmetic herbs

Herbs for health

History and traditions

Long before recorded history, men and women created patterns and rituals to accompany the essential tasks of plant gathering and animal hunting, and the commemoration of birth and death. Plant gathering, and later the sowing and harvesting of crops and herbs, were especially bound up with the power of the elements, the changing forces of the sun, moon and the seasons, and woven into myths of gods and demons and universal legends. Herbal medicine, which is traditional in every country, played an integral part in these legends as it gradually developed from the eating of herbs as part of the general diet – when sharp–tasting aromatic or bitter plants were instinctively gathered to satisfy the body's needs – to elaborate ceremonies directed by a powerful member of society.

It is easy to see that plants with appetizing, pleasant or innocuous tastes would play a vital part in man's diet, and that each would assume a strong character of its own according to its appearance, scent and habitat. Plantain for instance, although it has little flavour and a modest aspect, nevertheless assumed a powerful and widespread reputation as a protective and magical herb, probably because it flourished in the most hostile conditions on paths and trackways, withstanding constant crushing. It is vividly described in an old pre-Christian charm:

Over you chariots rolled, over you queens rode,
Over you brides cried, over you bulls belled;
All these you withstood and these you confounded,
So withstand now the venom that flies through the air.

It is at first more difficult to understand why plants that are clearly poisonous and dangerous, such as henbane with its foetid smell, sticky leaves and unpleasant taste, began to be used medicinally. But if the old connection between illness and evil spirits is considered, then it seems quite rational to use a nauseous medicine to drive the devils out, and a plant that has the power to provoke delirium and frenzy (and even death) in the patient would surely

The high cost of spices meant that even in the wealthiest households they were locked away in special cupboards or boxes.

have a violent effect upon demons. Guilt, too, was connected with illness, the powerful gods smiting man as a punishment for his sins, so a nauseous medicine would become a penance, a propitiation to the gods. Even today there is a basic and instinctive feeling that medicine should be nasty in order to be effective.

During these early and unrecorded times, two simple ideas for herbal treatment developed that were later extended and called the 'doctrine of similars' or 'signatures' and the 'doctrine of contraries'. The first used the appearance or character of the plant as a clue to its use as a medical treatment, for instance, the red juice that can be pressed from the flowers of St John's wort indicated its use as a wound herb, and the fact that parsley piert (or breakstone) often grows on stony ground was a sign that it was a treatment for gravel or stone in the bladder or kidney. This doubtful premise was carried to great lengths by some 16th- and 17th-century herbalists, particularly by an Austrian doctor known as Paracelsus, an Italian called Giambattista Porta, and an Englishman, William Cole. Porta made exaggerated claims for the signature doctrine, insisting that plants with short lives, would shorten the lives of men, and that those with curved, jointed shoots would cure scorpion stings. An allied and popular idea was that, in the words of a 17th-century herbalist, 'For what Climate soever is subject to any particular Disease, in the same Place there grows a Cure' – or that the cure is to be found with the cause. The second idea, the doctrine of contraries, attempted to restore the natural balance within a diseased body by using herbs with properties opposed to the symptoms of the illness; thus, cool, moist herbs would be used to counteract a hot, drying fever. This theory was allied to the later Classical division of all matter into four elements, air, water, fire and earth, with their corresponding bodily humours, sanguine, phlegmatic, choleric and melancholic, which was fundamental to Western medicine until the late 17th century.

The earliest surviving illustrated herbal is a copy of Dioscorides' De Materia Medica, *the* Codex Vindobonensis *of AD 512, which displays a standard of botanical accuracy that was not to be surpassed for centuries. The dog rose* **above** *and bramble* **opposite** *are two examples of the fine watercolour illustrations.*

Of the first known herbal, said to have been written by the legendary Chinese emperor, Shen Nung, nearly 5,000 years ago, only part of the text survived long enough to be recorded by subsequent writers though many later Chinese herbals were based upon it. Other existing herbal texts from these early times include a list of a thousand plants inscribed on tablets in Sumeria in about 2200 BC, and Egyptian papyri recording the medicinal uses of herbs, dating from 2800 BC. The latter mention marjoram, mint, juniper and other familiar herbs, together with aromatic gums such as frankincense, spices such as cinnamon and cassia, and unguents and ointments made by expressing the oil from herbs or by macerating them in fatty oils such as castor oil. In Egypt the dividing line between medicinal and cosmetic recipes was often blurred, and the priests, who generally controlled the manufacture of these substances, were also in charge of the lavish offerings of incense and fragrant oils in the temples and the precious ointments that were used for embalming the bodies of high-ranking Egyptians.

Spices and aromatics were imported into Egypt in quantity from about 2000 BC, carried from southern Arabia and the East to trading posts established on the eastern borders of the Mediterranean, and taken from there, by camel and mule, to Egypt. The sea-faring Phoenicians also took on cargoes from these ports and sailed with them to Spain and north up the Atlantic coast, trading spices and cloth for tin and salt.

The Phoenicians were still trading in the Mediterranean during the great period of Greek culture, and supplied the city states with spices and aromatics during the long lifetime of the famous Greek doctor, Hippocrates (born c. 460 BC), whose scientific writings and practical work ridiculed the supernatural aspect of primitive medicine. His straightforward, modest books emphasized the importance of diet and hygiene; he included about 400 simple herbal remedies and was also the first to set out the theory that disease is caused by an imbalance between the four bodily humours. (This was further developed by Galen, another influential Greek physician and biologist, in the 2nd century AD.)

A century after Hippocrates, Theophrastus (born 370 BC), a pupil of both Plato and Aristotle, wrote his *Enquiry into Plants*, a study of the structure of plants and the first attempt at plant classification. But although some important theories arose from this 'Aristotelian' botany, it was in those treatises written from a medical rather than from a botanical viewpoint that really practical advances were made towards the identification of herbs and their properties. One most important medical treatise was *De Materia Medica*, written during the 1st century AD by a Greek physician living in Rome, Dioscorides. In it he described 600 herbs with their names and healing virtues. A copy of the manuscript was illustrated in about AD 512 with naturalistic watercolour drawings, and the complete work provided the basis for herbal writing, illustration and medical theory for at least 1,600 years. A contemporary of Dioscorides was Pliny the Elder, a Roman civil servant, whose *Natural History* included several volumes on medical botany. Although his scientific observations were heavily larded with superstition, the sheer size of the work has made it a valuable source of reference for herbal writers.

As the Roman Empire grew and extended northwards through Europe to Britain, so the distribution of many Mediterranean herbs also spread, their seeds and roots being planted by Roman settlers in northern villa gardens, both as food and as medicines. The hardier plants such as fennel and

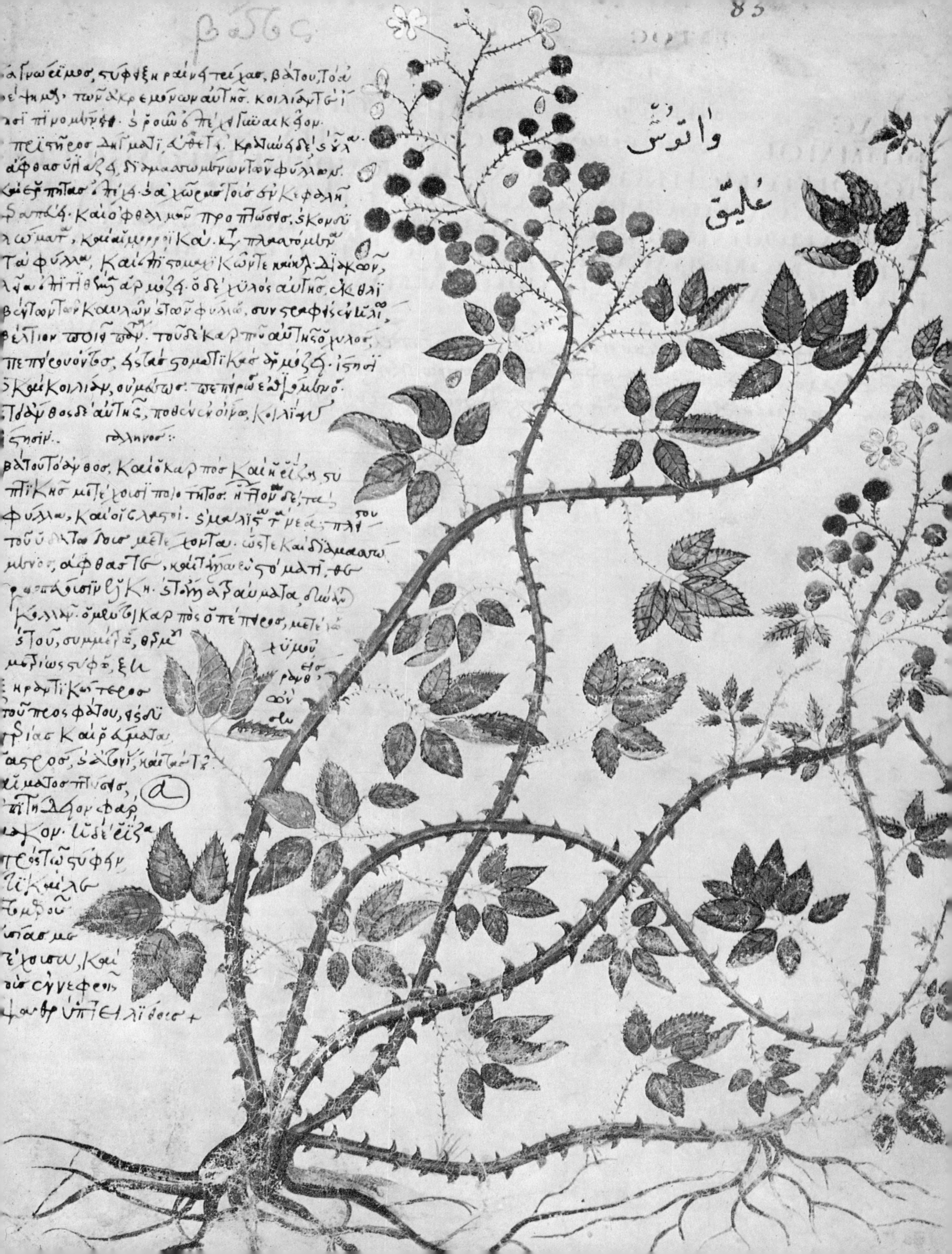

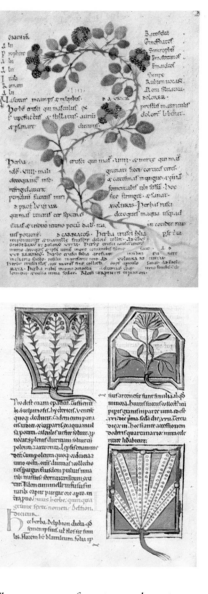

These pages are from two 12th-century English manuscript herbals based on the influential Latin Herbarium of Apuleius Platonicus. *The bramble* **top** *is an unusually naturalistic illustration for this period.*

alexanders soon escaped and became naturalized on open ground along the coasts and round human habitations, while herbs such as dill, savory, rosemary, parsley, garlic, mustard, garden mint and garden thyme, hyssop, sage and many others, have probably remained in continuous cultivation in the north ever since. (The only parallel to such a large-scale introduction of herbs came 1,500 years later during the European colonization of North America.) Spices were also becoming familiar in the north as the Romans imported these as seasonings and medicines, pepper and ginger being among the most important.

After the fall of Rome, during the period known as the Dark Ages, trade in spices continued to some extent between the East and southern Europe, both by sea, and in heavily defended caravans overland. Venice became a natural trading centre, and remained so for a thousand years. Cloves, cinnamon, ginger, cardamom and pepper, which reached Constantinople from Asia along the ancient spice routes, were loaded into the waiting Venetian galleys and transported to countries bordering the Mediterranean. In exchange, the Levantine traders received salt and salted meat.

Northern European countries conducted little trade after the departure of the Romans, their routes to the south being blocked by pirates and robbers and their economies disrupted by constant war and invasion. Consequently spices became extremely expensive. In Britain the only organized communities were those of the scattered monasteries, which were run on Roman and Byzantine lines, their Christian precepts still heavily influenced by paganism. The herbal remedies recorded by the monks often took the form of charms and incantations, but nevertheless the early Saxon herbals show a wide knowledge of herbs and their uses, being much influenced by southern-European herbals that had descended from *De Materia Medica*. The most famous was the 10th-century *Leech Book of Bald*, which included herbal prescriptions sent to Alfred the Great by the patriarch of Jerusalem.

The spice trade increased again during the late 8th century as the great Muslim Empire engulfed the Mediterranean and the bordering countries of Spain, North Africa and Egypt and east to Persia, thus breaking pirate control of the seas. Arab scholars studied and translated the teaching of Aristotle and other Classical philosophers and Muslim physicians revived and advanced the cause of rational medicine during a period when theology was stultifying medical practice in other parts of Europe. A Persian called Avicenna (born AD 980) was one of the best known of these physicians, his *Canon* becoming a standard medical text book of the Muslim and civilized Western world. While studying herbal properties he discovered the means of obtaining the volatile oil of herbs and flowers by distillation.

A famous medical school was founded at Salerno in Italy by four legendary 'Masters', an Arab, a Roman, a Jew and a Greek, which reached the height of its renown in the 13th century. There the humoral doctrine of Hippocrates and Galen was taught, and the diet, temperament and situation of the patient taken into account before diagnosis. A set of rules was published for treating illness or preserving health called the *Regimen Sanitatis Salerno*, which was to be translated into many languages over the next few hundred years, including a rhyming doggerel English in 1608.

Salerno became a regular stopping place on the crusading route, and from the 11th century many wounded crusaders must have been treated at the hospital there and have returned to the north with respect for the medical care they had received. They will also have brought home new ideas about cookery and living standards, particularly to Britain where the renewal of foreign trade, increased freedom of movement abroad and the introduction from 1066 of the more sophisticated Norman food all combined to bring about a revolution in cooking. In even the simplest farmsteads a pepper horn became an essential piece of kitchen equipment, and in wealthy households food was heavily spiced with ginger, galingale, cloves, grains of paradise, mace, cubeb pepper and many other spices from the Moluccas (the Spice Islands), southern China, India and Africa. The Arabs had begun to grow commercial crops of liquorice, saffron and sugar in Spain, and this was transported north. Spicy seeds of plants that could grow in northern climates such as coriander, fennel, cumin, caraway and mustard were widely cultivated, and crops of saffron and liquorice were grown on a limited scale in Britain. Medieval cookery books emphasize the importance of the colour of food – in winter, red or yellow food was recommended, coloured with red sanders (sandalwood), alkanet, cinnamon, saffron, marigold petals and ginger. In summer, the food was coloured with green herbs, especially parsley juice, and spiced with cardamom. Other food colourings included indigo and turnsole (*Chrozophora tinctoria*) for purple food, dried blood for black food and almond milk and cream for white dishes.

The reason most often given for the lavish spicing of food is that the powerful spices disguise the flavour of tainted meat and fish. This they certainly do, as well as adding zest to a dull dish, helping the digestion of tough, salted and dried meat and acting as a disinfectant on meat that is high. But this does not altogether explain why barley pottage was cooked with seven different spices nor why a recipe for fresh strawberries included pepper, ginger, galingale, saffron and vinegar, coloured with the root of alkanet. There seemed to be a habit, almost a necessity, for very strongly seasoned food at this period, although the high cost of spices meant that even in the wealthiest households they were locked away in special cupboards or boxes. In poorer homes food would be seasoned with pepper, garlic, mustard, fennel and peony seed, while aromatic herbs, both cultivated and wild, were cooked as potherbs or used as flavourings. Middle Eastern cookery today is similar to that of medieval Europe, with its composite, spiced dishes of meat, fruit, grains and pulses.

The Moluccas or Spice Islands

The first direct sea route from Europe to the Far East was established by the Portuguese in 1498, who thus opened the way to the East Indies for their own traders and weakened the Arab domination of the ancient overland routes to the West and the Venetian monopoly of the spice trade in the Mediterranean and Europe. The famous Spice Islands, which were the chief source of nutmeg and cloves from very early times, were now held by the Portuguese who remained in control for a hundred years until they were driven out by the Dutch in the early 17th century. The Dutch kept the price of nutmeg and cloves artificially high by restricting their cultivation to only a few islands, and it was not until the end of the 18th century when plants were smuggled out of the Moluccas and established in the West Indies and elsewhere that the Dutch monopoly was finally broken and the high cost of spices eventually fell.

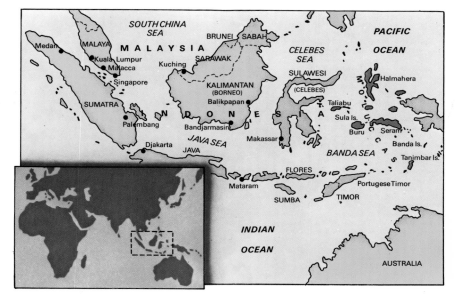

The Arab–Venetian monopoly on the spice trade from Constantinople now became so tight as to be intolerable and, at the same time, the overland spice routes from the East were disrupted by Turkish wars in Asia Minor. Christopher Columbus searched to the West for a new sea route to the Spice Islands, and ended up in America. However a few years later, in 1498, the Portuguese navigator Vasco da Gama sailed south round the Cape of Good Hope and into Calcutta harbour, and Europe was no longer dependent on the long, overland trade route and dozens of middlemen for her spices. Prices nevertheless remained extremely high in Europe, and although Magellan, on his prodigious voyage in the early 1520s, finally discovered the western route to the Spice Islands for Spain, the Portuguese continued to control most of the spice trade for a hundred years.

During these early years of the Renaissance, the science of medicine was beginning to develop in northern countries as the influence of the Arab physicians and the school at Salerno slowly spread. It was observed that the recurring epidemics of plague that were supposed to fall as Divine punishment upon a sinful population, fell equally heavily upon God's chosen instruments, his priests. At the same time a belief grew that pestilence might be due to 'fowle contageous ayre' and purifying fumigants made from spices and the seeds and roots of aromatic herbs were burned in public places and private houses. Greater attention was being paid to diet, living conditions and public hygiene, especially in the cities, and some physicians began to

*The mandrake **above**, whose root was often pictured in human form, and the vervain **centre** are charming examples*

of the woodcut illustrations in the first printed herbals. These are from the Ortus Sanitatis, published in 1497.

*The plantain **above**, from Otto Brunfels's Herbarum Vivae Eicones, 1530, and the hand-coloured woodcut of*

The frontispiece to Otto Brunfels's Herbarum Vivae Eicones, 1530.

*borage **above** from Leonhart Fuchs's De Historia Stirpium, 1542, are in a more naturalistic style.*

scorn the old superstitious practices that still surrounded the use of medicines – the stuffing of herbs into keyholes and shoes, herb amulets worn around the neck and the muttering of incantations and charms. As Andrew Boorde, one of the most sympathetic of these early Renaissance doctors wrote, 'my beloved Physicke . . . is gloriously re-rising after twelve centuries of swoon.' However the old medicine based on astrology and a literal translation of the doctrine of signatures took a long time a-dying and was still popular in Europe during the 16th and 17th centuries. As a 3rd-century Chinese physician, Ko Hung, once sadly wrote, 'When I tell the common people that . . . coltsfoot and aster can cure a persistent cough . . . angelica and peony for colic . . . they doubt it or deny it and prefer to believe in wizardry.'

With the invention of printing, the manuscript herbals of Europe – often derived from *De Materia Medica* and copied and recopied by generation after generation of monks – began to reach a wider public. One of the first to be printed was the *Herbarium* of Apuleius Platonicus, published in Italy in about 1481. This Latin text, first put together in about AD 400, relied heavily on Greek material. The stylized and usually unrecognizable woodcuts of the herbs, with their stencilled green and brown colouring, follow the tradition of the manuscript illustrations. Three other important herbals were published in Germany during the late 15th century, the *Latin Herbarius* and the *German Herbarius*, published by Peter Schöffer and the *Ortus Sanitatis*, published by Jacob Meydenbach, which also includes animals, birds, fish and minerals in its scope. They were probably all based on existing manuscript herbals and were illustrated with charming, simplified woodcuts.

The elegant woodcuts in a herbal by Otto Brunfels, *Herbarum Vivae Eicones*, published in Strasbourg in 1530, made a dramatic contrast, with their finely observed details and flowing lines. These were drawn by the artist Hans Weiditz and are similar in style to those of his contemporary, Dürer. In fact, much of Brunfels's information is derivative, but the herbal of Jerome Bock, published in 1539 with the encouragement and support of Brunfels, is written in a direct style and contains obviously first-hand information. Leonhart Fuchs was the third of these well-known German 'Fathers of Botany', whose *De Historia Stirpium* was published in 1542. Although a physician himself, Fuchs echoes the indignation of many herbal writers in deriding the ignorance of practising doctors who 'so shrink from [the investigation of herbs] that it is scarcely possible to find one among a hundred who has an accurate knowledge of even so many as a few plants'. He listed about 500 herbs with well-observed descriptions accompanied by fine illustrations, which were later much copied.

As the science of botany began to develop, this determination to personally follow all lines of enquiry is clearly seen in many later herbals. The English doctor and Dean of Wells, William Turner, for instance, travelled widely in Britain and 'into Italye and into diverse partes of Germany, to knowe and se the herbes my selfe', before writing his *New Herball*, published in three instalments in the mid-16th century. And in the Low Countries the herbals of the Belgian Rembert Dodoens, Charles de l'Ecluse from Arras, and Mathias de l'Obel from Lille (who spent much of his life in England), set new standards in descriptive botany and plant classification. Their influential herbals were all published by the great printer Christophe Plantin at Antwerp, who produced many other illustrated botanical books.

Meanwhile, of course, herbs were grown in the gardens of cottages, monasteries and castles, and recipes for their use in food and medicine and as

The frontispiece to the famous English herbal of John Gerard, The Herball or Generall Historie of Plantes (first published in 1597), from an edition printed in 1633. The figures of Theophrastus and Dioscorides show the continued reference back to the Classical writers.

scents and fumigants were handed on from generation to generation. A belief that wild herbs possessed more powerful properties than cultivated species meant that herb women and root gatherers could make a living by collecting herbs from the countryside and selling them in the marketplace and to apothecaries. The single herbs were called 'simples' and from these the apothecaries 'compounded' their drugs. Many apothecaries and physicians also grew herbs in their own physic gardens – they were in fact advised to do so in the *Book of Compounds* drawn up for apothecaries in 1576 by an English doctor, which said that 'his garden must be at hand, with plenty of herbs, seeds and roots' to 'sow, set, plant, gather, preserve and keep'.

One of the best-known European physic gardens must be that of John Gerard at Holborn in London, which he carefully catalogued and described as 'the little plot of myne owne especiall care and husbandry'. Gerard, whose *Herball or Generall Historie of Plantes* was published in 1597, had a direct and charming style of writing, and though he committed the sin of lifting a good deal of his information from an unpublished translation of Dodoens's herbal without acknowledgment, his book still gives much pleasure today. In his garden grew many of the new species that were brought to England by seafaring navigators and explorers, especially from the Americas.

Seeds and roots of plants native to North America were sent back to Europe in increasing numbers during the 16th and 17th centuries – by French settlers in Canada to the *Jardin des Plantes* in Paris, by Puritan settlers to the Chelsea Physic Garden or Oxford Botanic Garden in England, to the Italian botanical gardens at Florence, Padua and Ferrara. In 1672 a book was published of *New Englands Rarities*, written by an English visitor to America, John Josselyn, which included American flora and 'The Physical and Chyrurgical Remedies wherewith the Natives constantly use to Cure their Distempers, Wounds, and Sores'. Further species were described in a later book by Josselyn as having a generally 'more masculine vertue than any of the same species in England, but not in so terrible a degree as to be mischievous or ineffectual to our English bodies'.

At the same time, herbs were travelling in the opposite direction across the Atlantic, and the seed lists of useful herbs to be brought by the settlers to the new country make interesting reading. A typical order by the younger John

These illustrations of the flowers and leaves of the coltsfoot were originally printed in the Eicones Plantarum of J. T. Tabernaemontanus, and were later used by Gerard in his Herball of 1597.

Nicholas Culpeper, whose popular herbal emphasized the astrological significance of medicinal herbs.

An astrological map of the heavens from the Arati Solensis Phaenomena *of 1499.*

The Jardin des Plantes, *originally the* Jardin du Roi, *had a fine collection of new herbs raised from roots and seeds sent back by French settlers in Canada in the 16th and 17th centuries.*

Winthrop, from a London grocer in 1631, contains 48 species of herbs, both familiar plants such as parsley, rosemary, savory and thyme and the less familiar alexanders, clary, mallow and aconite (monkshood). The medicines Josselyn considered necessary to take on the Atlantic crossing, 'in case you, or any of yours should be sick at sea', included conserves of roses, clove gillyflowers, wormwood, green ginger, nutmeg, mace, cinnamon, pepper and 'juice of Lemmons well put up to cure or prevent the Scurvey'. Large, well-organized medical herb gardens were later established by religious communities in America, especially by the Shaker sect who planted their famous garden in New York in 1820 and made a thriving business of drying, mixing and selling their herbs.

Many of these early colonists carried with them the three most popular herbals of the period – the herbal of Gerard, now considerably enlarged by the apothecary-botanist Thomas Johnson; the *Theatrum Botanicum*, 'An Herball of a Large Extent' by John Parkinson, Herbalist to Charles I, published in 1640; and Culpeper's herbal, *The English Physitian*, published in 1652. The latter included an unauthorized English translation of the Latin *Pharmacopoeia* issued by the College of Physicians and accused those gentlemen of being 'a company of proud, insulting, domineering Doctors, whose wits were born above five hundred years before themselves' and urged his readers to depend instead upon 'Dr Reason' and 'Dr Experience'. This would have been all very well if Culpeper had not interwoven his often sensible advice on herbal remedies with quite outrageous astrological observations such as this description of the virtues of agrimony. 'It is an herb under Jupiter and the sign Cancer; and strengthens those parts under the planet and sign, and removes diseases in them by sympathy; and those under Saturn, Mars, and Mercury, by antipathy, if they happen in any part of the body governed by Jupiter, or under the signs Cancer, Sagittary, or Pisces, and therefore must needs be good for the gout.' This sends us right back to pre-Renaissance days when a French medical treatise could begin 'In the name of the Lord, Amen! Here begins a brief treatise to direct physicians in the practice of medicine with reference to the influence of the sky.' But although Culpeper's herbal was attacked not only by the insulted physicians but by contemporary herbalists and botanists, it is still in print today.

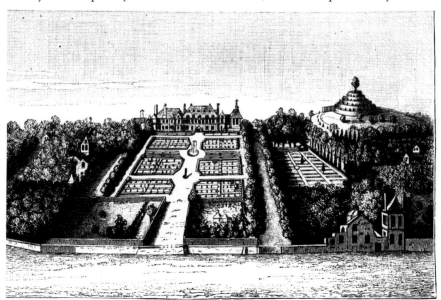

A cardamom nursery spread over a hillside in Nepal. The fruits are harvested before they ripen and dried very slowly to preserve the rich oil of the seeds.

Chilies drying in the sun in India. Although introduced to the country only comparatively recently, they are now an important crop, and have become a common ingredient in Indian cooking.

During the 17th century, there were changes in eating habits in Europe. Spices and sugar at last became cheaper following the establishment of such trading companies as the British East India Company, and with the much wider cultivation of spices. Then, as sugar from the West Indies became increasingly available and popular, spices began to lose their importance as vital ingredients in north-European cookery. Pickles, preserves, sweet dishes, cakes and drinks still relied on spices but they were no longer added impartially to every savoury dish. Three cookery books published in France in the 1650s, written by François Pierre de La Varenne, typify the new cuisine. Heavily spiced 'messes' of meat, dried fruit and nuts to be eaten off shared plates were replaced by individual dishes of fresh vegetables only lightly seasoned, cuts of roast meat accompanied by simple sauces made from the juices of the meat mixed with lemon and herbs and, perhaps, bowls of eggs, stuffed mushrooms, puff pastries (a new invention) and fresh picked fruit.

Towards the end of the century herbalism and botany began to part company, and medicinal remedies were now confined to pharmacopoeias. At first these were lists of drugs with notes on preparation and dosage produced locally by universities and other academic bodies; later official, national pharmacopoeias were published, the first *British Pharmacopoeia* in 1864, the first *United States Pharmacopoeia* in 1907. The early drug lists simply record the use of certain drugs for specific diseases without questioning how or why the drugs should work. Then, in the 18th century, Dr William Withering produced the first detailed study of the action of a drug, digitalis, in the *Account of the Foxglove*, and the development of chemistry and biology in the 19th century led to the beginning of modern, systematic pharmacology.

Until this time an exact herbal prescription had never been possible because of the widely varying strength of the active principle possessed by each individual plant. That the general climate, local weather conditions, habitat, soil, time of gathering and methods of preserving, all have an effect upon the properties of the plant has always been known by herbalists, and the customs and superstitions surrounding the growing and harvesting of herbs, although on the face of it bizarre, in fact often concealed a sensible method for preserving these properties as well as possible. Indeed, Dioscorides wrote in his herbal nearly 2,000 years ago, that 'it is proper to use care . . . in the gathering of herbs each at its due season, for it is according to this that medicines either do their work or become quite ineffectual.' But now chemistry made it possible to extract a measured quantity of the active principle from a plant and to make it up into exact doses. Chemistry also provided the means for reproducing the isolated principles synthetically, which has led to the modern development of thousands of potent, synthetic drugs produced by an enormous and thriving pharmaceutical industry. Although many are of great value, there has been little time to discover the long-term action of such complex drugs, and only too often the benefits are countered by unpleasant side effects. This problem has led, during the present century, to a revival of interest in medical botany.

Among the active principles that have been isolated from herbs, those most useful in medicine include essential oils (such as thymol), alkaloids (such as morphine from the opium poppy) and glycosides (such as digitalis from the foxglove). Medical biologists working in America today believe that less than half the active principles to be found in plants, that could benefit mankind, have yet been identified, and that by studying the traditional herbal medicines of the past and contemporary tribal medicines, many more

Lavender, well adapted to the stony fields of Provence, is a major crop for the French perfume trade.

A pepper farm in the humid tropics of Sarawak, North Borneo. Black peppercorns are harvested unripe and dried in the sun until wrinkled and dark; white peppercorns are left to ripen on the vine, then picked and the outer flesh soaked and rubbed off before the pale inner corn is dried.

useful species can be identified and analysed. This important line of research collects clues from legendary, historical, anthropological and archaeological sources, and especially from herbaria – collections of dried plants that have been gathered from all over the world during the last two or three centuries and preserved with notes on habitat and folklore. Apart from numerous private herbaria there are 1,800 public collections in the world, containing 175 million plants, which are being systematically studied.

Two world wars have contributed to the revival of herbalism in the West, for the halt in industry and foreign imports meant that people had to fall back on their own resources and became suddenly aware that the traditional skills and knowledge necessary for survival were almost lost. Herbs were needed as a vital addition to a dull and poor diet, rose hips were picked on a grand scale for their Vitamin C content and herbal remedies were used again, both at home and on the front. During World War I herbs were especially important – thymol as a disinfectant, sphagnum moss for wounds, and lily-of-the-valley as a treatment for poison gas.

The increasing popularity of all aspects of herbalism led to the publication of Mrs Grieve's *A Modern Herbal* in 1931, and since then quantities of books have appeared on the identification and uses of herbs. Today herbs are once more widely cultivated, both on herb farms and at a domestic level, and are bought and used by those who are dissatisfied with monotonous synthetic foods and artificial cosmetics and medicines that are widespread in Western countries today, and which sometimes produce unexpected and unpleasant side effects. This book attempts to increase an awareness of the old empirical knowledge of herbs, combined with a scientific and above all open-minded and practical approach towards their enjoyment and use.

Spice-producing countries

The map below shows the main spice-producing countries of the world and their products. Nutmeg, so long exclusively grown in the Spice Islands, is now principally cultivated in the West Indies, while flavourings from the New World, such as vanilla, have travelled in the opposite direction.

Trade in herbs and spices flourishes all over the world today, from Bolivia **top left**, *where a woman sorts an enormous variety of chilies in the street, to the Seychelles* **top right**, *where newly harvested cinnamon bark is dried in the sun. Cinnamon is not native to the Seychelles, but was brought there by the French at the end of the 18th century from the Dutch East Indies. Chili is an almost universal flavouring from East to West,* **above** *it is sold in a floating market in Kashmir. The mint seller* **left** *is a common sight in Morocco. His mint will be used in cookery and for the famous mint tea, which is drunk throughout the Arab world.*

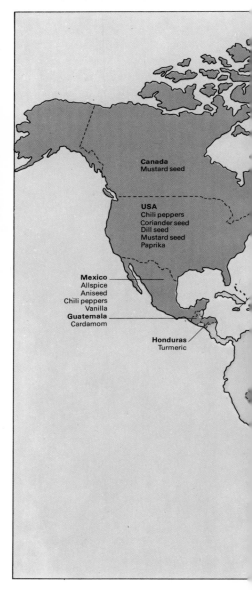

Canada
Mustard seed

USA
Chili peppers
Coriander seed
Dill seed
Mustard seed
Paprika

Mexico
Allspice
Aniseed
Chili peppers
Vanilla
Guatemala
Cardamom

Honduras
Turmeric

Ground cumin and paprika are displayed in the hot Moroccan sun **left**, *while* **above** *dried medicinal herbs are sold in a shady street in Brazil.*

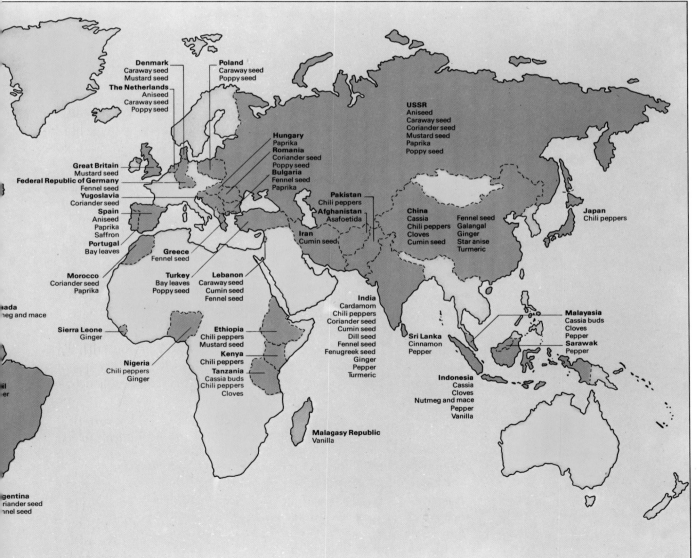

Denmark
Caraway seed
Mustard seed

Poland
Caraway seed
Poppy seed

The Netherlands
Aniseed
Caraway seed
Poppy seed

USSR
Aniseed
Caraway seed
Coriander seed
Mustard seed
Paprika
Poppy seed

Hungary
Paprika

Romania
Coriander seed
Poppy seed

Bulgaria
Fennel seed
Paprika

Great Britain
Mustard seed

Federal Republic of Germany
Fennel seed

Yugoslavia
Coriander seed

Spain
Aniseed
Paprika
Saffron

Portugal
Bay leaves

Morocco
Coriander seed
Paprika

Greece
Fennel seed

Turkey
Bay leaves
Poppy seed

Lebanon
Caraway seed
Cumin seed
Fennel seed

Pakistan
Chili peppers

Afghanistan
Asafoetida

Iran
Cumin seed

China
Cassia
Chili peppers
Cloves
Cumin seed
Fennel seed
Galangal
Ginger
Star anise
Turmeric

Japan
Chili peppers

Sierra Leone
Ginger

Ethiopia
Chili peppers
Mustard seed

Kenya
Chili peppers

Tanzania
Cassia buds
Chili peppers
Cloves

India
Cardamom
Chili peppers
Coriander seed
Cumin seed
Dill seed
Fennel seed
Fenugreek seed
Ginger
Pepper
Turmeric

Sri Lanka
Cinnamon
Pepper

Malayasia
Cassia buds
Cloves
Pepper

Sarawak
Pepper

Nigeria
Chili peppers
Ginger

Indonesia
Cassia
Cloves
Nutmeg and mace
Pepper
Vanilla

Malagasy Republic
Vanilla

ada
neg and mace

il
er

gentina
riander seed
nnel seed

21

A modern herbal

Nearly 300 herbs and spices are included in this modern herbal, the majority of which are illustrated and described in detail. They are listed alphabetically under their Latin names, each entry including the common name or names, the names of other closely related plants, habitat, methods of cultivation when this is relevant, harvesting and storage instructions, uses, historical references, myths and legendary powers. Each plant can be followed through later chapters by referring to the index.

The old herbalists generally divided their plants into three categories – sweet or flavouring herbs, potherbs and medicinal herbs – but the defining line between them is often indistinct and some of the plants described here combine all virtues. They cover a wide range, from wild herbs that are generally regarded as weeds, such as goosegrass, nettles and yarrow, to those that were once cultivated, such as ground elder and bistort, to the many common and uncommon species that are still grown today. To include all plants that are edible or medicinal would be like writing a universal *flora*; there are few plants that cannot be used for one or other purpose. The choice made for this book is as comprehensive as possible. Some herbs that did not seem worthy of a detailed entry, having perhaps only one specialized application, are covered in other parts of the book under their use as dye herbs, cosmetic herbs, medicinal herbs etc.

Spices are easier to define as they are usually dried, aromatic parts of plants that will only grow in the tropics. Some that are more difficult to classify, fenugreek and chili peppers for example, have also been included.

Many powerful herbs belong to three large families, the daisy family or *Compositae*, the thyme family or *Labiatae* and the parsley family, the *Umbelliferae*. Members of the daisy family can usually be recognized by their flowerheads, which are composed of tiny flowers packed together, sometimes with long, petal-like rays. These plants often have astringent, bitter and antiseptic properties. The Labiate herbs, such as thyme and mint,

are often strongly aromatic with long-throated, sweet-smelling flowers that attract bees, and many have soothing, tonic properties. The Umbellifers are easy to distinguish by their umbels of small flowers with flower stalks that radiate from a central point like spokes of an umbrella. Their seeds often contain potent oils that act on the stomach and digestive organs.

The specific or second Latin name of each herb will often give a clue to its uses. *Officinalis*, or *officinale*, is one of the most common specific names for herbs and means 'of the shop', showing that it was sold by apothecaries. *Sativus* indicates that the plant was cultivated, *tinctoria* that it was used as a dye, *fragrans* and *odorata* that it has a sweet scent.

Over half the plants listed grow wild in Europe and North America. It is now illegal to uproot any wild plant in Great Britain, nor should they be picked in any quantity. Only a few leaves or flowers should be taken from plentiful species that are growing away from polluted roads or sprayed fields. Make sure that they are absolutely, positively identified before using them and, for a regular supply, collect some seed and sow it in the garden – taking note of the conditions in which the plant is growing. Umbellifers should be collected with caution from the wild as several species, such as hemlock and fool's parsley, are extremely poisonous.

Botanical terms are kept to a minimum and those used are listed in the glossary at the end of the book. It is botanically correct to call the seeds of umbelliferous plants 'fruits' but, to simplify matters, they are here always referred to as seeds.

When reference is made to an infusion, then standard quantities of $15g/\frac{1}{2}oz$ dried herb or 25g/1oz fresh herb to 600ml/1 pint of boiling water are used unless other quantities are given. Detailed instructions for cultivation, drying and storage and many individual recipes are given in later chapters. Read the chapter on medicinal herbs and spices before using the medical treatments described in the herbal.

Achillea millefolium

Yarrow, knight's milfoil

Family: Compositae

The tough, adaptable yarrow grows in most climates as a perennial weed. The leaves are long, narrow and finely divided into feathery leaflets, the downy stems can grow 60cm/2ft tall. Clusters of small, greyish-white or occasionally pink flowers bloom throughout the summer.

Yarrow can be grown easily from seed or root. Use the leaves and flowers fresh or harvest the whole plant for drying as the flowers begin to open. The young leaves have a pleasant, fresh taste, but become peppery with age. Chop them in salads or boil like spinach.

Yarrow is a wound herb, astringent and healing, and rich in vitamins and minerals. Bind bruised, fresh leaves to cuts, or make an ointment by pounding the flowers and mixing with cold cream and beeswax, or bathe wounds with yarrow tea. The tea is also a good tonic drink, it restores lost appetite and promotes perspiration during colds and fevers. Chew fresh leaves to soothe toothache.

When grown in the garden, yarrow is said to increase the health of nearby plants. As a compost activator, it encourages fermentation, and a strong infusion can be used as a fertilizer that is especially useful for soils deficient in copper.

Yarrow has always been regarded as a plant of great power, both as a protection against evil and to invoke black magic. It was used as a herb of divination by the early Chinese – whose ancient book, *I Ching*, is also known as *The Yarrow Stalk Oracle* – and by the Druids and Anglo-Saxons. Dried, powdered yarrow leaves were used in Europe as a medicinal snuff, as were the leaves of the related sneezewort, *A. ptarmica*, to 'cleanse the head of tough slimy humours'.

Acorus calamus

Acorus calamus

Sweet flag, sweet sedge

Family: Araceae

Originally from the East, the perennial sweet flag now grows in marshy places in temperate regions round the world. The iris-like leaves have crinkled edges and stand about 1m/3ft high. The tiny green flowers bloom in midsummer, packed into a curving spike that projects from halfway up the stout stalk. These generally appear only when the plant is standing in water and seldom ripen in northern climates.

Plant the knobbly rhizome in rich, wet soil in a sunny position. Harvest and dry 2-year-old rhizomes in the late autumn and dry the leaves in the summer.

The whole plant smells sweetly spicy with a sharp tang, and was used in Europe as a culinary flavouring and strewing herb. Chew a piece of the rhizome to counteract acidity, to relieve dyspepsia, flatulence and indigestion. Or take an infusion of 15g/½oz powdered root to 600ml/ 1 pint boiling water.

Achillea millefolium

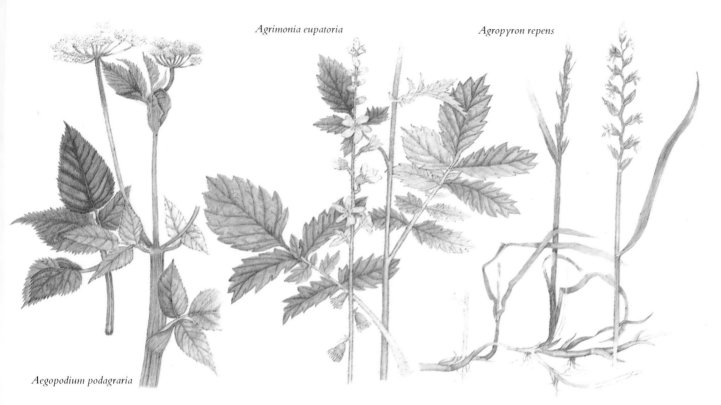

Agrimonia eupatoria

Agropyron repens

Aegopodium podagraria

Aegopodium podagraria
Ground elder, goutweed
Family: Umbelliferae
A familiar and widespread perennial weed in Britain, most of Europe, northern Asia and the U.S.A., ground elder is all too easy to cultivate. It grows about 50cm/20in high, with broad, smooth, serrated leaflets, creeping roots and umbels of white flowers in midsummer.

Harvest the pale rootstock for drying in the autumn, and dry the young leaves in late spring.

The aromatic leaves can be simmered in a little water and served as a spring vegetable with butter and lemon juice. Treat aching joints, rheumatism and gout with a warm poultice of boiled roots and leaves. Infuse a handful of fresh or a tablespoon of dried leaves in 300ml/½ pint boiling water and drink twice a day as a gentle, sedative tea.

Ground elder was cultivated in the Middle Ages, especially in the physic gardens of monasteries and castles, and often grows among their ruins today.

Agrimonia eupatoria
Agrimony, church steeples
Family: Rosaceae
A common roadside plant in Britain and Europe and introduced by early settlers to the U.S.A., perennial agrimony grows up to 60cm/2ft high with roughly hairy stems and leaves divided into toothed leaflets. Many small yellow flowers bloom on tapering spikes in high summer, followed in autumn by little bell-shaped burs. The whole plant has a faint, sweet smell.

Agrimony is easily propagated in dry soil by seed or by root division. Harvest and dry the leaves just before the flowers open.

An infusion made from the leaves is a common country tea, especially in France, and has a delicate scent and flavour. It is astringent, useful for clearing the skin, cleansing the blood, for liver complaints, as a gargle for sore throats and as a wash for wounds. It is one of the oldest recorded wound herbs.

Agrimony yields a fawn dye when mordanted with chrome.

Agropyron repens
Couch grass, twitch, quickgrass
Family: Gramineae
The perennial couch grass is found in most temperate regions and is familiar to gardeners as a weed that spreads rapidly across open ground. It grows about 1m/3ft high, with flat, sharply pointed leaves, tall flower spikes and a creeping, branching rhizome.

Dig up the pale rhizomes in the spring, wash, dry and slice into short lengths. These are rich in minerals, potassium and silica, and in Vitamins A and B.

A tea or decoction can be drunk as a general tonic or for bladder complaints and cystitis. To make the decoction boil 100g/4oz root in 1 litre/1¾ pints of water until reduced by half, then leave to steep for 10 minutes. Flavour this rather tasteless tea with lemon juice and drink a cupful twice a day.

A strong tea can be used as a liquid fertilizer in the garden and the minerals are beneficial in the compost heap.

Alchemilla vulgaris

Alkanna tinctoria

Alchemilla vulgaris
Lady's mantle, dew cup
Family: Rosaceae
The beautiful lobed leaves of lady's mantle are downy, pale green and finely toothed, often holding a dew drop in the centre. From early summer the inconspicuous yellow-green flowers grow in small clusters with no petals but prominent yellow stamens.

It is a perennial, growing about 30cm/12in high in Britain, northern Europe, North America and northern Asia, usually on high ground and in shady places, and can be propagated by seed or root. The cultivated variety is larger, grows easily from seed and is tolerant of the shade.

The slightly bitter leaves can be eaten fresh in a salad. Gather them for drying as the plant comes into flower and dig the root for drying in the autumn.

The whole plant is astringent and styptic, the root especially so. Drink an infusion of the leaves or a decoction of the root as a fortifying tonic drink (a cupful twice a day) or to control a heavy menstrual flow. Use it as a wash to dry up bleeding wounds and to draw poison from boils and other inflammations.

As a skin tonic apply the juice directly onto oily skin; for dry skin, mix it with cold cream.

The generic name *Alchemilla* indicates the herb's connection with alchemy and magic. It was used as a pagan protection against elves and demons and later given the blessing of Our Lady as a woman's herb, taken for all troubles of the womb, to help conception, to prevent miscarriage and to protect the unborn child. Several old herbalists go so far as to say that the drying properties of lady's mantle can be used to shrink and harden bosoms that 'be too great and flaggie'. It also had a reputation as an aphrodisiac, to inspire 'lust to the worke of generacyon'.

Alkanna tinctoria
Alkanet, dyer's bugloss
Family: Boraginaceae
The perennial alkanet from southern Europe belongs to the same family as borage, and has similar large rough leaves and thick root, though the small, bright blue flowers, blooming in early summer, are more like forgetmenots. It can be grown easily from seed or by root division in the autumn, and tolerates some shade.

Before the advent of modern antiseptics a wound ointment used to be made by pounding the root with olive oil and earthworms. The roots give a grey-green dye when mordanted with alum, and when mixed with oil or alcohol can produce a fugitive red dye for cloth, for colouring liquids and ointments and for staining wood and stone. The red dye was used as a face paint in ancient Egypt, and more recently as a rouge.

There are several closely related species whose roots also give a red dye – the tall garden *Anchusa azurea*, the naturalized *A. officinalis*, and the evergreen *Pentaglottis sempervirens*.

Allium cepa var. *proliferum*

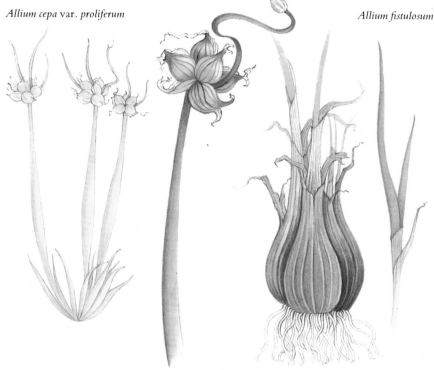

Allium fistulosum

Allium sativum
Garlic
Family: Liliaceae

Probably originating in central Asia, garlic is one of the oldest cultivated plants. It is perennial, the familiar bulb divided into many fat cloves each covered with papery white skin. The leaves are flat, growing about 30cm/12in high, and in late summer the pink or whitish flowers are grouped into a round head among little bulblets.

Plant garlic as winter ends, each clove about 15cm/6in apart and 3cm/1in deep in a sunny position in light, rich soil. The clove multiplies and grows leaves that turn yellow in late summer, when the bulb should be lifted and stored in a dry place. If the bulbs are left unharvested, the leaves will provide a green garlic flavouring the following year.

Garlic cloves have an infinite variety of uses in the kitchen, from a squeeze of juice from a clove to flavour a salad dressing, to the simmering of a whole bulb in a rich stew, when each clove will emerge plump and saturated with the juices of the dish. A small quantity of garlic will heighten existing flavours; a large amount, used fresh, will produce a tingling sensation in the mouth. If the breath smells strongly of garlic, chew a sprig of parsley or peppermint.

Garlic is a powerful disinfectant and antiseptic. Apply the diluted juice externally to wounds on sterilized lint or pound the cloves as a poultice for sores. Used internally, the antiseptic action is valuable in preventing infection and the formation of harmful bacteria in the intestines and stomach, also in preventing or treating coughs, colds and bronchitis. Take garlic regularly in food as a general tonic. Nursing mothers should not eat quantities of garlic as it flavours their milk.

Rich in sulphur, garlic has a

Allium species
Family: Liliaceae

Perennial garden onions have been cultivated for so long that their origins are uncertain. They are among the most basic of foods, infinitely adaptable and containing rich supplies of Vitamin C, minerals, sulphur and other trace elements.

As a medicine onions are antiseptic and stimulant. Eaten raw they have a cleansing and purifying effect on the body, helping digestion, stimulating the kidneys and clearing the blood, though they can cause wind. Use roasted onion warm as a soothing and effective poultice for sprains, boils or earache. Fresh onion juice can be rubbed onto insect or dog bites, between the toes for athlete's foot and, mixed with salt, onto chilblains. Dried onion skins yield a good, bright yellow dye.

The tree onion or Egyptian onion, *A. cepa* var. *proliferum*, is thought to have developed in Canada in the 19th century. The leaves are hollow and the sturdy, thick stems grow well over 1m/3ft high, bearing only

1 or 2 flowers on a head of little bulblets. These bulblets will drop in late summer and root on their own, or can be planted out in rich soil, 25cm/10in apart. The large parent bulbs multiply like shallots, and can also be separated and planted out. Use the leaves for onion greens, the bulbs as scallions and the bulblets for flavouring and pickling.

The Welsh onion, or ciboule, *A. fistulosum*, probably originates from east Asia and was introduced into Europe in the Middle Ages. It resembles large, coarse chives, but remains green all year and is invaluable for onion greens and scallions. It is very hardy and easy to grow from seed; divide and space out the multiplying bulbs every few years.

The leek and mild-flavoured shallot are closely related to the onion and have similar properties.

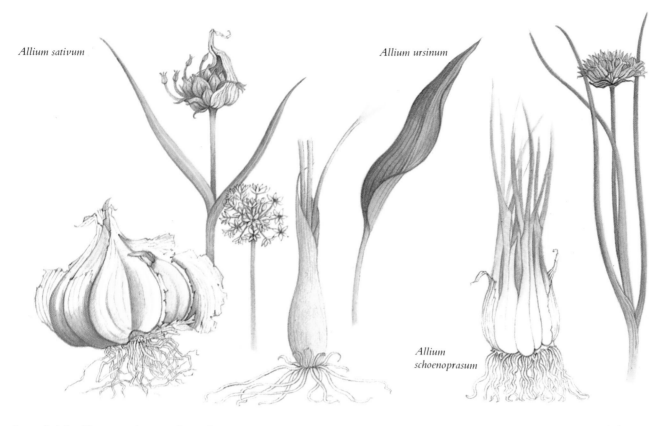

Allium sativum

Allium ursinum

Allium schoenoprasum

beneficial effect on the garden, the excretions and secretions from its roots encouraging the growth of other plants, especially roses. The only exceptions are peas and beans, which seem antipathetic. Sprinkle dried, powdered garlic round seedlings to protect them from birds, moles and insects, and use strong, freshly made garlic tea as an insecticide.

Garlic was first recorded by the Sumerians nearly 5,000 years ago. Many writers have referred to it since – Virgil praised it, but Horace and Shakespeare were disgusted by its effect on the breath. It was often regarded as the food of labourers and peasants (the builders of the pyramids, and Greek and Roman soldiers and sailors were issued with a daily ration of garlic), but it has always been recognized as a valuable strengthening medicine and as a potent protection against disease. The protective power of garlic extended to its use in magic; in many countries cloves of garlic were hung round the necks of children and livestock to avert evil spirits.

There are several wild species of onions and garlic and all are recognizable by their pungent smell. Ramsons, *A. ursinum*, is one of the most useful and common of these, growing in masses in damp woods in Britain and Europe, with broad leaves like those of lily-of-the-valley and a pretty white head of starry flowers. Its properties are similar to those of the cultivated variety.

Although unrelated to garlic, the wild garlic mustard, *Alliaria petiolata*, should be mentioned. A member of the cabbage family, it is native or naturalized in most temperate climates. Its edible leaves have a garlic scent and flavour.

Allium schoenoprasum
Chives
Family: Liliaceae
Perennial chives grow wild in most temperate, northern regions and occasionally in Britain. The smallest of the onion family, its narrow, hollow leaves grow about 30cm/12in tall from small bulbs. In early summer the round flowerheads are purplish pink and in autumn papery bracts contain small black seeds.

It is possible to grow chives from seed, but they are generally propagated by dividing the bulbs. Plant them out in small clumps of 4 or 5 in rich, damp soil 25cm/10in apart and divide them again every 3 years. They need some sun, but moisture is essential. Although easy to grow, chives often become yellow early in the year and this usually means that they have exhausted the soil and need feeding with rich compost, or that the soil has become too dry. Nip off any flowers to encourage leaf growth. Cut fresh leaves throughout the summer; they have a delicate onion flavour.

Alpinia officinarum

Althaea officinalis

Alpinia officinarum
Lesser galangal, China root
Family: Zingiberaceae

Lesser galangal is native to China, with slender leaves growing about 1.5m/5ft high and a spike of white, red-veined flowers. It resembles the closely related ginger and has a similar fat, knobbed rhizome.

The rhizome was brought to Britain and northern Europe from the East by crusaders in the 13th century, and became a popular spice with its strong, hot flavour and scent of roses. Though often mentioned in medieval and Tudor recipe books, it had fallen out of favour in European cookery by the 18th century and was used only as a medicine. Like ginger it is a stimulant, and can also be used to treat flatulence and indigestion. Infuse 25g/1oz of powdered root in 600ml/1 pint boiling water and take a tablespoon at a time.

English galingale, *Cyperus longus*, has similar medicinal uses. The greater galangal, *A. galanga*, from Java is often confused with lesser galangal, but has an inferior flavour.

Althaea officinalis
Marsh mallow
Family: Malvaceae

Marsh mallow generally grows near the sea, by river estuaries and in salt marshes in Britain, Europe and the U.S.A. It is a rather sprawling plant, growing about 1m/3ft high. The stem and large lobed leaves are covered with a soft velvet down. Pale pink flowers bloom in late summer, followed by round, flattened fruits and the long perennial roots are cream coloured.

Plant sections of fresh root, each carrying a bud, in light, damp soil, about 60cm/2ft apart, or sow seed in the spring. Harvest and dry the leaves just before the flowers blossom. Dig the roots for drying in the autumn.

There are many species of mallow growing around the world, often used as food or medicine and possessing similar properties. The young leaves of all the European mallows can be eaten in salads, the older leaves in soups, the roots boiled or fried and the seeds, known as cheeses, chewed fresh. They are all wholesome and their flavour faint and delicate.

All mallows, including the garden hollyhock, contain quantities of mucilage and the marsh mallow is an especially soothing, healing herb, useful in treating bronchitis, internal inflammation and irritation, for stimulating the kidneys and as a gentle laxative. The roots contain most mucilage and can be taken as a decoction, a spoonful 3 times a day. (Soak 100g/4oz dried root overnight in 3 litres/5 pints water, boil until reduced by nearly half and strain.) Inhale the steam for sinusitis. Alternatively, infuse a tea from the leaves and take a cupful twice a day; this also makes a soothing eye bath. The fresh leaves or crushed fresh root make an excellent hot poultice for inflammations, sprains, stings and aching muscles. The original marshmallow sweets were sucked for sore throats and made by soaking a mixture of powdered root and sugar in water until it became a jelly.

Anethum graveolens

Anethum graveolens
Dill
Family: Umbelliferae

Dill is native to southern Europe and Russia and is now cultivated and often found wild in Britain and northern Europe, North America and Australia. The fine, thread-like leaves usually grow from a single stem; the comparatively large, flat umbels of tiny yellow flowers bloom in midsummer, followed by light, flat, winged seeds with narrow ridges. The plant generally grows up to 1.5m/5ft high.

Dill is a hardy annual. Sow the seed in a sunny but sheltered place in the spring, if growing for seed, and from spring to midsummer for the leaves. Thin the seedlings out to 20cm/8in apart. They do not transplant well, having small and delicate root systems and a tendency to shoot into premature flower if disturbed. Keep well watered and free from weeds. In common with several other umbellifers, dill may prove difficult to grow until the right place in the garden is found for it, but will then flourish and self-sow prolifically. Do not grow near fennel, as the two can cross-fertilize.

Dill leaves can be picked fresh at any time but are difficult to dry. For pickle flavourings, harvest the flowerheads when they are carrying both flowers and unripe seeds together. Harvest the seeds as they begin to turn brown and hang the heads upside down in a dry, airy place with a cloth beneath to catch the ripe seeds as they fall.

Dill seeds are warming, strong-tasting and aromatic, slightly reminiscent of caraway seed, and contain a volatile oil that is similar to oil of caraway. Use them to flavour root vegetables, cakes and sweets. The leaves have a lighter, less bitter taste. Use them raw or add to a dish towards the end of the cooking time, to avoid destroying the flavour. The fresh leaves are especially popular in Scandinavian cookery with fish, in soured-cream sauces, potato salad and with other vegetables. The unripe seeds and flowers of dill have been used for many hundreds of years to flavour vinegar and pickles, especially pickled cucumber. Dill vinegar is made by steeping a seedhead in 600ml/1 pint of vinegar and straining after a week or two.

The old Norse name for dill was *dilla*, which means 'to lull', and the oil from the leaves, and especially the seeds, contains a gentle sedative. It is also a soothing digestive and relieves flatulence; dill water has been used to calm colicky babies for centuries. Make this by steeping a teaspoonful of bruised seeds in a glass of hot water for several hours, then strain and sweeten the liquid with honey; give 1 tablespoonful to adults and 1 teaspoonful to children. This drink will also stimulate the appetite and encourage milk production in nursing mothers. The seeds can be chewed as a digestive.

Dill is rich in minerals, potassium, sulphur and sodium. It is sometimes grown as a companion plant with cabbages but has a suppressive effect on carrots.

Dill is mentioned in a 5,000-year-old Egyptian medical treatise and has been used constantly as a medicine since. It appears in all old herbals, especially as an effective remedy for 'hicket', 'hisquet', 'hickocke' or hiccup. It is always spoken of as an entirely beneficial plant, a plant of good omen.

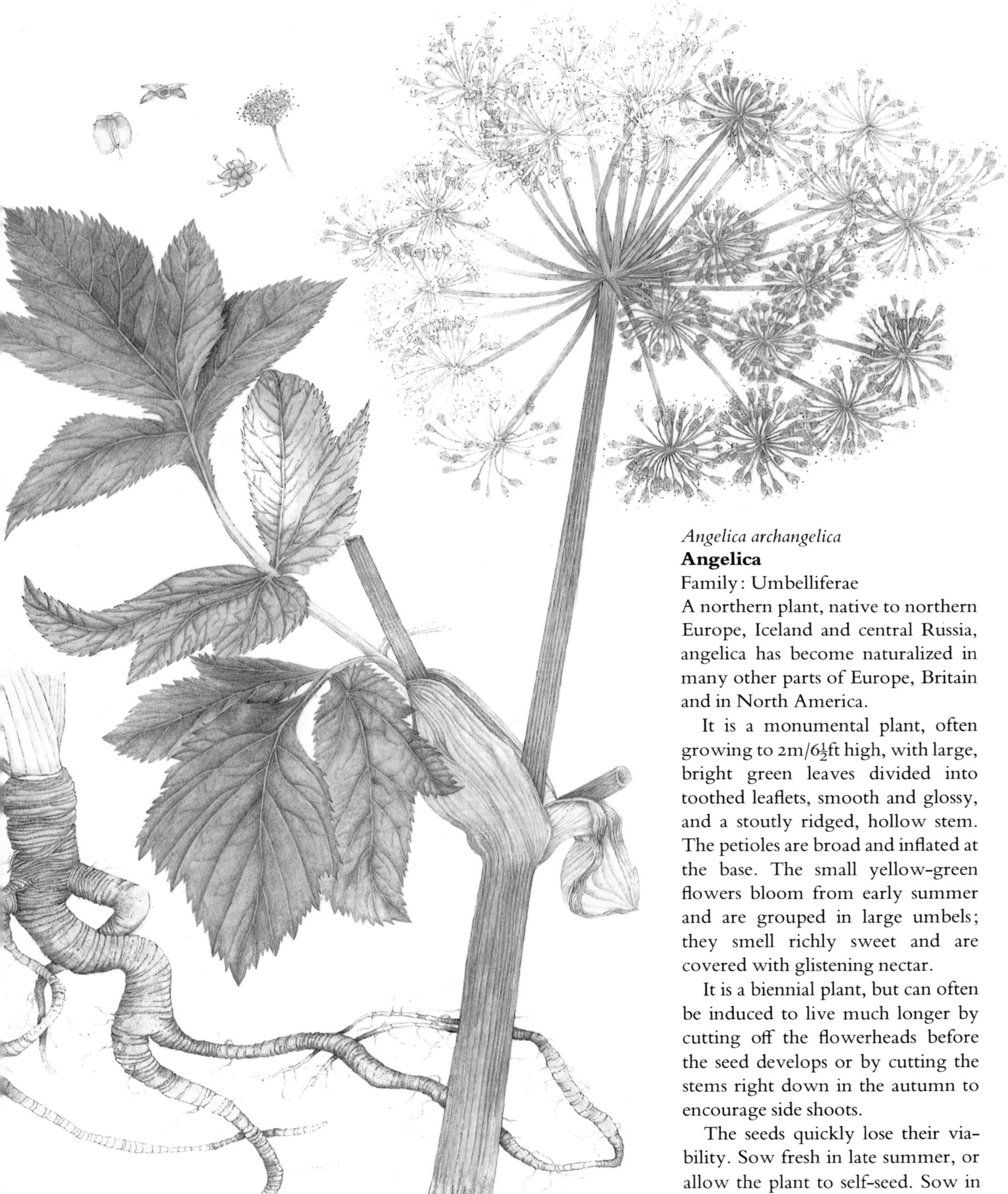

Angelica archangelica

Angelica

Family: Umbelliferae

A northern plant, native to northern Europe, Iceland and central Russia, angelica has become naturalized in many other parts of Europe, Britain and in North America.

It is a monumental plant, often growing to 2m/6½ft high, with large, bright green leaves divided into toothed leaflets, smooth and glossy, and a stoutly ridged, hollow stem. The petioles are broad and inflated at the base. The small yellow-green flowers bloom from early summer and are grouped in large umbels; they smell richly sweet and are covered with glistening nectar.

It is a biennial plant, but can often be induced to live much longer by cutting off the flowerheads before the seed develops or by cutting the stems right down in the autumn to encourage side shoots.

The seeds quickly lose their viability. Sow fresh in late summer, or allow the plant to self-seed. Sow in shallow drills as light helps their germination. It is sometimes possible to plant out the offsets that may develop round the base of the stem; these should be spaced at least 1m/3ft apart in rich soil in a damp, half-shaded position.

Harvest the leaves before the plant flowers, while they are fresh and green, and dry carefully in the shade to preserve their colour and scent. Harvest the stem and larger leaf ribs in early summer, dig the root in the autumn of the first year, before it is attacked by insects, and collect the seeds as soon as they ripen.

Angelica has a strong aromatic and pungent flavour. When biting into the fresh stem, there is at first a bitter taste, then an intense warmth pervades the mouth. The most common use for angelica is as a candied decoration for cakes and puddings, but the leaves and roots can also be used for flavouring fish dishes and for sweetening stewed fruit, and the leaf ribs peeled, blanched to remove some bitterness, then boiled as a vegetable. Infused dried leaves taste like a scented China tea and the seeds are used to flavour drinks – vermouth, chartreuse and especially gin. Preserves, jam and marmalade are given an interesting flavour by small quantities of the peeled, chopped, fresh stem. Diabetics should avoid eating quantities of angelica because of its sugar content.

A strong, volatile oil is present in all parts of the plant, but especially in the root, and angelica is effective as a general tonic, a stimulant, digestive and expectorant, and can be taken for anaemia, flatulence, and for bronchitis and chest complaints. It will also promote urine and perspiration. Make the tea by infusing 15g/½oz seeds or dried root in 1 litre/1¾ pints boiling water – but drink only 1 cupful twice a day after meals, to avoid over-stimulation and insomnia. The tea is reputed to cause

Angelica sylvestris

a strong dislike for alcohol and is sometimes used as a treatment for alcoholics. The stem can be chewed as a digestive but the flavour is too strong to be pleasant.

Strain the tea to make a cool bath for tired eyes or a wash to cleanse the skin. The scented leaves are an ingredient in pot pourri. Bees and wasps are attracted by the abundant nectar on angelica flowers and it is sometimes possible to catch and destroy queen wasps as they come to feed.

Although angelica is seldom used as a medicine today, it had a reputation as one of the most powerful of herbs, known by early herbalists as the 'Root of the Holy Ghost'. It was believed to be a panacea, under the protection of Michael the Archangel, a certain defence against evil spirits, witchcraft and, as Gerard said, 'all infections taken by evill and corrupt aire . . . yea, although that corrupt aire hath possessed the hart, yet it driveth it out again by urine and sweat'. Angelica was commonly carried to ward off the plague.

Angelica sylvestris
Wild angelica
Family: Umbelliferae
Wild angelica grows in damp, shady places on woodland borders, marshlands and river banks in Britain and Europe. Although it grows as tall as garden angelica, the wild species has a more slender stem and a head of white, pink-tinged flowers. It can be distinguished from other umbellifers by its aromatic scent, inflated petiole bases and branching stems, but should never be used unless identification is certain as some similar umbellifers are poisonous. Wild angelica has similar, but weaker, medicinal properties to the cultivated species, and a more acrid flavour.

In North America the great angelica, *A. atropurpurea*, grows in damp meadows and on the banks of streams and rivers. It closely resembles the European species, but has a purple root. Great care should be taken to identify the plant accurately. The properties are similar to those of *A. archangelica*.

Anthriscus cerefolium
Chervil
Family: Umbelliferae

Native to eastern Europe and western Asia, chervil is now cultivated and often naturalized in other parts of the world, especially in France, where it is regarded as an indispensable culinary herb. It is believed to have been introduced to northern Europe and Britain by the Romans.

The lacy, finely divided leaves are a bright, light green, turning a pinky red as the plant reaches maturity; the stem is finely ridged and slightly hairy above the nodes, and the root long, pale and tapering. The white flowers bloom from early summer in small umbels and are followed by dark, hairless attenuated seeds, similar to those of cumin. It is an annual and generally grows about 60cm/2ft high.

The site of the chervil bed is important, and it may be necessary to sow seed in several different places round the garden before finding the right spot, but once it has become established it will flourish and self-seed prolifically from year to year. Most soils are suitable, as long as they are well drained and not too heavy. As the plants should be sheltered from direct wind and from direct sun, a dappled shade is ideal, near a small tree or tall herbaceous plants, whose leaves will fall and allow only the winter sun to reach the chervil. Keep the plants well watered, for if allowed to become too dry the leaves will quickly redden and the plant shoot into flower before the leaves can be harvested.

Sow the seeds fresh in late summer, by sprinkling them onto finely raked soil and covering thinly. Or hang bundles of ripe chervil heads upside down above the bed, to scatter their seeds. The seeds will quickly germinate. Thin the seedlings to about 20cm/8in apart. These

Anthriscus cerefolium

seedlings will winter well and produce lush foliage in the spring – in early spring if covered with a cloche – or if the seed is sown in the greenhouse the leaves will be available throughout the winter. Avoid transplanting if possible, as this encourages early flowering, and quickly nip off any flowering stems. Seed can also be sown in the spring, but it is always difficult to prevent flowering and to keep the leaves lush in midsummer. Ideally seed should be sown in succession so that the herb is available throughout the year.

As chervil leaves are so fine and light, large quantities are often needed in the kitchen. It is worth setting aside a good-sized bed for it, perhaps 1m/3ft square, or a large tub in a shady place outside the kitchen door. Leaves can be cut at any time but are difficult to dry satisfactorily.

The flavour of chervil is fresh, subtle, slightly sweet, with a touch of aniseed. In small quantities it enhances the flavours of other herbs – it is one of the *fines herbes* mixture – and it can be used lavishly on its own. Delicate white fish, eggs, cream cheese, sauces and soups, fresh salads and spring vegetables are all suited to this light, delicious herb. Add the leaves towards the end of the cooking time – they lose their subtlety with long simmering – or use them raw, either chopped or broken into sprigs, or as a garnish.

As chervil is one of the earliest spring herbs and also has blood-cleansing properties, it is the ingredient of many traditional Lenten dishes. Like many other umbellifers it is a digestive, and can also be used to increase perspiration during colds and fevers and is reputed to lower blood pressure. An infusion can be made by pouring a cup of boiling water onto a tablespoon of the fresh herb, but it is so delicious eaten raw that this is hardly necessary. Chervil vinegar, made by macerating a handful of bruised seeds in 600ml/1 pint vinegar is recommended by Pliny for hiccups.

Use fresh chervil juice or the infusion as a lotion to clear and cleanse the skin.

Aphanes arvensis

Apium graveolens var. *dulce*

Aphanes arvensis

Parsley piert, parsley breakstone
Family: Rosaceae

The annual parsley piert is closely related to lady's mantle and looks similar, though much smaller. It grows at low altitudes in dry, stony places in Britain, Europe and North Africa and is naturalized in North America. The tiny, downy, lobed leaves are a pale green-grey and the stems either creep or grow upright. The height can vary from 1cm/½in to 20cm/8in. The yellowish flowers grow in minute clusters in early summer.

Transplant young plants to a dry, sunny corner of the garden and leave them to seed themselves.

The leaves can be eaten as a salad herb; they have a slightly astringent, pleasant taste and are cooling in the mouth. Drink a regular infusion 3 times a day in wineglassful doses to treat bladder and kidney complaints and to promote the flow of urine. Parsley piert was widely thought to act on bladder stones, a use perhaps first suggested by its stony habitat.

Apium graveolens var. *dulce*
Celery

Family: Umbelliferae

This is the cultivated celery, introduced into Britain in the late 17th century from Italy, replacing as a potherb the acrid little wild celery, known as 'smallage', that grows in salt marshes and river estuaries in Britain and Europe.

The leaves are smooth, shining, yellow-green and feathery, and the fleshy ridged stem is a bright green unless blanched pale. It is a biennial, umbels of white flowers appearing in late summer during the second year, followed by dark, ridged seeds.

Sow the seeds in boxes of fine soil indoors in early spring, or sow outside in late spring. They are slow to germinate. Plant out the seedlings 40cm/16in apart in a rich, moist soil, then keep well watered. The stems can be blanched, but this eliminates their Vitamin A and C content. The stems will be ready to eat in the autumn, traditionally after the first frost, but the leaves can be picked and used fresh at any time, or dried carefully in the shade to preserve colour and flavour.

Harvest and dry the roots in the autumn of the first year leaving a few plants to produce seed the following year.

Celery has an individual, fresh flavour and crisp texture. Eat the leaf stems raw (Evelyn places it 'in the middle of the Grand Sallet . . . as the Grace of the whole Board'), or braised or boiled, and chop the leaves fresh into salads or add to cooked dishes towards the end of the cooking time. The seeds are warming and aromatic, use them and the root to flavour stews and casseroles.

Unblanched celery is rich in vitamins and mineral salts. It is a digestive and stimulant with a reputation for lowering blood pressure and has been used as a treatment for rheumatism.

Apium graveolens
var. *dulce*

Arctium lappa

Burdock, beggar's buttons
Family: Compositae

This large biennial is common on dry roadsides and wasteland in temperate climates. The big, oval leaves are dull green above and downy beneath. In its second year it grows over 1m/3ft high, with small, purple flowerheads in midsummer. These have sharply hooked bracts that later become the burs.

Sow ripe seed in the autumn in a light, dry soil, and dig and dry the roots in the autumn of the following year. The young leaves can also be dried. Peel the tender leaf stems for braising or to add to soups; mix the leaves with dandelion to make an excellent beer.

The roots are most astringent and contain inulin, sugar, mucilage and volatile oils. Infuse the leaves or make a decoction of the root and take a small glass before meals to settle the stomach and cleanse the blood. Use as a face rinse to cleanse and freshen the skin. Apply boiled or crushed leaves to aches and bruises.

Armoracia rusticana

Horseradish
Family: Cruciferae

Horseradish probably originated in eastern Europe, but has been cultivated for thousands of years and now grows wild in many parts of the world, especially on roadsides and dry banks.

It is perennial with large, narrow, sometimes deeply cut leaves and a thick, tapering, fleshy root. In temperate climates long, loose panicles of white, four-petalled flowers occasionally appear in midsummer, but the seeds seldom ripen.

Plant out sections of the root 25cm/10in apart and 30cm/12in deep in richly manured ground in early spring. Horseradish easily spreads and becomes a pest, so lift the roots each autumn and store in moist sand, planting some out again the following year.

The root contains similar oils to those in mustard seed and can taste powerfully, even painfully hot, especially near the outer rind. Always use it raw or dried as the flavour is lost when cooked (or when exposed to the sun). Use freshly grated or dried and powdered in sauces, with hot and cold meat and fish, sausages and vegetables, or macerate slices in vinegar. The hot, young leaves are one of the bitter herbs of the Jewish Passover.

A tea or decoction of horseradish is antiseptic, stimulant, laxative and strongly diuretic, but as it becomes a purgative when taken in large doses it is best used only externally. Apply grated fresh root to aching joints and chilblains, or infuse it in milk as a skin tonic. Traditionally taken to expel worms, horseradish has only been used as a food during the last two or three hundred years.

Armoracia rusticana

Artemisia species
Family: Compositae
There are nearly 200 species of artemisia, many of them tough, perennial, shrubby weeds, that survive in the dry, dusty conditions of North American prairies, Siberian steppes and the deserts of Turkestan. The European species are often found on roadsides, wastegrounds and bare tracts of land near the sea, and flower from midsummer. Many have been cultivated and used as medicines to expel worms, bitter tonics, digestives, antiseptics and insecticides. Some are used as flavourings, such as the aromatic Roman wormwood, *Artemisia pontica*, which flavours vermouth; others make decorative border and rock plants, such as *A. stelleriana*, with its silvery, lobed leaves, and the little *A. granatensis*.

Artemisia abrotanum
Southernwood, lad's love, old man
Family: Compositae
Southernwood is a native of southern Europe, introduced to Britain in the mid-16th century and carried to America by the early colonists. It is perennial and grows up to 1.2m/4ft high. The finely divided, feathery leaves are a soft grey-green, and the yellow flowers, which are rayless and look like small buttons, often fail to appear in northern climates. The foliage has a powerfully sweet and penetrating scent.

Take cuttings in the spring or hardwood cuttings in the autumn, and when these are established plant them out in a dry, light soil in a sunny position. Southernwood will need regular clipping to prevent straggling growth. It is hardy, but never harvest the leaves after midsummer, for the grey foliage is protective and a newly clipped plant will die if exposed to cold winds or frost. The leaves dry easily hung in an airy place.

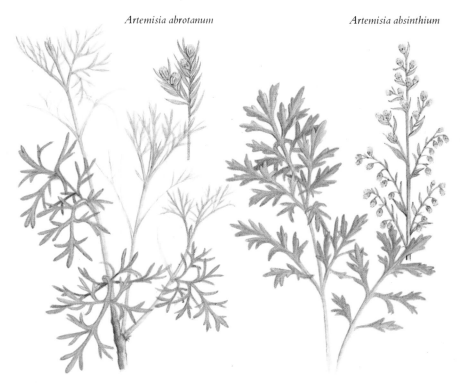

Artemisia abrotanum

Artemisia absinthium

The young tips can be used as a culinary flavouring, but have a strong smell and bitter taste. Like other wormwoods, southernwood possesses a strongly antiseptic and disinfectant oil, absinthol, which efficiently expels worms. Infuse a very weak tea from the young tops and take by the tablespoon to promote menstruation and as a general tonic. The name 'lad's love' derives from an ointment made from the ashes of the herb to encourage growth of the beard and other hair.

Southernwood was carried in the streets as a protection against infection and set in courts to ward off jail fever. Bunches of the dried herb among clothes act as a moth deterrent and a plant growing in the chicken run will discourage chicken lice. Plant it near roses to prevent aphis, near fruit trees against moth and with cabbages against the cabbage white butterfly.

Southernwood makes a compact hedging plant.

Artemisia absinthium
Wormwood, common wormwood, old woman
Family: Compositae
Native to Europe and Russia, and introduced in the U.S.A., perennial wormwood grows on roadsides and wasteground. It has aromatic leaves which are deeply cut and downy, downy stems with a silvery sheen and small greenish-yellow flowers.

Plant seeds, cuttings or divided roots in dappled shade, 60cm/2ft apart and away from tender herbs, which can be affected by its toxic substances.

Bitter wormwood, unusable and unsafe in the kitchen, is the notorious flavouring of absinthe. It was widely used as a worm expeller and tonic, but as strong doses produce convulsions it should not be taken.

Wormwood was strewn on floors as an insecticide, hung among clothes and in the granary, and a strong infusion used to disinfect hospital floors. Use a weak infusion as an insecticide spray but never directly onto other plants.

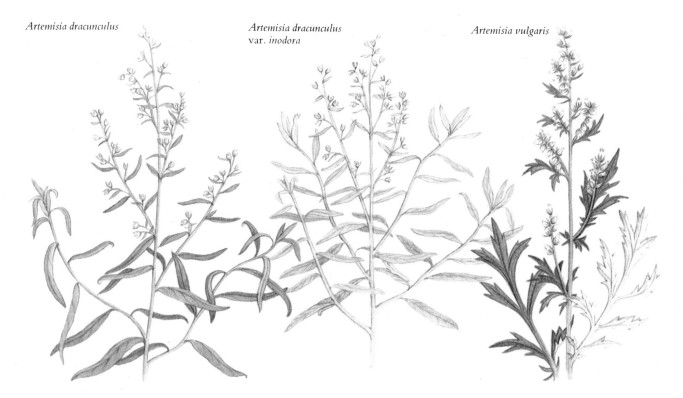

Artemisia dracunculus

Artemisia dracunculus var. *inodora*

Artemisia vulgaris

Artemisia dracunculus

Tarragon, French tarragon
Family: Compositae
Unlike other artemisias, tarragon has entire leaves, narrow, pointed and smooth. It grows about 1m/3ft high and is a dark green southern-European plant. The small greenish flowers barely open in cool climates, so it can only be propagated by cuttings or root division. Plant the cuttings out in late spring, about 60cm/2ft apart, leaving plenty of room for the spreading roots. They need a sunny position in a rather poor but well-drained soil, for the roots must be prevented from growing too fast and lush – they must be strong and hardy to withstand the winter and wet soil will weaken them. It is best to cut the whole plant down in the autumn and cover the roots with straw, uncovering them only when the danger of frost is past and new growth has begun. Lift, divide and replant the roots every 2 years in the spring, otherwise the flavour will deteriorate.

Pick the leaves fresh during the summer. They do not dry successfully but their flavour can be preserved in oil or vinegar. Bring a plant into the greenhouse in late summer to prolong growth.

The flavour of tarragon is warm and subtle, with a sharp, bitter bite to it, and it is one of the most useful culinary herbs. It heightens the flavours of other herbs and on its own will give a distinctive flavouring to sauces, salads, egg and fish dishes. Like basil, it goes well with tomatoes. Use only a few leaves at a time, for they contain a strong oil that can easily dominate a dish. It is a warming herb but has seldom been used medicinally.

The vigorous Russian tarragon grows taller than French tarragon and has slightly paler leaves and a coarser flavour. It is quite difficult to distinguish between the plants and packeted tarragon seed is invariably the Russian variety, *A. dracunculus* var. *inodora*.

Artemisia vulgaris

Mugwort, St John's plant
Family: Compositae
The perennial mugwort is a rampant weed in Britain, Europe, Asia and the U.S.A. The broad, deeply cut leaves are dark green above with silver down beneath; the stems are often reddish and the small yellow flowers bloom from early summer. It is easily propagated by seed or root.

Gather and dry the leaves and tops just before flowering; dig the roots in autumn and dry whole. The leaves were used to flavour and preserve ale before the introduction of hops. They taste less bitter than wormwood, and can be used to counter fatty meat. The flowering tops were a traditional Continental ingredient of goose stuffing. The root and leaves have similar properties to wormwood and, though less potent, should only be taken in small doses. Take a weak infusion of leaves, tops or root as an antiseptic tonic. A strong infusion added to the bath has an invigorating effect.

Balsamita major
Costmary, alecost, bible leaf
Family: Compositae

The perennial costmary was introduced into European gardens from the Orient hundreds of years ago, and was taken to North America by the early colonists.

The long, graceful, oval leaves are finely toothed and a soft green in colour. In midsummer loose clusters of small yellow flowers appear – with white daisy-like outer rays in some strains. These flowers seldom set seed in northern climates and when growing in the shade the plant seldom blossoms at all, only producing vigorous leaves. It grows about 1m/3ft high, often becoming straggly and needing support.

Propagation is by seed in the spring or, more commonly, by root division in the spring or autumn. The plants should be set out about 60cm/2ft apart in a well-drained soil. Like the closely related tansy, the roots will spread fast and may need containing in a buried, bottomless pot or bucket.

Harvest and dry the leaves just before flowering, when the oils are most concentrated. They smell sweet and soft, like balsam and lemon, and their flavour has a bitter edge, reminiscent of mint and tansy. Use only small amounts for flavouring food as it can easily overpower other, more delicate flavours. Add a chopped leaf to salads or stuffings or mix with melted butter and serve with new potatoes and carrots. As the name 'alecost' implies, the traditional use was as a popular spicy flavouring for ale.

The leaves have astringent and antiseptic qualities and were used in a wound ointment – pounded with olive oil and the little adder's tongue fern. Take an infusion made from the leaves, a glassful twice a day, for colds, upset stomachs, as a general tonic and to promote menstruation.

Balsamita major

The crushed, fresh leaves soothe insect bites and stings.

The sweet, long-lasting scent and insect repellent qualities of costmary made it a popular strewing herb. Dried branches were hung in cupboards and laid in presses to discourage moths and other insects. Parkinson says that 'the flowers also are tyed up with small bundels of Lavender toppes, these being put in the middle of them, to lye upon the toppes of beds, presses etc, for the sweete scent and savour it casteth.' He also speaks of its use 'with other sweet herbes to make sweete washing water'. This was one of costmary's most popular uses. An infusion of the leaves or the fresh leaves themselves give a delicious scent to rinsing water for the hair, for linen, or to bath water. The dried leaves can also be used in pot pourri to strengthen the scents of other herbs.

The name 'bible leaf' comes from its use as a scented, pressed bible marker. 'Cost' is derived from the Greek word for 'spicy herb', so costmary means 'the spicy herb of Mary'. It appears to have been used as a woman's herb since early times, for all uterine complaints and to ease childbirth. Culpeper says that during labour it 'moisteneth the hardness of the mother'.

A similar though smaller herb called 'maudlin' is often mentioned by old herbalists and another closely related variety still grown today is the camphor plant, almost identical to costmary but with slightly larger leaves that are camphor scented. Although not the source of the commercial oil, this makes a good insecticide laid dried among clothes or used as a spray in the garden.

Borago officinalis
Borage, bee bread
Family: Boraginaceae
Believed to have originated in Syria, borage is now widely cultivated in Europe and America, and often escapes to grow in hedgebanks and by roads. On rich ground it grows at least 1m/3ft high, with stout prickly stems and broad, rough, wrinkled leaves covered with stiff hairs. Borage blooms from midsummer. The star-shaped flowers open pink, then become bright blue. Their prominent black anthers carry quantities of pollen, which is very attractive to bees.

Borage is an annual, but occasionally survives the winter indoors or in a greenhouse. Sow seeds in the spring – they will quickly germinate with 2 large seed leaves – and plant out in a sunny position about 50cm/20in apart. It self-sows readily and will tolerate most soils, but flourishes on a loose, rich and limy ground.

Use the leaves and flowers fresh, as they quickly lose their flavour and goodness when dried. The flowers can be preserved by crystallizing.

Pick the young leaves to eat as a salad before they become rough; they taste refreshing and cooling, with a slightly bitter, cucumber flavour. The larger leaves can be boiled in the same way as spinach, chopped in stuffings, or fried in batter as fritters. Eat the flowers raw in salad or crystallize them as decorations for puddings and cakes. They are especially well known as cooling additions to summer drinks – either steeped with a few young leaves in fruit cups, cider, beer or wine, or frozen into ice cubes and added as decorative 'conceits'.

Borage has always been associated with courage and cheerfulness, 'to exhilerate and make the mind glad', 'to drive away all sadness', and Parkinson adds that it is 'of known Vertue to revive the Hypochondriac and chear the hard Student'. Recent research suggests that borage does in fact stimulate the adrenal glands.

The leaves and flowers are rich in potassium, calcium and salts and are an excellent tonic and blood cleanser. It is also refrigerant – a fresh leaf will lower the temperature in the mouth – and thus useful for fevers. The mucilage it contains is helpful for coughs and bronchitis. Drink an infusion of the leaves and flowers, a cupful at a time, or inhale as a vapour treatment. The pulped leaves make a poultice for swellings and bruises.

Borage was introduced to northern Europe by the Romans, and is first recorded as growing in England in the 13th century. A list of necessary seeds to be taken to New England in 1631 includes '1oz Buradg seed at 4d'.

The closely related viper's bugloss, *Echium vulgare*, has similar properties. It is a biennial, grows wild in dry places, especially near the sea, and will grow from seed in the garden.

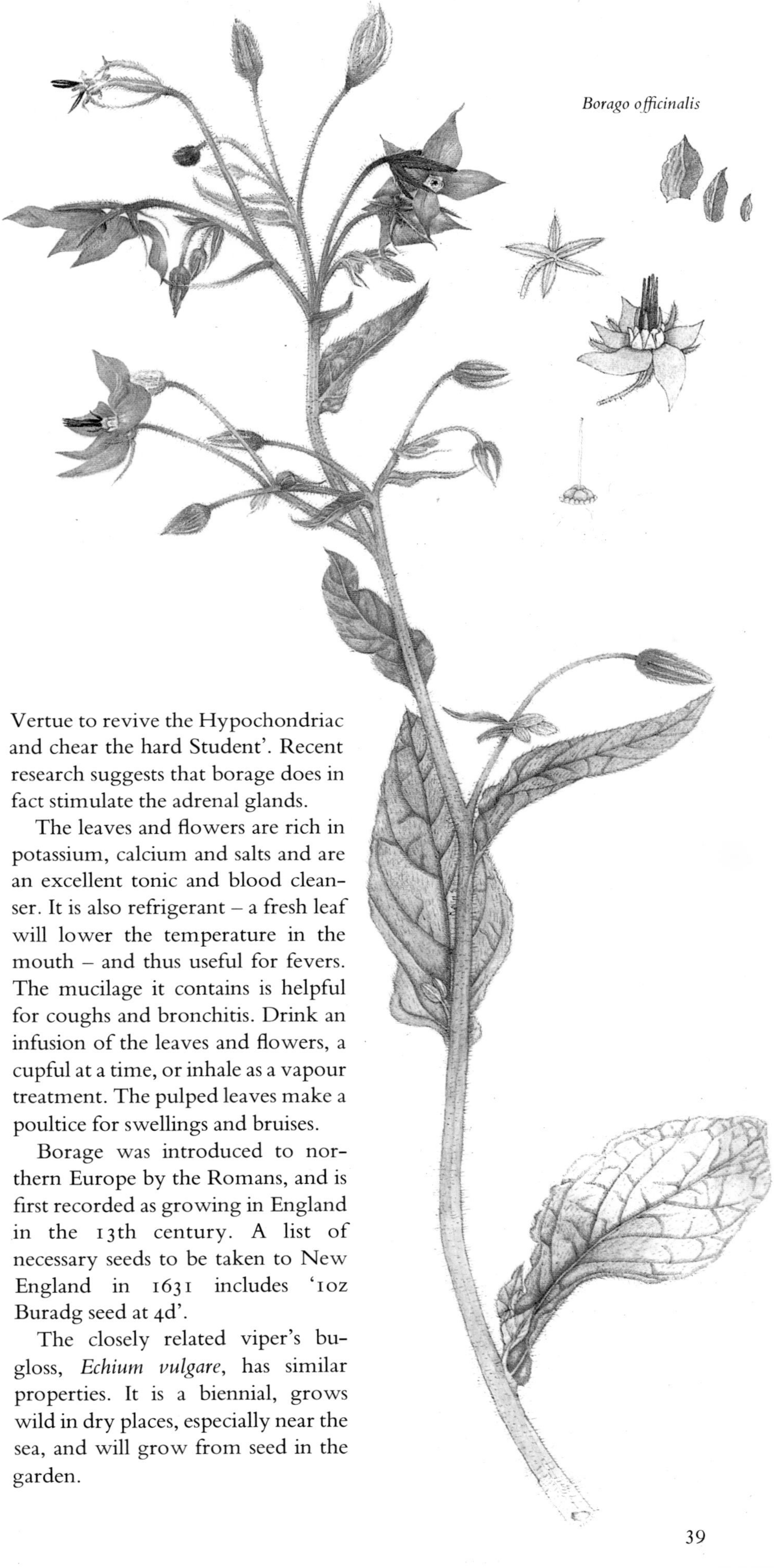

39

Brassica nigra

Calendula officinalis

Brassica nigra
Mustard, black mustard
Family: Cruciferae
The annual black mustard can grow 2m/6½ft high with bristly lobed leaves. Yellow flowers are followed by smooth, erect seed pods. Probably originally from the Middle East, it is widely cultivated. Sow the dark, round seeds in a sunny position in rich soil in spring and harvest just before the pods open in late summer. Dry the seeds in their pods.

The seeds are hotter and more pungent than those of white mustard, and contain an acrid oil and sulphur (which discolours silver spoons). It is stimulant, irritant and emetic – a tablespoon of mustard flour in lukewarm water provokes vomiting. Used as a poultice the oil draws blood to the surface of the skin, thus soothing the part. Make this by mixing 25g/1oz mustard flour and 25g/1oz bran to a paste with hot water; it can also be applied to the chest for bronchitis. Pour hot water over bruised seeds to make a soothing bath for tired feet.

Calendula officinalis
Marigold, pot marigold, Marygold
Family: Compositae
The garden marigold is a native of southern Europe, but grows well in northern climates, being tolerant of most types of soil. It flowers from early summer to late autumn and self-sows easily.

The bright orange variety has most value, but there are many others, all with round daisy heads and petals varying from pale yellow to deep orange. The long, rounded leaves are pale green and clasp the downy stems, which grow about 50cm/20in high.

Sow the seeds in the spring and thin the seedlings to about 25cm/10in apart. Marigold is an annual, though the plants occasionally survive the winter in a sheltered position. Use the leaves fresh; collect the petals as the flowers are opening and dry quickly in the shade to preserve their colour.

The leaves are edible, but have too strong and acrid a flavour to be pleasant. The petals give a piquant, distinctive flavour to salads, cheese, soups and stews. They are often used like saffron, soaked in water or milk, then added to rice, cakes and puddings to colour them yellow. Gerard describes barrels packed with dried petals 'kept throughout Dutchland against Winter' for 'broths and Physicall potions'.

The petals have stimulant properties and promote perspiration; an infusion, taken a tablespoon at a time, was recommended by many herbalists to comfort the heart and spirits. The mucilage in both flowers and leaves makes them valuable for the complexion and as a healing, soothing wound lotion. Beat 1 part bruised petals into 2 parts cold cream or infuse the petals in baby oil for the complexion. For wounds, chilblains etc, simmer 120g/4oz fresh petals in 400g/14oz lard and 150ml/¼ pint water until the water has evaporated. Strain, pressing to expel the juice, and store in a tightly stoppered jar.

Marigold petals produce creamy yellow dyes.

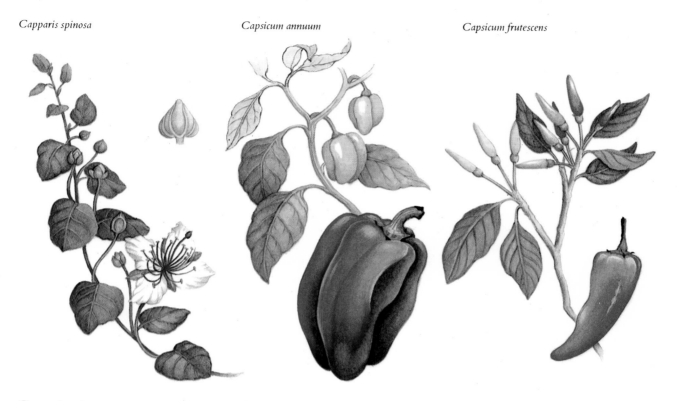

Capparis spinosa
Caper

Family: Capparidaceae

The small, trailing perennial caper bush grows wild around the Mediterranean, in stony places. The thick, shiny leaves withstand hot sun; the large, short-lived flowers bloom from early summer, with prominent purple stamens and white, frilled petals tinged with pale pink. Cuttings can be taken and grown under glass, in northern climates, in well-drained soil.

The characteristic flavour of capric acid only develops when the flower buds are pickled. Use it to complement salty or oily foods, olives, salted meat and fish. Capers add a refreshing, unexpected flavour to casseroles, or can be sprinkled with parsley over a rich daube of beef. They have a tonic and appetizing effect and aid digestion.

Do not confuse the true caper with caper spurge, whose seeds are sometimes recommended as pickles. All members of the spurge family are poisonous.

Capsicum annuum
Sweet pepper

Family: Solanaceae

Originally from tropical America, many varieties of sweet pepper are now cultivated in warm climates all over the world. It grows into a sturdy little annual bush, up to 1m/3ft high, with large shining leaves and small white flowers in midsummer. The immature fruits are green, turning red as they ripen, glossy, fleshy and slightly segmented, and up to 25cm/10in long.

In temperate climates sow the seeds of hardy varieties indoors in early spring and plant out after the frosts 60cm/2ft apart in a greenhouse or sunny, sheltered place.

The fruits contain large quantities of Vitamin C. Eat raw, baked or stewed with their acrid seeds discarded. The dried and ground flesh is paprika pepper, of which there are many grades from sweet to hot, with endless culinary uses, especially in Spanish and Hungarian cookery. It does not keep well, so buy in small quantities.

Capsicum frutescens
Chili pepper

Family: Solanaceae

Bought to Europe from South America by Spanish explorers, chilies are cultivated in most tropical regions. They are perennial, growing up to 2m/6½ft high, with smaller leaves than sweet pepper and narrower fruits. They need artificial heat in temperate climates.

Use the fruit fresh, or dry in a warm oven and store in a shady, airy place. Different varieties vary in strength. Fresh chilies are used in hot dishes from India to Mexico, and dried chilies, for pickling and flavouring. Cayenne pepper, made from ground dried fruits, is the basis of Tabasco sauce; chili powder is cayenne mixed with cumin, garlic or marjoram. Juice from fresh chilies can sting the eyes.

Chilies are stimulant, digestive, tonic and disinfectant. Take warming cayenne for chills, fever and indigestion. Sprinkle on suspect food or burn slowly in a heavy pan to fumigate a room.

Carthamus
tinctorius

Carthamus tinctorius
Safflower, dyer's saffron
Family: Compositae
Safflower has been cultivated in India, China, Egypt and southern Europe for so long that its origins are unknown. The plants grow up to 1m/3ft high, with a shaggy head of orange florets in midsummer and pointed, prickly leaves. There are several species that can be grown in northern climates on poor, dry soil, in full sun. It is an annual; seeds are sown in the spring, but the seedlings do not transplant well.

The oil is extracted from the large white seeds commercially for cooking and contains a low percentage of cholesterol. The petals make a substitute for saffron when colouring food; their flavour is slightly bitter.

As a medicine safflower also resembles saffron. Infuse a tea from the dried petals as a laxative and to induce perspiration and reduce fevers.

The florets produce a good yellow dye with water, and can give a red dye with alcohol, though the method is complicated and difficult.

Carum carvi
Caraway
Family: Umbelliferae
Caraway grows wild in Europe and in the cooler Asian countries and is naturalized in parts of the U.S.A., though seldom found wild in Britain. It is cultivated on a large scale, especially in Holland and the U.S.S.R.

The long, bright green leaves are divided and feathered, like carrot leaves; the stem is smooth, and the white or pink flowers grow in umbels. The dark and rounded seeds have 5 paler ridges. Caraway is a biennial, but once established will self-sow from year to year. Sow the seeds ripe in the autumn or in early spring in good soil, and thin the seedlings to about 20cm/8in apart.

During the first summer the leaves grow lush and thick, about 20cm/8in high, and can be cut fresh, a few at a time. The plant will die back in the autumn, or can be cut down, and will spring up early the following year to flower in the early summer. If prevented from flowering, caraway plants often live for another year with heavy foliage and many thick roots. When the seeds are almost ripe, cut the heads and hang above a cloth to catch the seeds as they fall.

The strongly aromatic, warming taste of caraway seeds is a familiar flavouring for bread, cake, biscuits, apples, cheese and cabbage, and is especially characteristic of German, Austrian and Scandinavian cookery. The flavour of the stems and leaves is also warming but milder, rather like parsley. Eat the leaves fresh, chopped in salads, mixed with cream cheese or with freshly boiled vegetables, or cooked in soups and stews. The carrot-shaped tap roots can also be eaten; they taste similar to parsnips, a rather drying flavour. The seeds were used to flavour the old-fashioned caraway comfits, and their oil for liqueurs such as kümmel.

The seeds are rich in protein and are well known for their digestive properties. They are often eaten with heavy, fatty foods. Chewed before meals they help digestion and stimulate the appetite, and $\frac{1}{2}$ teaspoon of bruised seeds infused in a cup of hot water can be given, a teaspoonful at a time, to colicky children. Chew the seeds or fresh leaves to sweeten the breath and disguise the strong smell of garlic.

Varieties of caraway have been used as food and medicine since very early times; the seeds have been found among the rubbish on prehistoric sites in southern Europe. They were a common ingredient in 15th-century English cookery (Falstaff is invited to 'a pippin and a dish of caraways'), and Gerard writes that 'it consumeth wind' and 'is delightfull to the stomacke and taste'. Later they became unpopular but revived during the reign of Queen Victoria when everything German was the fashion.

Such an ancient plant will inevitably gather legendary and magical powers. Caraway was thought of as a protective and binding herb, used against evil and witchcraft and as an ingredient in love potions, to bind the affections. The seeds were added to the chicken feed to prevent the fowls from wandering, and are still sometimes given to homing pigeons today.

Cassia marilandica

Carum carvi

Cassia marilandica

Cassia marilandica
American senna, wild senna
Family : Leguminosae
This hardy perennial species grows in temperate North America, up to 2m/6½ft high with yellow flowers, followed by long, dark pods, and leaves divided into narrow leaflets. Sow fresh seed in the autumn in light, sunny ground and thin to 60cm/2ft apart. Harvest leaves from midsummer, when the plant is in bloom.

American senna acts as an efficient laxative, but should be taken with some aromatic flavouring to prevent griping. As the strength of the pods may vary, it is safer to use the leaves. Cover 25g/1oz leaves and a teaspoon of coriander seed or ginger with 600ml/1 pint boiling water and leave to infuse for 15 minutes. Take a glassful, hot or cold, 3 times a day.

Alexandrian senna, *Cassia senna*, grows in North Africa and has a more powerful laxative action. Steep 3–10 pods in a glassful of cold water for an hour. Neither senna should be taken on a regular basis.

Chamaemelum nobile

Chamomilla species
Family: Compositae

There are many species of chamomile growing in temperate climates, all with finely divided leaves and daisy-like flowers with conical yellow centres, blooming from midsummer. The Roman and German chamomiles are most valuable in the herb garden, but there is some controversy over their properties. The flowers of both can be used for medical purposes, but the German is cultivated most often as a medicine, as it has a stronger and less acrid oil, while the Roman, with its mat-forming leaves, is grown as a scented turf.

Roman chamomile, *Chamaemelum nobile*, is a perennial and has tough, jointed stems that grow low or prostrate, and strongly aromatic, finely divided leaves. The flowers bloom from early summer, with many white rays surrounding a solid yellow centre. This is a sure way to distinguish the Roman from the German species, for the yellow centre of the German chamomile is hollow.

In order to form a good, dense turf, all flowerheads should be nipped off to prevent the plants straggling. To overcome this problem a new variety has been developed, *C. nobile* 'Treneague', which is non-flowering and propagated by division of the runners in the spring or late summer. The seed of the double- or single-flowered varieties is sown in late spring, either in the herb garden or broadcast over the prepared ground for lawns or paths. The soil should be a good, lightly composted loam. Plant out or thin the seedlings to about 10cm/4in apart for chamomile turf and avoid treading on them until they are well established and beginning to bind together. Once established, the turf should be regularly walked upon and rolled to encourage the plants to spread and to discourage flowering. Weeding can be a tiresome job, especially during the first year.

The first recorded description of a grass lawn in Britain dates from the 17th century; earlier lawns were often of chamomile, which makes a

thick, sweet-scented carpet when the plants are well established. John Evelyn describes October as the month when it will 'be time to beat, roll and mow carpet walks of chamomile'.

The annual German, true or wild chamomile, *Chamomilla recutita*, grows wild in Europe and is naturalized in parts of the U.S.A., often as a cornfield weed. It is similar to the Roman species, but has upright stems, growing 1m/3ft high. The flowers have a single border of white rays, which droop down around the high, rounded, hollow yellow centres as the flowers mature.

Sow the seeds in autumn or spring, cover thinly with fine soil and keep well watered until the plants are established. Gather the young flowers for drying on a fine sunny morning as soon as the dew has evaporated, and dry as quickly as possible in an airy place at a low temperature.

Chamomile is seldom used in cooking, although in Spain the bitter flowers are used to flavour sherry.

Chamomilla recutita

There the plant is called *manzanilla*, which means 'little apple', and a reference to its apple-like scent occurs in many other languages.

Both Roman and German chamomiles possess a powerful, aromatic oil, which is especially potent in the flowers. It has healing, warming and digestive properties. The most common use for the dried flowers is as a soothing, sedative tea to calm the nerves, prevent nightmares and promote menstruation. Inhale the steam from the infusion for its calming effect, and use a strong infusion (50g/2oz dried flowers to 600ml/1 pint boiling water) as an antiseptic and cleansing steam treatment for the skin. Add a strong infusion or decoction to bath water for its soothing effect. For inflammations, abscesses and rheumatism, wrap the flowers in a cloth, soak in boiling water for 10 minutes, then apply as a warm poultice.

A soothing oil can be made by bruising the fresh blossoms and leaving to soak in a mild, tasteless oil for several weeks in a warm place or on a sunny windowsill. Add the oil to bath or washing water or rub onto aching joints, or into the scalp as a hair conditioner. For a blonde rinse, use a strong infusion of the flowers. Pour several times over newly washed hair, catching in a bowl placed beneath.

Both German and Roman chamomiles are beneficial in the garden and have been called 'physician's plants' as they sometimes revive nearby, ailing plants. Use chamomile tea as a health-giving spray and to prevent seedlings from 'damping off'. A strong infusion works well as a compost activator, in the same way as the related yarrow.

One of the most ancient medicinal herbs, chamomile or mayweed is praised in all herbals. The Anglo-Saxon Nine Herbs Charm includes chamomile. 'Remember . . . that he never yielded his life because of infection/ After Mayweed was dressed for his food.' Turner says that common chamomile was consecrated 'unto the Sonne' by Egyptians, and Tusser includes it in his list of 21 aromatic strewing herbs.

Dyer's chamomile, *Anthemis tinctoria*, is another popular species. The bright yellow flowers yield an orange-brown dye, and it is a decorative herbaceous plant, its silvery foliage growing about 50cm/20in high. Corn chamomile, *A. arvensis* and stinking mayweed, *A. cotula*, grow in fields and waste places, but lack the aromatic apple scent and beneficial properties of the Roman and German species.

Chelidonium majus

Chenopodium album

Chelidonium majus
Greater celandine, swallow wort
Family : Papaveraceae

The greater celandine is a member of the poppy family and unrelated to lesser celandine. It grows in Britain and throughout Europe and was taken by early colonists to America. It is seldom cultivated now and grows outcast, in hedgebanks, near villages and ruins.

The hollow stems grow about 1m/3ft high, the leaves are divided into ovate leaflets, pale green above, silvery beneath. The flowers bloom from late spring and have 4 flimsy yellow petals followed by long seed capsules. It is perennial, and can be cultivated from seed. The leaf stalks and stems contain a strongly acrid, poisonous, yellow juice, which was universally prized as an eye treatment – mixed with fennel and wormwood, tempered with mother's milk and dropped in the eye to remove specks and 'slimie things'. This is not to be recommended, but the juice works well used externally as a wart remover.

Chenopodium species
Family : Chenopodiaceae

Many edible plants and familiar weeds belong to this large family, including spinach and all the garden beets, the colonizing goosefoot and orache, and the succulent little glassworts that can survive in extremely exposed conditions in salt marshes. These are all edible plants, but other species, such as the American wormseed, *Chenopodium ambrosioides*, can be poisonous. In appearance this wormseed is similar to fat hen, and an oil extracted from the seeds is used in the preparation of a vermifuge – to expel worms – which should only be bought from reputable chemists.

The flowers of most species are insignificant, and the leaves often triangular and lobed or toothed. The generic name *Chenopodium* comes from the Greek words meaning 'goose foot', and refers to the resemblance of the leaves to a broad, webbed foot.

Chenopodium album
Fat hen, white goosefoot, dungweed, pigweed, lamb's quarters
Family : Chenopodiaceae

The annual fat hen is a prolific weed. In temperate climates it springs up on any disturbed ground, road embankments or farm middens, growing over 1m/3ft tall with erect, often reddish stems. The leaves are roughly diamond-shaped with a white, mealy covering, which is especially dense on the underside; the flowers are insignificant, growing in greenish spikes in midsummer and followed by tiny green or reddish fruits.

The leaves have been eaten as a potherb since prehistoric times and are exceptionally rich in iron and other minerals, proteins and vitamins. The seeds, which contain fat and albumen, can be ground as flour or gruel, and make a nutritious poultry food. They were included in the last meal eaten by the Iron Age 'Tollund man', whose perfectly preserved body was discovered in a Danish peat bog in 1950.

Chenopodium bonus-henricus

Chenopodium bonus-henricus
Good King Henry, mercury
Family: Chenopodiaceae
Good King Henry is a perennial, slower growing than fat hen. It is found in temperate climates, in farm yards, on roadsides, near old buildings and often as a relic of an old kitchen garden. The leaves are fairly large, halberd-shaped and glossy and the small greenish flowers grow in spikes in midsummer.

Until the introduction of spinach, Good King Henry was grown regularly as an extremely nutritious potherb, and is worth cultivating. Plant the seed in spring, or roots in spring or autumn, in rich, manured soil and keep well watered.

The flavour is less pronounced and slightly sweeter than spinach, and the leaves can be used in similar ways – boiled, puréed or in tarts and stuffings. Bruise the leaves as a poultice for sore skin.

In Germany the poisonous dog's mercury of the woods is called 'Bad Henry', so the good potherb mercury took the name of 'Good King Henry'.

Cichorium intybus
Chicory, succory, barbe de capucin
Family: Compositae
Chicory is widely cultivated and grows wild on limy soil in Britain, Europe and the U.S.A. It is a large, perennial plant, often growing well over 1m/3ft high, with long, pointed, dandelion-like leaves. The flowers also resemble dandelions, but are sky blue, and only open in the mornings. The tap root grows thick, long and fleshy.

Sow the seed 3cm/1in deep in early spring, thin out the young plants 30cm/12in apart and keep well watered. Large leaves grow during the summer; in the autumn lift the roots in succession, cut the leaves off (they make nutritious poultry food) and bury the roots in a deep box or tub of damp soil. Keep this in a fairly warm place and cover either with at least 20cm/8in sand or ash or with a lid, to exclude all light. Cut the new, fat, blanched leaves as the tips appear above the sand, leaving the roots to produce a second crop. Plant some roots about every 2 weeks to give a continuous supply of leaves throughout the winter. In early spring, heap earth over any remaining plants in the garden to blanch a final crop before the stems thicken and toughen for flowering, then compost any remaining plants.

Eat the juicy, blanched leaves as a crisp salad, or braised in butter or oil. The thick roots can be dug in the autumn of the first year, dried and ground and used as a coffee substitute.

Chicory is a tonic and digestive herb; take a small glass of tea made from the leaves for anaemia and digestive troubles, to clear the skin and purify the blood, or boil 15g/½oz dried root for 5 minutes in 1 litre/ 1¾ pints water and infuse for 10 minutes.

Many Roman writers mention chicory as a vegetable and tonic.

Cichorium intybus

Cinnamomum aromaticum   *Cinnamomum verum*   *Coriandrum sativum*

Cinnamomum aromaticum
Cassia, bastard cinnamon
Family: Lauraceae

The evergreen cassia tree is native to China and Burma and is grown commercially in many subtropical countries. It has long shining leaves, small pale green flowers and a loose, thin, peeling bark.

The trees are grown in plantations and coppiced, for the new long shoots provide the scented bark. The stripped bark curls into 'quills' as it dries, and is exported in bundles; the dried unripe fruits are sold as Chinese Cassia Buds, and the dried leaves used as a flavouring, *tej pat*, in Indian cookery.

The flavour of the bark is not as subtle as true cinnamon, but strong and pungent and often used as a substitute. The buds have a similar flavour and are used in the manufacture of drinks and sweets, and for scenting pot pourri.

Cassia has been used as a spice in Europe since the Middle Ages, and also to treat indigestion and to increase the flow of milk.

Cinnamomum verum
Cinnamon

Family: Lauraceae

The cinnamon tree is smaller than cassia, with similar tough shiny leaves, small yellowish-white flowers and a dark blue berry. It is native to Sri Lanka, but cultivated in the West Indies and in many eastern countries.

The bark is harvested from the young shoots, the palest bark being of the finest quality. The quills are thinner and more fragile than those of cassia. Buy ground cinnamon in small quantities as the flavour soon deteriorates.

Use the delicate, sweet flavour of cinnamon to spice sweet creams, cakes and chocolates; cassia is better suited to richer dishes of meat and rice. Cinnamon is stimulant, digestive and antiseptic; mix a teaspoon of ground cinnamon in a glass of warm water as a mouthwash. Add $\frac{1}{2}$ teaspoon to a cup of tea for diarrhoea and stomach troubles, and take a teaspoon of cinnamon brandy with hot milk for colds and 'flu.

Coriandrum sativum
Coriander, dizzycorn
Family: Umbelliferae

One of the most ancient culinary herbs, coriander grows wild in south-east Europe and has been cultivated for thousands of years in India, China and Egypt. It is grown in many temperate countries today. A hardy annual, growing up to 60cm/2ft high, it has a fine stem, shining lower leaves divided into broad segments, and thread-like upper leaves. The flowers bloom in midsummer in small, pink-tinged umbels and are followed by largish round seeds. The pungent leaves and unripe seeds smell almost unpleasantly strong.

Sow the seeds in early spring, or in autumn for the plants to survive the winter. They need a fairly light, dry soil and sunny position. Like other annual umbellifers, such as dill and chervil, the seedlings do not transplant well, as they tend then to shoot too quickly into flower. Pick the leaves fresh at any time from early summer; they are not suitable for drying. Gather the seedheads as the seeds change from green to light brown, and hang in an airy place above a cloth for the seeds to ripen.

The ripe seeds are strongly aromatic, sweet and pleasant, with a slightly bitter edge like zest of orange. They can be used to flavour both sweet and savoury food, liqueurs and sweetmeats, stews, pickles and marinades and especially curries. Buy the seeds whole as they are easy to crush. The fresh leaves can also be used lavishly with curries. Eaten on their own, they do not suit many palates, having a strong, almost foetid taste, but when combined with chilies and other hot foods they provide a cool, pungent and unique foil to the hot spices. A common and delicious Indian chutney is made by pounding quantities of coriander leaves with chilies, garlic, mustard oil and salt. In Thailand the roots are crushed with garlic and used as a flavouring.

The first monks included coriander among their medicinal herbs. Today coriander seeds are occasionally used to disguise the taste of other unpleasant medicines and the aromatic oil in the seeds acts as a stimulant and digestive. Chew the seeds or eat as sugared comfits, or make coriander water in the same way as dill water. Mix a few pounded seeds with honey for coughs. They can have a narcotic effect when eaten in very large quantities, which explains the name 'dizzycorn'.

The name 'coriander' originates from the Greek *koriannon* meaning 'bug', a reference to the smell of the leaves and unripe seed. They were a common ingredient in early Greek medicine and recommended by Hippocrates. Later Pliny recorded that coriander of the highest quality was grown in Egypt. Late Bronze Age invaders brought coriander to Britain, to flavour their barley gruel, and the seeds were used in medicines, cookery and love potions during the medieval and Renaissance times. Gerard describes it as a 'very stinking herbe', but admits that the dried seed is 'convenient to sundry purposes'. The first American settlers carried the seed to the New World where it became naturalized in many places and is widely cultivated today. Spanish conquistadors introduced coriander to Mexico and Peru, and there it soon became an indispensable companion to the native chili. In England coriander was used less in the 19th century, but has regained popularity this century, with the renewed interest in spicy cooking and with the increase of immigrants from India and Pakistan.

Coriandrum sativum

Crocus sativus
Saffron
Family: Iridaceae

The saffron flower resembles an autumn-flowering garden crocus, with long, fine leaves sprouting from a corm and blue or purple flowers that grow to a height of 15cm/6in. There are several varieties growing wild in the hills of Italy, across Greece, Iran and as far east as Kurdistan, but the cultivated form can be distinguished by its large stigmas and style that often hang out loosely from the flower. It should never be confused with the poisonous meadow or autumn crocus, *Colchicum autumnale*, a member of the lily family, which has similar flowers.

Saffron grows best in rich, sandy, well-drained soil in a sheltered position. Seed can be sown, but as the corm will take 3 years to develop sufficiently to flower, it is easier to propagate by dividing a group of corms in autumn. Pull off the 3 bright orange stigmas (and the part of the style that comes with them) when the flowers are fully open in early autumn. As they can only be picked by hand and 70,000 to 80,000 are needed to provide 450g/1lb of saffron, it is not surprising that saffron is extremely expensive.

Saffron from Valencia is considered to be of the highest quality. It is cheaper to buy the little dried filaments whole rather than powdered, and they should be stored in a dark place. Good saffron is a fresh, bright orange colour and smells strongly sweet and pungent – when old it becomes musty. Add the dried threads to a little warm water, milk or cooking liquor and leave for a few minutes to colour, scent and flavour the liquid, then add the liquid, either with the threads or strained, to the dish. Alternatively leave the threads in a low oven for a few minutes to crisp, then crumble into the food. A

Crocus sativus

pinch will colour and flavour 450g/1lb of rice. When too much saffron is used a bitter taste overpowers the subtle flavour. Saffron is the traditional flavouring of many European dishes such as French bouillabaisse, Spanish paella, Milanese risotto and Cornish saffron cake, and is used extensively in Middle Eastern cookery. Safflower, marigold petals and ground turmeric are other yellow food colourings that have been used to adulterate saffron or as substitutes, but they will completely change the character of the dish.

As a medicine, saffron tea is a warming, cordial drink that can be used as a digestive or to induce menstruation or perspiration. Gerard writes that the 'moderat use thereof is good for the head, and maketh the sences more quicke and lively, shaketh off heavy and drowsie sleepe, and maketh a man merry'.

A bright yellow dye is produced from the stigmas, but this is soluble in water.

Saffron was recorded in a Theban medical papyrus in 1552 BC, and in Classical times the scent, colour and flavour were praised extravagantly by poets. The Romans probably brought saffron to Britain and northern Europe. In the 8th century Muslims introduced saffron into Spain and it was reintroduced to Britain by returning crusaders. Although very costly, about 15s a pound in Britain in the 13th century, saffron became one of the most common ingredients recorded in European medieval recipes, used to spice and colour fish and meat dishes, puddings, pies and wine. It began to be cultivated in the 15th century, often grown in rotation with coriander and teasels, but the price remained high because of the labour involved in harvesting. In Britain, by the end of the 17th century, saffron was only used for puddings, buns and cakes, although it was still a common flavouring on the Continent.

Cuminum cyminum
Cumin
Family: Umbelliferae

A small annual, seldom growing more than 30cm/12in high, cumin has a slender stem, and leaves divided into thread-like segments. There are only a few white or pale pink flowers in each partial umbel. These appear in early summer and are followed by narrow, ridged seeds that resemble caraway in appearance.

Cumin is indigenous to Egypt, but has been cultivated in eastern and European countries since earliest times. As the plants take about 4 months to reach maturity, it is advisable to sow seed in early spring, in a hot bed or under glass in northern climates. Transfer the seedlings to a sunny position in a well-drained, rich soil. Handle them delicately as they dislike being transplanted, and keep well weeded. Cut the seedheads as they begin to change colour, and hang to ripen and dry in an airy place, with a cloth beneath to catch the seeds.

There are several varieties of cumin with seeds of varying strength and colours. The seeds have a powerful, warming, aromatic flavour, stimulating and appetizing, and are an indispensable spice in the kitchen. They are a typical and constant ingredient of Indian curries and appear often in Middle Eastern and Moroccan cookery, with lamb, chicken, yoghurt and aubergines. Flavour a beef stew with $\frac{1}{2}$ teaspoon of warmed cumin seed or spice a chicken stuffing with a few crushed seeds. A traditional appetizing and digestive drink is made in India by mixing ground cumin, mint, ginger, salt, sugar and lemon juice with tamarind water. Keep both whole and ground cumin in the store cupboard, as it is difficult to grind the seed finely in a mortar. Buy ground cumin in small quantities to ensure freshness.

Cumin seed shares the digestive and anti-flatulent properties of dill, caraway and some other umbellifers, and its warming effect is felt when taken, as Gerard describes, 'in a supping broth . . . for the chest and cold lungs'. He also suggests sewing the seeds into a little bag with bay salt, heating it on a bed pan, sprinkling with vinegar and applying it to 'the stitch and paines thereof'.

Cumin is mentioned in the Bible, by Pliny (who recommends smoking the seeds to cultivate an impressive scholastic pallor), and by many Classical poets. The Celts along the Atlantic coast of France baked fish with cumin in the 1st century BC, and cumin was a common plant in the medieval herb garden.

Cuminum cyminum

Curcuma domestica

Cytisus scoparius

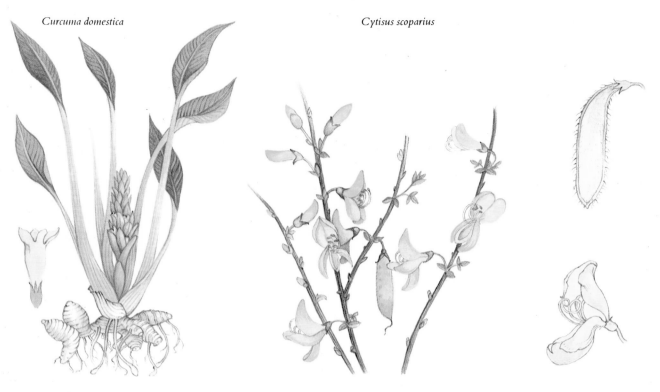

Curcuma domestica
Turmeric
Family: Zingiberaceae

Turmeric is closely related to ginger and has a similar knobbly rhizome, which is bright orange beneath the rind. The large leaves are about 50cm/20in long, broad, smooth and shining. The flowers grow in yellow-green spikes in early summer. Like ginger, turmeric is a tropical plant cultivated in China, India, Java and Peru. Propagation is from pieces of rhizome; the mature rhizomes are boiled, peeled, dried and powdered.

The deep yellow powder has a pungent, characteristic smell, a mild, warming flavour and colours food a rich gold. Its main culinary use is as a curry ingredient and to colour mustard and pickles. Turmeric will keep its colouring properties for a long time but quickly loses its flavour, so buy only small quantities at a time. In India turmeric is used as a mild digestive. The rhizomes produce strong yellow or orange dyes when mordanted with chrome.

Cytisus scoparius
Broom
Family: Leguminosae

Broom grows on sandy heaths in Britain, Europe, northern Asia and along the coast of North America. Although young plants have small leaves, many of these drop off and the long green stems act as leaves. The sweetly scented bright yellow pea-flowers appear in early summer; later, long pods develop, which blacken as they ripen, then twist open with a popping sound, scattering the dark seeds.

Grow broom from seed or propagate by layering or from cuttings. An open, sunny situation on a dry bank is ideal, but the soil must not contain lime.

Although the young buds and flowering tops of broom have been used in cooking and as a medicine for centuries, they contain a principle called sparteine, which can have a narcotic and dangerous effect, so that broom should not be taken internally.

The bitter buds were eaten as a salad, either fresh or pickled; Gerard writes that they 'stirre up an appetite to meate'. He also mentions that a water distilled from the flowers was drunk by 'that worthy Prince of famous memory Henry VIII' against the 'surfeit'. A tea made from the flowering tops is recommended in all the old herbals as a treatment for dropsy and the ague, and as one of the most popular tonics.

The use of the stiff stems bound together as brooms and the narcotic effects of the plant may have suggested the old association between witches and broomsticks. Certainly the plant was powerfully associated with black magic from earliest times, and also used as a protection against enchantments. Perhaps it was as a protection that the Count of Anjou first wore it in his cap, whose son became Henry II, the first Plantagenet king. The old herbalists' name for broom was *Planta genista*.

The flowering tops of dyer's broom, *Genista tinctoria*, make a good yellow dye when mordanted with chrome or tin.

Dianthus caryophyllus

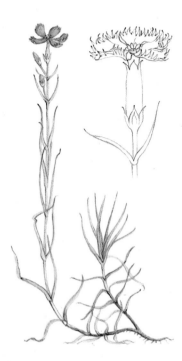

Dianthus caryophyllus

Clove carnation, gillyflower, clove-scented pink

Family: Caryophyllaceae

A favourite perennial garden flower in Britain, Europe and the U.S.A., it has narrow, bluish-grey leaves, stems about 60cm/2ft long and, in mid-summer, deep, purplish-red or rich pink blossoms with a deliciously spicy scent. Take cuttings or sow seed in the spring; layer the plants or divide the roots in late summer. Plant in a sunny position in well-drained soil.

The petals, with their bitter white 'heels' snipped off, will scent and flavour food and especially drinks. Used in Britain since Norman times, and later carried to the New World by colonists, the petals were preserved in sugar, syrup or vinegar and drunk as a cordial, a 'comforter of the heart'. The petals were floated in wine – sops-in-wine – and the flowers bound into chaplets for weddings and coronations. The name 'carnation' probably derives from this tradition.

Elettaria cardamomum

Cardamom

Family: Zingiberaceae

There are several varieties of cardamom, each with a slightly different flavour, but the one most commonly imported into Europe is grown in southern India. Long, spear-like leaves grow from 3m/10ft stems; the flowers are yellow and blue, followed by rounded capsules containing small dark seeds. To preserve the rich, essential oils of the seeds, the fruits are harvested before they ripen to prevent them from splitting, and dried whole, very slowly.

The dried fruits vary in colour from pale green to brown. Always store whole in a dark cupboard and extract the seeds just before use. Easy to crush or grind, the seeds are strongly pungent, rich and warming, and can be used to spice sweet or savoury dishes. They are a constant ingredient in Indian cookery, especially in curries, are ground with coffee by Arabs and are a universal flavouring for liqueurs and sweets. In Scandinavia and other cold, northern European countries, cardamom is used as a warming spice in mulled wine, with stewed fruit, in batters and puddings and with some meat dishes. Chew the seeds to sweeten the breath, as an aid to digestion and to stimulate the appetite.

The Normans brought cardamom to Britain in the 11th century. Another type of cardamom was introduced at the same time, called grains of paradise or melegueta pepper, *Aframomum melegueta*, which has a very powerful flavour and is often mentioned in medieval and Tudor recipes. This was exported from the coast of West Africa – hence the name 'Grain Coast' – but it is difficult to obtain today.

Elettaria cardamomum

*Equisetum
arvense*

Equisetum arvense
Common horsetail, bottlebrush,
pewterwort
Family: Equisetaceae
The horsetail family is a relic of an
otherwise extinct type of plant that
flourished during the Carboniferous
era. A tough, perennial weed it is
extremely difficult to eradicate and
spreads by fast-creeping rhizomes
and floating spores. Horsetails grow
in most temperate northern regions,
some species in marshland; *E. arvense*
is the most common and is found in
dry and stony places.

Fertile stems appear early in the
year, each topped by a spore-bearing
cone. Later an erect stem grows
about 30cm/12in high, circled by
whorls of stiff little green branches.
Harvest and dry these infertile stems
in midsummer.

The fresh stems have an acrid,
salty flavour and contain quantities
of silica and other minerals and
vitamins. For this reason they are
used in many countries as a remedy
for anaemia, to enrich the blood and
as a powerful tonic. Take a small
glass of horsetail tea or decoction
twice a day. To make the decoction
soak 25g/1oz dried herb in 600ml/
1 pint cold water for 2 hours, boil for
30 minutes, strain and cool. Horsetail
is also an effective treatment for
bladder complaints such as cystitis
and removes the white spots on
fingernails. It is very astringent;
apply a poultice of the bruised, fresh
herb to stop bleeding or bathe with a
strong decoction (50g/2oz dried
herb to 600ml/1 pint water). Gerard
writes that it cures wounds 'yea
although the sinues be cut in sunder'.

Species of horsetail can be used to
scour metal and wood because of
their high silica content. A strong
decoction used as a garden spray
prevents mildew, rust and other
fungi. Horsetail gives a light yellow
ochre dye when mordanted with
chrome or alum.

*Eryngium
maritimum*

Eryngium maritimum
Sea holly, eryngo
Family: Umbelliferae
The stiffly spiny sea holly that used to
be common along seashores in
Britain and Europe is only occasionally found in Britain today,
though there is a cultivated variety.
It is a thistly-looking plant with pale-
veined, silver-bloomed leaves and
soft blue flowerheads surrounded by
spiky bracts. The perennial roots are
very long, growing several metres
through sand and shingle to reach
fresh water. Dig the roots from the
garden in the autumn and use fresh as
a flavouring for jams and jellies or
peel, boil and candy them.

The roots contain iron, silica and
other valuable minerals and were
eagerly collected and candied as a
cough sweet, an aromatic stimulant
and nerve tonic. They were also
thought to restore health, vigour and
sexual appetite. The vogue for
candied eryngoes reached its height
in the 18th century. The American
water eryngo, *E. aquaticum*, is an
expectorant and emetic.

Eucalyptus globulus

Eugenia caryophyllata

Eugenia caryophyllata

Eucalyptus globulus
Eucalyptus, blue gum, fever tree
Family: Myrtaceae
The Australian eucalyptus is cultivated all over the world. Leaves from young trees are rounded and blue-green with a silvery bloom, those from mature trees are longer, pointed, tough and glossy green. They contain a strongly scented oil in small translucent glands. The woody flower bud has a lid that is pushed off as the mass of stamens emerge. The bark frequently peels off in characteristic ragged strips.

The oil is a powerful antiseptic and disinfectant. Rub it onto the chest for bronchitis and chest complaints, and sprinkle on the pillow to soothe coughs, colds and asthma. Several drops in warm water make a gargle for sore throats. To clear the nose and bronchial tubes, boil 25g/1oz fresh leaves in 1 litre/1¾ pints water, then inhale the steam with a towel over the head.

The bark produces a beige dye and when boiled for about 2 hours the fresh leaves give a beautiful red.

Eugenia caryophyllata
Clove

Family: Myrtaceae
Zanzibar is now the centre of the clove trade, but the clove tree is native to the famous Moluccas islands. The trees only thrive in a tropical climate near the sea, growing to a height of about 9m/30ft. The evergreen leaves resemble bay and the flower buds (though seldom allowed to bloom) are a bright pinky-red, opening to reveal yellow petals and a mass of stamens. The flower buds are harvested and dried in the sun until they turn brown.

Cloves contain a highly scented oil and should be used with restraint – one clove in an apple pie will flavour a whole dish or embedded in an onion will subtly spice a casserole of beef. Warming and aromatic, cloves are found in many spice mixtures and are an essential sweet spice. A good quality clove will ooze a glistening oil when the 'stalk' is pressed with a fingernail. Buy both whole and powdered cloves as they cannot easily be ground by hand.

Cloves have stimulating, warming and digestive properties. They are also antiseptic with a slightly anesthetic action, which is why cloves are chewed to ease toothache. They were a constant ingredient in 16th-century body and sachet powders. For a sweet-smelling antiseptic, make a pomander by pressing cloves into oranges or use powdered in pot pourri. A few cloves heated in a dry pan will scent and fumigate a room.

Listed in early Chinese herbals and well known in Europe in Classical times, cloves were rare in Britain until the advent of Norman cooking and remained expensive until the Portuguese broke the Venetian monopoly on spices. By the mid-17th century the Dutch had seized the Moluccas and prevented the export of clove seed or seedlings until the 18th century, when widespread cultivation began at last.

Cloves are named after the Latin word for nail – *clavus*.

Euphrasia officinalis

Eupatorium perfoliatum

Ferula assa-foetida

Eupatorium perfoliatum

Boneset, thoroughwort, agueweed

Family: Compositae

Boneset grows over 1m/3ft high in marshy places in eastern North America. A perennial weed, it has a rough, hairy stem and pairs of pointed leaves joined at the base and dotted with glands. The greyish-white flowers grow in clusters in late summer.

Gather and dry the leaves and tops as the flowers begin to open. They contain a strong oil and bitter principle. Take a tea made from the dried herb in small doses as a tonic for indigestion and especially for fever, as it promotes perspiration. Keep the doses small as large doses are emetic. This was one of the favourite medicines of North American Indians.

Several other *Eupatorium* species with medicinal value grow in North and South America. In Europe the hemp agrimony, *E. cannabinum*, which has thick heads of dull purple flowers, has been used medicinally but is now considered toxic.

Euphrasia officinalis

Eyebright

Family: Scrophulariaceae

Eyebright is a semi-parasite, nourished partly from grass roots, and found in grassy places in Britain, Europe and the U.S.A. It is a tough, bushy little annual plant, growing from 5cm/2in to 20cm/8in high, with toothed, slightly hairy leaves and wiry stems. The white or pinkish flowers have a yellow spot on the lobed lower lip and fine red or purple lines to direct insects down the throat to nectar. Gather and dry the whole flowering plant in mid-summer.

Its use as an eye herb was suggested perhaps by the resemblance of the red lines on the flower to a bloodshot eye. It has an astringent and soothing action; soak clean lint in an infusion and lay warm over the eyes and temples to relieve tired or inflamed eyes and headache, or express fresh juice onto the compress. Eyebright is also an ingredient in herbal tobacco. *Euphrasia* derives from the Greek for 'gladness'.

Ferula assa-foetida

Asafoetida, devil's dung

Family: Umbelliferae

There are several *Ferula* species with similar properties, but this is the best source of the official drug asafoetida. A perennial, it grows 2.5m/8ft high in Afghanistan and eastern Iran, with pale yellow-green flowerheads in summer, divided leaves and a long, fleshy root. When the stems and roots of the mature plants are cut in early summer, a thick resinous gum accumulates and hardens. This is collected and sold in lumps or ground to a powder.

The whole plant smells strongly foetid and the dried gum is a powerful seasoning that should be added only in small quantities. It was used by the Romans and is a common spice in Eastern cookery – especially in southern India for flavouring vegetarian dishes and fish. The leaves, stems and immature flowerheads are eaten fresh.

Asafoetida is a sedative, expectorant, digestive and laxative. The related garden *Ferula* is poisonous.

Filipendula ulmaria
Meadowsweet, meadwort, queen
of the meadow
Family: Rosaceae
Throughout Britain and Europe,
Asia and eastern North America,
meadowsweet grows in water meadows, damp woods and ditches,
often in large colonies. The stem is
1m/3ft high, stiff and reddish, the
toothed leaves are dark green,
wrinkled above and downy white
beneath, and the creamy flowers
grow in massed clusters from
midsummer.

Propagate by root division in
spring or autumn. The smell of the
flowers is almost too sweet and
heady, like almonds and honey; the
leaves have a different scent, a clean
smell that changes as they dry to that
of new-mown hay. This change is
due to the presence of the chemical
coumarin, which is also found in
woodruff, melilot and certain grasses, giving a characteristic, long-
lasting hay-smell as they dry. This
scent is easily communicated to
liquids and meadowsweet was a
traditional flavouring for mead.
Chaucer describes meadwort as an
ingredient in a drink called, simply,
'Save', and Gerard writes 'that the
floures boiled in wine and drunke do
make the heart merrie'. Today
meadowsweet is still used in the
brewing of herb beers.

Collect and dry the whole plant as
it begins to flower, including the
perennial root. All parts are astringent, and an infusion of leaves
can be given as a gentle corrective
medicine for diarrhoea. The flower
contains salicylic acid, which is an
ingredient of aspirin (whose name
derives from the old generic name
for meadowsweet, *Spiraea*), and this
is valuable for the treatment of fevers
and 'flu, for rheumatism and gout, to
soothe the nerves and to encourage
restful sleep. Use a strong decoction
made by boiling 50g/2oz dried root

in 600ml/1 pint water as an astringent, healing wash for wounds
and sore places. For the complexion,
soak the flowers in soft water for
several hours, strain the liquid and
use as a washing water.

The strong hay-like smell that
develops as the plant dries made
meadowsweet popular in the house
as a strewing herb. Gerard says that
'The leaves and floures farre excell all
other strowing herbes . . . for the
smell thereof . . . delighteth the
senses'. The flowering tops produce
yellow-green dyes.

The dropwort, *F. vulgaris*, has
similar but larger flowers and is a
much shorter plant than meadowsweet, growing on dry downland. A
Filipendula species in North America
is known as 'queen of the prairies'.

Filipendula ulmaria

Foeniculum vulgare
Fennel
Family: Umbelliferae
Native to Mediterranean countries, fennel was introduced to northern Europe by the Romans, and to North America by early European settlers. It now grows wild in most temperate climates, especially on limy soil near the sea.

A perennial, often growing over 1.5m/5ft tall, fennel is easily recognized by its long, finely cut, feathery leaves, stiff smooth stems and large umbels of yellow flowers, which bloom from midsummer. The aromatic seeds are broad, slightly curved and ridged.

There are several varieties with similar flavours and properties – the annual Florentine fennel, *F. vulgare azoricum*, has swollen bases to the stalks, another Italian variety is grown for its tender stems and a large perennial for its decorative bronze leaves – but the common fennel is most useful in the herb garden, being hardy in northern climates, with fine flavoured leaves and seeds.

Sow the seeds in the spring in a sunny position and thin the seedlings to 50cm/20in apart, or divide the roots of established plants in the autumn. It has been said that fennel will cross-pollinate with dill if they are grown together and also that it will inhibit the growth of coriander, tomatoes and beans. As with lovage, it is advisable to grow several fennel plants so that some can be allowed to seed, while others are grown solely for their leaves.

The leaves and stems can be picked fresh throughout the summer. Collect the seedheads as the seeds change colour and hang in an airy place to dry, with a cloth beneath to catch the ripe seeds. Cut the stems in late summer and dry slowly in a cool oven. The leaves are not suitable for drying but the dried stems and seeds will give a flavour of fennel to winter dishes.

Fennel seeds have a subtle, slightly bitter, aniseed flavour, warming and appetizing. The fresh leaves taste sweeter and richer. Fennel is a traditional seasoning for fat meat, such as pork, and oily fish, but it also suits lamb, chicken and ham, fresh vegetables and creamy sauces. As an alternative to mint, add fresh chopped leaves to hummus or other pulse dishes or to yoghurt. The leaves and peeled stalks make a refreshing salad. The seeds give a good flavour to bread and cakes. Alternatively, bread can be baked on a bed of dried fennel stalks. Place a few dried stalks inside a fat, butter-basted roasting chicken, or beneath roasting meat or fish to give the dish a delicate and subtle flavour. Soak them in brandy and flame beneath fish for the Provençal *grillade au fenouil*.

In more northern parts of Europe, the annual Florentine fennel will only grow fat leaf bases in a warm summer, but the succulent 'bulbs' can be bought and are delicious raw in a salad or braised as a vegetable.

The seeds, with their rich oil, have stimulant and digestive properties in common with many other umbelliferous herbs. Chew them, or make a tea by infusing a teaspoonful of bruised seeds in 300ml/$\frac{1}{2}$ pint boiling water. For tired or inflamed eyes boil a handful of fennel leaves in water for 15 minutes, then pour the decoction onto a piece of lint and lay lukewarm over the eyes for 10 minutes.

Fennel has a long tradition as an eye herb. Pliny tells a story of snakes eating and rubbing against fennel to restore and sharpen their sight after casting their skins, and Gerard quotes an old recipe for a distilled water to preserve the eyesight made from fennel, roses, vervain, rue and celandine. Culpeper recommends that the fresh juice 'dropped into the eye cleanses them from mists and films that hinder the sight'.

The Greeks used fennel as a slimming herb and called it *marathron* from *maraino*, to grow thin. Several thousand years later in 17th-century Britain, William Coles, the botanist and gardener, wrote that fennel is much used 'for those that are grown fat, to abate their unwieldiness and cause them to grow more gaunt and lank'. Another general use was to increase the flow of mothers' milk, and the Romans, Chinese and Hindus all considered fennel an antidote for snake bite and other poisons.

The Romans held fennel in high regard as a food and medicine; Pliny suggested it as a treatment for 22 ailments and it was supposed to increase strength, courage, and prolong vigorous youth. When the legions finally left Britain, fennel was thought by the natives to be not only a powerful medicine but powerful against all evil. In the ancient Nine Herbs Charm, fennel is described as 'great in power'. 'It stands against pain, resists the venom, It has power against three and against thirty, Against a fiend's hand and against sudden trick, Against witchcraft of vile creatures.'

Later, during the Middle Ages, fennel was stuffed in keyholes and hung over doors as a protection against witches, especially on Midsummer Eve. And always the seeds were eaten in quantities with fish and with hard fruit because of their digestive qualities. In the 11th century a large household is recorded as having consumed $8\frac{1}{2}$ pounds of fennel seed in a month.

Foeniculum vulgare

Galium species and related herbs
Family: Rubiaceae

The bedstraws are all very closely related and easy to recognize as they have such similar characteristics: long, sprawling, usually weak stems, with whorls of leaves at intervals and clusters of small flowers. Many species are useful to man, being sweetly scented or edible or medicinal (especially as wound herbs), able to curdle milk and with roots that yield variable red dyes. Several species were used by North American Indians.

Among those formerly prized as a medicine, though seldom used today, is the tiny squinancywort, *Asperula cynanchica*, which was used to treat the quinsy or sore throat. This grows locally on dry downland in Europe and southern Britain. Crosswort, *Cruciata laevipes*, is a very common species among long grass, with 4 downy leaves and whorls of yellow flowers. It is a herb for wounds and aching joints and grows on limy soil in Britain and Europe.

Although a red dye can be obtained from the roots of most species, the madder, *Rubia tinctorum*, is one of the most famous dye plants and is the largest of the bedstraws. It is a perennial, with prickly angular stems that will grow 1m/3ft long, scrambling over rocks and among low scrub in southern Europe. The prickly evergreen leaves are dark and shiny, growing in whorls; the flowers, appearing in midsummer, are yellow and clustered, followed by largish berries. It is cultivated for its thick fleshy root, which has a dark rind and ruddy-coloured flesh. This yields a rich orange dye when mordanted with tin, a carrot red with alum and a red-brown with chrome. The wild madder, *R. pergrina*, grows in France and south-west Britain and is similar to madder, but produces a weaker red dye.

Galium aparine

Goosegrass, cleavers, hedgeheriff
Family: Rubiaceae

The most common of the bedstraws, goosegrass is an annual that grows as a weed throughout Britain, Europe and North America on cultivated or disturbed ground, on banks and in hedgerows. The weak stems grow over 1m/3ft long and each leaf ends in a sharp point and is covered with tiny bristles that cling to the surrounding vegetation and to the clothes of passersby. The clusters of small white flowers bloom in the early summer, followed by prickly round seeds that are caught and transported on fur and clothing.

Dry the whole plant as it is coming into flower.

The fresh leaves and young tops of goosegrass make a wholesome and nutritious vegetable when boiled like spinach, and John Evelyn advises using the tops in soup. The dried seeds can be roasted and ground as a coffee substitute.

Goosegrass is a tonic herb, rich in silica and other minerals, and will enrich the blood, strengthen teeth and bones and clear the complexion. It is also a gentle laxative and will promote urine, but as it increases the sugar content in the blood it should not be taken by diabetics. The soothing properties of the herb make the tea suitable as a treatment for insomnia and, externally, as a wash for easing sunburn and sore skin. Crush the fresh herb as a poultice for blisters and sore places. The tea can also be used as a hair rinse to treat dandruff.

Culpeper says that 'it is a good remedy in the spring . . . to keep the body in health, and fitting it for that change of season that is coming'. The name 'hedgeheriff' derives from the Anglo-Saxon word meaning 'hedge robber'.

Galium aparine

Galium odoratum　　　　　*Galium verum*　　　　　*Gaultheria procumbens*

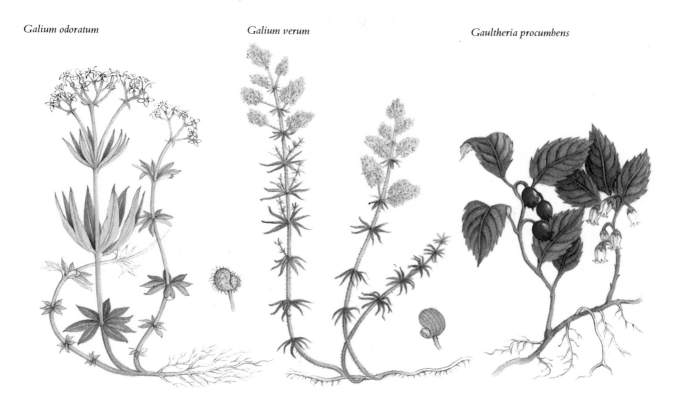

Galium odoratum
Woodruff, sweet woodruff
Family: Rubiaceae
Woodruff grows about 30cm/12in high, with broader leaves than goosegrass, dark green and smooth. The loose heads of star-shaped flowers bloom in late spring; they are larger than those of the other bedstraws and brilliantly white. It is an erect woodland plant, native to Britain, Europe and Asia and cultivated in the U.S.A.

Sow the rough, round seeds as soon as they ripen in the summer in a moist, partly shaded place, or plant out pieces of the perennial creeping root in autumn. Harvest and dry the whole herb as it begins to flower.

The German 'Maywine' is made by macerating woodruff in white wine. Taken as a tea it is a cordial, cheering herb and the bruised, fresh leaves can be used on wounds. Valued for its sweet smell, which strengthens as it dries owing to the presence of coumarin, it was used for strewing, to scent linen, for stuffing mattresses and in pot pourri.

Galium verum
Lady's bedstraw, cheese rennet
Family: Rubiaceae
Lady's bedstraw begins to bloom in midsummer, the masses of tiny yellow flowers appearing among the grasses on dry sunny banks and roadsides throughout Britain, Europe and North America. The wiry stems grow about 1m/3ft high, with whorls of narrow shining leaves. The tough perennial root yields a rusty-red dye. Gather and dry the whole plant as the buds open; dig the root in autumn.

Many country names in Britain and Europe refer to the milk-curdling properties of this herb. It does not seem effective with modern milk, but can be added with rennet to colour cheese a rich yellow. Like goosegrass it is a wound herb, promotes urine and is a soothing, cleansing treatment for the skin. A sweetly scented strewing herb, it possesses coumarin, and was used to stuff mattresses and pillows. According to legend, lady's bedstraw was put in Christ's crib.

Gaultheria procumbens
Wintergreen
Family: Ericaceae
A perennial evergreen of the heather family, wintergreen grows about 15cm/6in high in woods throughout North America, and was a favourite medicine of the North American Indians. It has dark, serrated leaves and scattered, white, bell-shaped flowers in midsummer, followed by scarlet berries. Propagate by seed, layering or cuttings in spring or autumn, and plant in a well-drained, shady place.

The bitter berries can be used as a flavouring for sweets. The powerfully aromatic leaves are astringent and stimulant. Apply warmed and pulped as a poultice to boils and swellings or as a treatment for rheumatism. Gargle the tea for sore throats. Oil distilled from the leaves was a common rub for rheumatism and sore muscles, but a synthetic substitute is usually used today.

The European wintergreens belong to the family *Pyrolaceae*, but have similar astringent properties.

Gentiana lutea

Gentian, yellow gentian, bitterwort
Family: Gentianaceae

Species of gentian grow throughout the world and all possess very bitter properties, but the perennial yellow gentian is the one chiefly used in medicine. Native to mountainous areas in Europe and Asia Minor, it grows over 1m/3ft high with long, usually ovate leaves, prominently veined, and large, deep yellow flowers in midsummer. The fleshy root can grow 1m/3ft long.

A striking garden plant, it can be grown from fresh seed but takes many years to flower. It is easier to plant root cuttings in deep, rich, moist soil in a sheltered but sunny position. Harvest the rhizome and roots in autumn.

Gentian root is profoundly bitter and is used to flavour aperitifs and occasionally beer. A valuable tonic, it has been administered for over 2,000 years as a fortifying medicine, a treatment for fever and all digestive troubles and as an antiseptic wound herb. It should be taken in small quantities. Soak a teaspoonful of dried root in a cup of wine or water and take a teaspoonful half an hour before meals to help the digestion, or give 3 times a day to convalescents to strengthen the stomach and purify the blood. Sweeten with honey or flavour with orange peel to overcome the bitterness. Apply bruised, fresh leaves as a cooling, antiseptic poultice for wounds and inflammations.

Blue gentians include the American gentian, *G. catesbaei*, and the little, purple autumn gentian, *Gentianella amarella*. The European centauries belong to the gentian family and share their properties. The name derives from the centaur physician, Chiron. An old name for all gentians is 'felwort', which comes from *fel terrae* or 'gall of the earth'. As Culpeper says: ''tis very wholesome, but not very toothsome'.

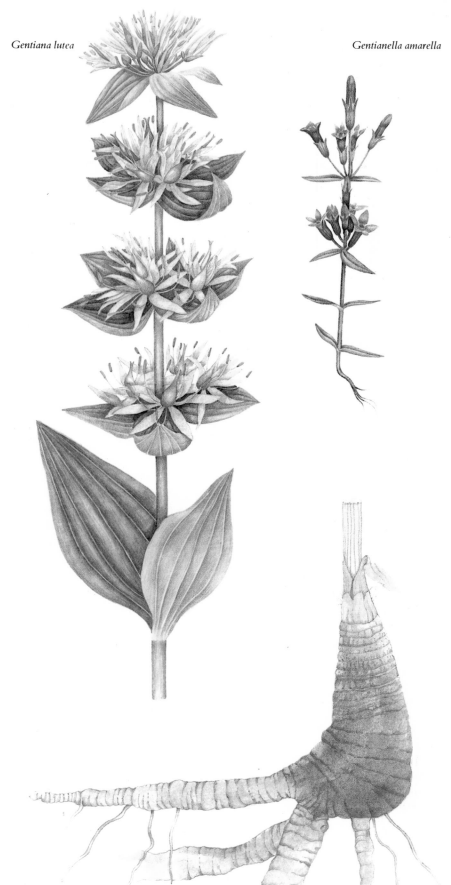

Gentiana lutea

Gentianella amarella

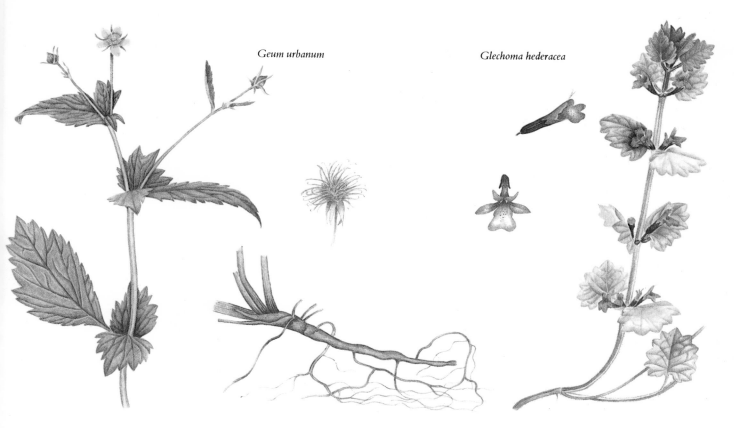

Geum urbanum

Glechoma hederacea

Geum urbanum

Wood avens, herb bennet, clove root

Family: Rosaceae

The leaves of wood avens are downy, toothed and irregularly cut, broader at the base of the plant and narrow higher up. The stem is downy and often reddish, sometimes growing 60cm/2ft high, and topped in midsummer by delicate, symmetrical, yellow flowers with long sepals. These are followed by hooked fruits that catch onto passersby, The root is perennial, dark and fibrous, with an aromatic scent. Wood avens grows in shady places, woodland and hedgebanks, in Britain, Europe, Russia and central Asia, and there is a similar species, *G. aleppicum*, in the U.S.A.

The leaves can be dried but the root is more frequently used. Harvest it in spring and dry slowly, whole, then slice or powder as needed.

Wood avens was a common potherb in Europe in the 16th century and often cultivated in gardens; the fresh leaves give a slight but pleasant taste to soups and stews. Both leaves and root contain tannin and an astringent oil, and are antiseptic. Make a tea from dried leaves or powdered root, leave to cool, then take a small glassful 3 times a day as a tonic or for diarrhoea, sore throat, colds or fevers. As a washing water, this infusion is astringent and refreshing and will help to clear the complexion.

Leave a scrubbed root in wine for a few days to give it a dry, rather vermouth-like flavour. This is said to settle an upset stomach and Culpeper writes that it 'comforteth the heart and strengthens . . . a cold brain'. A dried root laid among linen acts as a moth repellent.

The name 'herb bennet' derives from the medieval Latin *herba benedicta*, the 'blessed herb', as the fragrant root was thought to repel both infection and the devil.

Glechoma hederacea

Ground ivy, alehoof, gill-over-the-ground

Family: Labiatae

Native to temperate Europe, Asia and Britain and introduced in the U.S.A., perennial ground ivy spreads by long runners and grows in shady places. The leaves are downy, dark green and kidney-shaped, with glands that contain an aromatic, bitter oil The deep-throated flowers are purple or blue.

Pieces of rooting stem planted in the garden will quickly spread. Pick and dry the plant as the flowers begin to open in late spring.

The tea – known as 'gill tea' – is a most versatile country remedy; take a small cupful 3 times a day as an effective spring tonic or use to treat coughs and colds, kidney complaints, to ease menstrual pains or externally as a wash for tired eyes. Crush the fresh plant as a poultice for bruises and swellings.

An ancient ale herb, bitter ground ivy was used to clear and flavour ale before the introduction of hops.

Glycyrrhiza glabra

Liquorice

Family : Leguminosae

The perennial liquorice is native to southwest Asia and southeast Europe, and there are other similar species in southern Europe and the U.S.A. The bushy plants grow up to 1m/3ft high, with leaves divided into fine, sensitive leaflets that fold and droop each evening. In late summer pale cream or mauve peaflowers grow from the leaf axils, followed by smooth or sometimes hairy seed pods. Many long, horizontal rhizomes grow from the deep rootstock, each producing aerial shoots.

Liquorice was often cultivated in Britain in the 16th and 17th centuries, especially at Pontefract in Yorkshire, but needs long hot summers and some protection from frost to prevent the roots from becoming woody. Plant pieces of rhizome, each with a bud and about 15cm/6in long, in spring in light, rich soil, 10cm/4in deep and about 1m/3ft apart. The young plants need plenty of moisture. Collect the roots and runners in their third or fourth year, putting some aside to plant out the following spring. In countries such as Spain and Italy, where liquorice is cultivated on a large scale, the root is crushed and the juice extracted and solidified to make the familiar glossy black sticks.

Liquorice can be eaten as a sweet, used to flavour drinks and also to treat coughs, colds, sore throats and bronchitis. It is a mild laxative. Make a soothing tea by dissolving 8cm/3in black liquorice stick in 300ml/$\frac{1}{2}$ pint hot water or a decoction by boiling 25g/1oz bruised, peeled root in 600ml/1 pint water for 5 minutes, and drink a small glassful 3 times a day before meals. Liquorice can be taken safely by diabetics.

In the 3rd century BC Theophrastus observed that chewing a piece of root will prevent thirst.

Hamamelis virginiana

Hamamelis virginiana

Witch hazel, snapping hazelnut

Family : Hamamelidaceae

Witch hazel is a small tree, seldom growing more than 4m/13ft high, with branching, crooked stems and smooth, greyish bark. The leaves are similar to hazel, but smaller and downy, with more prominent veins. The scented flowers usually appear after the leaves have fallen in the autumn and have narrow, yellow, ribbon-like petals. Seed is seldom produced except in its native North America where dark nuts follow the flowers and snap open to eject edible white seeds. The species *H. mollis* from China is a common garden tree and flowers early in spring.

Witch hazel is hardy in cool climates and grows well· in rich, moist soil. All parts are strongly astringent; use to check bleeding and as a treatment for bruises, swellings and sprains. An extract distilled from leaves, twigs or bark can be bought for use as a skin tonic, to soothe and cool painful swelling and, diluted, to soothe sore eyes.

Glycyrrhiza glabra

Helianthus annuus

Helianthus annuus
Sunflower
Family: Compositae

The familiar giant sunflower is native to Mexico and Peru, and was first brought to Europe by Spanish explorers. Rough heart-shaped leaves grow alternately up the thick stem. The great flowerheads can measure more than 30cm/12in across and are composed of hundreds of small florets packed together and glistening with nectar and honeydew. The outer or ray florets are long and yellow.

The seeds are about 2cm/¾in long, white, dark brown or irregularly striped. Sow under glass in the spring and plant out the seedlings when all danger of frost is past, about 60cm/2ft apart. In rich soil they will grow 4m/13ft high or more and should be staked early. Cut the seedheads in the autumn and leave in a dry, airy place until the seeds fall easily from their sockets.

The oil extracted from the seeds has little taste or smell but is rich in vitamins and minerals, especially iron, and low in cholesterol. The seed kernels have a pleasantly nutty taste and are 25 per cent protein. They are delicious raw, tossed in oil or roasted golden in a medium oven. The lesser flower buds that often grow off the main stalk can be eaten like artichokes, with butter and vinegar.

Sunflowers draw large quantities of potash from the soil, so when the seeds have been harvested burn the dry stalks and use the ash as a garden fertilizer. Sunflowers can also be planted to help drain wet ground, as they absorb a great amount of water. As a bee plant, they provide rich nectar and the green leaves and seeds make a good poultry food.

Many Inca paintings and carvings depict the sunflower, which was revered as an embodiment of the sun.

Humulus lupulus
Hop
Family: Cannabinaceae

The thick, fibrous stems of the hop grow up to 7m/23ft long each year from the perennial root and twine clockwise round scrubby trees and through hedges in most temperate climates. The rough leaves are pale green, shaped like vine leaves. The male and female flowers grow on separate plants in late summer, the male flowers in loose clusters, the female in shorter, rounder heads, developing into papery cones that contain valuable properties.

Hops are cultivated on a large scale in many countries and can be grown in the garden in deeply worked, rich soil in an open, sunny situation. Grow female plants only, propagating from cuttings or suckers; these should bear well by the third year. Cut the whole plant right down each autumn, dry the cones in a warm, airy place and store. Use within a few months, before the flavour becomes unpleasant.

The buds and new leaves can be eaten; blanch first to remove some bitterness. Boil or steam the young, tender sideshoots like asparagus. The female flowers are made up of many overlapping papery bracts with a small fruit at the base of each bract. The bracts contain tannin and among them lie loose powdery yellow glands that contain a bitter oily substance called lupulin. The dried heads are used whole to flavour beer and preserve the liquor longer than other natural additives. They can also be used to leaven bread. Gerard recommends that water in which hops have been boiled should be added to the dough 'that the lumpe be sooner and easilier leavened'. (Boil a few hops in potato water, add a little live yeast, and leave the liquid to ferment.)

Hop tea makes a good general tonic and has a gentle sedative

Humulus lupulus

Hydrastis canadensis

action; it will also help the digestion and stimulate the appetite. Alternatively, add a few dried hops to ordinary household tea or make a wholesome aperitif by infusing dried hops in sherry. Pillows stuffed with hops are said to calm the nerves; use a warmed pillow to soothe earache.

A brown dye can be produced from the leaves and flowers.

The word 'hop' derives from the Anglo-Saxon *hoppan*, to climb. Although hops were used in the brewing of beer in northern Europe from the 8th century, they were thought unwholesome in Britain and did not become common until the 16th century, traditional bitter brewing herbs such as ground ivy, bog bean and broom being used instead. The controversy concerning the wholesome qualities of hops continued for several hundred years and even in the late 17th century John Evelyn wrote that the hop 'preserves the drink indeed, but repays the pleasure in tormenting diseases and a shorter life'.

Hydrastis canadensis
Golden seal, yellow root
Family: Ranunculaceae
A woodland plant with a thick, perennial, bright yellow root, golden seal grows up to 30cm/12in high in moist ground in eastern U.S.A. It has been heavily collected from the wild and is now uncommon, and can be difficult to cultivate.

Two leaves grow from the rough stem and a large leaf from the base, all deeply cut, hairy and wrinkled. The solitary flower appears in late spring with greenish sepals that fall away as the flower opens leaving a mass of stamens. Divide the roots and plant out in rich, damp, shaded ground. Lift and dry both roots and rhizome in autumn.

The root was used as a medicine by the Cherokee Indians and later by European settlers, but large doses are poisonous. A fluid extract can be bought for gastric troubles, catarrh and general debility.

The Indians dyed their skin and clothes a brilliant yellow with the root, which also acts as an insecticide.

Hypericum perforatum

Hyssopus officinalis

Hypericum perforatum
Perforate St John's wort
Family: Guttiferae

Dedicated to St John the Baptist, this is one of the most valuable of the St John's wort species and can be recognized by the many, tiny, transparent glands in the leaves. It is perennial, growing throughout southern Britain, Europe, Asia and the U.S.A. in woods and shady places. About 1m/3ft high it has an erect stem, paired leaves and star-shaped, yellow flowers with masses of stamens. Gather the tops and leaves from midsummer.

Make an astringent oil by filling a glass jar of leaves and flowers with good-quality oil and leaving it for a month on a sunny windowsill before straining. This is a soothing treatment for wounds, cuts and sprains, or massage for sore joints and muscles, and was carried by crusaders to the Holy Land. A tea made from the dried herb is useful for insomnia and coughs.

The tops produce an orange dye when mordanted with chrome.

Hyssopus officinalis
Hyssop
Family: Labiatae

A bushy plant growing up to 1m/3ft high, hyssop has narrow entire leaves and flowers growing in one-sided spikes. These are usually blue, though there are pink and white varieties. Although native to southern Europe, it will grow in northern climates in a sunny position on a light, well-drained soil, and was introduced by European colonists to the U.S.A. Sow the seeds in early spring – they are slow to germinate – or take cuttings or divide the roots in the spring or autumn. Plant out about 1m/3ft apart. Harvest and dry the leaves and flowering tops in midsummer, just as the plant comes into flower.

The aromatic, slightly bitter flavour of hyssop counteracts fatty, oily meat and fish and the herb helps to digest them. A few chopped leaves go well with stuffings or sausages, or add them fresh to salads or to stewed fruit and fruit pies. The tops are used as a flavouring for some liqueurs such as chartreuse.

Hyssop possesses a healing oil, which is a useful treatment for coughs, asthma and catarrhal colds, and will strengthen a weak stomach and help digestion. Make a tea from the fresh or dried herb and drink warm several times a day or use as a gargle. Take hyssop baths and tea for rheumatism and bruise the green leaves as a poultice for cuts and wounds. The oil is antiseptic and cleansing and the whole plant was used as a strewing herb and, in Classical times, for the ritual cleansing of temples; it is referred to in the Old Testament: 'Purge me with hyssop and I shall be clean.'

The oil is used in perfumery, an ingredient in eau-de-Cologne.

Hyssop responds well to pruning and will make a strong, thick, summer hedge about 1m/3ft high, though most leaves will drop in the winter. The flowers are very attractive to bees and butterflies.

Illicium verum

Indigofera tinctoria

Inula helenium

Illicium verum
Star anise
Family: Illiciaceae

Star anise is a small, evergreen tree native to southwest China, with large, shiny magnolia-like leaves and small yellow flowers. These are followed by large and beautiful fruits that form a star shape when ripe, each point of the star containing a hard shiny seed. They are harvested just before ripening and dried in the sun. As they store well and will retain their flavour for several years, they can be bought in quantity and stored in an airtight jar.

The strongly aromatic oil contained in the star anise is similar to that of aniseed, but less subtle and slightly more bitter.

A characteristic Chinese spice, it has a delicious permeating flavour; one star will scent a large joint of beef when cooked beneath it in the roasting tin, and one seed will flavour a large fish.

Indigofera tinctoria
Indigo
Family: Leguminosae

This famous dye plant is native to the East Indies and cultivated in many warm countries. Belonging to the pea family, it is small and shrubby with purplish flowers. In temperate climates it can only be grown in a greenhouse.

There are several processes used for producing the rich blue dye from the plant; all are complex, involving fermentation. Traces of the dye have been found on cloth in ancient Egyptian tombs and it has probably been used for at least 3,000 years. When the trade routes from Europe to the East Indies became established in the 16th century, indigo was brought to northern Europe and began to supplant the native woad, and in the 18th century seeds were carried to the U.S.A.

Two other members of the pea family growing in North America yield a weaker blue dye: wild indigo, *Baptisia tinctoria*, and *B. australis*, the false indigo.

Inula helenium
Elecampane, scabwort, horseheal
Family: Compositae

This large, perennial plant grows wild in damp meadows and on roadsides throughout temperate Europe and Asia, and occasionally in Britain. It was taken to North America by early settlers. It grows over 2m/6½ft high, the basal leaves 30cm/12in long, in a rosette, the upper leaves broader, clasping the stem, smooth above and downy beneath. The clusters of yellow flowers bloom from midsummer, each flower is 5cm/2in across with narrow rays that droop as the flower matures. The roots are large, fleshy and aromatic.

Sow seed in spring or divide the roots in early spring or autumn, or take offsets in the spring, each with a bud. A rich, moist soil is suitable and the plant will tolerate some shade.

Harvest and dry the root in the autumn of the second year. When chewed it has a powerful, warming, bitter flavour and was used in Roman cookery for sauces, and eaten salted as an hors d'oeuvre and at the end of the meal to aid digestion. The bitter, aromatic leaves have been used as a potherb. Elecampane root is often mentioned in medieval recipes and was candied and used in confectionery until the beginning of this century.

The pungent oil in the root is astringent, expectorant and strongly antiseptic; it is a treatment for coughs, bronchitis and asthma, and a digestive and tonic. Soak 7g/¼oz dried root in 1 litre/1¾ pints of water overnight, boil for 30 minutes, cool, and take a small glassful 3 times a day or use as a mouthwash or gargle. The root can also be chewed raw, or candied as cough lozenges. Steeped in wine it is a cordial and cheering drink; Pliny advises that it helps the digestion and 'causes mirth'. Another popular use was as an antidote to poisons and infection;

Inula helenium

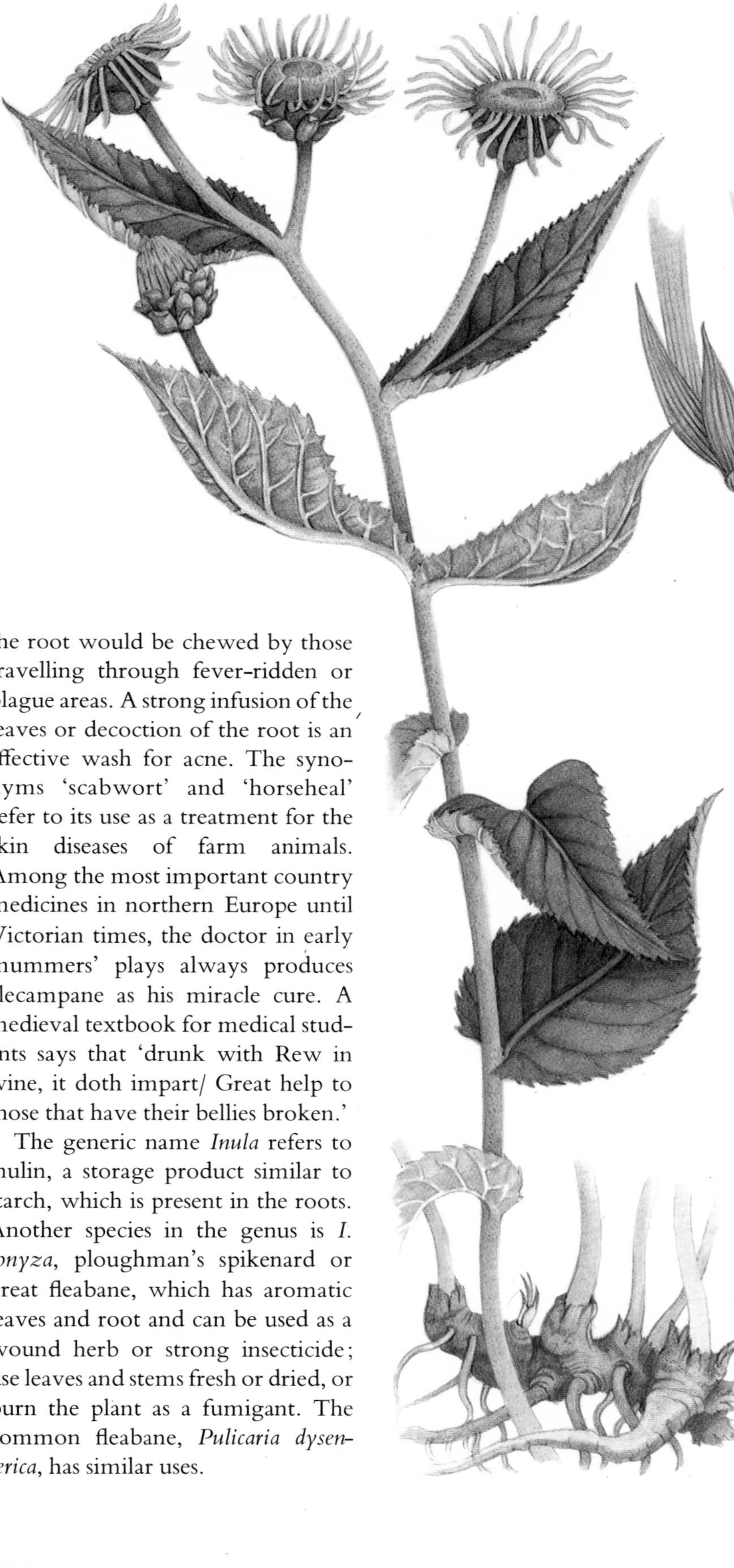

Iris florentina

the root would be chewed by those travelling through fever-ridden or plague areas. A strong infusion of the leaves or decoction of the root is an effective wash for acne. The synonyms 'scabwort' and 'horseheal' refer to its use as a treatment for the skin diseases of farm animals. Among the most important country medicines in northern Europe until Victorian times, the doctor in early mummers' plays always produces elecampane as his miracle cure. A medieval textbook for medical students says that 'drunk with Rew in wine, it doth impart/ Great help to those that have their bellies broken.'

The generic name *Inula* refers to inulin, a storage product similar to starch, which is present in the roots. Another species in the genus is *I. conyza*, ploughman's spikenard or great fleabane, which has aromatic leaves and root and can be used as a wound herb or strong insecticide; use leaves and stems fresh or dried, or burn the plant as a fumigant. The common fleabane, *Pulicaria dysenterica*, has similar uses.

Iris florentina
Orris, white flower de luce
Family: Iridaceae
This white-flowered iris grows 1m/3ft high, a native of the eastern Mediterranean. Its rhizome has the strongest scent among *Iris* species. It is propagated by division of the rhizomes in the spring and will grow in most soils. Harvest and dry the rhizomes in the autumn; the sweet violet scent increases and lasts for many years.

Although formerly used as a medicine, the rhizome should not be taken, as it is purgative. Its chief use is in perfumery and oil of orris is used for most violet scents. Powdered orris has been mixed with rinsing water and used to scent linen since Biblical times. It acts as an efficient scent fixative and can be added, grated or as a powder, in pot pourri.

Yellow flag, *I. pseudacorus*, is native to Europe and introduced in North America. Its astringent rhizome yields a grey or black dye when mordanted with iron and the flowers produce a yellow dye.

Isatis tinctoria

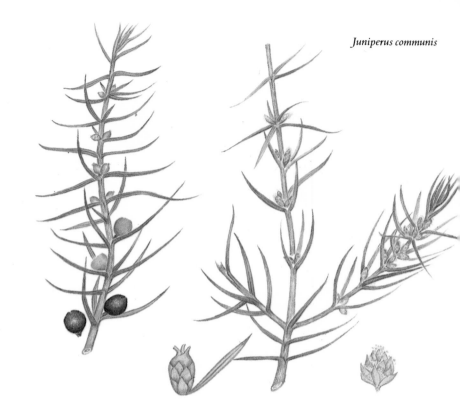

Juniperus communis

Isatis tinctoria

Woad

Family: Cruciferae

Woad plants still grow in some parts of Britain and northern Europe as relics of their former cultivation; their true home is in southern Europe and western Asia. A biennial plant, it grows a rosette of long broad leaves during the first year and produces panicles of small yellow flowers the following midsummer. The flowering stems grow at least 1.5m/5ft high. Later, dark fruits appear that dangle like earrings.

Sow seed in the spring on rich, well-drained ground in a sunny position and plant the seedlings 1m/3ft apart. It flourishes in most climates and will readily self-seed.

Pick the leaves for dyeing during the midsummer of the first year. The leaves are astringent and styptic and were used as a wound herb. The Ancient Britons must have taken this into account when dyeing their bodies with woad. The process of dyeing cloth was complex, involving repeated, smelly, fermentations.

Juniperus communis

Juniper

Family: Cupressaceae

The shrubby, perennial juniper with its little, sharp-tipped, grey-green leaves and aromatic scent grows according to its situation – almost prostrate when exposed to the wind on mountains and downland and to a height of 3m/10ft or more in protected places. It is widespread throughout Europe, North Africa and Asia and North America, and on limestone and chalk hills in Britain.

Small cones grow in early summer at the base of the leaves, the male and female on different plants. The male cones are yellow, the female bluish-green. The female cones become fleshy berries, taking up to 3 years to ripen and gradually turning from green to blue-black. A hardy plant, it will grow well on a dry soil in an open position in the garden. As the seeds take a long time to germinate, it is easier to propagate from cuttings.

Pick the berries when thoroughly ripe; dry in the sun or in an airy place. They have an aromatic resinous flavour that goes particularly well in marinades and with wild game such as venison, hare and partridge. They will sharpen and enrich beef and pork, stuffings and pâtés, sauerkraut and hot potatoes. As the flavour is strong add them with discretion; crush before use. The leaves can also be used, fresh or dried, especially with grilled fish, and the burning wood and leaves give a subtle fragrance to barbecued meat and fish. Oil distilled from the berries flavours Hollands gin.

Take 1 cupful a day of an infusion of 25g/1oz crushed berries in 1 litre/1$\frac{3}{4}$ pints boiling water for flatulence and indigestion, or to promote urine. Juniper branches can be used as a fumigant and were commonly burned in public places in times of plague and pestilence. This was still the practice in French hospitals a century ago during the smallpox epidemic of 1870.

The berries produce pale creamy-brown or khaki dyes when mordanted with alum or chrome.

Laurus nobilis
Bay, noble laurel, sweet bay
Family : Lauraceae

This is the true laurel, not to be confused with the poisonous cherry laurel of garden shrubberies. In sheltered warm places and in its native Mediterranean countries it may grow into a tree at least 9m/30ft high, but often remains short and shrubby. The leaves are strong, shiny and evergreen, about 8cm/3in long; small greenish flowers bloom in late spring and are followed by shiny black berries. The bark is smooth and dusty green.

Bay is difficult to grow from seed, but cuttings taken in early summer usually succeed, especially in a close atmosphere. Plant out established saplings in a sunny, sheltered spot in well-drained, lightly composted soil. In northern Britain and Scandinavia it is advisable to plant in a tub so that the tree can be put in a greenhouse or indoors during the winter; even in warmer climates young trees may need some protection during frost. Growth is slow. The trees respond well to trimming.

Harvest the leaves at any time and dry in the dark to preserve their strong oils and colour; dry the berries when they ripen. The leaves taste slightly bitter when fresh, but sweeten as they dry and become strongly aromatic. They have in-numerable uses in the kitchen, as an essential part of the *bouquet garni*, as a flavouring for marinades, stews, cooked tomato dishes, fish, and infused in milk for sweet or savoury puddings and sauces. The flavour is strong so use only half a leaf or less to begin with. A leaf is usually included with potted meats, pâtés and pickles, and packed with liquorice and dried figs as a flavouring and for its preservative and antiseptic qualities.

Rub the oil expressed from the berries into the skin for bruises and sprains, but do not take internally as it is emetic and provokes abortion. The berries used to be taken as a medicine for flatulence, but the whole plant has narcotic qualities. The oracle at Delphi uttered her prophecies with a leaf held between her lips and it is possible that her trance was induced by bay.

The smell from the leaves, either fresh or burning, was considered a protection against infection, and branches of bay were burned with juniper in public places in times of plague. It also acts as a protection against insects; keep a few leaves in grain and flour bins to discourage weevils and gnats.

The bay has always had a repu-tation as a protective tree, against lightning, witchcraft and all evil. In Classical times the tree was dedicated to Apollo, the patron of music and poetry, and Greek and Roman heroes were crowned with wreaths of bay. The title 'Poet Laureate' and the French *baccalauréat* derive from this.

Laurus nobilis

Lavandula species
Family: Labiatae

The most valuable lavender oil is obtained from *L. angustifolia*, which grows wild along the dry, stony hills bordering the Mediterranean, but is well adapted to milder climates and especially to that of southern England. The shrubby bushes grow about 1m/3ft high and live for many years, their stems becoming twisted and woody. The long, narrow leaves are downy when young and the flowers grow on tall, stiff stalks from midsummer. Each inflorescence has many bluish-mauve flowers. The flowers and leaves are covered with shining glands of oil.

Propagate lavender by cuttings in the spring or autumn, using strong little shoots of new growth about 15cm/6in long. Once rooted, plant out in a rather poor, sandy, limy, but well-drained soil in full sun. A south-facing, sloping bed is ideal. Pick off all flower buds during the first year to encourage a bushy growth. Lavender bushes tend to straggle as they mature, so trim the old growth back every few years as soon as the flowers have been harvested.

Gather the flowers as the buds begin to open, picking with long stems on a fine, sunny morning after the dew has evaporated. Hang loosely bunched in a shaded, airy place to dry, or spread on a drying tray, then store the flowers with or without their stems.

Lavender is seldom thought of as a culinary herb, but the leaves can be used to flavour stews, especially of wild game such as rabbit, and in marinades. In the past the flowers were popular in conserves – lavender conserve is reputed to have been a favourite of Queen Elizabeth I – and they can be crystallized or substituted for mint in a savoury jelly.

Oil pressed from the stalks is of a coarser quality than oil from the flowers. Both are strongly antiseptic and were once a treatment for palsy. The diluted oil can be used for cleaning wounds, on bites and stings, and for rubbing on aching or bruised limbs and stiff joints. It is best known, however, as a cure for headaches, an ancient remedy still used today. All the old herbalists describe the refreshing effect of lavender for 'a light migram' and 'swimming of the braine'. For this purpose sniff the oil like smelling salts, or rub the oil, lavender water or lavender vinegar on the temples. To soothe the head and nerves and to relieve dyspepsia, take a few drops of oil on a lump of sugar or a small glass of a very weak infusion made with 7g/$\frac{1}{4}$oz dried flowers to 1 litre/ 1$\frac{3}{4}$ pints boiling water. Large doses can become narcotic.

The disinfectant and insect-repellent qualities of lavender, combined with its sweet smell, have led to its domestic use as a fumigant in the sickroom (a bunch of dried twigs was set alight to smoulder like joss sticks) and as a protection against moths and other insects among linen. The diluted oil rubbed onto the skin will repel mosquitoes and flies, rubbed into the scalp it is said to encourage the growth of hair. Its use for scenting washing water goes back to Classical times (the name originates from the Latin *lavare*, 'to wash') and the flowers are a famous ingredient of pot pourris and scent.

There are many forms of the hardy English lavender, *L. angustifolia*, and a good deal of confusion in its nomenclature. Alternative names include *L. officinalis*, *L. vera* and *L. spica*. The old herbalists distinguish English lavender from spike lavender, which was apparently the most popular medicinal lavender and possibly the plant used in Classical times. It was known as 'sticadore' and its abundant, but slightly inferior oil was called 'oil of spike'.

Lavandula angustifolia 'Hidcote'

L. stoechas, the French lavender, is less hardy and grows into a smaller, more compact bush, flowering early with purple blossoms. Each spike has several long purple bracts at the tip. A delicate white variety, *L. angustifolia* 'Alba', needs to be cultivated with care. A dwarf form of 'Alba', growing only 15cm/6in high, can be planted with the little, purple-flowered 'Dwarf Munstead' on walls and rockeries and as a low border hedge. For a hedge about 60cm/2ft high use the semi-dwarfs such as *L. angustifolia* 'Hidcote' or the highly scented 'Twickel Purple'; use the English Lavender for a hedge of 1m/3ft or more. Grow *L. dentata* indoors or under glass. It has delicate round, toothed leaves, a balsamic scent and grows 1m/3ft high.

Lavandula angustifolia

Lawsonia inermis

Lawsonia inermis

Henna

Family: Lythraceae

This shrubby, perennial plant grows on dry hillsides in Eastern countries and can only be cultivated in temperate climates under artificial heat. It grows up to 3m/10ft high, with narrow, grey-green leaves and small, sweet-scented, pink or cream flowers, followed by blue-black berries.

The dried, powdered leaves are cooling and astringent. Mix to a paste with water and apply as a compress to the forehead for headaches and fevers, and to swollen, hot or aching parts of the body, bites or stings.

Best known as a hair dye, henna produces a strong red colour and should be used with care. Test a small piece of hair first to make sure the colour is not too brilliant and subdue if necessary with chamomile or other herbs. Rub oil into the hair after dyeing to counteract the astringent effect. Henna was used as a dye and skin oil by the ancient Egyptians and is still popular today.

Levisticum officinale

Lovage

Family: Umbelliferae

Lovage was probably one of the many Mediterranean plants introduced to Britain and northern Europe by the Romans. It grows wild along the coasts and on the mountainsides of southern Europe and was particularly abundant in the province of Liguria in Italy, from which may come its old generic name, *Ligusticum*. It is a hardy perennial, growing after a few years to a height of 2m/6½ft, with stout, hollow stems and large leaves divided into broad, toothed leaflets – shiny on their upper surfaces and a duller grey-green beneath. Umbels of yellow flowers blossom in midsummer, glistening with nectar; later curved, oval seeds develop, each shaped like a shallow boat with three ribs as the keel. The root is thick and fleshy, becoming tough and woody with age and multiplying each year until the plant base can measure 50cm/20in in diameter.

Lovage will tolerate most soils but grows best in a rich, well-drained loam in a sunny or slightly shaded position. Propagation is by seed or root division. Sow seed in late summer, as soon as it has ripened, and thin the seedlings to about 60cm/2ft apart. Space out again after a year or two, as the mature plants need about 1.5m/5ft between them. Divide the roots in late autumn or early spring, each piece with a bud or 'eye', and plant out in their permanent positions. Water the plants in dry weather, keep clear of weeds and give a feed of well-rotted compost or manure each year. Lovage dies down in the autumn but the tough roots will survive bitter weather unless in waterlogged soil. Strong bronze-coloured shoots appear in the early spring.

Two plants provide sufficient leaves and seeds for most families.

Remove all flowerheads from one to encourage the growth of leaves; leave the other to flower and fruit. Pick fresh leaves at any time or cut the plant down to 30cm/12in above the ground 2 or 3 times a year for drying. Dry in a warm, airy, shady place then store the leaves in airtight jars. Cut the seedheads as they are turning brown and hang to dry above a cloth to catch the ripe seeds.

The seeds, leaves and leaf stems have a strong, earthy, celery flavour that enriches soups and stews and is particularly useful in vegetarian dishes, with rice, vegetable stuffings and nut roasts. The leaves preserve their flavour during long simmering, unlike celery, which soon develops a sour taste. Add fresh leaves to salads and vegetables. In winter use the seeds in bread and savoury pastries, in hot potato and cabbage soups and in all cheese dishes. The pungent flavour suits robust dishes and is less successful with fish or eggs. The roots can be harvested and boiled, but their flavour is very strong and they must first be peeled of all bitter skin. The young stems can be candied like angelica, but lack its slightly aniseed sweetness.

Lovage was grown in the earliest monastic physic gardens. It acts as a digestive, relieves flatulence, and has deodorant and antiseptic properties and a warming, soothing and cleansing effect. Take an infusion of dried leaves for sore throat and fever or use as an antiseptic mouthwash or gargle. Add a strong infusion or a decoction of the root to the bath water to make a cleansing and aromatic bath.

Scotch lovage, *Ligusticum scoticum*, has also been used as a potherb. It grows wild along the sea cliffs of Scotland, northern Europe and on the North Atlantic coast of America. It is stockier and tougher than garden lovage, with white umbels of flowers and a bitter aromatic flavour.

Levisticum officinale

Alexanders, *Smyrnium olusatrum*, is also called black lovage or black potherb. This tall, Mediterranean umbellifer was introduced to Britain and northern Europe by the Romans and taken to North America in the 16th century. About 1.5m/5ft high, it grows along sea coasts of southern Britain and northern Europe. The leaves resemble angelica but are bright, glossy and aromatic, the flowers are yellow, shining with nectar, and the seeds a dark brown. The perennial root can be boiled or candied, the young stems stewed or braised, the leaves used as a salad or potherb, the seeds for flavouring and the buds as a salad.

Alexanders have a particular affinity with fish and were a common vegetable on the many fish or fasting days that were once compulsory in Britain. A typical Elizabethan recipe begins with 'Alexander buds cut long ways, garnished with whelks'. Alexanders are well worth growing in the garden; sow fresh seed in the late summer.

Levisticum officinale

Linum usitatissimum

Smyrnium olusatrum

Linum usitatissimum

Linum usitatissimum
Flax, linseed
Family: Linaceae
A graceful annual with blue flowers
in midsummer, narrow grey-green
leaves and a wiry stem up to
50cm/20in high, flax has been cultivated for so long and in so many
countries that its origin is obscure.
Sow seeds in rich soil in spring and
keep the seedlings well weeded.
When grown for cloth, plants are cut
after flowering and the stems soaked
to rot the tissues so that they can be
beaten from the tough fibres. Gather
the seeds as they ripen. Their oil has a
warming effect and was formerly
used to treat coughs and colds and as
a laxative. It is now considered
unsafe to take internally as it may
irritate the intestine or act as an
abortifacient. However, it is valuable
as an external poultice for inflammations or boils – mix bruised or
crushed seed with boiling water and
apply, lukewarm, on lint. A decoction of the seed in bath water
softens and soothes the skin. Linseed
is an ingredient in furniture polish.

Lippia triphylla   *Marrubium vulgare*

Lippia triphylla
Lemon Verbena
Family: Verbenaceae
Lemon verbena rarely grows more than 2m/6½ft in temperate climates, but in its native countries in South and Central America it can reach a height of 8m/26ft. It is a graceful, perennial, deciduous shrub with long, pale green, pointed leaves and faded purple flowers that grow in terminal clusters during late summer.

Plant lemon verbena in a sunny position. The soil should be poor and dry in order to keep the roots hardy; too lush and soft a growth will weaken the shrub and it may not withstand the winter. Take softwood cuttings in the summer; they should be well established by the autumn. In autumn either cut down the plant and cover the roots with protective straw or leaves until the spring, or take the whole shrub indoors in a pot. On the other hand, it may survive in a warm sheltered corner for many years without any special care being taken.

The sweetly lemon-scented leaves can be harvested at any time, but are at their best as the flowers are coming into bloom. Store in an airtight container and they will retain their flavour and scent for several years. Use chopped in stuffings or to flavour fish, poultry, jams, jellies and puddings. Tea made from the leaves is refreshing and delicious. It has a gentle, sedative effect and will soothe bronchial and nasal congestion and settle the stomach. In pot pourri, the leaves give a sharp, long-lasting fragrance.

When first introduced by the Spaniards to Europe, the oil from lemon verbena was used in perfume and to scent soaps and cosmetics. It has been superseded to some extent by lemongrass, *Cymbopogon citratus*, a species of edible grass from tropical southeast Asia that yields a strongly lemon-scented oil.

Marrubium vulgare
Horehound, white horehound
Family: Labiatae
A member of the large mint family, white horehound is a hardy perennial, growing in dry waste places in Europe, occasionally in Britain, and naturalized in the U.S.A. It grows 1m/3ft high, with wrinkled leaves covered in dense hairs and whorls of white flowers from midsummer.

It is easy to grow either from seed or cuttings on a poor, dry soil. Harvest and dry the leaves as the plant comes into flower. They are extremely bitter and have no recorded culinary uses, but have been grown as a valuable cottage medicine for thousands of years. Take a small glass of tea 3 times a day for colds, coughs and croup, as an expectorant tonic and for all troubles of the lungs. As the taste is disagreeable, a syrup or cough candy can be made, or the fresh leaves chewed with honey.

Black horehound, *Ballota nigra*, has an offensive smell and was used as an antidote for dog bites.

Melilotus officinalis

Melissa officinalis

Melilotus officinalis

Melilot, sweet clover, hart's clover
Family: Leguminosae

A naturalized fodder crop, melilot grows wild on wasteground and roadsides in Britain, Europe, Asia and the U.S.A. It grows over 1m/3ft high with stiff stems and narrow, trifoliate leaflets. Spikes of bright yellow peaflowers bloom from midsummer. Melilot is either an annual or a biennial, depending on the time of year it is planted. Harvest and dry the flowering tops and leaves. They contain the chemical, coumarin, which gives a strong, sweet, almond smell, similar to woodruff. Use melilot to scent and flavour sausages and stuffings, especially rabbit stuffing, and to give an original flavour to marinades and beers. A blue-flowered species, *Trigonella caerulea*, is used to flavour gruyère cheese.

Melilot tea will aid digestion and relieve wind; use the fresh leaves as a poultice for rheumatism and cuts. The dried leaves will scent and protect clothes from moths. It is an excellent bee plant.

Melissa officinalis

Lemon balm, sweet balm, bee herb
Family: Labiatae

A familiar garden plant with its fresh, green, nettle-shaped leaves and strong bushy growth, lemon balm is native to southern Europe and was probably introduced to the north by the Romans. The creamy flowers are undistinguished and grow in loose clusters from midsummer. The hardy root is perennial.

Easy to grow and tolerant of most soils, it does especially well on a fairly rich, moist ground in a sheltered, sunny position. Sow seeds in the spring or late summer; divide the roots in the autumn or early spring; take cuttings in the summer. Keep the plants well weeded; they should grow at least 1m/3ft high.

The fresh leaves can be gathered at any time; harvest them for drying as the flowers begin to open. Dry quickly and carefully in the dark to preserve their colour.

The lemon-flavoured, minty leaves can be used fresh in stuffings, salads, sauces and omelettes and with fruit salads and cooked milk puddings. A bruised leaf or two will flavour a fruit or wine cup.

Tea made from the fresh or dried leaves is delicious, perhaps the best flavoured of all herb teas. Take it particularly for fevers, colds and headaches, as it promotes perspiration and is soothing and refreshing. A strong infusion added to the bath water is relaxing and said to promote menstruation and to 'comfort the sinews'. Crushed, fresh leaves bound to a wound will help prevent infection.

John Evelyn describes the leaves steeped in wine as having a 'cordial and exhilerating effect', and Gerard says that it 'driveth away all melancholy and sadness'.

The most famous of all bee herbs, the generic name *Melissa* derives from the Greek for 'bee' and many herbalists from Dioscorides onwards recommend it. Gerard suggests rubbing the hives with 'Bawme' to attract new swarms. Planted round orchards, lemon balm will attract bees to pollinate the fruit trees.

Mentha species
Family: Labiatae
There are numerous mint species, both wild and cultivated, and a confusing number of hybrids, but all share certain characteristics. They are perennial, with 4-sided stems, paired leaves, whorls of small flowers in midsummer, varying in colour from white to purple, and a strong fragrant oil. They spread by seed and creeping underground rhizomes.

As they hybridize readily, it is wise not to propagate by seed but by planting 15cm/6in pieces of the rooting stem horizontally, 5cm/2in deep in moist, loamy soil in the spring. Plants may need to be confined in a buried, bottomless bucket or by surrounding the bed with a deep barricade of some sort. Most varieties tolerate some shade. In the autumn, fork manure compost over the bed and chop the runners a few times with a sharp spade to encourage a vigorous growth. To reduce the likelihood of disease, move the plants every few years to fresh soil and plant different species as far apart as possible. The plants die down in the winter and in cold areas the roots should be protected with straw. A few runners can be buried in a box of rich earth in a heated greenhouse to force leaves during the winter.

Mint rust is a fungus disease, especially common in spearmints. It grows from within the plant, and soon the lower shoots become contorted and speckled with orange. These outbreaks of spores spread up the plant as the fungus destroys it. Harvest the unaffected parts, dig up and destroy the rest and then grow fresh stock in another place.

Most mints respond well to regular picking. For drying, cut the stems and leaves about 5cm/2in above the ground as the flower buds begin to form, take care to avoid bruising and dry quickly in loose bunches or on frames in a warm, shaded, airy place. Strip the leaves from the stems and store in an airtight container.

Mint is a traditional accompaniment to lamb, duck and young vegetables in northern Europe, and is common in Middle Eastern cookery combined with yoghurt and pulses and in India in chutneys and highly spiced dishes; mint tea is a universal cooling drink. Mints have been used for many centuries as digestives, antiseptics and appetizers, and as cordial, cheering herbs. In Classical times the fresh leaves were rubbed over tables 'to stir up . . . a greedy desire of meate', and used to scent the body and bath water.

The most common wild mint in temperate climates is the water mint, *M. aquatica*, which grows in marshy places, about 60cm/2ft high. It has a strong peppermint smell and acrid taste, rounded leaves, often tinted purple, and lilac-coloured flowers. Spearmint or garden mint, *M. spicata*, is the most common culinary species, used in mint sauces and jellies.

The peppermint, *M. x piperita*, is probably a cross between water mint and spearmint. The two varieties, black and white, grow about 1m/3ft high with mauve flowers and long, narrow leaves. The black has a purple stem and purple-tinged leaves; the white has a green stem and leaves and a more delicate though less plentiful oil. Their oil contains menthol, which is an antiseptic and anesthetic, numbing and cooling the mouth. Chew the leaves to relieve toothache or infuse as peppermint tea, a refreshing, safe treatment for indigestion and dyspepsia, colds and 'flu. It is best not to drink it at night as it can cause insomnia. The oil is used to flavour confectionery, liqueurs and toothpaste. Make a flavoured oil by macerating fresh leaves in oil for 6 to 8 weeks.

Eau-de-Cologne mint, *M. x piperita* n.m. *citrata*, has rounder leaves edged with purple and a sharper, lemony scent. Use in washing waters, pot pourri, or add an infusion of the leaves to citrus jellies. The green and yellow ginger mint, *M. x gentilis* 'Variegata', has a spicier scent. Apple or Egyptian mint, *M. suaveolens*, has rounded, downy leaves, a fresh apple flavour and flowers of faded pink. The delicious variegated variety, pineapple mint, *M. suaveolens* 'Variegata', is dappled cream and pale green, and has a more fruity flavour.

Bowles mint, *M. x villosa* n.m. *alopecuroides*, is one of the largest, growing 1.5m/5ft high with broad leaves covered with a pale, woolly down. It is the best all-round culinary mint with a fresh scent and flavour, vigorous and hardy.

M. requienii, the Corsican mint, has mauve flowers the size of a pinhead and tiny rounded leaves. It seldom grows higher than 3cm/1in and will form a soft, peppermint-scented carpet in a sheltered, damp, warm position. Another small mint, *M. gattefossei*, grows about 23cm/9in high with lilac flowers and small, pointed leaves.

Pennyroyal, *M. pulegium*, is also known as 'pudding grass' and 'organie'. The upright varieties grow little over 30cm/12in high, the creeping ones make good carpeting herbs, with small, smooth leaves. Plant in damp, rather shaded places. Pennyroyal is as pungent as peppermint, but with a coarser flavour. An ointment was made with the leaves against fleas and other insects; rub fresh leaves on the skin as a protection against midges and scatter in the bedding of animals, among clothing and on larder shelves against ants. Take an infusion for coughs, hoarseness and indigestion or add to washing water to refresh and cleanse the skin. Sailors used to purify their drinking water with dried pennyroyal.

Mentha x piperita

Mentha x villosa
n.m. *alopecuroides*

Mentha aquatica

Mentha spicata

Mentha pulegium

Menyanthes trifoliata　　　*Monarda didyma*　　　*Myrica cerifera*

Menyanthes trifoliata

Bogbean, buckbean, water trefoil
Family: Menyanthaceae

Bogbean grows in northern climates across Britain, Europe, Russia, North America and along the borders of the Arctic. An aquatic perennial, up to 50cm/20in high, the stalks rise from creeping, submerged roots and the large, smooth leaves resemble those of the broad bean, growing in groups of three. The spikes of pink-and-white flowers bloom in early summer, each with 5 petals and delicately fringed within with long white hairs.

Divide the creeping roots and plant out in a marshy place or in shallow water by a garden pool. The dried leaves can be used as a bitter tonic drink and for flavouring ale. The infusion promotes the appetite and cleanses the skin and blood; the bruised leaves can be applied to swellings and inflammations.

To make a spring tonic, rich in iron, infuse equal quantities of bogbean, dandelion and nettle for about 45 minutes, then strain.

Monarda didyma

Red bergamot, bee balm, Oswego tea, Indian plume
Family: Labiatae

One of several varieties, all native to North America but now widely grown as garden plants, this is a tall, herbaceous perennial, growing about 1m/3ft high. The leaves are broad, slightly toothed and highly scented; the flowers bloom from midsummer in shaggy heads of scarlet blossoms with long hoods and cleft lips. Propagate by root division in damp, rich soil and divide every few years.

Dry the leaves and flowers at midsummer. A few fresh leaves can be included in salads or stuffings or floated in summer drinks; their flavour is aromatic and fresh. An infusion of the dried leaves resembles a scented China tea and was a favourite drink of the Oswego Indians in North America. It is refreshing taken cold with a slice of lemon. The name 'bergamot' derives from the Italian bergamot orange, which has a similar scent. It is a good bee plant.

Myrica cerifera

Bayberry, candleberry, wax myrtle
Family: Myricaceae

A large evergreen shrub of up to 4m/13ft high, the bayberry grows wild in temperate North America in poor, damp places. The shining leaves are aromatic, tough and sharply pointed; the inconspicuous, pale green flowers bloom in early summer, followed by clusters of bluish nutlets that are encrusted with a pale wax.

Propagate by seed, layering or from suckers, in a moist, lime-free soil. Dry the bark from the roots in autumn and the leaves in summer. Use a decoction of the bark as a gargle for sore throats, or take in small doses as a tonic or for diarrhoea – in large doses it is emetic. When the nutlets are boiled in water the wax separates and can be removed from the surface. This can be made into brittle candles or used in soap.

The related European sweet gale, *Myrica gale*, is deciduous. Its leaves produce an inferior wax. The leaves of both yield a yellow dye.

Myristica fragrans

Myristica fragrans
Nutmeg and mace
Family: Myristicaceae

The tall, evergreen nutmeg tree is native to the Moluccas and is cultivated in the West Indies and many other tropical countries. There are male and female trees, a few males being included in each plantation. Both grow up to 8m/26ft high, have smooth, grey bark, long, dark, aromatic leaves and small, pale yellow flowers. The fruit is large and succulent with a yellow skin. Inside is the heavy seed, the nutmeg, which is protected and enclosed by a bright red fleshy network, the aril or mace. The trees are harvested several times a year and will bear for at least 70 years. The nutmeg and mace are dried separately. When dried, nutmegs are dark, or sometimes whitened with lime, which is a protection against nutmeg worms and insects. The dried mace is flattened into orange 'blades'.

Nutmegs quickly lose their strength when cut, so buy whole and grate when needed with a fine cheese grater or a special nutmeg grater. As mace is impossible to grate, keep small quantities in powdered form in an airtight jar. A few whole blades can be stored and used for flavouring soups, vinegars and fish dishes, when they can easily be removed at the end of the cooking time. Both nutmegs and mace vary in quality. When pressed with a thumb nail a blade of mace should exude a little oil and a cut nutmeg should have an oily surface within.

Nutmeg and mace have similar flavours but that of mace is stronger and more pungent, nutmeg being sweetly spicy and warming. Mace was more popular than nutmeg until the 17th century, when strong spices became less necessary with the increasing use of sugar. Use ground mace in cakes, potted meat, fish and cheese and other savoury preserves. In the 18th-century *Country House-wife*, the author describes how a strong mace-flavoured liquor was added to give 'true relish' to 'the famous Stilton cheeses'. Nutmegs are indispensable, blending well with other spices and an ingredient in sweet and savoury dishes. Use in cakes and sweet cream or milk puddings, to spice cream cheese, cheese or onion sauces and soufflés, and with apple pie, stewed fruit and vegetables, especially potatoes and spinach. Use it to flavour mulled wine and other spiced or chocolate drinks. In Italy it is one of the most popular spices and Dutch food is often heavily spiced with nutmeg.

Nutmeg has a good effect upon the digestion and is useful for countering flatulence, diarrhoea and nausea. Taken in large quantities it can become dangerously narcotic, but in small quantities acts as a mild sedative. Grate into hot milk or take a teaspoonful of nutmeg brandy in hot milk as a digestive and nightcap. This is made by steeping about $1\frac{1}{2}$ grated nutmegs in 600ml/1 pint brandy and leaving for 2 to 3 weeks, shaking daily. Strain through fine muslin.

Myrrhis odorata

Sweet cicely, anise fern, great chervil

Family: Umbelliferae

Resembling a scented cow parsley, sweet cicely grows along roadsides and hedgerows in mountainous districts in the north and west of Britain and on high ground in Europe and Russia. It can easily be identified by the aniseed or liquorice smell and taste of the leaves and, in midsummer, by the clusters of erect, pointed fruits. These are about 2cm/¾in long, deeply ribbed, and turn dark brown and glossy. The flowers are white, growing in umbels, and the fern-like leaves are a fresh green above and softly downy beneath, with downy stems. The plant can grow up to 1m/3ft high.

Once established in a partly shaded corner of the garden in moist, loamy soil, sweet cicely will freely self-seed. Propagate by fresh seed sown in the autumn or by root division. The plants grow large, 1.5m/5ft high, with thick, perennial roots, so space the seedlings about 60cm/2ft apart. The new green leaves appear early in the spring, one of the first herbs in the garden, and the flowers blossom from spring to early summer. All green parts die down in late autumn.

The leaves do not dry well, but the aromatic fruits can be dried as a flavouring. The leaves can be chopped in salads. They have a markedly sugary taste and if cooked with sour fruit such as rhubarb or gooseberries will reduce the need for sugar. As a natural sweetener it is a useful addition to a diabetic diet. The seeds (fruits) have a more powerful, sweetly liquorice flavour and when green and unripe can be chopped for salads, ice cream or whipped cream. Put whole ripe seeds into apple pies, like cloves. One herbalist recommends them served boiled with oil and vinegar. Use the roots peeled, chopped raw and dressed as a salad or steamed or boiled as a vegetable and served with butter.

Sweet cicely was considered an altogether wholesome herb, for strengthening the lungs, for warming 'old and cold stomachs oppressed with wind and phlegm', and for stimulating the appetite. The strongest oil is present in the seeds, which have a mildly laxative effect. The whole plant is tonic and digestive. An infusion made from the leaves has a mild, pleasant flavour and should be taken twice a day, a small glassful at a time. The roots are most praised by herbalists – as a protection against the plague when candied or boiled, and as a warming comforting dish when 'sodden' (boiled).

In the north of England the seeds were crushed and the oil used as a scented polish for oak furniture.

A North American species, *Osmorhiza longistylis*, looks similar but has broader, divided leaves. The scent is also like sweet cicely and the root has similar uses.

Myrrhis odorata

Myrtus communis

Nasturtium officinale

Myrtus communis
Myrtle
Family: Myrtaceae
A bushy, evergreen shrub, myrtle grows about 3m/10ft high in temperate climates, but in its wild state on dry hillsides in southern Europe, North Africa and the Middle East may reach at least 5m/16ft. The leaves are aromatic and glossy, the creamy flowers with prominent stamens blossom in early summer, and the berries are black with a blue bloom. Take cuttings from young shoots in midsummer or propagate by seed or by layering. A sunny protected position against a south-facing wall is ideal. The young plants should be protected with straw or sacking in the winter, and even mature bushes can be killed by sharp frosts if not covered.

Dry the flowers for pot pourri. The leaves and berries have been used fresh or dried for thousands of years as a stuffing and spice for game, and the branches burned as a flavouring beneath roasting meat. The leaves are available all year.

Nasturtium officinale
Watercress
Family: Cruciferae
Watercress grows in fresh, running water in most temperate climates, and especially where the soil has a high lime content. The divided leaves are bright green and glossy, the hollow stem grows up to 30cm/12in long and the white flowers bloom from midsummer. The perennial roots are submerged in mud or shallow water. *N. x sterile*, a hybrid between this and a bronze-leaved species, *N. microphyllum*, is cultivated on a large scale.

Sow seed at any time during the summer in boxes of moist compost or on the muddy banks of a stream, or plant out portions of the rooting stem in shallow, moving water or in a moist trench. Each plant will spread rapidly, sending out new roots. The sterile hybrid has brownish-bronze leaves that can be picked throughout the winter, except in very frosty weather; gather the green-leaved *N. officinale* during the summer; in both cases the

mature leaves have a better flavour than the younger sprigs. Do not pick wild watercress from polluted streams or in sheep country where the eggs of an unpleasant sheep parasite may be hidden in the stems. Be careful to identify the plant accurately as a similar but umbelliferous water plant, 'marshwort' or 'fool's cress', is poisonous.

Watercress has a hot, tangy and refreshing taste. It is delicious as a salad herb, in soups, blanched and sieved as a purée or chopped and salted with brown bread and butter. It contains a high proportion of Vitamin C and also valuable minerals, especially iron. For this reason it is a tonic herb and taken for anaemia, rickets, weak heart and eyesight and to increase the flow of milk. In the 17th century a popular anti-scorbutic drink contained orange juice, scurvy grass, brooklime and watercress. As an antiseptic cleanser, apply the juice of pulped leaves to the skin and leave for at least 15 minutes; this will help remove spots and blemishes.

Ocimum basilicum
Basil, sweet basil
Family: Labiatae

The cultivation of basil spread from its native India through Asia to Egypt at least 4,000 years ago, and from there to Rome and southern Europe. It does not appear to have reached Britain until the 16th century and was then carried by early settlers to North America.

In India it is perennial, but in cooler climates is treated as a tender annual. It grows about 50cm/20in high with broad, juicy, aromatic leaves and a long spike of creamy-white or purple-tinged flowers in midsummer. Sow the seeds indoors or in a heated greenhouse in early spring and keep well watered. Transplant the seedlings into individual pots or boxes, among tomatoes in the greenhouse, or out of doors in a sheltered, sunny corner of the garden when all danger of frost has passed. Protect under glass to be sure of a good lush growth during a cool summer. The soil should be well drained, light and rich, and dressed with rotted manure or compost. The plants need plenty of moisture but do not like to stand in water. Pinch out the tops as the flower buds begin to form to encourage bushy growth. If kept indoors or in a greenhouse, plants should survive well into the winter. It is a good bee herb.

The leaves lose their special pungency when dried and a minty flavour dominates. Cut the plant down to the second pair of leaves as the buds begin to form; a second cut can be made before the first frosts. Dry the whole stems loosely bunched or on a rack in a shaded, airy place.

There are many varieties of sweet basil with differing flavours and a decorative purple variety, 'Dark Opal', with toothed leaves and a gingerish, spicy flavour. The flavour of true basil is deliciously pungent and strong, warming, slightly spicy, fresh and appetizing. To preserve the flavour during winter, macerate in oil or fine vinegar for about a month, leaving it on a sunny windowsill and covered with a cloth, then strain and bottle the oil. If the flavour is not strong enough, repeat with fresh basil. In India the leaves are sometimes salted in layers like beans in an earthenware crock, then rinsed as needed. In Italy basil is preserved whole in oil but the result is somewhat slimy. For those who like the flavour, fresh basil will improve almost every savoury dish – salads, soups, vegetables, fish, meat, poultry, cheese, marinades, sauces and dressings, stuffings, pâtés and potted meats and all tomato dishes. Add the leaves towards the end of the cooking time. Fresh basil is essential for the famous pesto sauce, made by pounding leaves to a pulp in a mortar and combining with salt, garlic and olive oil; parmesan cheese and pine nuts or walnuts can be added, and the result stirred into minestrone soup or hot pasta.

A strongly tonic and antiseptic herb, basil is a stimulant and digestive, good for settling an upset stomach and relieving nausea. The oil rubbed on the temples is said to relieve headaches and the dried leaves were used as a medicinal snuff to clear the head. In the past there have been passionate advocates for and against its use in medicine, some physicians asserting that even smelling basil causes scorpions to breed in the brain, others that it gives strength and courage and will draw poison from the body. Its associations with poisons probably accounts for the repeated advice against planting basil near rue, the well-known poison antidote. It is often cited as an aphrodisiac and it is still used in many countries as an aid to childbirth.

Ocimum basilicum

Basil was used as a strewing herb and it is traditional to keep a pot of basil on the windowsill to deter flies. The oil or fresh leaves were commonly used to scent 'sweet or washing waters' and it is still used in perfumery.

The sacred Indian basil, *O. sanctum*, is dedicated to Krishna and planted round temples, and laid on the breasts of the dead as a powerful protection. In France it is the *herbe royale* and the name 'basil' derives from the Greek word meaning 'kingly'. In ancient Greece the planting of basil seeds was accompanied by shouts and curses, hence the French phrase '*semer le basilic*', meaning 'to slander'.

Bush basil, *O. minimum*, is a hardier and more compact plant growing no more than 25cm/10in high with small leaves. It has a slightly weaker flavour than sweet basil, but makes a satisfactory little pot plant that should survive indoors well into the winter.

Ocimum minimum

Ocimum basilicum 'Dark Opal'

Oenothera biennis

Oenthera biennis

Oenothera biennis
Evening primrose, tree primrose
Family: Onagraceae
Native to North America, the evening primrose grows in dry and waste places and was brought to Europe in the 18th century. A biennial with a strong, deep, tap root, it forms a rosette of leaves during its first year, and a hairy stem, 1m/3ft high, of large, pale yellow blossoms in its second. The flowers are sweetly scented with flimsy, poppy-like petals, which open throughout the summer, especially in the evenings when they are pollinated by insects.

There are many species. Sow seed in a sunny position on a light well-drained soil; they will readily self-sow. Harvest and dry the whole plant in the early summer of its second year. Boiled, the root tastes sweet, like a parsnip. The leaves and stalks are astringent and contain much mucilage. Take an infusion to soothe coughs and asthma and as a mild sedative. Scientists are investigating the root as a possible source of treatment for multiple sclerosis.

85

Origanum species
Family: Labiatae

There are many cultivated species and varieties of marjoram, including variegated, golden and prostrate plants, but two South Mediterranean species are commonly cultivated in herb gardens – the sweet or knotted marjoram, *Origanum majorana*, which is treated as an annual in temperate climates, though perennial in the south, and the hardy perennial pot marjoram, *O. onites*. The wild marjoram, *O. vulgare*, often called 'oregano', is a tough perennial that grows on limy soils in southern Britain, northern and southern Europe, Asia, North Africa and North America. Its flavour and growth vary tremendously according to climate and habitat. Dittany of Crete, *O. dictamnus*, is another species, grown more as a decorative plant than as a herb, with downy leaves and curious pink flowerheads. Winter marjoram, *O. heracleoticum*, is native to Greece.

All marjorams possess varying quantities of a strong, warming, aromatic oil and have been used as flavouring herbs since ancient times. They are easy to dry and retain their flavour well. The oil has an antiseptic effect, is mildly tonic and digestive, will provoke menstruation and soothe and calm the nerves. An infusion will settle the stomach and is helpful in cases of morning sickness. Macerate the plant tops in oil, and use this as a rub for rheumatism and aching joints or headache, or apply a hot poultice of bruised fresh leaves. The oil or fresh leaves will soothe toothache, and a pillow stuffed with the dried herb may help insomniacs. Marjoram was popular as a sweetly scented disinfectant strewing herb and the oil was used to polish wooden furniture. The flowering tops were a flavouring and preservative for ale and produce a rusty red dye that is soluble in water. The flowers bloom from midsummer and are very attractive to bees and butterflies.

The name 'oregano' derives from Greek words meaning 'joy of the mountains' and in Greece bridal couples were crowned with marjoram and it was planted on graves to ensure a happy afterlife.

Sweet or knotted marjoram grows about 25cm/10in high with a fine, often reddish stem and pairs of small, greyish leaves covered with oil glands. The pale mauve or white flowers are almost hidden by knotted bracts. Sow the fine seeds early in the year under glass. Plant out the seedlings in a warm, sunny, sheltered place in a light soil and keep well weeded. Only sow out of doors when all frost is past, and thin the seedlings to about 20cm/8in apart. Cut the plants for drying about 5cm/2in above the ground as the buds are about to burst, and again in the autumn. Dry in loose bunches or on a rack. This is the most delicately flavoured of the marjorams with a fine, sweet scent. It is most suited to salads, egg or light meat dishes, summer vegetables, and in stuffings and cream sauces. It was a common ingredient in 'sweete powders, sweete bags, and sweete washing waters' and as Gerard says, 'excellent good to be put into all odoriferous . . . broths and meates'. The tea was used against all 'cold diseases of the braine and head'.

Pot or French marjoram is more commonly cultivated and grows up to 60cm/2ft high, forming a strong, spreading, perennial clump. The white or pink flowers are borne in clusters and bloom in midsummer. Propagate by seed in the spring, by cuttings, or by root division or offsets in the autumn. Plant the seedlings out in a sunny position in good, well-drained soil and keep well weeded. Divide the clump

Origanum majorana

every few years or the flavour will deteriorate. Harvest in the same way as sweet marjoram. It has a more robust flavour and is used in soups and stews, sausages and stuffings.

Wild marjoram is less compact, tall and leggy, spreading by rhizomes among grasses on dry banks and stony hillsides. The flowers are similar to those of pot marjoram and it can be cultivated and harvested in the same way. When grown in hot, dry conditions the flavour is far stronger, more peppery and with a more bitter tang. It should be used with discretion in the kitchen. In Italy oregano is one of the most popular flavouring herbs, for pizzas, pasta and all tomato and cheese dishes. In Greece the many wild species are known collectively as *rigani* and grilled with meat and fish, the bitterness countering heavy olive oils. In Mexico it flavours chilies, spicy soups and bean dishes. It is the wild species that is chiefly used as a medicine and had a reputation since Classical times as an antidote for poisons, venom and hemlock.

Panax quinquefolius

Origanum vulgare

Origanum onites

Panax quinquefolius
American ginseng
Family : Araliaceae
American ginseng grows in woodland in eastern North America. The seeds take nearly 2 years to germinate; the fleshy root produces a few leaves with 5 leaflets, small, greenish-yellow flowers in midsummer and bright red berries, and is ready for harvesting after 6 years. It measures up to 60cm/2ft long and is often shaped in a roughly human form; the name 'ginseng' derives from the Chinese word meaning 'man-shape'. The wild root began to be cultivated in North America in the 1880s and has been exported since then to China and Europe.

A similar species, Chinese ginseng, *P. pseudoginseng*, has been used medicinally in China and Tibet since about 3000 BC. Ginseng has a reputation as a universal panacea, aphrodisiac and elixir, and appears to adapt to the needs of the body. Research so far has found no scientific proof of these powers. It can be chewed or taken as a tea or powder.

Papaver somniferum

Pelargonium graveolens

Petroselinum species

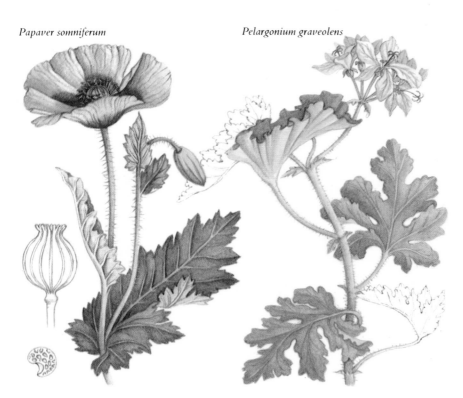

Papaver somniferum
Opium poppy
Family: Papaveraceae

Cultivation of the opium poppy spread from the Middle East to China over 1,000 years ago and opium was used as a medicine in ancient Egypt, Greece and Italy. A tall annual, 1.2m/4ft high, with large, pale mauve or white flowers from midsummer, this poppy is easily grown from seed in most climates in a rich, moist soil and sunny position. The drug is obtained by making an incision in the unripe seed capsule and collecting the thick juice that oozes out, as soon as it has dried hard in the sun. In cool climates the drug collected is very weak. Opium is a dangerous and addictive poison. Several important drugs are obtained from it, including morphine and codeine.

The ripe seeds are not narcotic; shake the seeds from the capsules of any poppy species and use to flavour bread and cakes, curries and noodles, or use their expressed oil in cooking.

Pelargonium graveolens
Rose-scented geranium
Family: Geraniaceae

This is one of the most popular and adaptable varieties from the large *Pelargonium* genus, which includes all the cultivated geraniums. They originated in South Africa but have been cultivated in Europe for nearly 200 years and are now popular in most countries. The rose-scented variety grows up to 1m/3ft high with deeply lobed, fragrant leaves and loose clusters of small, mauve or pink scentless flowers, which bloom from early summer. Other varieties have a whole range of scents from lemon to peppermint and grow in every shape and size.

All species are perennial, and easily grown from cuttings taken at any time from spring to autumn. They thrive in well-rotted, well-drained compost, but will not survive frost. Bring indoors during the winter, put in a cool place and seldom water. Use the leaves fresh or dried to flavour sweet cakes, jellies and puddings or add to pot pourri.

Petroselinum species
Family: Umbelliferae

Parsley is probably native to countries bordering the eastern Mediterranean, but has been cultivated for thousands of years. Introduced to Britain by the Romans, it vanished during the Dark Ages and was re-introduced in medieval times. The original wild variety is likely to have been plain-leaved, similar to the cultivated French and Italian parsleys. Later the familiar curly-leaved *P. crispum* was developed and later still the Hamburg parsley, *P. crispum* 'Tuberosum'.

All species are biennial, developing a thick clump of leaves during the first year and a tall flowering stem about 1m/3ft high during the second. The leaves of the *crispum* varieties are tightly curled, the French, Italian and Hamburg varieties deeply cut but flat. The flowers grow in midsummer in umbels about 5cm/2in across and are a pale yellow-green colour; the seeds are greyish brown; the pale tap roots are sweet and fleshy, like spindly carrots. The roots of Hamburg parsley are much larger. Take care not to confuse plain-leaved parsley with fool's parsley, *Aethusa cynapium*.

The seeds take at least 6 weeks to germinate. To hasten the process leave overnight in warm water then sow in a well-raked seed bed that has been previously soaked with boiling water, and cover thinly with fine soil. Thin the seedlings to about 25cm/10in apart and transplant carefully on a wet day. The parsley bed can be in full sun though the plants tolerate some shade. Sow in spring or late summer. Flower stalks will appear the following spring and should be nipped off to encourage leaf growth; if they are allowed to seed, parsley will readily self-sow. For a supply of fresh leaves during

the winter, sow seeds in the greenhouse in midsummer or pot some
roots of spring-sown plants and
bring indoors. Otherwise a cloche
over outdoor plants will prolong the
growth of leaves. To ensure a steady
supply, sow seeds every year.

The leaves are at their best during
the first year and can be picked and
dried at any time; spread on a tray in
a cool oven until just crisp and store
in an airtight jar in a dark place to
preserve their colour. Parsley roots
take much longer to dry. Store these
for flavouring.

Parsley is a universal herb, en-
hancing most flavours, an indispensable part of *bouquet garni* and used
in soups and stews, with meat and
fish, vegetables, marinades, sauces
and stuffings. Use both stems and
leaves. As a garnish, the leaves can be
used raw or fried until crisp. The
curly parsley has the finest flavour
but is less hardy than the plain-leaved
varieties, which have a slightly
coarser, stronger taste. The young
roots can be boiled or eaten raw with
a dressing and taste like sweet, earthy
carrots. Treat the roots of Hamburg
parsley like parsnips.

All parts are rich in Vitamins A, B
and C, also iron, calcium and other
important minerals. Take as a general tonic and for anaemia. It will
stimulate the digestive system and
kidneys and is said to relieve menstrual pains. The crushed leaves
make a soothing, antiseptic dressing
for bruises, sprains, insect bites and
wounds and will ease the sore breasts
of nursing mothers. Steep parsley in
water overnight to make a cleansing
rinse for the skin. The leaves are well
known as a breath sweetener, being
the traditional antidote for garlic.
The seeds contain a strong oil, apiol,
and are considered unsafe to take
internally.

Parsley leaves and stems give
greenish-yellow dyes when mordanted with chrome or alum.

Petroselinum crispum

Pimenta dioica

Allspice, Jamaica pepper, pimento
Family: Myrtaceae

An evergreen belonging to the myrtle family, the allspice tree grows about 9m/30ft high in the tropical forests of South America, the West Indies and, most prolifically, in Jamaica. There they grow in plantations along the hillsides above the sea and, once established, need little care besides the clearance of the undergrowth. The trees are grown from fresh seed and will continue to bear for about 100 years. The leaves are thick and leathery, the small white flowers grow in clusters in midsummer and the ripe berries are a rich, dark purple. The berries lose their spicy aroma as they mature, so are harvested while green and unripe and dried artificially or in the sun. When dried they resemble large, brown, wrinkled peppercorns.

The rind of the berries is particularly aromatic and to obtain the spice at its full strength it is best to buy whole dried berries rather than the ground powder. They are easily crushed in a mortar or ground in a pepper mill. The flavour, as the name implies, is like a blend of several spices, being rather hot and peppery with a touch of cloves and nutmeg, and can be used in both sweet and savoury dishes. It blends well with other spices and is an ingredient in most spice mixtures, though it is seldom necessary to add cloves when using allspice. Use whole in slow-cooking stews, soups, bean dishes and marinades, and ground with ham, curries, meat loaf, pâtés, sweet cakes and biscuits, and whole or ground as a warming ingredient in mulled wine. The early Central American civilizations used allspice as a flavouring for chocolate. In Jamaica it is added lavishly to numerous dishes – sweet potatoes, soups, stews and curries. The Spanish explorers of the 17th century gave allspice the name *Pimenta* because of its peppery flavour and later the dried berry was included in cargoes sent back to Europe from the West Indian colonies. As the only real spice that grew relatively close to the newly established colonies in North America, allspice was used in quantity in pumpkin pies, pickles and cakes by the early settlers.

As a medicine, allspice has much the same uses as cloves and their oils are similar. It works well as a digestive and has an antiseptic and slightly anesthetic action. A comforting and warming infusion can be made from a few crushed berries. Add allspice to pot pourri to provide a long-lasting spicy scent. Several other species from the *Pimenta* genus grow in tropical South America and the West Indies, including *P. racemosa*, which is used in the manufacture of 'bay rum'.

Pimenta dioica

Pimpinella anisum
Anise
Family: Umbelliferae

Like so many aromatic herbs, anise is native to the southern Mediterranean and has been cultivated in warm climates since the earliest times. The seeds seldom ripen successfully in northern regions, but it has been grown in herb gardens in Britain since the 15th century, or possibly since the Roman occupation, and seeds were carried to North America by the first European settlers. It is a tender annual, seldom growing more than 50cm/20in high. Like coriander, the basal leaves are broad and lobed and the upper leaves finely cut and feathery. The small creamy flowers grow in umbels in midsummer, followed by pale brown, ribbed and hairy seeds.

Sow seed in late spring in a light, dry soil in a sunny, sheltered position and thin the seedlings to 20cm/8in apart. They do not transplant well and should be kept carefully weeded. The seeds take a long time to ripen and need a long warm summer and favourable conditions to succeed, but the leaves can be used and the plants themselves are pretty and well worth growing. Gather the seed-heads as the seeds change colour and hang in a sunny place to ripen, with a cloth beneath to catch the seeds as they fall.

The seeds have the strongest flavour, an aromatic, penetrating sweetness that is warming and pervasive. There is some similarity with the flavour of fennel – both contain the same oil, anethol – and anise can be used in the same way with fish, poultry, and in creamy soups and sauces. Sweet cakes, biscuits and confectionery can also be spiced with anise and it has an affinity with some fresh fruit, especially figs. Aniseed is an important flavouring for sweet liqueurs such as anisette and for pastis

such as Pernod and Ricard. These pastis have many culinary uses; add them to soups, sauces, basting liquor, fruit syrups and sweet creams when the whole aniseeds would be less suitable. The leaves have a more delicate and subtle flavour, eat fresh in salads, with vegetables or cream cheese.

Anise is one of the best-known digestive herbs and will also soothe coughs and headaches, and relieve catarrh. Make a delicious tea by infusing the leaves, or $7g/\frac{1}{4}oz$ bruised seeds for 10 minutes in 600ml/1 pint boiling water or hot milk. Chew the seeds after meals to sweeten the breath and help digestion. In Roman times a special cake heavily spiced with anise, cumin, fennel and other digestive seeds was eaten after rich meals. Aniseed is also said to increase breast milk.

As aniseed has antiseptic qualities, anise oil is sometimes an ingredient in toothpastes and insect repellents, and is also used in the manufacture of scent. Rubbed on cheese, it is an efficient bait for mousetraps.

Piper nigrum
Pepper
Family: Piperaceae

The pepper vine grows wild in the equatorial forests of India and Asia and is cultivated today in other tropical countries. The smooth, woody stems climb 6m/20ft up jungle trees, though in cultivated plantations they are limited to about half that height. The oval leaves are thick and dark green and the small white flowers grow in long clusters. The berries that follow are green, turning orange then red as they ripen. Some of these are harvested unripe and dried in the sun until wrinkled and black. Others are left to ripen, then picked and the outer flesh soaked and rubbed off before the pale inner corn is dried. The former are sold as black pepper, the latter as white.

The flavour of pepper quickly deteriorates when the corn is ground, so both black and white peppercorns should be bought whole and ground just before use in a pepper mill. Whole pepper stores well and can be bought in quantity. Powdered pepper is sometimes adulterated. Green peppercorns are unripe fresh berries, which are often marketed packed in brine, vinegar or their own juices.

The hot pungency of pepper is neither sweet nor savoury and has an enormous range of uses. The black peppercorns are the most popular with the best aroma and strongest flavour; those from the Malabar coast are of especially high quality. The white have a powerfully hot flavour and the green are freshly hot and spicy.

Add whole peppercorns to marinades, stock, *court bouillon* and stews, and use ground pepper for dishes with a shorter cooking time or add just before serving so that the flavour does not become too bitter. Roughly crush peppercorns in a mortar for dishes such as steak *au poivre* when the pepper should tingle and crunch in the mouth. Pepper can also be ground into sweet dishes, fruit cakes, fruit tarts and pies.

Medicinally, pepper is a stimulant and can be used to increase the flow of gastric juices, to help digest rich foods and to prevent constipation. A formerly well-known medicine, called *Diatrion Piperion*, consisted of a mixture of white, black and long pepper, thyme, ginger and aniseed boiled in hyssop syrup and taken for the digestion and for restoring the memory.

Pepper is the most popular and important spice in Europe and has been since Roman times. It was often used as a substitute for money, ransoms, tributes and rents (peppercorn rents are still referred to in Britain today). In the 15th century it was the enormous value of pepper that inspired the dangerous voyages of the Portuguese mariners.

Other *Piper* species include cubebs or tailed pepper, *P. cubeba*, which has bitter, pungent fruit, and the hot and acrid long pepper, *P. longum*.

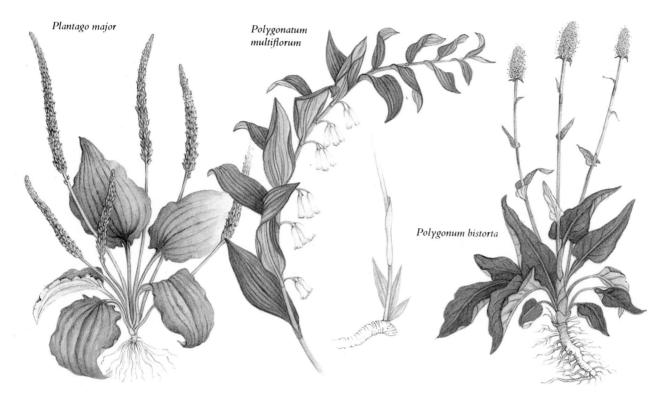

Plantago major

Polygonatum multiflorum

Polygonum bistorta

Plantago major
Great plantain, waybread, rat's tail
Family: Plantaginaceae

Great plantain is one of the most widespread herbs, growing in grassy places in temperate climates around the world, and is generally considered a weed. A perennial, and the largest of the plantains, it has broad, heavily veined leaves and long greenish spikes of flowers that bloom from midsummer on stalks about 50cm/20in high.

The leaves are edible with little flavour, but as a medicine they are included among the first recorded herbs and were listed in most old recipes for vulnerary and soothing ointments.

Plantain is astringent and refrigerant. Take an infusion of the leaves or decoction of the root for fevers, diarrhoea, thrush and bladder and kidney troubles, or use the infusion externally as a cleanser for the skin or as a compress for tired eyes. Apply the bruised leaves to insect bites and stings, burns and bleeding wounds.

Polygonatum multiflorum
Solomon's seal, lady's lockets
Family: Liliaceae

Native to northern Europe but rarely found wild in Britain, Solomon's seal grows in woods and moist, shady places. The curving stems are at least 60cm/2ft high and clasped by oval, ribbed leaves. Creamy, bell-like flowers grow from the axils in early summer, to be followed by black berries. The perennial rootstock is pale, thick and twisted and covered with knobbed joints and stem scars that can resemble seals. There are several species, all with similar properties; the garden variety is often a cross between *P. multiflorum* and *P. odoratum*.

Sow fresh seed in autumn or divide the creeping rootstock from late autumn to spring. Plant in a shady position in light soil dressed with leaf mould.

Do not take the root internally, but use either fresh or dried and powdered as an efficient, astringent, mucilaginous poultice for bruises, inflammations and wounds.

Polygonum bistorta
Bistort, Easter ledges
Family: Polygonaceae

Bistort grows in damp meadows and grassy places on high ground from northern Britain to the Himalayas. Up to 1m/3ft high, it has smooth broad leaves and tight little spikes of pink flowers in early summer. The twisted, perennial rootstock quickly spreads and bistort is easily propagated by root division in a moist, shady corner of the garden.

The leaves appear in early spring and make a nourishing vegetable or salad. Harvest and dry the root in the autumn. It is an extremely powerful astringent and can be taken as a decoction for coughs, sore throats and dysentery. To make the decoction boil 25g/1oz root for 10 minutes in 300ml/½ pint water and drink half a glassful twice a day. This can also be used as a gargle or mouthwash for ulcers and as a wash for wounds or sores. The dried, powdered root is an effective styptic. The related buckwheat and knotgrass are irritants.

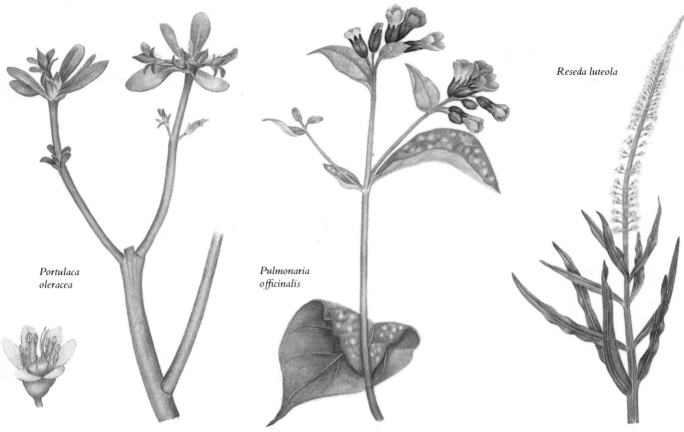

*Portulaca
oleracea*

*Pulmonaria
officinalis*

Reseda luteola

Portulaca oleracea

Purslane, green purslane

Family: Portulacaceae

A sprawling annual about 30cm/
12in high with thick, fleshy leaves,
purslane grows wild in India, but has
been cultivated for centuries in
Britain and Europe and was taken to
North America by early settlers. The
blunt green leaves grow from succulent reddish stems and yellow flowers bloom in midsummer. Sow
seed in spring and in succession
during the early summer months in a
rich soil and sunny position; keep
well watered. Golden purslane, *P.
oleracea* var. *sativa*, is a less hardy plant.

The young leaves have a sharp,
cooling flavour and texture and can
be eaten in salads or boiled or
steamed as a vegetable. Use the
older, tougher leaves to flavour
soups and stews; pickle the stems for
winter salads. Purslane was used as a
cooling herb – the leaves held
beneath the tongue to allay thirst or
bruised and applied to a hot
forehead or to inflamed eyes. It is also
an antiscorbutic.

Pulmonaria officinalis

Lungwort, Jerusalem cowslip

Family: Boraginaceae

Lungwort is native to Europe,
growing in woods and shady places,
and has been cultivated in Britain for
centuries. A member of the borage
family, it is a hardy perennial that
appears in the early spring with
large, pointed, silver-spotted and
roughly hairy leaves and, in late
spring, flowers that change from
pink to blue. It grows up to
30cm/12in high and makes good
ground cover in the garden, in
moist, shaded places, and can be
propagated by seed or root division.
There are many cultivated varieties.

The young leaves can be eaten as a
salad or potherb in the same way as
borage leaves and, like them, contain
quantities of mucilage. For this
reason it is helpful for coughs and the
infusion of the leaves had a high
reputation as a treatment for all
pulmonary complaints. The spotted
leaves were thought to resemble
diseased lungs and to be a clue to the
uses of the plant.

Reseda luteola

Weld, dyer's rocket

Family: Resedaceae

Native to Britain and Europe, weld
is biennial, growing over 1m/3ft
high on basic soil. The leaves are
smooth, long and lanceolate with
wavy edges. During its second year
long, narrow spikes of pale yellow-
green flowers appear from midsummer. It used to be grown as a catch-
crop with barley and was widely
cultivated as a dye herb. In Britain
the demand was so great that dried
weld was often imported from
France. It can easily be mistaken for
the closely related wild mignonette,
R. lutea, which has a sweet scent and
toothed leaves.

Grow in a light, limy soil in a
sunny position. The seeds remain
fertile for many years and colonies of
weld occasionally spring up when an
old site is disturbed by roadworks.

Weld is one of the oldest known
dyes, yielding a strong yellow when
mordanted with alum or tin and
once used with woad to produce
'Saxon green'.

Rheum rhabarbarum

Rosa canina

Rheum rhabarbarum
Rhubarb, English rhubarb, garden rhubarb
Family: Polygonaceae

Cultivated garden rhubarb may have developed from a wild Siberian species or from a hybrid. The roots grow large and woody, dark red outside and fibrous within, and last for many years. From them grow thick leaf stalks, up to 1m/3ft long, and enormous, dark green, veined leaves. The creamy-white flowers are clustered in a spike in mid-summer.

Rhubarb can be grown from seed but is most easily propagated by root division. Plant out pieces of root, each with a bud, in deeply worked soil that has been dressed with well-rotted manure. The stalks should not be pulled during the first year, and in subsequent years only pick until midsummer to ensure healthy, productive crowns. The stems can be forced early in the year beneath inverted pots or boxes surrounded by manure or straw.

Rhubarb stems are generally stewed with sugar as a pudding and can also be taken as a gentle laxative. They are acidic, so do not eat large quantities at a time. The leaves contain strong concentrations of oxalic acid and must not be eaten at all. The dried and powdered root is an astringent medicine for stomach and bowel troubles.

Other species of rhubarb were used medicinally before the introduction of the garden species to Britain from Italy in the 17th century. These came from China where the roots have been used as a purgative medicine since 3000 BC and have a stronger action than the garden species.

A decoction of the root of garden rhubarb, or the powdered root mixed to a paste, can be used as a yellow hair dye. Because of its acidic action, rhubarb acts as a descaler when boiled in a kettle or pan, and the crushed leaves make a good scourer for brass or copper.

Rosa canina
Dog rose
Family: Rosaceae

The dog rose is the most common wild rose of northern Europe, a deciduous shrub growing 3m/10ft or more, with curving, prickly stems, toothed leaves and delicate, white or pink flowers. Oval, red rose hips ripen in late summer. It can easily be grown in the garden from seed or cuttings.

Eat the delicate, scented petals fresh in salads or sandwiches, cook in jam and jellies, or use as a flavouring for butter, vinegar or sweets. Rose hips contain Vitamin C and make nutritious syrups, purées or jellies (strain well to remove irritant hairs). The dried leaves can be used for tea.

The deep, red petals of the cultivated damask rose, *R. damascena*, are the most useful medicinally, being astringent, tonic and cordial. Take in honey for sore throats and apply in vinegar to the forehead for headaches. Add dried petals to pot pourri. The distilled water is used as a condiment and scent.

Rosmarinus officinalis

Rosmarinus officinalis

Rosemary

Family: Labiatae

Rosemary grows wild in Mediterranean countries and is cultivated in temperate climates. In sheltered places it may grow 2m/6½ft high and live for 20 years. Related to lavender, rosemary has a similar twisted and woody stem; the aromatic leaves are evergreen, dark above and silvery beneath; the pale blue flowers bloom in midsummer and are attractive to bees.

Cuttings will usually take easily and rosemary can also be propagated by seed, layering or root division. Plant in a light, well-drained soil in a sheltered, sunny position beside a wall. In northern climates it is wise to grow rosemary in a large pot, drained with broken crocks, which can be sheltered in a greenhouse or indoors during the winter.

Rosemary bushes make good hedges if grown about 50cm/20in apart and trimmed and shaped immediately after flowering. They can also be trained against a wall; a visitor to Hampton Court in the 16th century described rosemary 'so planted and nailed to the walls as to cover them entirely'. Dry and store the hedge trimmings and cut for drying in the usual way as the plant comes into flower.

Other varieties include *R. officinalis* 'Alba' with white flowers; a bright blue-flowered variety; and a small prostrate, rather delicate variety, suitable for rockeries or pots.

Rosemary is strongly pungent and should be added to food with care. The leaves are sharp and spiky, so use a sprig to flavour marinades, stews and strong game dishes, and remove it before serving. Lay a sprig beneath roast or baked meat or fish, or add to barbecued lamb or beef. Infuse the leaves in milk for sweet puddings and custards and add a sprig to a jar of sugar to flavour it. The flowers can be used to garnish salads or crystallized or pounded with sugar to make a conserve. Rosemary was one of the most popular ale-flavouring herbs.

Rosemary is a cheering, cordial, antiseptic herb that soothes the nerves, stimulates the digestion and strengthens the heart and the head. The oil was used as a rub for tired, gouty limbs and aching joints, and a distilled water of rosemary, Hungary water, was invented for a Hungarian queen to restore the use of paralysed limbs. Infuse a tea from fresh or dried leaves and tops for headaches; if the flavour is too strong it can be combined with a sweeter herb, such as lemon balm.

Many herbal hair preparations contain rosemary, which has a stimulating effect on hair roots, gives body and lustre and helps get rid of dandruff. The infusion can be used as a skin rinse; the first printed English herbal includes instructions to 'boyle the leves in whyte wine and wasshe thy face therwith . . . thou shall have a fayre face . . . wash thyself and thou shalt waxe shiny'. The belief in rosemary as a preserver of youth is recorded in every herbal since Classical times. Even smelling the wood of rosemary was said to 'keep thee youngly'. It was also the herb of fidelity, love and abiding friendship, worn in wreaths at weddings and planted on graves. Branches of scented rosemary were burned in the house against infection and dried twigs laid among linen against moths. Bouquets of rosemary and rue were traditionally used in the courtroom as a protection against jail fever.

The name 'rosemary' derives from the Latin *ros marinus* meaning 'dew of the sea'.

Rumex acetosa

Rumex obtusifolius

Rumex acetosa
Sorrel, garden sorrel, sour dock
Family: Polygonaceae
This is the most common sorrel, growing wild in grassy places in Britain, Europe and Asia, and naturalized in the U.S.A. It is a perennial, nearly 1m/3ft high with broad, arrow-shaped leaves and spikes of tight, clustered, red flowers from early summer. The French sorrel, *R. scutatus*, is often cultivated for its succulent leaves.

Propagate by seed or by root division and set out 30cm/12in apart in rich soil in a moist, semi-shaded position (French sorrel in a dry, sunny place). Pick the sharp-tasting leaves from early spring for salads, or cook them in butter or purée with cream or add to soups and sauces. Take this cooling, cleansing herb for fevers, and for bladder, liver and kidney complaints, or use juice from the leaves as a poultice for skin troubles. A strong infusion will remove stains from linen, wicker and silver. The leaves and flowering tops produce greenish-yellow dyes.

Rumex obtusifolius
Dock, broad dock, butter dock
Family: Polygonaceae
Larger and coarser than the related sorrels, the broad dock grows at least 1m/3ft high with rough leaves and tall, green flower spikes. It is a common weed in most parts of the world, and one of many dock species with similar properties.

The young leaves can be eaten as potherbs but are bitter and unpalatable. In common with the closely related rhubarb, the root has a slightly laxative and astringent effect and, taken in small doses as a decoction, is a cooling, blood-cleansing drink. An infusion of the leaves has a similar effect, but is most popular as an external dressing for burns, stings, inflammations, swollen breasts and skin complaints. Apply pulped or boiled fresh leaves as a poultice, or mix them with cold cream as a cleansing ointment. The leaves are a traditional, cool, country wrapping for butter pats and both root and leaves can be used for dyeing.

Ruta graveolens

Ruta graveolens
Rue, herb of grace
Family: Rutaceae

The rue that grows wild on the hillsides of southern Europe is harsher and more potent than the garden varieties. These grow up to 50cm/20in high, perennial evergreens with tough, woody stems and beautiful, rounded, compound leaves that have a soft bloom. The flowers blossom from midsummer and are yellow with 8 prominent stamens. One of the most common cultivated varieties is 'Jackman's Blue', which has an almost metallic blue sheen to the leaves.

Rue is easily raised from seed, cuttings or rooted slips; sow in the spring and thin to 50cm/20in apart. It prefers a well-drained soil and a sunny but slightly sheltered position. Like many other southern species, excessive moisture will encourage lush growth but reduce the hardiness and aromatic properties of the plant. Occasionally the leaves may fall during a hard frost, but they generally persist throughout the winter

and the plants can be grown as a compact evergreen hedge. This can be trimmed in the early summer, but never in the autumn when the leaves are needed for protection. Rue is said to be incompatible with sweet basil, but early writers suggest planting it beneath a fig tree as 'it becomes more sweet and milde in taste, by reason it taketh as it were some part of the sweetnesse of the fig tree'.

All parts of rue contain rutin and powerful oils, which are extremely bitter and have irritant properties that occasionally cause skin rashes. The leaves are sometimes added in very small amounts to salads, cheeses or drinks such as grappa, to give an aromatic, bitter flavour, but if eaten in quantity become slightly poisonous and can cause abortion.

Rutin is said to strengthen blood vessels and this may provide the basis for the reputation rue has as an eye herb, although this is not recommended today. Most herbalists since Pliny recommend an infusion as an eye bath and rue tea was popular with artists until comparatively re-

cent times to improve and strengthen the sight. Another popular use was as an antidote to poison and infection. Dioscorides suggests drinking the seeds in wine against the bites of serpents, scorpions and hornets, and it was the most common ingredient in medicines taken to counteract the plague.

Rue is the 'herb of repentance'; the twigs were used to sprinkle holy water during Mass and were an important part of the ceremony. It was also associated with witches and black magic, which extended to its use as a cure for epilepsy and insanity. As a disinfectant and insecticide and a protection against evil, rue was strewn in houses, churches, courtrooms and public places. Sprinkle dried and powdered rue on insect-infested plants or hang dried twigs in the larder against flies. Rue roots produce red dyes.

Goat's rue, *Galega officinalis*, is unrelated to rue. It is a perennial legume with prolific white, lavender or pink peaflowers and has a reputation for encouraging lactation.

Salvia officinalis
Sage, garden sage
Family : Labiatae

Sage grows wild along the northern shores of the Mediterranean, a shrubby, woody plant with long, greyish leaves, finely wrinkled and veined. The flowers are generally purple or blue, deep throated and attractive to bees. Sage has been cultivated for so long that many varieties have been developed. There is a red sage, *S. officinalis* 'Purpurascens', with soft, deep purple leaves; a golden sage with yellow and green leaves; a dwarf variety; and white- or pink-flowered forms, variously scented and flavoured.

Seeds can be sown in the spring but many varieties do not breed true and can only be propagated by cuttings and layering. Plant out seedlings and established cuttings 50cm/20in apart in well-drained rather limy soil in a sunny position. Most species grow about 60cm/2ft high and begin flowering in the midsummer of their second year. They can be trimmed after flowering; this is often necessary for leggy, straggling plants, or for those grown in pots or window boxes.

Sage is easy to dry in the usual way; pick the leaves as the buds begin to open. They have a strong, dry, pungent flavour with a bitter tang that is particularly welcome with fatty foods. They are used in sausages and in stuffings for goose and pork and as a flavouring for cheeses, such as Sage Derby and Vermont sage cheeses, and in rich eel dishes. Although uncommon in French cookery, sage is often used in Italy with veal and game and in the Middle East it is threaded with lamb and onions on kebabs.

Sage was considered one of the most important medicinal herbs – *Salvia* derives from the Latin 'to save' or 'salvation'. It has an astringent and tonic action, stimulating the digestion, cooling fevers and cleansing the blood. The disinfectant action has led to its use as a fumigant. Take an infusion of the leaves for headaches, nervous tension or to promote menstruation, or use as an antiseptic gargle and mouthwash for sore throats, mouth ulcers or bleeding gums. There are many old recipes for sage tooth powders, or the leaves can simply be rubbed over teeth and gums to cleanse and strengthen them. To revitalize and darken thin or greying hair, rinse regularly with a strong infusion.

Sage tea and sage ale have been recommended by herbalists since Classical times for many ailments. John Evelyn ends his list: 'In short, it is a Plant endu'd with so many and wonderful Properties, as that the assiduous use of it is said to render Men Immortal.'

The related clary, *S. sclarea*, is a decorative, biennial or perennial plant with coloured bracts. The bitter, aromatic leaves were used in ale and as fritters; and the seeds as an eye treatment.

Salvia officinalis 'Purpurascens'

Salvia officinalis

Salvia sclarea

Sambucus nigra

Elder, black elder
Family: Caprifoliaceae

The elder tree grows in Britain and from Scandinavia to the coast of Africa, a twisted, shrubby tree, seldom more than 9m/30ft high and common in hedgerows and waste places. The strong-smelling leaves are divided into broad leaflets, creamy flowers grow in sweetly scented clusters in midsummer and in the late summer black juicy berries ripen and fall. There are other, similar elder species in Europe and North America but these have different properties.

Elder grows easily from cuttings or by root division and can be pruned or shaped into a thick, deciduous hedge. Pick and dry the leaves as the tree comes into flower; gather the blossoms as soon as they are fully open and dry quickly in a cool oven – this takes less than an hour. Fresh berries store satisfactorily in plastic bags in a deep freeze.

There are many 18th- and 19th-century recipes for pickled or boiled elder shoots, the new green growths that appear among the old stems in the spring. Eat the blossoms whole as sweet fritters, or add their fragrant, muscatel flavour to stewed fruit (especially gooseberries), to jams, jellies, and vinegars or use them to make elderflower wine or the sparkling 'champagne'. A popular medieval recipe was for a 'sambocade', a tart of elderflowers, curds and egg white. Quantities of berries should not be eaten raw as they will have a strong purgative effect, but can be cooked in jams and jellies, combined with apples in tarts and made into syrups, vinegars and wine.

The bark and leaves of elder have a violent purgative action when taken internally and are not safe. However, used externally, the juice of the leaves is cooling, soothing and healing and has been a common and efficient domestic remedy for several thousand years. Stew a double handful of fresh leaves in a little water for at least 15 minutes, then strain the liquor and use to bathe inflammations, bruises, sprains, eczema and other skin complaints, burns, scalds or boils. Alternatively, boil crushed leaves in lard and beeswax and strain well, or crush fresh leaves in linseed or olive oil.

Elderflower tea calms the nerves, soothes headaches, is cooling for fevers and will help to cure a throat infection. Use externally as a compress for tired and inflamed eyes and as a wash for the complexion. Boiled in lard and strained like the leaves, the flowers will also make a soothing ointment. They are often used in cosmetic preparations.

Elderberries have the gentlest action of all the parts, they are mildly painkilling and are best known as a treatment for sore throats and coughs. Hot elderberry juice, flavoured with honey and lemon, is ideal for colds, 'flu or bronchitis, and the spiced, bottled syrup or vinegar added to hot water makes a delicious, healthy winter drink.

Among other domestic uses, the berries, leaves and root yield strong dyes and the leaves can be used as an insecticide. Fresh elder branches were hung in the dairy during cheese making and the leaves rubbed on the skin against midges. Use a strong decoction of the leaves as an insecticide spray in the garden, and build the compost heap around the tree as it is said to benefit from excretions from the roots.

The elder was closely associated with protective magic, and elder wood thought variously to be the wood of the Cross and of the tree from which Judas hanged himself. In Denmark, Hylde-Moer, the Elder-tree Mother, lived in its branches and her permission had to be begged before the wood was cut or burned.

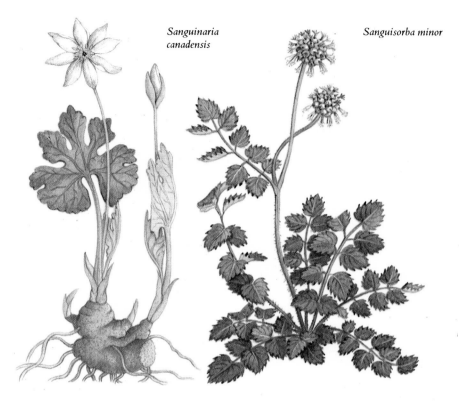

Sanguinaria canadensis

Sanguisorba minor

Sanguinaria canadensis
Bloodroot, Indian paint, puccoon
Family: Papaveraceae
Bloodroot grows on rich soil in the woods of Canada and North America, a beautiful plant with single, white flowers in early spring, a broad, lobed leaf and a creeping, perennial rootstock. Propagate by seed or by division of the roots and plant in rich, moist loam in a shady corner of the garden. It grows about 15cm/6in high.

Although used as a common medicine by the North American Indians, the action of bloodroot is violently emetic and it should not be taken internally. An ointment made from the powdered root was used externally to treat wounds and sores.

All parts of the plant yield an orange-red sap and the root especially was used as a body paint by the Indians. It produces a good, fast, red dye for cloth.

Sanguisorba minor
Salad burnet, lesser burnet
Family: Rosaceae
A hardy perennial, native to Britain and Europe, salad burnet is especially common in grassy places on chalk and limestone. The leaves are long and graceful, with finely toothed leaflets. From midsummer, tiny green flowers grow tightly bunched in round heads, the red styles appearing before the stamens. The height varies from 10cm/4in on thin soil to 1m/3ft on deeper ground. Sow fresh seed in the autumn or spring in a sunny position, and thin to about 30cm/12in apart. The plants usually retain their leaves in winter.

The young leaves are fresh, cooling and slightly bitter, like the rind of cucumber, and are refreshing in mixed salads, chopped in herb butters and cheeses, with vegetables, in soup and in cooling summer drinks. A healing and wholesome plant, the infusion can be drunk as a tonic or used as a wash for sunburn and skin troubles. Salad burnet was one of the prime cordial herbs.

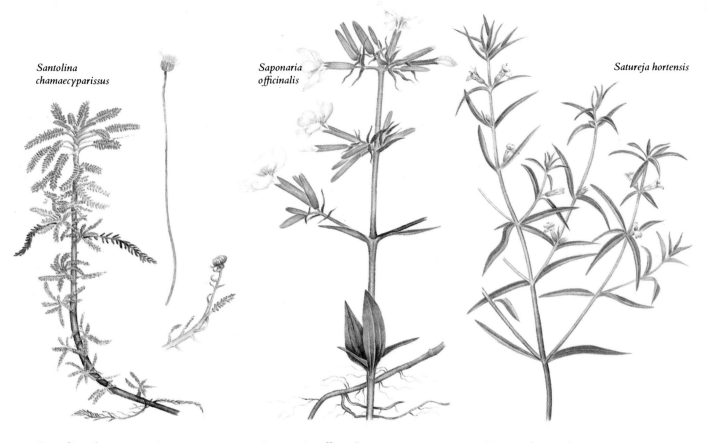

Santolina chamaecyparissus

Saponaria officinalis

Satureja hortensis

Santolina chamaecyparissus
Santolina, lavender cotton
Family: Compositae
Santolina grows wild on dry hillsides in Mediterranean countries and has been cultivated for hundreds of years as a wound and strewing herb, a disinfectant and insecticide, and as a decorative garden plant. It is a shrubby perennial whose downy grey leaves have rows of rounded teeth resembling coral. The small, yellow, button flowers grow from midsummer on tall flower stalks about 60cm/2ft high.

Take cuttings in the summer and plant out the following spring in a sunny position in light, dry soil. Santolina is not thoroughly hardy; in cold climates it is wise to protect with straw during the winter. Clip hedges of santolina only in late spring or summer, never in the autumn.

Strongly aromatic and disinfectant, santolina is generally used as an insecticide; hang dried branches in cupboards and lay beneath carpets against moths.

Saponaria officinalis
Soapwort, bouncing bet, fuller's herb
Family: Caryophyllaceae
A perennial European plant, though uncommon in the British Isles, and introduced in the U.S.A., soapwort grows by streams and roadsides, about 1m/3ft high with creeping roots, sprawling, pale green stems, and smooth, lanceolate leaves. The wild species has single pink flowers from midsummer, each growing from a long calyx; the cultivated variety is often double flowered. Propagate by seed or root division. It tolerates some shade and should be planted out in moist, rich soil.

The root should not be taken internally, but a decoction made from root shavings can be used as a wash for scabby skin or acne. European settlers in North America used this to treat the rash raised by poison ivy. The whole plant contains saponin and when simmered for half an hour the leaves or root will produce a soapy liquid that can be used for washing delicate fabrics.

Satureja hortensis
Summer savory
Family: Labiatae
There are several aromatic *Satureja* species, all native to southern Europe. Summer savory is an annual, growing about 60cm/2ft high with pale purple, slightly downy stems. The narrow leaves are dotted with oil glands and the small white or lilac flowers are attractive to bees.

Sow seed in spring in very shallow drills in lightly composted soil; germination is slow. Thin to about 20cm/8in apart and keep fairly moist. Summer savory grows well as a pot plant. Pick the leaves throughout the summer or dry the whole plant as it comes into flower.

The flavour resembles both thyme and mint, with an added hot, peppery bite. Traditionally eaten with beans, the savories give a spicy, warming flavour to sausages, stuffings, meat pies, soups and boiled vegetables, and a leaf or two can be chopped in salads, cheese dishes or added to herb mixtures.

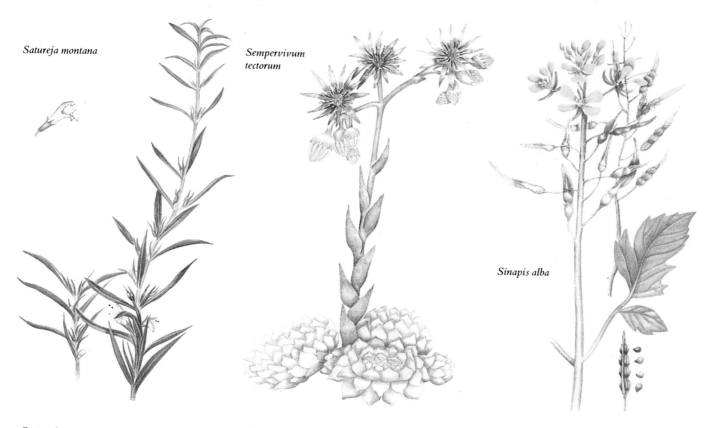

Satureja montana

Sempervivum tectorum

Sinapis alba

Satureja montana
Winter savory
Family: Labiatae

Winter savory is perennial, a woody shrubby plant growing about 30cm/12in high. The leaves are similar to summer savory, but sharp-tipped and shinier on their upper surfaces. The pale purple or white flowers bloom from midsummer to autumn and are attractive to bees.

Sow seed in shallow drills or take cuttings in summer, each with a woody heel. Set out in a sunny position in poor, dry soil, about 60cm/2ft apart. The plants often become straggly and need sharp pruning, but respond well to this and can be shaped into a low, compact hedge. The leaves generally survive the winter, though occasionally drop off during frosts; the plants may need protection during cold weather.

Aromatic, digestive and antiseptic herbs, both savories dispel wind and regularize the bowels. Fresh leaves rubbed on wasp stings are immediately soothing.

Sempervivum tectorum
Houseleek, hen-and-chickens, singreen
Family: Crassulaceae

The houseleek has been grown as a protective plant round human dwellings for so long that its origins are obscure. It has a thickly succulent rosette of leaves that spread by offshoots across roofs, walls and other stony places. Occasionally, in midsummer, a 20cm/8in flower stem appears, bearing clusters of pink blossoms. The rooting offshoots can be planted in a little earth on rockeries or walls.

Houseleek was believed to be a defence against thunder and lightning and all black magic, and is also one of the oldest domestic medicines. The fleshy leaves are cooling and astringent; use crushed or pulped as a poultice or dressing for all inflammations of the skin, wasp and nettle stings, burns and scalds, boils, ulcers, warts and corns – or mix with lard as an ointment. Crushed leaves laid on the temples are cooling for headaches.

Sinapis alba
White mustard
Family: Cruciferae

The annual white mustard grows up to 1m/3ft high and has larger yellow flowers and more deeply cut leaves than black mustard, but the seed pods are the distinguishing feature. They are hairy and rounded with a long beak, and project horizontally from the stem. Each contains about 5 yellow seeds, which are dried in the pod and threshed out. Sow seed in rich soil in a sunny position.

Originally from the Mediterranean, white mustard has been cultivated for centuries and has much the same culinary and medicinal uses as black mustard, although it is less pungent. The seedling leaves can be used in salad. The seeds are more bitter and have stronger disinfectant and preservative properties; use in pickles and infuse in boiling water as a gargle for sore throats.

White mustard can be used to supply humus for poor soil by sowing broadcast and digging in as the first buds show.

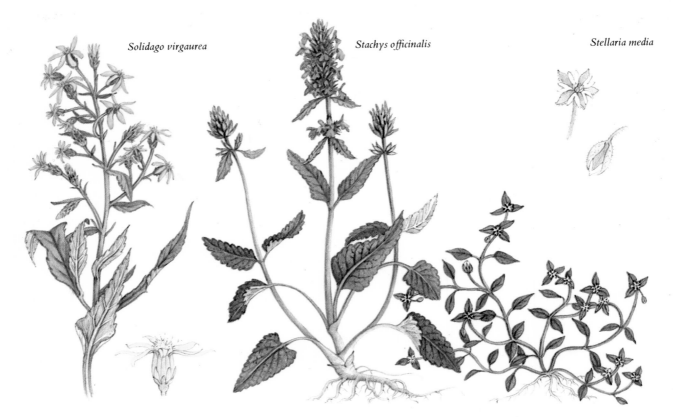

Solidago virgaurea   *Stachys officinalis*   *Stellaria media*

Solidago virgaurea
Golden rod
Family: Compositae
Golden rod is the only member of
the large *Solidago* genus that is native
to Britain; it also grows in dry
woods and heaths in Europe. A
variable plant, it grows up to 1m/3ft
high with lanceolate leaves and
clusters of small yellow flowers in
late summer. Varieties of this species
and some North American species
are often cultivated in gardens and
have similar properties. All are
perennial and easy to grow from
seed or by root division in the spring
or autumn. Gather and dry the leaves
and tops as the plant flowers.

A strong infusion of these makes a
cleansing, astringent and styptic
wash for wounds, or crush the leaves
and use directly on the part. Golden
rod was famous as a wound herb –
praised in all old herbals, and carried
by the Saracens into battle against
the crusaders. The generic name
derives from the Latin *solidare*, 'to
unite'. The flowers produce strong
yellow dyes.

Stachys officinalis
Betony, wood betony
Family: Labiatae
Betony grows wild in grassy places
in Britain and Europe, a perennial,
upright plant about 50cm/20in high,
with dark, regularly spaced, round-
toothed leaves and reddish-purple
flowers. Propagate by seed or division of the creeping roots and dry
the whole herb as it is coming into
flower in midsummer.

Do not use the root or take the
fresh leaves internally. An infusion of
the dried herb is a tonic, nervine and
cure for headaches, and makes an
acceptable substitute for household
tea. Smoke from the dried herb was
inhaled for bronchitis and headache
and the powdered leaves used as a
medicinal snuff. The fresh leaves
contain a bitter, astringent oil and
make a good poultice for wounds,
stings and poisonous bites. The plant
was considered a powerful protection against witches and enchantments. The related woundworts and
the garden donkey's ears, *S. byzantina*, have similar properties.

Stellaria media
Chickweed
Family: Caryophyllaceae
This is the most succulent of the
chickweeds, a variable, little annual
with weak, jointed stems and
small, white, starry flowers. It is a
common weed in most parts of the
world, springing up on disturbed
ground, often flowering and seeding throughout the year. It is a
thoroughly wholesome plant and
can be used fresh or dried.

Strip the leaves from the stem and
eat fresh or simmer as a vegetable
with butter and lemon juice. As an
infusion, its cooling, healing properties and rich copper and iron content
make it a valuable tonic drink and a
treatment for coughs, internal inflammation and irritation, and a
gentle laxative. Use also to bathe
sore eyes and inflammations of the
skin, or make a poultice for boils and
swellings from crushed, fresh leaves,
or by boiling the chopped herb with
lard. Gerard describes 'little birdes in
cadges' being fed chickweed 'when
they loath their meate'.

Symphytum officinale
Comfrey, knitbone, boneset, blackwort
Family: Boraginaceae

Comfrey grows in colonies on river banks and in damp places in Britain, Europe and temperate Asia, and was introduced to North America by early European settlers. A perennial, the basal leaves grow at least 30cm/12in long, and are broad, lanceolate and hairy. The leaves diminish in size up the stem. In early summer the bell-shaped flowers bloom progressively up the curving stalk – white, pink or purple. A species with cream-coloured flowers, *S. tuberosum*, is more common in northern regions and there are other species that have escaped from cultivation onto wasteland and road-sides such as the prickly comfrey, *S. asperum,* native of the Caucasus with bright blue flowers, and *S. x uplandicum*, a hybrid often cultivated today.

Comfrey can be grown from seed, but as the plants take a long time to mature, it is easiest to propagate by planting root offsets, each with a bud. These will flourish on rich, deeply worked soil in a shady position, and each plant may last as long as 20 years. As every scrap of root will develop into a new plant in the manner of the horseradish, comfrey may need to be restricted.

The succulent leaves are difficult to dry, but the root can be dug in the early spring, dried slowly and stored whole or powdered. Both roots and leaves are astringent and contain quantities of mucilage and a healing substance called allantoin. Although it is not now considered safe to take comfrey internally, an in-fusion of the leaves or a decoction of the root (made by boiling 25g/1oz bruised root in 1 litre/1¾ pints water until reduced by half) can be used as a gargle and externally as a wash for inflammation, acne and chapped and rough skin – or add a strong brew to the bath water. Apply bruised leaves or a mash made from the grated fresh root as a soothing poultice for bruises, swell-ings, sprains, aching joints, wounds and sores, burns and scalds. The hairy leaves can irritate so it is advisable to protect the skin with thin, clean cotton. Comfrey is one of the best herbs for reducing swellings and if applied to the area around broken bones will soothe and reduce the inflammation, thus helping the bones to unite. For this reason it was given the country names 'knitbone' and 'boneset' and exaggerated stories were told of minced meat becoming steak when boiled in a pot with comfrey, and of virginity restored in comfrey baths.

Because of its quick, lush growth and high mineral content, comfrey is grown as a composting plant, used for nutritious mulches and as a liquid fertilizer.

The fresh leaves and flowers produce yellow and orange dyes.

Tanacetum parthenium

Tanacetum vulgare

Tanacetum parthenium
Feverfew, featherfoil
Family: Compositae

Feverfew is a familiar cottage garden plant, introduced into Britain long ago as a domestic medicine and now growing wild in hedgerows and stone walls in northern Europe and the U.S.A. The divided leaves are rounded, strongly aromatic and a bright yellowish-green; the pretty single or double daisy-like flowers bloom from midsummer. It is a herbaceous perennial, forming a compact little clump up to 60cm/2ft high, self-seeding readily, tolerant of most soils but preferring a dry sunny corner of the garden. Propagate by seed, root division or by taking cuttings of young shoots.

An infusion of the herb used to be taken as a tonic and nervine, but is only recommended in small quantities today. Use the fresh leaves bruised or pulped as a soothing poultice for swellings and insect bites. A strong infusion in the bath soothes aches and pains and encourages menstruation.

Tanacetum vulgare
Tansy, bachelor's buttons
Family: Compositae

Native to Britain and northern Europe and naturalized in North America, tansy grows on roadsides and in waste places, up to 1m/3ft high, with dark, feathery, strong-smelling leaves and rayless, yellow flowers in late summer. It is a hardy perennial that can be grown from seed or by division of the creeping roots and is tolerant of most soils. Cut the plant for drying as it is coming into flower; the heads can also be cut and dried as 'everlasting' flowers.

Although now considered dangerous to take internally, tansy used to be popular as a cleansing, tonic medicine and was a traditional ingredient in 'Tansies' – cakes and puddings eaten at Easter to purify the system after the heavy winter diet. Externally, an infusion of the leaves can be used as a wash to clear the complexion, or a warm poultice of the crushed leaves applied to aching joints, sprains,

inflammations and varicose veins.

Tansy was used as a strewing herb for its insecticide and disinfectant properties, and the dried leaves were laid among clothes and in the bedding of humans and animals to repel fleas and other vermin. On larder shelves and hung over windows and doors, tansy acts as a fly deterrent, and rubbed on meat discourages blow flies. In the garden it can be planted near fruit trees against insect pests. It is rich in potassium and other minerals and should be used on the compost heap. The leaves and flowering tops produce yellow dyes.

Athanasia is one of the names given by the old herbalists to tansy; it is the Greek word meaning 'immortality' and may refer to the everlasting qualities of the dried plant, to its medicinal virtues or to its use for embalming corpses. Tansy was in the drink given to Ganymede by order of Jupiter to immortalize him as cup bearer to the gods.

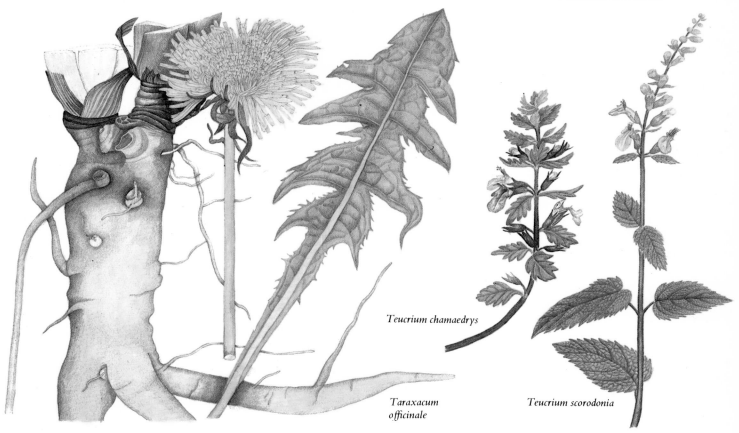

Teucrium scorodonia

Teucrium chamaedrys

Taraxacum officinale

Teucrium scorodonia

Taraxacum officinale

Dandelion, piss-a-bed

Family: Compositae

One of the most familiar wild plants, dandelions are tolerant of most climates and conditions and grow as weeds in every garden. Variable, hardy and perennial, they grow up to 30cm/12in high producing golden flowerheads from late spring, each followed by a 'clock' of seeds. The leaves are long and toothed, the stems filled with a milky juice and the root is long, thick and fleshy.

Seeds from wild species can be sown in the garden, but the cultivated variety has thicker, broader leaves and a less bitter flavour. Thin the seedlings to 30cm/12in apart; they will need little attention. Dig and dry the roots in the autumn of their second year.

Eat the leaves when very young, as they soon become too bitter. Blanching improves the flavour, although they will then lose some of their goodness. They can be eaten in salad, tossed in butter as a vegetable or cooked as a potherb. The flowers are used in dandelion wine and the leaves in herb beers; the dried root can be ground and roasted as a substitute for coffee.

All parts of the plant are wholesome, especially the root, containing a rich store of minerals and vitamins. Make an infusion from the leaves and flowers or a decoction of the root – by boiling 50g/2oz root in 1 litre/1¾ pints water until reduced by half – and take a small cupful 3 times a day as a tonic, to promote urine, for all kidney and liver disorders or as a mild laxative. It also acts as a digestive, stimulating the gastric juices and increasing the appetite.

Simmer the flowers for 30 minutes in soft water and use the strained liquid as a cleansing wash for the skin or add to the bath water.

The roots and leaves produce yellowish-fawn dyes.

Teucrium scorodonia

Wood sage, sage-leaved germander

Family: Labiatae

Common in shady places on acid soils in Britain, Europe and North Africa, wood sage grows up to 60cm/2ft high, a downy, dark herb. The regular leaves are wrinkled and oval and the pale greenish flowers have long purple anthers and no upper lip. Sow seed in the spring or divide the creeping perennial rhizome. Dry the leaves as the plant begins to flower in midsummer.

Wood sage is a bitter, astringent, tonic herb. The tea is bloodcleansing, diuretic, and can be taken for fevers and to promote menstruation. Use a poultice of the fresh, bruised herb for skin troubles and wounds.

The hardy, perennial wall germander, *T. chamaedrys*, has similar properties and was a popular treatment for gout. Native to much of Europe, it is a sweet-smelling, decorative, purple-flowered plant, that can be clipped to form a hedge and was popular in knot gardens and as a strewing herb.

Thymus species
Family: Labiatae

The most aromatic thyme is the common garden species, *Thymus vulgaris*, which grows wild in southern Europe on stony hillsides and has been cultivated for hundreds of years. A perennial, shrubby, woody plant, it grows about 30cm/12in high with narrow, grey, paired leaves and small, whitish or pale purple flowers that bloom in midsummer and are attractive to bees. Propagate by seed, cuttings, layering or root division. Sow the seed in early spring in shallow drills and plant out or thin to 25cm/10in apart in well-drained soil in a sunny position. The plants may need some protection from frost in cold climates; cover with straw or heap earth around them.

Harvest the leaves for drying as the flower buds begin to open, cutting the stems about 5cm/2in above the ground. Hang or lay to dry in a warm, shady place and store in an airtight jar.

Like marjoram, the thyme that grows on warm, dry southern hillsides has a far more powerful flavour than the same species growing in a damp, northern climate. It is one of the most basic and important herbs used in Mediterranean food, its warm and pungent flavour blending naturally with the garlic, olives, tomatoes and wine of southern cooking. The strong flavour survives long simmering in rich stews of beef or lamb, or in hot pots of rabbit and mushrooms and other game dishes. As the tough little leaves retain their aroma so well when dried, they should always be stored as a winter herb for flavouring thick soups and root vegetables, and as an indispensable ingredient in *bouquet garni* and other herb mixtures and stuffings. In addition to its flavour, the preservative qualities of thyme are valuable in sausages and salamis, pâtés, potted meats and strong potted cheeses, and in pickles, vinegars and marinades.

The leaves contain several strong oils of which the most important is thymol, an antiseptic and preservative. An infusion of the leaves makes a good tonic drink and a cupful can be taken 3 times a day for all digestive troubles, flatulence, and to stimulate the appetite. Thyme has had a reputation as a strengthening herb since early times and is useful for anaemia and exhaustion, coughs and bronchitis, colds and 'flu. The extracted oil makes an antiseptic ointment, dressing or rub and is an invigorating bath oil. Use the infusion as a mouthwash or gargle for sore throats and ulcers, as a wash for infected wounds or as a strengthening rub for the scalp.

Other thyme species and their many varieties share the properties of garden thyme. Among the broad-leaved species, lemon thyme, *T. x citriodorus*, is particularly useful as a culinary herb, having a sharp lemon scent and warm flavour that go well with fish or eggs, in creamy sauces and in some sweet dishes. It is less hardy than garden thyme and usually needs some protection during the winter. It grows into a compact, cushion shape with rounded green leaves and pale purple flowers, and is propagated by cuttings or division in the spring or autumn.

The species native to the cooler climate of northern Europe is *T. serpyllum*, a prostrate, mat-forming plant that is hardier but less aromatic than the southern species. This creeping thyme grows wild on downland and heath and can be planted in rockeries, between paving stones, or used to make a turf for paths and lawns. Varieties of *T. serpyllum* include lemon-scented, variegated, and there is a woolly, grey-leaved plant, *T. pseudolanuginosus*.

There are golden varieties of the garden and lemon thymes, as well as dappled silver varieties, such as 'Silver Queen', a variety of lemon thyme, and 'Silver Posie', a variety of garden thyme. *T. herba-barona* has a caraway scent and was used in Britain to flavour the traditional baron of beef; it is semi-prostrate and grows well on rough walls and as a pot plant. There are numerous other varieties with colours ranging from white to deep purple and whose growth varies from the prostrate to compact, upright plants that can be clipped to form low hedges.

In ancient Greece thyme was used as an invigorating scent to anoint the body and add to the bath, and considered a symbol of courage, style and elegance. As an incense and fumigant, faggots of thyme were burned in temples and other public places. The association with courage was strong in northern Europe at the time of the Crusades, when ladies embroidered a bee with a sprig of thyme on the scarves of their knights as a badge of bravery. The 16th-century herbalists give long lists of ailments to be treated with thyme, recommending its use for 'wambling and gripings of the bellie', to 'stayeth the hicket', and to 'helpeth against the biting of any venomous beast'. Culpeper adds that it is 'a certain remedy for that troublesome complaint, the night-mare'.

Thymus serpyllum

Thymus vulgaris

Thymus x citriodorus

Thymus pseudolanuginosus

Thymus herba-barona

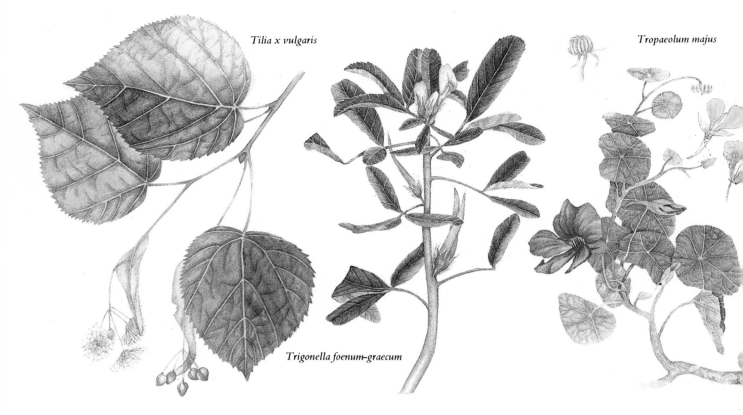

Tilia x vulgaris

Tropaeolum majus

Trigonella foenum-graecum

Tilia species
Family: Tiliaceae
The tall, deciduous common lime, *Tilia x vulgaris*, is a fertile hybrid between the small-leaved and broad-leaved species, *T. cordata* and *T. platyphyllos*, and grows in Britain and Europe to a height of about 30m/100ft. In central and eastern U.S.A. there is a species known as basswood, *T. americana*. All have broad, toothed leaves and scented, yellow flowers that bloom in midsummer, hanging in clusters with a long, leaf-like bract.

Gather both flowers and bracts and dry carefully in the shade to use for lime tea, one of the most popular herbal infusions. This delicately flavoured drink contains mucilage and acts as a gentle sedative, nervine and digestive. It promotes perspiration and is valuable for colds, 'flu, bronchitis and catarrh. A strong infusion added to bath or washing water will cleanse, refresh and relax the skin. The soft, young leaves are edible and cooling, and a delicious honey is produced from the flowers.

Trigonella foenum-graecum
Fenugreek
Family: Leguminosae
Originally from the eastern Mediterranean, fenugreek has been cultivated in Europe, Africa and Asia for thousands of years as a fodder plant, a medicine and a spice. It is an annual and grows about 60cm/2ft high with yellowish peaflowers in midsummer, trifoliate leaves and long narrow pods containing at least 10 square seeds, reaching maturity in a few months in warm climates. It is tender in temperate climates.

Fenugreek is best known as a powdered ingredient of curry powder, but it is also used for confectionery and as a pickle flavouring. Sprouted seeds can be included as a bitter but nutritious ingredient in mixed salads. They are rich in vitamins, nitrates and calcium, have a softening, soothing action and are said to encourage lactation. Infuse 15g/½oz seeds in 600ml/1 pint boiling water for a tonic tea, or apply soaked seeds as a poultice for inflammations of the skin.

Tropaeolum majus
Nasturtium, Indian cress
Family: Tropaeolaceae
Nasturtium seeds were brought to Europe from Peru by Spanish explorers in the 16th century and it quickly became a favourite, sprawling garden plant. Sow seed in the spring in a sunny position in well-drained soil and the bright yellow, orange or red flowers and round, flat leaves will flourish from midsummer until the first frosts.

Nasturtium leaves, buds and flowers add a sharp, peppery bite to salads and will flavour vinegars. The unripe fruits can be pickled like capers, but should not be eaten in large quantities as they may become purgative. The leaves contain valuable minerals and a high level of Vitamin C. Taken internally, they have a tonic, cleansing and antiseptic effect. Externally, the crushed fruits can be applied as a hot poultice for sores and boils.

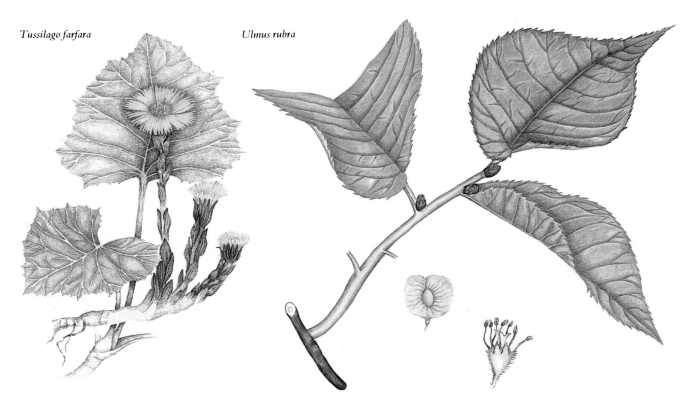

Tussilago farfara

Ulmus rubra

Tussilago farfara
Coltsfoot, coughwort, baccy plant
Family: Compositae

The perennial coltsfoot is a common weed on poor or heavy soil in temperate climates. The yellow flowers appear in early spring and are followed later by broad, hoof-shaped leaves whose undersides are covered with a heavy down. The plant grows about 30cm/12in high.

The generic name *Tussilago* means 'cough dispeller', and for at least 2,000 years coltsfoot has been used to treat coughs, catarrh and asthma. Pliny recommended that smoke from the burning plant should be sucked through a reed and the leaves are still used in herbal tobacco for bronchitis. A tonic tea can be made from the leaves and taken a cupful at a time, but this must be strained to remove all hairs. Use the infusion or juice from fresh leaves as an antiseptic wash for wounds and skin blemishes or apply the crushed leaves as a poultice, enclosed in fine muslin to prevent skin irritation.

Ulmus rubra
Slippery elm
Family: Urticaceae

A deciduous tree growing in North American woods and also widely cultivated, the slippery elm grows at least 15m/50ft high with dark, rough bark and rough, toothed leaves. The flowers are small tufts of red stamens, which appear in early spring. It can be propagated by seed or cuttings.

The pale, aromatic inner bark is the part used medicinally. To reach it the outer bark has to be stripped from a mature tree, then the inner bark is dried and sold either in pieces or ground as powder. This is rich in a nutritious mucilage. Leave 25g/1oz of powdered bark to soak for an hour in 600ml/1 pint water, sweeten with honey and take by the spoonful every hour or so as a soothing, healing medicine for sore throats, coughs, bronchitis, catarrh and stomach and bowel troubles, or make an infusion of pieces of bark. Internal irritation is reduced by slippery elm and it also acts as a treatment for cystitis and urinary complaints. A nourishing gruel can be made for invalids and children by mixing the powdered bark with water or milk and flavouring to taste. For external use, mix the powder with hot water as a poultice for skin inflammations, rheumatism, swollen glands and boils. This paste is sticky, so enclose in a clean cloth before applying to open wounds and poisoned abscesses. A healing ointment can be made by boiling the powdered bark with lard and beeswax.

The bark from the most common European elm, *Ulmus procera*, can also be used medicinally. A decoction, made by boiling 25g/1oz fresh, inner bark in 600ml/1 pint water until reduced by half, is an astringent, soothing wash for wounds, skin problems and for dandruff. The fresh, bruised leaves can also be used as a healing poultice for wounds or infused and used as a rinse for scurfy skin and dandruff.

Stripping the bark from an elm will kill the tree and must not be done unless a plantation has been cultivated for this purpose.

Parietaria officinalis　　　　*Urtica dioica*

Urtica dioica
Stinging nettle

Family: Urticaceae

Growing in most temperate climates from Japan to the Andes, perennial stinging nettles are tall, familiar plants, their dark, toothed leaves covered with stinging hairs. The dark, erect stems grow about 1m/3ft high, and from midsummer hanging clusters of green or reddish flowers are pollinated by the wind. They spread rapidly by seed and tough, creeping roots. Gather the whole plant just before flowering and hang to dry in a shady, airy place.

Young nettle leaves and shoots can be cooked like spinach (the stings become harmless when boiled or dried), and are quite palatable with a rather drying, furry texture. Add them to spring soups and stews as a wholesome potherb. Do not use old leaves as they can be irritating. Nettle beer is a popular homemade brew.

The astringent leaves contain more iron than spinach and quantities of Vitamins A and C, together with important acids, nitrogen and trace elements. An infusion of the leaves makes an excellent tonic medicine. Take a cupful twice a day as a treatment for anaemia, blood impurities, retention of urine, indigestion and skin disease. A strong infusion can be used as a healing wash for burns and rough skin, added to bath water or used as a scalp tonic to encourage the growth of hair and to eliminate dandruff. A decoction, made by boiling 100g/4oz nettle seed or root in 1 litre/1¾ pints water for 20 minutes, can also be used to strengthen the hair and as a skin cleanser.

The stinging leaves have been used as a rub for rheumatism and paralysis and are still used today. This has a similar effect to the treatment of rheumatism by bee stings.

Nettles have many domestic uses.

Fibre made from the stems has been found on Bronze Age sites and was used in some northern countries until the 17th century for cloth, rope and fishing lines. Paper can also be made from the pulped fibres. The leaves and roots yield a wide range of dyes. The seeds and boiled leaves can be chopped in poultry food and the juice or a strong decoction of the leaves is a substitute for rennet. Soft fruit, tomatoes and root vegetables will stay fresh longer when stored in nettle leaves.

The rich minerals, nitrogen and chlorophyll stored in nettles make them valuable in the compost heap and as a mulch, and a good plant feed can be made by soaking armfuls of nettles for several weeks in a butt of rainwater. Use a strong brew or decoction on plants against fungus diseases and aphids. The soil in an established nettle bed is always rich in nitrogen.

Another common species is the small nettle, *U. urens*, an annual plant, smoother than *U. dioica* but with similar properties. The Roman nettle, *U. pilulifera*, is rare in Britain and has violent stings. There is an old story that this was introduced by the Romans for use as a warming rub.

Pellitory-of-the-wall, *Parietaria officinalis*, belongs to the same family and grows in Britain and Europe on walls and in stony places. It is a softly downy plant about 60cm/2ft high with red stems, green flowers and untoothed leaves. The juice or an infusion of the whole herb is laxative and provokes urine, and the crushed, fresh plant makes a cooling, healing poultice.

Vaccinium myrtillus

Valeriana officinalis

Vaccinium myrtillus
Bilberry, whortleberry, crowberry
Family: Ericaceae
A tough little shrub growing up to 50cm/20in high in colonies like the related heather, bilberry has sharply pointed, glossy oval leaves, drooping, pink flowers from late spring and edible black berries. It is found on acid soil on heathland and in woods in Britain, northern Europe and northern Asia. Other *Vaccinium* species with edible berries include the North American blueberry, *V. corymbosum*, the cranberry, *V. oxycoccos*, and cowberry, *V. vitis-idaea*.

The berries and leaves can be dried; soak the dried berries in water before use. The ripe, juicy berries have a slightly acid flavour and are delicious eaten raw or stewed, or in conserves and jellies. Their astringent qualities make them an excellent treatment for all intestinal disorders, diarrhoea and nausea. Their vitamin content is high and they have been used to treat scurvy. A tonic tea can be brewed from the leaves. The berries yield a blue dye.

Valeriana officinalis
Valerian
Family: Valerianaceae
Perennial valerian grows in Britain and temperate Europe and Asia in woods and on open, stony ground. It has a stout stem, up to 1.5m/5ft high, and regular, toothed, divided leaves. The flowers bloom from midsummer in tight, pale pink clusters with prominent stamens. The plant has a slightly foetid smell when bruised.

The seeds are difficult to germinate but the roots can be divided and planted out and are tolerant of most soils. Dig and dry the roots in their second autumn. They have a strong smell of old leather that develops as they dry and is said to attract cats, rats and earthworms.

Valerian has a long tradition as a sedative, nervine and pain killer, but should be used with caution as large doses can produce bad headaches and shaking. Infuse 25g/1oz of root in 1 litre/1$\frac{3}{4}$ pints boiling water and take a small glassful 3 times a day. This infusion can be used externally as a wash for sore skin.

Vanilla planifolia

Verbascum thapsus

Vanilla planifolia
Vanilla
Family: Orchidaceae
The long seed pods from this tropical orchid were first brought to Europe from South America by the Spaniards in the 16th century, but cultivation in other tropical countries only began in the mid-19th century when a method of artificial pollination was developed. The perennial climbing plant is trained up posts or trees and long, yellow-green pods follow the white flowers. These are picked unripe, and cured until dark brown and covered with frosty crystals of vanillin.

The scented pods were originally used by the Aztecs to flavour chocolate drinks and are still popular today in sweet dishes and custards, creams and ices. Infuse the whole or part of the pod in milk or cream, then remove, wash and dry for re-use, or scrape seeds from the pod into the dish. A pod left in a jar of sugar will scent and flavour it for a year or more. A chopped vanilla pod is an ingredient in pot pourri.

Verbascum thapsus
Mullein, great mullein, hag's taper
Family: Scrophulariaceae
Mullein grows in most temperate climates in waste and grassy places. It is biennial and this species is easily recognized by its rosette of large, thick leaves covered with woolly, silver down and during its second year by the great flower spike growing 2m/6½ft high. The flowers open at random and are bright yellow with orange anthers.

Sow seed in the spring or autumn and transplant the seedlings to a sunny sheltered position in well-drained soil, at least 60cm/2ft apart. The leaves and flowers can be dried, though the flowers need gentle handling.

Mullein is soothing, emollient, astringent and slightly sedative. Infuse the leaves or flowers (which have a sweeter taste) in water or milk for coughs, colds, bronchitis, asthma, insomnia and diarrhoea. Strain well to remove any irritant hairs and take 3 glassfuls a day. Inhale the steam from a strong infusion for hay fever and sinus troubles. Pound or boil the leaves and use as a poultice for skin infections and irritations, protecting the skin from any hairs with a clean cloth. Steep fresh flowers in olive oil and leave in the sun or a warm place for 2 weeks, strain and store for use as a soothing rub for bruises and aching joints, earache and haemorrhoids. A tobacco made from the dried leaves used to be smoked as a treatment for consumption. Use a strong infusion of flowers as a rinse to brighten fair hair.

The down from leaves and stem used to be rubbed off and dried for use as tinder and lamp wicks. The tall hairy stem, coated with tallow or suet, made a primitive torch – hence the name 'hag's taper'.

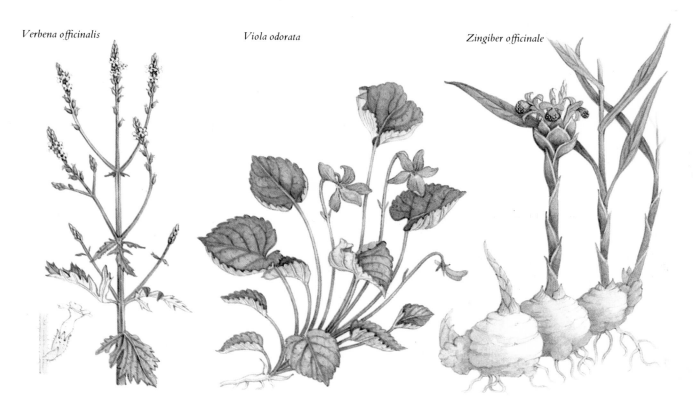

Verbena officinalis　　　　*Viola odorata*　　　　*Zingiber officinale*

Verbena officinalis
Vervain, holy herb
Family: Verbenaceae
Vervain grows locally on chalk and limestone in southern Britain and in temperate Europe, Asia and America in rough, dry places. It is an upright, graceful perennial, growing up to 1m/3ft high with toothed, lobed leaves and delicate spikes of pale mauve flowers from midsummer. Propagate by seed or root in a dry, open place in limy soil.

It is slightly astringent and diuretic. Infuse the fresh or dried leaves and flowering tops and take a small glassful 3 times a day for headaches, fever and delayed menstruation, add a stronger infusion to bath or washing water. Use as a cleansing wash for wounds and as a gargle for sore throats. In Classical Rome the collective name *Verbena* referred to plants used in religious ceremonies; in northern Europe vervain came to be regarded as one of the most important sacred herbs, used in holy ointments as a cleanser and defence against demonic illness.

Viola odorata
Violet, sweet violet
Family: Violaceae
This is the only sweet-smelling violet. It grows about 15cm/6in high in shady places, hedges and banks in Britain and temperate Europe, and is naturalized in North America. The single violet or white flowers appear early in the spring from among heart-shaped leaves. The perennial plants spread by creeping runners, which can be detached and planted out in a well-composted, half-shaded bed. The newly opened flowers can be dried; they have a delicate flavour and can be eaten fresh in salads, added to drinks or crystallized. An infusion of the flowers, or a syrup made by boiling a strong infusion with sugar, can be used to flavour cream puddings or ices. As a medicine the infusion or syrup have a gentle laxative action and are a soothing remedy for headaches, insomnia and nervous ailments. Bruise the leaves as a poultice or boil them with lard as an ointment for skin inflammations.

Zingiber officinale
Ginger
Family: Zingiberaceae
Ginger grows wild in the damp tropical forests of southeast Asia. A tall, perennial plant about 1m/3ft high, it has broad leaf blades, a spike of yellow, purple-lipped flowers and a fat, knobbed rhizome. It is cultivated in many tropical countries, including the West Indies.

The rhizome is sold fresh, dried, tinned, ground or preserved in syrup or vinegar and is an essential ingredient in Eastern cookery. Curries, pickles, spiced meat and fish, rice and vegetable dishes are flavoured with it. Introduced to northern Europe by the Romans, ginger was one of the most popular spices in medieval cookery and its warming, rich and pungent flavour is used in sweet dishes, cakes and biscuits today.

Its antiseptic properties and sulphur content made ginger a common antidote for the plague. It stimulates the gastric juices and is warming and soothing for colds and coughs.

Poisonous herbs

The fearful powers of these plants led to the use of many in witches' brews and ointments to induce delirium, frenzy and, often, a sensation of flying. Their association with magic meant that they were also considered a powerful protection against evil spirits, and plants such as mandrake and henbane were hung round human dwellings and the stables of animals until comparatively recent times. The plants listed here are among the best known of the poisonous herbs that have played an important part in the development of medicine, from the early days when the *Spongia Somnifera*, a sponge soaked in the juice of henbane, mandrake, poppy and wine, was given by surgeons to 'such as they cut, saw, burn or take off a limb' to 'causeth a dead sleep', to the modern use of atropine and digitalis. Several are employed in homeopathic medicine today, the extremely small doses being heavily diluted with milk sugar. Extracted drugs such as morphine and colchicine have important uses in orthodox medicine.

Aconitum napellus
Aconite, wolf's bane, monkshood
Family : Ranunculaceae
This tall, perennial European plant with deeply cut, palmate leaves and spikes of hooded, blue flowers is commonly grown in gardens and has been cultivated as a medicinal herb since ancient times. It grows about 60cm/2ft high in moist, shady places and can be propagated by seed or root division.

Although all parts are poisonous, the roots are especially potent and have been used as a deadly dip for arrows, spears and animal traps. Pliny called aconite 'plant arsenic'. An old antidote to the poison was to

take brandy mixed with quantities of flies that had fed upon the plant. It is used in minute quantities in homeopathic preparations as a sedative and pain killer.

Arnica montana
Arnica, leopard's bane, mountain tobacco
Family : Compositae
The yellow flowers grow up to 1m/3ft high from a low rosette of leaves in European mountain pastures. A perennial, it is easily cultivated and propagated by seed or division of the thick rhizome.

The flowers, or occasionally the rhizome, are used in a diluted tincture as a healing (but occasionally irritant) application for sprains and bruises. It is used internally in homeopathic doses for sickness, epilepsy and many other disorders, but is a powerful poison.

Atropa bella-donna
Deadly nightshade, belladonna
Family : Solanaceae
A shrubby plant, deadly nightshade can grow to a height of 2m/6½ft in shady places, or dwarfed on open ground. It is found throughout Europe and southern Britain on calcareous soil, a dark, perennial with pointed, oval leaves, dull purple, bell-shaped flowers and single, shining, black berries.

Although easy to cultivate, it is unwise to grow in gardens where children play as the poisonous berries are sweet and tempting. Gerard wrote 400 years ago, 'banish therefore these pernicious plants out of

your gardens . . . where children do resort.'

A distillation of the herb was used to dilate the pupils and beautify the eyes of Court ladies, at least as early as the 15th century. Since the 19th century it has been used to dilate the pupil during eye operations. The alkaloids atropine and hyoscyamine, generally extracted from the root, have been taken internally as sedatives and relaxants. All parts are poisonous however and have always been used as sedatives and to induce narcotic trances. The generic name derives from 'Atropos', the Greek Fate who holds the shears to cut the thread of human life.

Bryonia dioica
White bryony, English mandrake
Family : Cucurbitaceae
A familiar, perennial plant in the hedges and woodland borders of Europe and southern Britain, the white bryony climbs (like the related cucumber) with twisting tendrils, about 4m/13ft high. It has small, greenish flowers, smooth, ivy-

shaped leaves and, in autumn, clusters of red berries. Male and female flowers grow on separate plants. It is easily distinguishable from the unrelated black bryony, which has darker, heart-shaped leaves and climbs by twining its whole stem.

All parts are poisonous, the large perennial root especially so. This used to be taken in powdered form as a violent purgative and to relieve headaches and dropsy but, as Culpeper said, it is 'not rashly to be taken', and is extremely dangerous. The roots were often sold to the superstitious as mandrake roots.

Colchicum autumnale
Meadow saffron, naked ladies
Family : Liliaceae
The solitary, pale purple, perennial crocus flowers bloom in the autumn from North Africa to Britain, in damp woods and meadows. The long leaves (20cm/8in) and egg-shaped fruits appear in the spring and die down before the flowers appear. Propagate by seed or corm division.

The active and poisonous principles of the plant – colchicine is the most important of these – are contained in the corm and the seeds. Meadow saffron has been used since Classical times to treat rheumatism and gout, but nowadays the dose taken is minute and must be prepared by professionals. In medium doses it has a sedative action and a strong effect on the bowels; large doses can cause death.

Conium maculatum
Hemlock
Family : Umbelliferae
One of the most common of the really poisonous herbs, the biennial hemlock often grows at least 2m/6½ft high in roadside ditches and on waste ground in most temperate climates. The hollow stems are often streaked with purple, the graceful leaves are finely cut and white umbels of flowers bloom throughout the summer. It bears a dangerous resemblance to cow parsley and other umbellifers.

All parts are poisonous, but the seeds (fruit) and leaves are most potent, containing 5 alkaloids. Lethal doses were given in the past to condemned criminals, and it is thought that Socrates killed himself with hemlock juice. The generic name derives from the Greek word *konos*, meaning spinning top, as dizziness and vertigo occur before paralysis sets in. The extracted drug, conium, is used as a sedative and antispasmodic and externally to reduce inflammation.

Convallaria majalis
Lily-of-the-valley, lady's tears
Family: Liliaceae
This familiar, little perennial garden plant with white, sweet-scented bell flowers followed by scarlet berries, is found in temperate woods in many parts of the world. It grows up to 30cm/1ft high and is easily cultivated in moist, shaded soil and propagated by division of the creeping roots in the autumn or early spring.

The flowers have been used in medicine since the 4th century as a remedy for gout, palsy and inflammation of the eyes, and the extracted drug is used today to strengthen and regulate the action of the heart. All parts are poisonous.

Datura stramonium
Thornapple, jimson weed
Family: Solanaceae
The bushy, annual thornapple is an unmistakable plant, growing about 1m/3ft high with jagged leaves, large, white, trumpet flowers and strange, spiky fruit containing black

seeds. Its origin is uncertain but it now grows as a weed in waste places around the world.

Sow seed in the spring and, for large specimens, add plenty of manure.

Closely related to both deadly nightshade and henbane, thornapple has a similar action – sedative, dilating the pupils of the eyes and, in excess, causing delirium and death. A tincture of the seeds is still occasionally prescribed today for asthma and laryngitis.

Digitalis purpurea
Foxglove, dead man's thimbles
Family: Scrophulariaceae
This tall biennial grows wild throughout Britain and western Europe, mainly on dry, acid soils, in heathy woods and on banks. The spike of tubular pink flowers grows about 1.5m/5ft from a rosette of large, soft, wrinkled leaves. It is easy to cultivate from seed.

Digitalis, which is extracted from the leaves, contains several effective heart stimulants, and is an important drug given today to slow down, strengthen and regulate the heart

beat. In the past it was used externally as an ointment for swellings and internally as a treatment for dropsy, but these remedies were not widely popular. Gerard wrote, 'yet are they of no use, neither have they any place amongst medicines, according to the Antients.' It was Dr William Withering who first isolated foxglove from at least 20 other herbs included in an old medicine for dropsy and made a detailed scientific study of the drug. He recorded his findings in the celebrated *Account of the Foxglove*, published in 1795.

Include the leaves in a vase of cut flowers to prolong their lives.

Helleborus niger
Black hellebore, Christmas rose
Family: Ranunculaceae
Many varieties of perennial hellebore are cultivated in gardens, particularly the black hellebore with its long, smooth, dark leaflets and white or pink-tinged flowers, which can grow up to 50cm/20in high. This is the variety with the longest medical history and is a native of southern and eastern Europe. In Britain and northern Europe stinking hellebore, *H. foetidus*, and the smaller green hellebore, *H. viridis*, grow wild on calcareous soils and have similar properties. All flower in the early spring, often appearing in the snow.

Hellebores can be propagated by seed or root division and grow well in shady places in rich soil. Early medicinal uses were as an anesthetic, as a violent purgative and emetic, and to procure abortion. It was also given to children against worms – a drastic remedy that must occasionally have had tragic results. The entire plant and especially the rhizome is poisonous. A tincture of the rhizome is used today in homeopathic medicine to regulate the heart and calm nervous disorders, but the action is thought to be too unpredictable for orthodox medicine.

smoked, or boiled in vinegar and used as a mouthwash. This is extremely dangerous as internal use can lead to delirium and convulsions, or as an old herbalist put it, 'to an unquiet sleep like unto the sleepe of drunkennesse, which continueth long, and is deadly to the party'. The notorious Dr Crippen used the extracted drug to murder his wife. The drug contains strong alkaloids, generally obtained from the leaves and is used, by qualified practitioners only, as a sedative and narcotic.

propagated by seed or root division and may need some protection during cold winters.

Of all the medicinal herbs, the mandrake must be the one most shrouded in mystery and superstition. In early herbals the root is usually represented as a human figure often accompanied by a dog – dogs were used to pull the roots from the ground as by tradition the digger risked being struck dead in the process. As a protective and good luck talisman the roots were often kept wrapped in silk in a special box. As a medicine it was used since early Classical times as an anesthetic during operations, as a treatment for rheumatism and a strong emetic. Large doses are fatal.

Hyoscyamus niger
Henbane, hog's bean
Family: Solanaceae
An occasional weed on waste or cultivated ground in most parts of the world, henbane can grow as a biennial or annual, both forms occurring in seed from the same capsule. The biennial may grow over 1m/3ft high, the annual is a shorter, more straggling plant. The stout stems and long, toothed leaves are covered with pale, sticky hairs and have a slightly foetid smell; the flowers are handsome, a pale, dusky yellow traced with purple veins. The seed capsules are arranged along one side of the stem and, as they harden and mature, could be thought to resemble a row of large teeth.

In fact the most common medicinal use of henbane in the past has been as a remedy for toothache, the seeds or roots being chewed or

Mandragora officinalis
Mandrake, mandragora
Family: Solanaceae
A native of southern Europe, the mandrake has dark leaves about 60cm/2ft long that grow directly from the base of the plant, and, in midsummer, single, bell-shaped flowers of a faded yellow. These are succeeded by fleshy, yellow berries the size of a small crab apple. The perennial root can grow to a large size and may become forked and branched and occasionally assume a rudimentary human shape. Like most members of this family the mandrake will do well in a sheltered, slightly shaded, moist, rich soil. It is

Phytolacca americana
Poke root, Virginian poke
Family: Phytolaccaceae
The perennial poke root grows wild in North America, a shrubby plant that can grow as much as 3m/10ft high in damp, half-shaded places. The pale flowers grow in clusters and are followed by rich purple berries. The young spring shoots are said to be edible, but the whole plant becomes poisonous as it matures. Although the thick, fleshy root has a dangerous narcotic effect, it has been widely used as a purgative medicine and as an external poultice or poultice for inflammations, rheumatism and skin diseases.

The herb garden

In Europe and the Middle East early gardens of medicinal plants were generally attached to temples or sacred groves and were attended by priests, whose role gradually developed from that of primitive witch doctor to physician. This long and universal association between medicine and religion continued throughout recorded history until comparatively recently. The basic plan of such gardens was dictated by the necessity of growing numbers of plants in a confined space, tending them, protecting them and providing irrigation, so the plantings were in straight lines with regular paths between, a wall or fence around them and systems of water channels, a tank or a pool. These practical considerations combined to create the formal, rectilinear garden design familiar in ancient Egyptian frescoes, early Persian and Islamic paintings, and in the Roman *hortus* with its tidy divisions between vegetables and herbs, and colonnades and courtyards filled with terracotta pots of aromatic herbs.

After the fall of the Roman Empire these Roman villa gardens in northern Europe returned to the wilderness during the Dark Ages and only the hardiest herbs survived. In southern Europe they provided the pattern for the first monastery gardens, where the traditions of herb culture continued and were developed by monks with their standard of self-sufficiency and duty to the sick. An early plan survives of the gardens of a Benedictine monastery, St Gall in Switzerland. It was under the protection of the Emperor Charlemagne who was deeply interested in horticulture and who, in AD 812, sent out lists of herbs to be grown on all Imperial farms. The monastery vegetable garden at St Gall was divided into 18 narrow, rectangular beds, dill, coriander and chervil being included among the carrots and cabbages. The physic garden or *Herbularius* lay near the infirmary and consisted of 16 plots of herbs such as sage, rue and rosemary and also lilies and roses that we grow as ornamentals today. Scented flowers were grown in an open court known as 'Paradise' and used to decorate the church.

Many similar monasteries were established in Britain and Europe during the next 600 years, cuttings and seeds were exchanged between them and the properties of herbs recorded. In the monastic libraries lay the heavy manuscript herbals, which were laboriously copied by generations of monks. It was only with the Renaissance and the invention of printing that herbals became more generally available, together with many new books on garden design and 'the true Nature of every Soyle'. One of the earliest of these is *The Feate of Gardening* written by Ion Gardener in the 15th century, the first practical treatise on the 'sowing and settyng of Wurtys and of other maner Herbys' to appear since the 9th-century *Hortulus* of the Swiss abbot, Walafrid Strabo. The utilitarian domestic herb garden became increasingly popular and elaborate, the beds shaped into looping patterns and mazes, bordered with clipped hedges of lavender or germander, pebbles or bones, in the fashionable Italianate style. Cardinal Wolsey's garden at Hampton Court was 'so enknotted, it cannot be expressed'.

The physic gardens that provided medicinal herbs for apothecaries and monks now received an influx of new plants such as the nasturtium, sunflower and potato, brought home by the travellers and explorers of the 16th and 17th centuries, and in North America the first physic garden was founded by the Quaker George Fox 'for lads and lasses to know simples'. In Italy, Germany, France, Holland and Britain large botanical gardens were planted, attached to universities and medical schools and used for both medical and botanical study. The design of domestic herb gardens became generally less formal during the Romantic movement of the 18th century, when the fashion was for certain studied carelessness and a natural and asymmetrical aspect. During the tremendous revival of interest in the use and cultivation of herbs it is perhaps this informal impression of lush, barely controlled vegetation and subtle colour plantings that particularly influences the design of herb gardens today.

Formal herb gardens

The design of a formal herb garden usually follows a clear pattern, the paths and beds arranged to balance and complement each other and based on geometric shapes – regular curves, rectangles, triangles and circles. The focal point is generally in the centre of the garden, marked by a sundial, a seat, a large pot or statue or a trimmed shrub or tree. Plantings may be sparse, the herbs spaced well apart as they were in early herb-garden designs, often in straight lines or groups and contained within the beds by low walls or wooden planks. A common 17th-century border consisted of upright rows of bones, often the jaw bones or shank bones of sheep or pigs. A well-controlled low hedge of perennial herbs makes a traditional edging. Use silver santolina or cotton lavender, steely blue rue or glossy dark green wall germander to contrast with the foliage of the contained herbs, or, around a small bed, plant a border of close-growing chives, upright thyme or dwarf lavender to mark the boundary between bed and path.

The general effect of order and peace is determined both by the manner of planting and by the choice of herbs. Choose upright, compact varieties when possible, prune the roots as well as the branches of the fast-growing herbs such as costmary and tansy, and keep spreading herbs like mint to a minimum. The individual herbs are displayed more clearly here than in an informal garden, and garden pots and containers are more likely to contain a single plant than a mass of different species.

A well-trimmed rosemary hedge and 4 shaped bushes of variegated holly surround the small knot garden **below**. *The 2 designs within are picked out in box and wall germander with santolina and box at the corners. The knots contain a darker-coloured gravel than the path.* **Opposite:** *Set within a formal framework of tall box hedges, the freer and more luxuriant planting of this herb garden is balanced by square beds and straight, paved paths that lead to the central raised bowl of closely planted houseleeks.*

Examples of knot designs from The Country Housewife's Garden, *1617.*

Designs for a formal herb garden

There are many designs in 17th-century gardening books for garden knots, their twining, looping patterns defined by neatly clipped, compact hedges of grey, green and silver herbs. Fill tight knots with different coloured stones or sand, and the more open loops with many coloured herbs. Some of the complicated designs would need almost daily attention but a simple knot, used as the basic pattern for a herb garden, works very well and needs only a little more care than a more orthodox design.

Apart from planting straightforward borders or rows of herbs many pleasing, simple designs can be made for a garden based on a square, rectangle, triangle or circle. Square paving stones and small, square herb beds will make an unusual chequerboard terrace, while discarded ladders or old cartwheels – the rungs and spokes acting as divisions between the plants – will make attractive long or circular beds.

It is easier to cultivate and harvest herbs growing in raised beds. Herbs in the earliest monastic gardens were grown in rectangular raised beds and these generally provide better drainage as well as the pleasure of smelling the scents and watching bees without stooping. Plant ground ivy and nasturtiums to fall down the sides and houseleek and pellitory-of-the-wall to cling between the stones.

In larger gardens there is space for the more unusual herbs and for different varieties of the important ones. Large areas of contrasting colour and texture can be very effective – beds of silver-stemmed, blue-flowered borage, golden marigolds, the black and white horehounds – and the range of heights, from the monumental angelica to the tiny creeping mints, is easily exploited.

The wheel design **left** (used as a centre-piece) is picked out with silver-leaved herbs. The spokes are santolina with, from the right, sage, lavender and curry plant between them. The long, narrow bed of mature culinary herbs **right** is altogether more functional in design and should be positioned within easy reach of the kitchen door. All the plants are accessible from the path.

Three ideas for designs using raised beds. A neat retaining wall with stone coping **bottom left** provides a clean framework for the herbs in this formal garden. The mixed lavenders, silver santolinas and artemisias are all well trimmed. Granite setts have been used in the small, sunken garden **below** to slightly raise the height of the bed of rich purple lavender, while in an awkward corner of the kitchen garden **right** a mass of bright orange and yellow nasturtiums fills a triangular raised bed built from loose bricks.

Designing your own herb garden

Choosing the site

Whatever the design of your herb garden the first task is to choose the site. Culinary herbs must be easily accessible from the kitchen door, and near a path so they can be collected dryshod in wet weather. Part of the garden at least should have a southerly aspect as the majority of herbs need full sun and tender herbs such as tarragon or southernwood and tall rosemary and mullein need some protection from prevailing winds. Many aromatic herbs, particularly those native to southern climates, need a light, well-drained soil. A gently sloping site is ideal. In gardens of heavy clay or in city gardens with sour soil it may be worth building raised beds and filling these with fresh earth. Other herbs, such as the mints, prefer a moist soil, and there are many species, including some medicinal herbs, that do best in shady beds.

The basic plan

The plan opposite for a small but useful herb garden is based on a grid of 40cm/16in squares, as most mature perennial herbs will fit comfortably into this measurement and 40cm/16in is the minimum width suitable for a path. By using graph or squared paper any number of variations can be worked out on this basis. Measure up the squares in the garden and mark the design with lines and pegs. Although the design can work well on a much larger scale, this example is only 2·75m/9ft square and accommodates over 25 herbs. The only important species missing are a culinary mint and basil, the first because it is such a rampant grower that it is likely to suffocate everything else in a small garden, the second because it does not grow luxuriantly out of doors during most northern summers.

The herbs

The top right-hand bed contains perennial herbs for the kitchen; diagonally opposite are perennial medicinal and scented herbs. Most will need occasional trimming to prevent them becoming leggy and uncontrolled and the roots of the central tansy plant may need containing in a bottomless pot or bucket as they spread fast. For the first year or two annual herbs can be grown in the spaces between young perennial herbs, but as the perennials mature, spread outwards and grow to their full height, it is best to move the annuals to beds of their own.

The remaining beds are bordered by low-growing herbs. Parsley is the only one that will need replacing every year or so; the others are perennial. Within these borders grow essential annuals and caraway, a biennial. Both caraway and chervil will self-seed from year to year; sow the seeds of sweet marjoram and dill freshly each spring.

The central point

Choose a tall, narrow terracotta pot or a chimney pot for the centre of the garden or build a hollow heap of stones. Make sure this is set solidly into the earth, fill it with soil and plant a stout angelica or a rosemary or lemon verbena bush. Or plant a dark myrtle or bay tree and keep it well clipped. Alternatively, leave the centre open and place a bench at the end of one of the paths to give a view of the whole garden.

The paths

Lay paths of brick, stone, concrete slabs or crazy paving, leaving spaces between for creeping herbs. A gravel path is easy to make but it must have a raised border of bricks or wooden planks to contain it. Plant carpeting herbs – mint, chamomile or thyme – along the edge of the gravel path and they will soon grow across it and help to bind the pebbles. If there is space, set pairs of large pots at the end of each path and fill them with marigolds, nasturtiums or upright and trailing pelargoniums (scented geraniums) for the summer, or with small perennial herb shrubs or trees.

Raised beds

The basic design suggested here can easily be raised 30–60cm/1–2ft from the ground. Mark out the design with lines and pegs, dig a foundation trench at least 10cm/4in deep for stability (if possible), and build low walls of brick, stone or concrete blocks. Wide planks make good supports too, laid on their sides and pinned into position with upright posts that must be hammered firmly into the ground on either side. If the soil on the site is heavy and soured or clayey, spread a layer of broken crocks, stones or bricks over the bottom of the beds before filling them with good, light soil, mixed with well-rotted compost. This will help to give the beds adequate drainage.

Planting for height

One of the most obvious pieces of advice is the easiest to forget. Always plant tall species at the back of a border bed and grade the sizes progressively lower towards the front, and when planting a central bed begin with a large and striking plant in the middle and plant lower towards the edge. The basic garden plan given here is too small to allow for much gradation, but the perennial beds have tall bronze fennel and deep-green tansy at their centres and the annual beds have low borders.

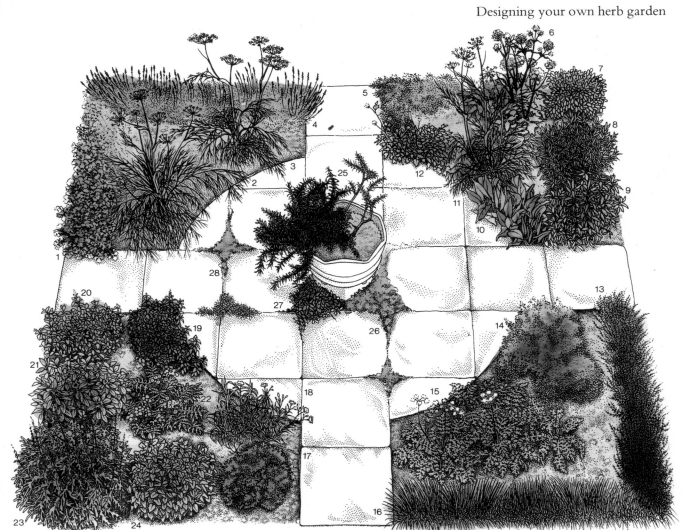

Planting key

Parsley (1) and dwarf lavender (4) border the top left-hand bed, enclosing a large dill (2) and caraway (3).

In the right-hand bed thyme (5) lovage (6) red sage (7) tarragon (8) and winter savory (9) grow into strong and bushy plants. The large, glossy leaves of sorrel (10) contrast with bronze fennel (11) and graceful salad burnet (12).

In the bottom right-hand bed rock hyssop (13) makes a small hedge beside sweet marjoram (14) and chervil (15) with a lower border of chives (16).

The bottom left-hand bed is framed by the contrasting leaves of rue (17) clove carnation (18) black peppermint (19) and white horehound (20) with bergamot (21) tansy (22) southernwood (23) and lemon balm (24) behind.

A large rosemary (25) grows in the central pot and creeping thymes (26) mints (27) and chamomiles (28) spread between the stones of the paths.

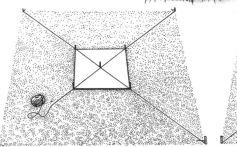

Marking out a formal garden

A square can be established by placing a square tile or piece of cardboard on the ground and stretching 2 strings diagonally across it and outward from a peg at each corner.

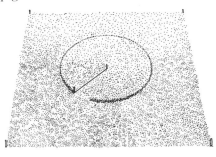

Circles are marked with 2 pegs tied to a piece of string. Plant 1 peg in the ground in the centre of the circle and draw around it with the other. Combinations of these techniques can be used to design your own knot garden.

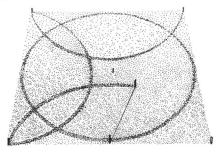

Informal herb gardens

Although an informal herb garden may give an impression of barely controlled abundance, of wandering paths half overgrown with creeping or trailing plants, of unexpected corners and hidden seats or pools, it needs to be planned and designed as carefully as the more rigid, formal garden. Use any existing slope or contour – building a rocky terrace to emphasize a bank perhaps, or digging a sunken garden – and plot out a winding path. Ideally any walls or paths should be made of stone, brick or other local, natural building material to blend with the site.

It is the planting especially that gives an informal garden its character. The herbs are usually grown close together and species chosen that will not entirely obliterate one another. The effect of colour and texture should be impressionistic and seemingly casual: broadcast seeds and encourage plants that self-seed naturally or that spread by roots and runners as much as possible. In the garden below the seeds of bronze and green fennel have been scattered at random over the gravel and the biennials mullein, angelica and foxglove have self-seeded and are thus at different stages of growth. Informal planting can be very successful on a small scale, even on a terrace or large balcony. Plant a few large, dramatic herbs – angelica and fennel for instance with their contrasting foliage. Allow clumps of hardy herbs to grow from among bricks and stones and fill to overflowing as many boxes, pots and tubs of the smaller herbs as the garden will hold.

*Some ideas for an informal herb garden. The old lead tank **above** makes an ideal container for trailing herbs, while in the garden **below** herbs have been encouraged to self-seed among the gravel. The bed **opposite** has been packed with contrasting herbs, including silver and garden thyme, lungwort and marjoram.*

Selecting the herbs

Colours and heights

Having decided on the plan of the herb garden, it is time to buy seeds or plants and to collect cuttings and roots from friends. Whatever your design, it is important to have some idea of the colours, textures and heights of herb species and their varieties before planting.

Herbs of a similar colour can look effective when planted in groups, but their leaves or type of growth should be contrasting. For instance, black peppermint with its long, purple-tinged leaves looks dramatic when planted by tall, feathery, dark bronze fennel, but fades into insignificance beside purple basil, whose similar leaves are glossier and have a richer colour. Variegated herbs tend to lose their character and become visually confusing when planted together. Grow them to their full advantage surrounded by plainer varieties. Herbs of contrasting colours are striking. Try growing golden marjoram with purple sage or plant a bed of black horehound with tall, yellow-flowered mullein.

Finally consider the background to the herb bed before planting. A mass of silver thyme will be thrown into relief against a dark hedge but may be barely visible against a white-washed wall.

The choice of plants for the herb garden must in the end be a personal one, dictated as much by a plant's use as by its appearance. However, these lists will give you some idea of the design possibilities and the many visual alternatives.

*In the garden **above** the green santo-lina in the foreground has been allowed to produce a mass of yellow button flowers, whereas the silver species behind the marigolds in the garden on the **right** has been tightly clipped and shaped. This late-summer garden shows some of the more dramatic large herbs including, from right to left, blue-flowered borage, yellow-flowered fennel, a mature bush of rosemary and, in the background, a great clump of elecampane, which can grow 3m/10ft high and spreads rapidly.*

Artemisia

Variegated lemon balm

Bronze fennel

Herbs with pale and silver leaves

Artemisias: southernwood *Artemisia abrotanum*, wormwood *A. absinthium*, *A. canescens*, *A. pedemontana*, *A. stelleriana*.
Camphor plant *Balsamita vulgaris*
Clove carnation *Dianthus caryophyllus*.
Costmary *Balsamita major*
Dittany of Crete *Origanum dictamnus*.
Donkey's ears *Stachys byzantina*
Eucalyptus *Eucalyptus globulus*
Lavender *Lavandula angustifolia*
Marsh mallow *Althaea officinalis*
Mints: apple mint *Mentha suaveolens*, horsemint *M. longifolia*.
Mullein *Verbascum thapsus*
Rue *Ruta graveolens* 'Jackman's Blue'
Sage *Salvia officinalis*
Santolina *Santolina chamaecyparissus*
Sea holly *Eryngium maritimum*
Thymes: woolly thyme *Thymus pseudolanuginosus*, and 2 varieties that are usually variegated to some degree, *T. × citriodorus* 'Silver Queen' and *T. vulgaris* 'Silver Posie', which is hardier but without the lemon scent.
White horehound *Marrubium vulgare*

Herbs with variegated leaves

Plant these less hardy herbs in a sheltered position but avoid shade as this may cause some species to revert slowly to green. Variegated herbs do not always breed true so it is wise to propagate them by cuttings, layering or division of the roots.
Lungwort *Pulmonaria officinalis* Most pulmonarias have dark green, silver-spotted leaves.
Mints: pineapple mint *Mentha suaveolens* 'Variegata', cream and green; ginger mint *M. × gentilis* 'Variegata', gold and green.
Pelargoniums: there are many variegated pelargoniums (scented geraniums) including *Pelargonium crispum* 'Variegatum', *P. graveolens* 'Variegatum' and *P. × fragrans* 'Snowy Nutmeg'. These are mostly cream and green.
Sage: golden sage *Salvia officinalis* 'Icterina', gold and green; red variegated sage *S. officinalis* 'Tricolor', purple, pink and white.
Thymes: these are already listed under pale- and gold-leaved herbs.
Variegated lemon balm *Melissa officinalis* 'Aurea', gold and green.
Variegated meadowsweet *Filipendula ulmaria* 'Variegata', cream and gold.
Variegated rue *Ruta graveolens* 'Variegata', cream and green.

Herbs with dark leaves

Bay *Laurus nobilis*
Black horehound *Ballota nigra*
Fennel *Foeniculum vulgare*, bronze variety.
Ground ivy *Glechoma hederacea*
Juniper *Juniperus communis*
Mints: black peppermint *Mentha × piperita*, eau-de-Cologne mint *M. × piperita* n.m. *citrata*.
Myrtle *Myrtus communis*
Peppermint-scented geranium *Pelargonium tomentosum*.
Purple basil *Ocimum basilicum* 'Dark Opal'.
Red sage *Salvia officinalis* 'Purpurascens'.
Tansy *Tanacetum vulgare*
Thyme *Thymus serpyllum* var. *coccineus*.
Wall germander *Teucrium chamaedrys*.
Woad *Isatis tinctoria*

Herbs with gold leaves

Feverfew *Tanacetum parthenium*
Golden marjoram *Origanum vulgare* 'Aureum'.
Golden purslane *Portulaca oleracea* var. *sativa*.
Thymes: golden lemon thyme *Thymus × citriodorus* 'Aureus', golden thyme *T. vulgaris* 'Aureus', both of which can be slightly variegated.

Bergamot

Herbs with bright flowers

Those few herbs with bright and showy flowers can be enlivening among the more usual subtle sage greens and silvers. Scarlet-flowered bergamot sets off the quieter mauves of lavender, clear yellow spires of mullein contrast with dark purple sage leaves, and massed, pale yellow woad flowers look well behind the stiffer, pink blooms of pot marjoram, *Origanum onites*. Rich red clove carnations make a good border to a bed of green curled parsley.

Red flowers

Bergamot *Monarda didyma*
Clove carnation *Dianthus caryophyllus.*
Hollyhock *Alcea rosea*
Rose *Rosa damascena, R. gallica*

Borage

Blue flowers

Borage *Borago officinalis*
Chicory *Cichorium intybus*
Hyssop *Hyssopus officinalis*
Viper's bugloss *Echium vulgare*

Dyer's chamomile

Orange and yellow flowers

American senna *Cassia marilandica*
Dyer's chamomile *Anthemis tinctoria*
Elecampane *Inula helenium*
Evening primrose *Oenothera biennis*
Gentian *Gentiana lutea*
Marigold *Calendula officinalis*
Mullein *Verbascum thapsus*
Nasturtium *Tropaeolum majus*
Safflower *Carthamus tinctorius*
Sunflower *Helianthus annuus*
Woad *Isatis tinctoria*

Other large-flowered species include the pink, mauve or white opium poppy, *Papaver somniferum*, pink soapwort, *Saponaria officinalis*, white orris, *Iris florentina*, and the white and yellow feverfew, *Tanacetum parthenium*.

Tall herbs

The majority of herbs do not grow more than 1m/3ft high, but it is often the tall species that provide the focal point in a garden. Plant one or more at the centre of a large bed, group them against a wall or fence or use them to flank garden steps. Hardy herbs such as sunflowers, hollyhocks and evening primrose will give some protection from the wind if they are properly staked.

Angelica

Herbs that grow over 1·25m/4ft high

American senna *Cassia marilandica*
Angelica *Angelica archangelica*
Chicory *Cichorium intybus*
Elecampane *Inula helenium*
Evening primrose *Oenothera biennis*
Fennel *Foeniculum vulgare*
Hollyhock *Alcea rosea*
Hop *Humulus lupulus*
Lemon verbena *Lippia triphylla*
Lovage *Levisticum officinale*
Mullein *Verbascum thapsus*
Rose *Rosa canina, R. damascena*
Rosemary *Rosmarinus officinalis*
Sunflower *Helianthus annuus*

Small trees and shrubs

Bay *Laurus nobilis*
Broom *Cytisus scoparius*
Juniper *Juniperus communis*
Myrtle *Myrtus communis*
Witch hazel *Hamamelis virginiana*
The larger eucalyptus, lime and elder trees will need heavy pruning in a small garden.

Sun and shade

Purple-flowered thyme needs the sun;
ramsons **far right** *flourishes in shade.*

Herbs in the sun

There are constantly repeated instructions in every book on herb cultivation to plant the majority of species in full sun, in well-drained, light soil. To understand why this is necessary it is helpful to know something about the natural habitat of these herbs.

Garden thyme, sage, savory, lavender and rosemary and other important culinary and aromatic herbs come from the hilly country surrounding the Mediterranean, where the plants are exposed to blazing sun and high winds and grow from thin, harsh soil. To prevent what little moisture they have from being evaporated by the sun and wind their leaves are usually narrow, thus reducing their exposed surface, and have a tough, greyish cuticle. Their sharp tips and strong flavours act as some protection against grazing animals and in very hot weather their potent, volatile oils form a protective vapour against the sun.

If plants that have adapted to such harsh conditions are grown in too rich and moist a soil, they become lush, losing much of their aroma, and their weakened roots are unable to withstand winter temperatures.

This does not mean that such herbs need *poor* soil. A herb that is to be picked and pruned several times a year must make a strong, shrubby growth. The ideal soil is a light-to-medium loam, lightly composted every year to maintain the essential mineral and organic content.

Herbs in the shade

Although so many herbs need full sun, there are some that will tolerate

Although so many herbs need full sun there are few gardens that face due south. Herbs are listed below that will grow in dappled shade and also a few that are adapted to the dense shade beneath shrubs and evergreens.

a little shade, such as parsley and mint, and others that grow best in a partly shaded position. Plant those listed below in dappled shade:
Alkanet *Alkanna tinctoria*
Angelica *Angelica archangelica*
Bistort *Polygonum bistorta*
Boneset *Eupatorium perfoliatum*
Burdock *Arctium lappa*
Celery *Apium graveolens* var. *dulce*
Chervil *Anthriscus cerefolium*
Garden sorrel *Rumex acetosa*
Lady's mantle *Alchemilla vulgaris*
Lungwort *Pulmonaria officinalis*
Marsh mallow *Althaea officinalis*
St John's wort *Hypericum perforatum*
Sweet cicely *Myrrhis odorata*
Valerian *Valeriana officinalis*
Wintergreen *Gaultheria procumbens*

These herbs will thrive in deep shade and make good ground cover:
Ramsons *Allium ursinum*
Solomon's seal *Polygonatum multiflorum.*
Woodruff *Galium odoratum*

Poisonous herbs

Many poisonous herbs grow naturally in the shade. Apart from their interesting history as drug plants their curious or beautiful flowers often make them fascinating to grow. It is not sensible to cultivate poisonous plants near herbs picked regularly for cooking, so give them a

shady corner of their own.

Plant some lily-of-the-valley, *Convallaria majalis*, and meadow saffron, *Colchicum autumnale*, along the front of the bed. The first flowers in the spring, the second has pale pink, crocus-like blossoms in the autumn. Behind them plant the dark mandrake, *Mandragora officinarum*, with its large, crinkled leaves and yellow-green flowers, then hellebores, the *Helleborus* species, at the back of the bed. Clumps of blue- or white-flowered monkshood, *Aconitum napellus*, with its narrow, graceful leaves will lighten the effect of dark foliage. In a less heavily shaded part of the bed grow the tall, familiar foxglove, *Digitalis purpurea*, and the perennial arnica, *Arnica montana*, with its dark yellow, daisy-like flowers. Two interesting members of the potato family, the *Solanaceae*, have strange flowers and poisonous leaves and seeds and have been grown for drugs for thousands of years. The thornapple, *Datura stramonium*, grows about 1m/3ft high, and the annual form of henbane, *Hyoscyamus niger*, is a slightly smaller plant. It is not advisable to grow the related deadly nightshade, *Atropa bella-donna*, in gardens where there are young children, despite its dusky purple flowers, as the ripe black berries can be tempting.

Herbs for a water garden

A stream or pond in the garden will provide the natural conditions for semi-aquatic herbs. The species listed below should be planted in shallow water. All are grown from pieces of creeping root or stem, which should be pressed into the wet mud. Plant them a good distance apart as they spread vigorously. If the pool has a fibreglass or concrete bottom, plant them in large containers and submerge these until the soil is at least 5cm/2in underwater.

Bog bean, *Menyanthes trifoliata*; sweet flag, *Acorus calamus*; watercress, *Nasturtium officinale* (which can only be grown in running water); water germander, *Teucrium scordium*; water mint, *Mentha aquatica*; yellow flag, *Iris pseudacorus*.

Grow the following herbs in moist soil along the bank: comfrey, *Symphytum officinale*; sneezewort, *Achillea ptarmica* (which has double-flowered forms); English mace, *A. decolorans* (a garden variety of sneezewort); marsh mallow, *Althaea officinalis*; meadowsweet, *Filipendula ulmaria*.

Herbs for a dyer's garden

Another specialized herb garden might be planted by those who use herbal dyes. Large quantities of flowers or leaves are needed for dyeing, so grow the herbs massed in individual beds or in big, circular plantings. Most herbs – and other garden plants – will yield some colour as a dye, but those listed here are traditional dye herbs, well tried and tested. Many are large, striking plants.

Alkanet, *Alkanna tinctoria*; bloodroot, *Sanguinaria canadensis*; dyer's chamomile, *Anthemis tinctoria*; dyer's greenweed, *Genista tinctoria*; golden rod, *Solidago virgaurea* (or other golden rod species); madder, *Rubia tinctorum*; safflower, *Carthamus tinctorius*; weld, *Reseda luteola*; woad, *Isatis tinctoria*.

A bed of soapwort, *Saponaria officinalis*, will provide the ingredients for a gentle washing-soap substitute that is suitable for fine wool.

Nutritious, glossy-leaved watercress **above** *will easily grow in running water. The uncommon sweet flag* **right** *should never be picked in the wild, but makes an ideal herb for a water garden with its scented leaves and strange, curving flowerhead.*

Herbs for bees

The long-throated flowers of bergamot can be pink, mauve or white, but red bergamot is the most common and strongly scented species.

Nectar from thyme flowers gives a richly aromatic honey, and many other members of the Labiate family are sought out by bees.

Thyme has been grown for bees at least since Classical times and was much praised by the poet and beekeeper Virgil. Thyme honey from Mount Hymettus in Greece has been justly famous for several thousand years and there are other well-known honeys that are strongly flavoured by certain flowers – rosemary honey from the south of France and Spain, eucalyptus honey from Australia, clover honey from Canada, Scottish heather honey and English lime-blossom honey. Most honeys, however, are flavoured by a mixture of flowers, and the flowers of aromatic herbs give a special richness and depth of flavour.

Although the task of beekeeping is absorbing and fascinating, it is not necessary to actually be a beekeeper to have the pleasure of a bee garden. Bees will travel at least 1k/½ mile to your garden to feed from their favourite flowers and it is possible to plant herbs that will supply them with food from spring to late autumn. Such a garden will be filled with bees throughout the season, except during bad weather, and vegetables and fruit will benefit by being thoroughly pollinated. Butterflies will be attracted to the garden too; a bank of flowering lavender or hyssop covered with peacock butterflies and humming honey bees is a lovely sight.

What to grow

Plant a bee garden in full sun, as the sunshine will help to stimulate the secretion of nectar, and grow the herbs in large, bold groups to attract attention. Do not plant double-flowered species as bees find these difficult to work. If hives are placed in the garden, provide a windbreak to shelter them from winter winds and to protect bees that are returning home heavily laden. Hedges of hawthorn, blackthorn or willow will all yield nectar and pollen early in the spring when it is especially needed. Tall sunflowers or hollyhocks make good temporary windbreaks, with flowers that are valuable for bees in the autumn.

For the herb beds choose both early-flowering species, such as hellebores and poppies (which yield only pollen), marigolds, and late-flowering plants, such as golden rod, mullein, and meadow saffron, *Colchicum autumnale*. Among the long-flowering, heavy nectar producers are catmint, either the usual *Nepeta mussinii* or the larger, upright, medicinal species, *Nepeta cataria*, borage and the related viper's bugloss and melilot, whose name derives from *mel* meaning 'honey' and *lotus* meaning 'flower'. Bergamot or bee balm is prized by many beekeepers though the flower tubes of some species are too long for honey bees. Labiate herbs are among the best bee plants. Thyme, mint, marjoram, hyssop, savory, basil, sage and horehound and herbs from the *Stachys* and *Teucrium* genera are just a few of these. Flowering chives make a good border herb.

Apart from those that produce pollen or nectar there are several herbs that have long been associated with the art of keeping bees. Pliny recommends rubbing hives with the leaves of lemon balm to attract bees and the scented oil can be added to the syrup used for introducing queen bees to the hive. The dried flowers, leaves and stalks of tansy make a strong-smelling and slow-burning fuel for bee-smokers. These resemble small bellows and are used to puff smoke over the bees to quieten them when they are disturbed by the beekeeper. Sunflower leaves and stems can be employed for the same purpose. Wormwood, *Artemisia absinthium*, is as unpleasant to bees as to other insects and if rubbed over the hands its bitter smell helps to prevent stings. Stored with honey it discourages wax moth and stroking a swarm of bees with bruised branches of wormwood will encourage it to move.

Hedging herbs

A low hedge of lavender on the left and southernwood on the right lead to magnificent rosemary bushes, flanked by well-trimmed Irish junipers.

Herbs on walls

The most dependable and traditional hedging herbs are lavender and santolina. Both respond well to clipping and are hardy in most climates. Old English lavender, *Lavandula angustifolia*, and the 'Grappenhall' and 'Hidcote Giant' varieties are among the tallest, growing about 1m/3ft high. Plant them in well-drained, limy soil 1m/3ft apart and clip each year immediately after harvesting the flowers, and also removing any dead wood. There are pink- and white-flowered lavenders, medium and small sizes, and dwarf varieties that make compact, low hedges. Plant these rather closer together. If you have plenty of room, plant double or triple lavender hedges, high lavenders at the back and low ones at the front, with different coloured flowers. These can be quite spectacular. Choose varieties that bloom at different times so the scented flowers open in succession, attracting bees throughout the summer.

Santolina chamaecyparissus is the most popular of the santolinas, with silver-grey foliage and yellow button flowers. Plant 30cm/1ft apart in light soil and clip into shape in early and late summer. Though clipping prevents flowering, the hedge will grow dense and compact and reach a height of about 60cm/2ft. *S. virens* has green foliage and a less powerful scent; plant it alternately with one of the silver species as an interesting hedge or use the green and silver for interlacing knot patterns. The dwarf form, *S. chamaecyparissus* 'Nana', makes a good, low, edging hedge.

A rosemary hedge needs a more sheltered position and the roots may require protection during cold winters. Plant 50cm/20in apart in well-drained soil and clip just after midsummer. For a tight, formal hedge plant the upright 'Miss Jessup's Variety' and clip when necessary during the summer. The looser *Rosmarinus officinalis* varieties, both blue- and white-flowered, make a more natural, flowing hedge that usually grows about 1m/3ft high.

For a low hedge of about 30cm/1ft high, grow wall germander, *Teucrium chamaedrys*, with its dark, glossy, scalloped leaves. This germander will tolerate some shade and was one of the most popular hedging plants grown in the old knot gardens. Space about 20cm/8in apart in light soil and clip as soon as the purple flowers are past their prime, or earlier in cold regions.

Hyssop makes a lovely hedging herb but will sometimes drop all its leaves in the winter, unlike the evergreens listed above. There are pink- and white-flowered varieties, as well as the more common rich blue, which is the hardiest. It will grow up to 1m/3ft high; plant 30cm/1ft apart in well-drained soil and clip in late spring. *Hyssopus officinalis* ssp *aristatus*, the little rock hyssop, grows to the same height as wall germander and can be grown with it to good effect. Its dark blue flowers bloom in late summer.

Other herbs that can be shaped to form low hedges and borders are winter savory, garden thyme, rue and some Artemisia species such as southernwood. These herbs may lose their leaves during hard winters but will grow thick foliage again in the spring. Southernwood needs regular trimming, but do not cut it at all after mid or late summer as this weakens the plant.

As so many of the aromatic herbs are well adapted to dry, stony conditions, a good selection can be grown along the top of a wall. This is especially useful for gardens with limited space.

You need a double wall 50cm/20in high, or more, of brick, stone or weathered concrete blocks. Leave a space of at least 25cm/10in between the walls and fill this with fine, lightly composted soil. Plant low, shrubby herbs such as thyme, savory, dwarf lavenders, the dwarf artemisia, *A. schmidtiana*

'Nana', and prostrate rosemary. Rock hyssop and wall germander will do well. If the wall is a suitable height for sitting on, leave occasional spaces, about 60cm/2ft long, and plant them with creeping thyme, the silver, gold or lemon-scented varieties as well as the common *Thymus serpyllum*. They will grow into cushioned, scented seats.

Larger plants usually need more nourishment and root space than is available on a wall, but the daisy feverfew, *Tanacetum parthenium*, will often grow 60cm/2ft tall, rooting happily between the stones. Pellitory-of-the-wall, *Parietaria officinalis*, is another herb that grows naturally on walls, and to a similar height. Its fresh green leaves and red stems are pretty in the spring but become rather dull by midsummer. Walls are the natural habitat for the fat-leaved rosettes of houseleek, *Sempervivum tectorum*, and for other stone-crops such as roseroot, *Rhodiola rosea*, and wall pepper, *Sedum acre*. These all spread quickly and withstand drought. One of the tiniest herbs, parsley piert, *Aphanes arvensis*, grows well along a wall top and is a healthy addition to salads and cooked vegetables. These last 4 herbs will also grow along any stone wall that has some earth tucked between the crevices and will seed themselves and spread without any trouble. The wallflower, *Cheiranthus cheiri*, is not usually regarded as a herb today, though oil from the flowers was a common remedy for ague and sold under the name of Cheirinum. Scatter wallflower seed along wall tops and the sweetly scented flowers will bloom in the spring in mixed colours – yellow, orange and brick red.

Hardy lavender will grow in rough, stony conditions. These mature plants are growing along a dry-stone wall.

Paths

Paths, lawns, seats and ground cover

Old bricks and weathered paving stones with their subtle colours and textures make ideal paths through a herb garden. Plant aromatic, creeping herbs in the earth-filled holes or cracks between the bricks and stones or allow taller plants to lean and fall across from the borders of the herb bed, to scent the air as they are crushed. Francis Bacon, writing in 1625, recommends wild thyme, salad burnet and water mints, 'you are to set whole alleys of them, to have the pleasure when you walk or tread.'

Since the 17th century, many thyme varieties have been developed from the wild carpeting species, *Thymus serpyllum*, all of which grow well in temperate climates. For good close mats that will spread across the path choose *T. serpyllum* var. *albus*, with white flowers and bright green leaves, *T. serpyllum* var. *coccineus*, which is not quite so vigorous but has attractive small, dark leaves and crimson flowers, or 'Pink Chintz' with its clear pale pink flowers. Towards the edges plant the grey-green woolly thyme, *T. pseudolanuginosus*, which is a good carpeter but less resistant to constant trampling. It has lilac-pink flowers.

Other scented herbs suitable for paths are salad burnet, *Sanguisorba minor*, with its faint cucumber scent and pretty rosette of leaves; the perennial *Micromeria filiformis*, a tough prostrate savory from Corsica with white flowers and a peppery, minty scent; and Roman chamomile, *Chamaemelum nobile*, which smells richly fruity. The medicinal herb, broad-leaved plantain,

A close carpet of creeping mint softens the outline of the concrete path **above**. *Chives, mint and parsley border garden steps* **below**, *while the broad steps* **opposite** *are covered with a thick, springy turf of white-flowering thyme.*

Plantago major, can withstand constant crushing but is usually considered a weed in the garden, and has no scent.

Thyme, burnet, savory and chamomile grow best in full sun. Along shadier paths plant the creeping mints, which need a richer, moister soil. Make a hole between the stones or bricks 15cm/6in deep with a dibber and fill it with good, loamy soil, then plant prostrate pennyroyal, *Mentha pulegium*, which will soon spread with rooting stems into a compact peppermint-scented mat. The smallest mint of all, *M. requienii*, grows in the same way but is less hardy and likes a sheltered position. *M. gattefossei* grows taller and should be planted along path edges.

Thyme, salad burnet and yarrow often grow wild in close turf on downs and dry hills and their seeds can be mixed with grass seed when sowing a garden lawn. Or try planting a massed carpet of thyme alone for an aromatic lawn or on a sunny bank. First drain the site well and use a rather poor, uncomposted soil that has been thoroughly weeded and raked finely. Sow one or many of the *Thymus serpyllum* varieties, scattering the seeds freely over the prepared ground in the spring, then thinning the seedlings to about 15cm/6in apart – or buy plants in bulk. They soon spread and will join together by the autumn when they can be regularly trodden on. The ground must be kept well weeded, at least once a fortnight during the first summer as once well established it is difficult to detach weeds without damaging the thread-like thyme roots. Weeding is the greatest drawback to any herb lawn, particularly during the first year. However, it is not necessary to mow unless you wish to prevent the thyme from flowering.

The first detailed directions for growing a grass lawn are given in John Rea's *Flora*, written in 1665, when turves were cut from a 'hungry Common ... where the grass is thick and short'. Before this time chamomile was the most common lawn plant and, despite the care required, is still sometimes used today, as it is hard wearing, will withstand drought and is deliciously scented. If you walk on it regularly it may not need to be trimmed at all and

Lawns

Several varieties of creeping thyme have been thickly planted here and allowed to flower, forming a bright, aromatic lawn.

the runners will be encouraged to root as in the old rhyme, 'Like a chamomile bed – the more it is trodden the more it will spread.'

Single-flowered Roman chamomile, *Chamaemelum nobile*, can be grown from seed; the double-flowered variety is better, having a more compact growth, but does not always breed true from seed so propagate by detaching the little plantlets from the runners of the parent plant. Another variety *C. nobile* 'Treneague' is non-flowering and therefore very suitable for lawns.

Clear the site for the chamomile lawn thoroughly of all weeds, dress with well-rotted compost, level and firm down. Sow seed broadcast in the spring, then thin the seedlings or set out the plantlets to 15cm/6in apart. When established, roll the lawn regularly and keep it well weeded and trimmed. If necessary cut with shears, otherwise mow by machine, the blades set high, and nip off any flowers that appear to keep growth compact and tight.

Seats

Carpeting herbs can also be grown as a scented covering for seats or along the tops of walls or on a patio or terrace. A herb seat will look attractive in the centre of a formal herb garden, at the end of a path, tucked into a hedge or arbour, around the base of a tree or cut into an earth bank. To make it, build a low bank of earth and lay slabs of stone paving, slate or wooden planks along the top, leaving spaces between for the herbs. If the seat is planted in the spring it should be completely covered by an aromatic carpet by the end of the first year.

Thyme will grow well on a sunny seat, the creeping varieties on the base and taller varieties behind. Tall garden or lemon thymes are the most suitable, or plant more unusual species such as *T. azoricus*, which smells of pine needles and forms a compact cushion with pale purple flowers, or *T. erectus*, a little upright, narrow plant with a camphor scent. Roman chamomile can also be planted, and any of the creeping mints described earlier will grow well in shady and protected situations.

Ground cover

Ground cover is often needed for bare patches under trees and there are several spreading, perennial herbs that grow in colonies in shady areas. They require little attention and, once established, will discourage weeds.

China-white woodruff flowers bloom in deep shade and the plants form a thick ground cover. When exposed to full sunlight the plants soon lose their colour, wither and die.

Most woodland plants spread by creeping roots as lack of light often prevents them from flowering. Woodruff, *Galium odoratum*, and ground ivy, *Glechoma hederacea*, are typical woodland species with long trailing stems that make good ground cover. Both are useful herbs – woodruff as a wound herb and a scented flavouring for drinks; ground ivy as a nutritious tonic and a bitter flavouring for beer. Propagate woodruff by planting out portions of the creeping root in the autumn and ground ivy by planting out pieces of rooting stem in the spring or autumn; both like a good, loamy soil.

Bistort, *Polygonum bistorta*, grows well in dappled shade, its broad, edible leaves appear early in the year and long, pink flowerheads bloom in late spring. Propagate by seed in the spring or by root division in autumn or springtime.

Two members of the borage family also form colonies in shady places, though they do not spread very quickly. Lungwort, *Pulmonaria officinalis*, with its long, spotted leaves and pink and blue flowers, can be grown from seed or by root division and the much larger comfrey, *Symphytum officinale*, by seed or root offsets. Both have edible leaves and healing properties.

Stachys byzantina, donkey's ears, is another healing plant, related to betony and the woundworts. This is one of the most tolerant of ground-cover plants, it thrives in sun or shade, on moist or dry ground, and keeps its thickly felted, silvery-grey leaves all the year round.

Herbs in winter

Herbs outdoors

The herbs that can be picked fresh throughout the winter include salad burnet, Welsh onion, watercress, celery, some hardy thyme species, sage, winter savory and marjoram, including the winter marjoram, *Origanum heracleoticum*. Unlike the curly-leaved species, the strong Hamburg parsley will go on providing leaves and stems for sauces and stuffings during early winter and the roots are always available for winter soups and stews. Chicory and dandelion will continue to produce leaves for salads or as cooked vegetables. Blanch them slowly outdoors under flower pots or mounds of earth, or bring them into the greenhouse or indoors where they can be blanched in about 10 days, buried in a covered tub or bucket.

Blanching

Growing herbs under cover

Cloches

Covering plants of parsley, mint, chervil and tarragon with a glass or plastic cloche will prolong their useful growing period for a few extra weeks, or longer during a mild winter. Move a few roots to the greenhouse for winter flavourings. Mint is especially easy to force in a warm greenhouse. Lift a long piece of creeping rhizome in the autumn, cut it into 3cm/1in pieces and lay these close together in a box of light, rich soil, covered with 3cm/1in of soil. They will produce leaves all winter but by spring will be exhausted and only fit for the compost heap. The little green crowns of parsley, caraway and fennel that may survive above ground should not be picked during winter, but if they are covered with cloches in the early spring they will spring up several weeks earlier than those left uncovered. With some thought and planning it is possible to have a selection of fresh herbs to pick even during the darkest winter months.

Straw and sacking

In cold regions small bay and myrtle trees and lemon verbena and rosemary bushes that have been planted in tubs out of doors should be pulled under cover before the first frosts, and those growing outside should be protected with straw or sacking around the base of the trunk or stem. Use straw, cloches or open-weave baskets or mats to protect French tarragon, thymes, especially lemon thyme, southernwood and lavender, liquorice and other southern herbs that are growing in cold, exposed places. It is worth making this effort, which may make all the difference to the survival of the plants.

Herbs to bring inside

As the air sharpens in the autumn, begin to carry tender herbs indoors or into the greenhouse for the winter. Pelargoniums and basil must come in and also some of the unusual, delicate species that belong to common herb families, such as fringed lavender, *Lavandula dentata*, with its softly scalloped leaves and blue flowers, which occasionally bloom during the winter, and dittany of Crete, *Origanum dictamnus*. This perennial herb has rounded, soft leaves that closely resemble those of sweet marjoram, but lack the strong flavour. The difference is most apparent when it flowers in late summer, as the hanging blossoms are small and pink with prominent stamens. Pineapple sage, *Salvia rutilans*, makes an ideal indoor herb for the winter. The graceful, pointed leaves have the typically rough sage surface and a strong and refreshing fruity scent. The spikes of long-throated red flowers begin to bloom in the autumn and continue throughout the winter. These last 3 delicate species may be kept in pots outdoors during the summer. Other hardy culinary species can be brought indoors for winter use. Dig up a few plants of thyme, parsley, mint and other favourites with plenty of earth around the roots and plant in roomy pots. Water them well and leave outside for a few days to become established before bringing them indoors to a cool room. They must be gradually accustomed to the change in temperature.

Tender herbs

Hardy species

A tub containing herbs for tisanes. In the centre grows a vigorous lemon balm whose leaves provide a refreshing and delicious tea. From left to right are German chamomile; yarrow, which can be eaten or taken as a tonic; the little rock hyssop and lady's mantle with lobed leaves, which also have both culinary and medicinal uses. The leaves of the trailing ground ivy make a slightly bitter, aromatic tisane.

This urn contains a selection of culinary herbs. Several large-leaved basil plants grow in the centre, surrounded by, from left to right, parsley, chives, dwarf golden sage and dwarf winter savory. Creeping thymes trail and hang over the brim. The basil is the only annual herb among them and is one of the most useful kitchen herbs with its powerful, often dominating flavour and lush growth.

Herbs indoors

Many herbs will grow well in pots on sunny windowsills, in window boxes, hanging baskets and in tubs or barrels in a sun room or on a balcony. There should even be enough space on one large, south-facing windowsill to grow a selection of the basic flavouring herbs or a row of scented herbs that can be used for making tisanes. If you have a sun room or balcony, then 4 tubs planted with mixed annuals and perennials and a good proportion of evergreen herbs for winter picking could provide most of the fresh herbs needed by a small household, as well as being decorative and sweetly scented.

Light and temperature

The first necessity is light. Few herbs suitable for indoor growing will thrive in the shade. Most need sunlight for at least half the day so set them in a south-facing window if possible, otherwise one facing east or west. It is possible to grow herbs in a shady room under special fluorescent tubes, which should be set about 15cm/6in above the top of the plant.

Temperature is important. It is useless to attempt to grow herbs directly above a radiator or stove or in an airless kitchen that is often steamy and full of fumes. Ideally there should be warmth during the day, lower temperatures at night and some humidity. In a centrally heated house humidity may be lacking so keep a bowl filled with water above the radiator or near the herbs. A direct draught may harm the plants though fresh air is necessary.

Clay and plastic pots

Plastic pots are often used today, being cheaper, lighter and less likely to break than clay. But there are some advantages in using an unglazed clay pot, the most important being that excess water will evaporate through the clay walls so the roots are not likely to become waterlogged. Drowning by over-watering is the most common fate of indoor herbs. Another advantage is that the moisture content in the soil can be discovered by tapping a clay container sharply: it will give a ringing sound if the soil is too dry and a dull thud if too wet. Whether of plastic or clay, the container should have an adequate drainage hole and be stood in a saucer or tray. A layer of gravel in the tray will ensure that the pot never sits in stagnant water.

Boxes and barrels

Wooden boxes or barrels make good containers if you have the space. Boxes should be at least 25cm/10in deep. Saw barrels in half and use them as tubs, or cut several holes about 5cm/2in across in their sides and grow a herb from each hole. If you use a large barrel in this way, put a narrow tube of wire netting down the centre, from top to bottom, before filling it with earth. By watering down the tube the moisture will spread evenly through the soil; with no tube the lower plants may suffer from drought. Do not creosote the insides of wooden containers to sterilize them as the fumes may damage the plants, instead make a small fire of newspaper inside the container, just sufficient to char and sterilize the surface of the wood.

Hanging baskets

To make the best use of all available space and light, plant a hanging basket with herbs, the upright species in the centre and trailing mints and thymes, nasturtiums or ground ivy round the edge. Special clay bowls or wire baskets can be bought for this purpose or even an old kitchen colander will do. To contain moisture, line the wire basket thickly with sphagnum moss or hay, or with a plastic sheet, before filling it with earth.

A large, unglazed, terracotta bowl with 6 or 7 5cm/2in holes bored in it will make an ideal hanging onion pot, if you can buy one or have one made.

Fill it with earth, plant chives in the top and press the bulbs of Welsh onions into the holes – you will be able to cut the hanging green shoots throughout the winter.

Soil, water, food and care

Potting soil

Put a layer of broken crocks or stones in the bottom of large containers before filling them with soil and sprinkle a few spoonfuls of granulated charcoal over them to prevent the soil souring. Then fill with a standard potting compost bought from a shop or good, loamy, garden earth mixed with a little coarse sand. Sterilize the garden earth for an hour in the oven if you wish, to kill insect eggs and weed seeds.

Watering

Be careful not to over-water, especially during the winter when plants are resting and should not be stimulated into unseasonal growth. It is best to water in the morning so that excess moisture can evaporate during the day, and to use only tepid water. During the summer it may be necessary to syringe the leaves of broad-leaved herbs such as sweet basil with tepid water to prevent them flagging. The leaves of herbs in city window boxes will also need occasional syringing to prevent their pores becoming clogged with grime and fumes.

Compost and fertilizer

Each spring spread a little well-rotted compost over the earth in the herb container and water well. If any other food is needed, use a herbal fertilizing tea (page 147).

Pruning

Although the restricted light and space will prevent herbs from growing as large indoors as they would outside, they will need regular cropping or trimming to keep them compact and controlled. Pinch out the centre shoots to encourage bushy growth and cut off any runners. Examine the drainage hole regularly and if root fibres are showing, transfer the plant to a larger pot.

What to grow

Culinary herbs

Many people will want to grow culinary herbs indoors that cannot be bought fresh and do not dry well. Three large pots, 30cm/12in in diameter, filled with the annuals, chervil, basil and coriander, will provide a good mixture with strong, distinctive flavours. Sow their seeds directly into the pots in the spring in moist, fairly rich soil and thin out the seedlings. The chervil and coriander will begin to shoot and grow leggy soon after midsummer, but basil, especially the compact bush basil, will continue into the winter months. Sweet marjoram and summer savory also grow well indoors and are both annuals. For a basic supply of perennial, evergreen culinary herbs plant thyme species, winter savory, a clump of Welsh onions and the prostrate rosemary. Decorative dwarf golden sage can be included, and the biennial parsley. None of these are very invasive herbs and can be planted together, but mint needs a pot of its own and plenty of moisture. If you have room for a deep tub or barrel on a balcony or roof then it may be possible to grow tall herbs such as angelica, deep-rooted caraway or horseradish; otherwise these species are obviously unsuitable for indoor growing.

Tisane herbs

Another series of pots or a large box could be used for growing herbs for tisanes. Plant peppermint and lemon balm (whose roots may need confining), the annual German chamomile, the little rock hyssop, *Hyssopus officinalis* ssp *aristatus*, lady's mantle and trailing ground ivy.

Scented herbs

Herbs grown for their scent might include dwarf lavender species, clove carnation, dwarf santolina and upright and trailing pelargoniums. There are literally hundreds of pelargonium varieties, each with leaves of a different scent and shape, and all make admirable houseplants, being easy to grow and easy to propagate from cuttings. Use the leaves to flavour custards, creams and jellies and in pot-pourri mixtures.

Pots of culinary herbs, including fennel, thyme, summer savory, sage, dill, marjoram and basil, are set out on a parapet to catch the afternoon sun.

Companion planting with herbs

'Rue and the Fig-tree are in a great league and amitie', wrote Pliny nearly 2,000 years ago. An early example of companion planting.

Herbal pesticides

The organic herb garden

A garden needs to be as well balanced as the human diet; that is, there should be a good and various mixture of plant species (or ingredients), each contributing something slightly different to the soil and to each other, building up a complex pattern of mutual benefits and interaction.

Common sense and experience will help the gardener to achieve this balance. It is clear, for instance, that a row of shallow-rooting, shade-tolerant plants will grow well between rows of tall, deep-rooting plants, as the former will take nutrients only from the surface of the soil and also benefit from the shade of the latter. Another sensible step would be to plant a herb that seems impervious to insect pests as a protection beside another that is prone to attack.

Much has been written on this subject recently as the old gardening lore is increasingly proved to have a firm scientific basis, but there is still a great deal to be discovered about the effects of plant exhalations, scents, root excretions and other plant substances on their surroundings. It is known that aromatic herbs have a particularly strong influence and play a large part in companion planting. When grown naturally they are seldom bothered by pests or disease themselves (with the exception of mint rust), and many species will increase the health and vigour of nearby plants, repel pests above and below ground and mask the scents of more vulnerable plants with their strong aromas.

Try growing rosemary and sage, thyme, mint and other labiate herbs among vegetables against insect pests. Plant nasturtium against the woolly aphis, chives against apple scab and southernwood and tansy around fruit trees against fruit moth. Garlic and other alliums protect most garden plants from a variety of pests and diseases, increase the scent of roses but inhibit the growth of peas and beans. Bitter wormwood and rue discourage insects, slugs and moles. Yarrow and the related German chamomile have high reputations as 'physician' plants: an ailing plant can sometimes be revived by moving a chamomile plant beside it although, as with so many medicines, too many chamomiles may have the opposite effect. Yarrow and German chamomile together with the stinging nettle are also said to increase the essential oils present in other herbs, thus improving their flavour and potency. The stinging nettle and foxglove are both 'preservative' plants, prolonging the lives and protecting the plants around them from fungus diseases. These are just a few of the many examples of companion planting that will benefit the garden.

To avoid altering the natural balance in the garden, use fresh or dried herbs in place of chemicals as pesticide sprays, especially on vegetables and herbs that are to be eaten. For a standard pesticide tea pour 1 litre/2 pints of boiling water over a double handful of fresh or 2 tablespoons of dried herbs, cover and leave for at least 10 minutes. Stir well, strain and use immediately. When spraying against aphids or other leaf pests, add a spoonful of washing-up liquid or soft soap.

For aphids use a tea made from stinging nettles, basil or garlic (4 crushed cloves to 1 litre/2 pints), or a strong brew of 225g/8oz rhubarb or elder leaves simmered for 30 minutes in 600ml/1 pint of water then diluted with 1 litre/2 pints cold water. To help to prevent mildew and fungus diseases use a spray of couch grass tea or a decoction made from a handful of fresh or 1 tablespoon dried horsetail, boiled for 20 minutes in 2 litres/4 pints water and left covered for a day before straining. Tea made from chamomile flowers is especially useful as a protection against the diseases of young plants and helps prevent the 'damping off' of seedlings. Wormwood tea, though effective against flea beetle, moth, caterpillars and aphids, should only be used directly on mature plants and diluted to half strength because of its toxic substances. At full strength it can be watered on open ground to discourage slugs. Fermented stinging-nettle water is a well-known control for black fly, mildew and other pests and at the same time acts as a rich fertilizer. It is made by soaking a bundle of nettles in rainwater for 3 weeks then straining the liquid and using it as a spray, or simply spreading the decomposed sludge as a healthy mulch.

Dried, aromatic herbs such as the disinfectant sage and garlic can be sprinkled around plants as a protection from lice and mildew. When planting seeds, mix them with dried and powdered aromatic herbs to repel mice, birds and slugs. So many herbs have useful properties that instead of throwing away last year's dried herbs when the new crop comes in, spread them on the herb garden.

Herbal fertilizers

To improve the quality and humus content of a barren or poor soil it is well worth growing a crop of white mustard as a green manure. Sow it broadcast, just cover the seed with fine soil and dig in the young plants as soon as the first buds appear. The rotting plants will enrich the soil and the secretions from their roots will also help to neutralize acid soils.

Herbs that are rich in various minerals and other valuable foods can be made into teas (the same recipe as for pesticides) and used in the garden. Some of the properties of these individual herbs are included in the encyclopedia, silica from horsetail, iron and nitrogen from stinging nettle, copper from dandelion and yarrow, sulphur and potassium from coltsfoot, and so on. A few lush comfrey plants will provide a rich liquid fertilizer that, among other benefits, will give the soil potash, nitrogen and phosphorus. Steep an armful of fresh comfrey leaves in rainwater for 4 weeks then use the liquid as a plant food and put the decomposed leaves on the compost heap or on tomatoes or potatoes as a fertilizer. Quick-growing comfrey leaves can be harvested at least 4 times a year.

Herbs on the compost heap

A compost heap is a necessity in every garden and a continual supply of nutritious humus, and herbs play an important part in its make-up, adding their nutrients and accelerating fermentation.

If there is an elder tree in the garden, build the heap beneath it as its leaves and root excretions will encourage fermentation. In order to convert kitchen and garden waste to a rich humus as quickly as possible, the heap needs some air, a little moisture, fresh, green organic material to heat up the heap and kill harmful weed seeds and a nutritious food for the bacteria and fungi that ferment and decay the rubbish down. This food is called the compost activator. Bio-dynamic compost activators include yarrow, chamomile, valerian, dandelion and stinging nettle. Only small quantities are necessary; lay several plants of one or a mixture of these herbs, fresh or dried, between 20cm/8in layers of composting material and occasionally sprinkle the heap with a herbal infusion.

If there is a shortage of fresh, green material in the garden, try growing a small crop of sunflowers, which will quickly provide a mass of greenery at little cost. Plant the seeds close together, pull up the plants when they are about 1m/3ft high and pile them on the compost heap. Long comfrey leaves also provide good, green composting material.

Cover the heap when it is full and the compost should be rotted down and ready to use in 6 to 8 weeks in the summer or 2 to 3 months in the winter.

Large comfrey leaves should be allowed to wilt for a day before composting.

The propagation of herbs

There is an ancient tradition that seed should be sown and seedlings transplanted during the waxing of the moon. Although the idea is often dismissed as cranky today, it appears to be based on common sense, for rain is more likely to fall at this time and, if lunar rhythms can affect not only the movements of the sea but also the movements of water in all living creatures, then it seems likely that they will have some effect on the growth of plants. Certainly the phases of the moon have guided the planting and harvesting of vegetables, corn and herbs since agriculture first began. Exact instructions vary through the centuries but the most common advice from the old herbalists is to plant aromatic herbs during the new moon and deep-rooted herbs when it is on the wane – as there is on average less rain during the waning of the moon, roots would be encouraged to grow deeper in dry soil.

Sowing seed indoors

Annual herbs that need a long growing season such as sunflowers, anise and sweet peppers, are best started indoors or in a warm greenhouse, and early crops of basil, sweet marjoram and borage can be sown indoors in the spring. If your garden is small or the seed is precious, then it is worth germinating herbs indoors in a sterile soil instead of exposing them to the hazards outside. Do not be tempted to sow the seed too early or the seedlings will outgrow their box and become weak and leggy before the weather is warm enough for them to be transplanted outside.

Wooden or well-drained plastic seed boxes are suitable for quantities of seeds, or plant 3 or 4 in a flower pot or any other suitable container, such as a yoghurt pot, with a hole punched in the bottom. Fill these about 4cm/1½in deep with bought seed compost or with sand mixed half and half with garden earth or the finely crumbled earth from molehills. Home-made mixtures should be sterilized in a hot oven for an hour.

Moisten the compost or earth thoroughly and sprinkle the seeds over it, well spaced, then cover with a fine sprinkling of earth, spray lightly with tepid water and label clearly. Cover the boxes with glass to hold in the moisture and newspaper to keep out the light – darkness will hasten germination – and put them in a warm place beside the stove or boiler or in an airing cupboard. Check them every day or two to make sure the compost is moist. As soon as the first sprouts appear, put the seed tray in a light place and when the seedlings are large enough to be handled with a little wooden spatula, prick them out into pots, a deeper seed box or peat pots filled with a more nourishing soil. Although the spores of the tiny fungi that cause the 'damping off' of seedlings are less likely to occur in sterilized earth, they may attack weakened, newly pricked out seedlings. Spray them with a weak chamomile infusion if the seedlings begin to flag or if white mould appears on the earth. Plant the sturdy young herbs outside as soon as the frosts are past and protect any that have become leggy with a cloche or windbreak for a few days until they have firmed up.

Sowing seed outside

The advantages of sowing seed outside are first that the seedlings suffer no setback by being transplanted and secondly that they do not need such constant attention. It is well worth sowing the seed of annual herbs under a plastic tunnel cloche out of doors to give them a good start and to protect the new seedlings from an unexpectedly late frost. Otherwise follow the usual procedure of outdoor planting, making sure the earth is finely raked and smoothed for the seeds and that the seedlings are thinned out in good time.

Seeds

A covering of glass will keep a moist atmosphere in the tray, encouraging the seeds to germinate. Remove as the first sprouts appear and prick out the seedlings as soon as they are large enough.

Self-seeding

Some herbs, especially some umbelliferous species, will readily self-sow. However, if the ripe seeds are merely left on the plant to fall naturally onto the surrounding soil, the dried remains of the parent plants cannot then be cleared away for fear of disturbing the germinating seeds, and the soil, which may have become exhausted from the previous crop, cannot be improved. The best answer is to gather the whole plants with their ripening seedheads, tie them into bundles with string and dangle them upside down from a pole above a prepared, well-raked bed, so the seeds fall as they ripen. This method is suitable for chervil, caraway, angelica, parsley and fennel. The annual borage, marigold, nasturtium and opium poppy and the perennial feverfew and thyme can generally be relied upon to seed themselves each year, though not always where they are wanted; borage particularly can become a pest.

Plants grown from seed, that is by sexual reproduction, are not bound to resemble their parent exactly. When perennial herbs are propagated by vegetative means – by cuttings, layerings, division etc – then the offspring are bound to be identical to their parent. This is extremely useful when growing varieties of mint, for example, which readily hybridize with each other, or special varieties of herbs that may not breed true. This method of propagation is generally easy and has quick results.

The simplest method of vegetative reproduction is by division of the roots in the early spring or autumn when the foliage is withered. This is suitable for herbaceous plants with creeping roots and stems such as the mints, tarragon, tansy and bergamot and those with bulbs, such as chives and Welsh onions for example. Dig up the whole plant, pull it gently apart and plant out each piece as soon as possible. If the roots are too closely tangled, cut through them cleanly with a sharp knife. Regular division will also prolong the healthy life of the plant.

Root division

When the foliage has died down in autumn, the roots of many perennial herbs can be divided to create new plants and to give new vigour to the parent. Dig up the roots and pull them gently apart, or use a sharp knife if necessary.

Cuttings

Soft cuttings

Shrubby herbs such as lavender, rosemary, santolina, sage and southernwood are especially suitable for propagation by cuttings. Take soft cuttings in late spring by slicing a vigorous little shoot of new growth, about 8cm/3in long, from the end of a branch with a sharp knife. Do not choose a shoot carrying buds. Strip off the lowest leaves leaving about 3 sets of leaves, press the cuttings around the edge of a pot filled with rooting compost or a light mixture of earth and sand, and firm down. Several cuttings together always do better than one alone; 4 to an average flower pot will do. Water the cuttings and set them in a shady place, among long grass or near a hedge outdoors or on a shady windowsill indoors. Keep the soil moist. Water loss from the leaves can be reduced and root growth speeded up by covering the

Soft cuttings are generally taken in the spring, though 'easy rooting' herbs can be propagated in this way throughout the summer. Take cuttings about 8cm/3in long with no buds and 3 sets of leaves and press about 4 into a pot of rooting soil. Cover with a plastic bag to speed growth.

whole pot with a roomy plastic bag. If the cuttings take, roots will develop within a few weeks and new leaves will begin to appear. The little plant should then be moved to a lighter and more spacious position and a more nutritious soil.

Cuttings from pelargoniums can be taken at any time from spring to autumn, they root so quickly and easily. Other easy-rooters such as sage will often take if soft cuttings are simply pushed into the earth in the shade of the parent bush outdoors.

Hardwood cuttings

Hardwood cuttings are taken in the autumn and may take longer to become established. Cut a woody shoot about 20cm/8in long, with a small heel to it. Push this into moist, sandy soil in a shady place and firm the soil around it well. Follow the instructions for soft cuttings and plant them in their permanent positions the following spring. Bay, myrtle and lemon verbena are suitable for hardwood cuttings.

Offsets

In some species a shoot springing from the base of the stem or the crown of the root will form its own small roots and, at the beginning or end of the summer, can be pulled carefully from the parent, planted out and kept moist for a few weeks. Angelica, lovage and comfrey are among the herbs that will produce these offsets.

Layering

Herbs suitable for layering in the late spring include clove carnation, thyme, winter savory, pennyroyal and many others whose stems form roots when kept in contact with the earth for a time. Press a portion of a long stem

Layering: Press a long stem onto the ground or a pot of earth or compost and secure it with a wire loop. Leave to root and then cut the newly formed plant from its parent.

onto the surface of the soil and hold it down with a stone or, better still, with a loop of wire. When roots have formed, cut the new plant from its parent and plant it out. If the stem is pressed into a pot of earth then the new plant can be cut and moved in its pot with the minimum of disturbance. Sometimes root development can be hastened by cutting a tiny slit in the stem.

Harvesting herbs

Superstitions surrounding the harvesting of herbs are legion and often elaborate and daunting. Many will have been originally spread by professional herb gatherers to frighten amateurs off their pitch, such as the shrieking of mandrake and peony roots as they are pulled from the ground and the blinding or subsequent death of the puller. The rituals that were associated with the collection of medicinal herbs – at night, naked, with no iron tools and so on – would make a great impression upon the mind of an apprehensive patient. St John's Day, Midsummer's Day, is often recommended in the old herbals as the day for harvesting herbs. Apart from pagan associations with the summer solstice, many species will in fact be about to flower at this time and therefore ready to harvest.

Harvesting for immediate use

When gathering small quantities of fresh herbs for immediate use in the kitchen, pick the centre tip of single-stemmed herbs such as basil, sweet marjoram and summer savory, to stimulate bushy side growths, and nip off and use the tops and flower buds of herbs such as chervil, thyme and mint. Pick the outside leaves and stalks from herbs such as parsley and lovage, leaving the crown to grow undisturbed. Gather leaves from the salad herbs purslane, salad burnet and dandelion before they become bitter and tough. This will encourage new, tender growth.

Harvesting for drying

The ideal time to harvest herbs that are to be dried and stored is on a sunny morning, immediately after the dew has evaporated and before the sun has had a chance to lessen the oil content in the leaves. Handle them as gently and as little as possible and gather small bundles at a time to prevent damage by bruising. Carry them indoors immediately, out of the sun. Do not be tempted to gather more herbs than you have space to dry at once; any delay in drying, any crushing or exposure to moist air, will reduce the properties and effectiveness of the herbs.

Details of the harvesting of individual herbs are given in the encyclopedia

These herbs harvested in early autumn include, from front to back, dill, tree onion, costmary, chervil (for seed to be sown later), red bergamot, marjoram, lemon balm, feathery tansy and yellow-flowered santolina.

Leaves and stems

Flowers

Seedheads and roots

Harvesting lavender in the old style in Spain. This will be distilled for its valuable oil.

and harvesting chart, but there are some general principles that should be borne in mind. Most aromatic herbs reach the peak of their condition just as their buds are about to burst, when the oil glands in their leaves are rich and full of flavour; these include the thymes, basils and other labiates, lady's mantle, costmary and the artemisias. Cut the perennials back by about one third, trimming and shaping them at the same time. Annuals can be cut down to about 8cm/3in above the ground. Both annuals and perennials should yield another 2 or 3 cuts before the end of the season. Take the last harvest in early autumn, so that the new growth has time to harden up before the frosts.

The flowering tops of other herbs, such as agrimony, yarrow, golden rod, meadowsweet and St John's wort, are dried together with their leaves, so gather these when the flowers are half open. Harvest lavender when the first flowers open and cut them with long stems, trimming the bushes at the same time.

When flowerheads alone are to be dried, gather them when they are well out but just before they reach maturity and handle them with particular care. Marigold, rose, mullein, German chamomile, lime and elderflower are all valuable but can be easily bruised.

Cut seedheads with stalks for easy handling, just as the seeds begin to turn brown and ripen and before they begin to fall. Apart from the culinary seeds such as dill, coriander, caraway, fennel and lovage, remember to collect the seeds of annuals to sow the following year.

Most herb roots are dug for drying in the autumn, when they are plumped out and stored with food for the winter, though the narrow rhizomes of couch grass are at their best when gathering new strength in the spring.

Harvesting Chart

Late Spring

Chervil	leaves	Ground ivy	leaves	Wood avens	root
Couch grass	rhizomes	Violet	flowers, leaves	Woodruff	leaves

Early Summer

Angelica	leaves, stems	Lemon balm	leaves	Rose	petals
Clove carnation	flowers	Lovage	leaves	Rue	leaves
Coriander	leaves	Mugwort	leaves	Southernwood	leaves
Goosegrass	leaves	Parsley	leaves	Tarragon	leaves

Midsummer

Agrimony	leaves, tops	Horehound	leaves	Nasturtium	fruits
American senna	leaves	Horsetail	whole herb	Rosemary	leaves
Basil	leaves	Hyssop	leaves, tops	Safflower	flowers
Bergamot	leaves, flowers	Lady's bedstraw	whole herb	Sage	leaves
Betony	whole herb	Lime	flowers & bracts	St John's wort	leaves, tops
Borage	leaves, flowers	Marigold	flowers	Stinging nettle	whole herb
Chamomile	flowers	Marjoram	leaves, tops	Tansy	leaves
Costmary	leaves	Marsh mallow	root	Thyme	leaves
Elder	leaves, flowers	Meadowsweet	leaves, tops	Vervain	leaves, tops
Eyebright	leaves, tops	Melilot	leaves, tops	Weld	whole herb
Feverfew	leaves	Mint	leaves	Woad	leaves
Flax	stems	Mullein	leaves, tops		

Late Summer

Anise	seeds	Golden rod	leaves, tops	Mustard	seeds
Boneset	leaves, tops	Hops	female flowers	Onions	bulbs
Caraway	seeds	Juniper	berries	Poppy	seeds
Elder	berries	Lavender	flowers	Sweet cicely	seeds
Flax	seeds	Lemon verbena	leaves		

Early Autumn

Bistort	root	Elecampane	root	Rose	fruit (hips)
Celery	seeds	Fennel	seeds, stalks	Saffron	stigmas
Coriander	seeds	Gentian	root	Savory	leaves
Cumin	seeds	Liquorice	root	Soapwort	root
Dandelion	root	Lovage	seeds	Sunflower	seeds
Dill	seeds	Orris	rhizome		

Late Autumn

Angelica	root	Chicory	root	Solomon's seal	root
Burdock	root	Horseradish	root	Valerian	root

Drying and storing herbs

Drying herbs

Herb drying is simple for those living in a warm climate. Suspended from a high, dark kitchen ceiling above the open window, herbs are thoroughly dried in a day or two. Upstairs the chamomile and lime flowers for tisanes are spread over tiled floors while a hot wind blows through the closed, slatted shutters. In a cool and damp climate more care needs to be taken, though the resulting home-dried herbs are far superior to most packeted or bottled products.

Shade, temperature and ventilation

Shade, a good current of air and some warmth are necessary for successful herb drying. Shade, because bright light will draw the oils from the leaves and cause discolouration and bleaching – the colouring substances are connected with the properties of the herb. Air must freely circulate to prevent mustiness and rotting, and warmth and air together will drive off all water contained in the herb. To preserve the characteristic flavour and essential goodness, the whole drying operation should be done as quickly as possible, the temperature being the critical factor.

The simplest method is to separate the herbs into small bunches, tie them loosely with string and hang them in a warm, shady, airy part of the house such as an attic, or in an outbuilding, a dark barn or tool shed. The bunches should hang freely, away from the wall. If a lot of herbs are to be dried in this way it may be worth putting up a line to hang them from or, better still, an old-fashioned, wooden, clothes drier that can be raised and lowered by a pulley. The disadvantages of this method are that the herbs are likely to become dusty and to take too long to dry, especially during a rainy summer.

Artificial heat

Some artificial heat will speed up drying and therefore give better results. Suspend the bunches in a well-ventilated airing cupboard or near (but not above) a boiler or kitchen range that gives off a steady heat. It is possible to dry herbs in a very cool oven with the door left ajar, a method that works especially well for rather tough herbs such as lovage and parsley, and for delicate flowers that must be quickly dried to retain their colour. Lay the herbs or flowers on cake cooling racks covered with perforated brown paper or on drying trays. The oven temperature should never exceed 90°F/30°C. Check the drying herbs regularly for overheating.

Microwave ovens

Those with microwave ovens should try experimenting with herb drying. Juicy-leaved mints and basil will take about 3 minutes to dry by microwave, and herbs such as savory, rosemary and thyme, with small, dry leaves, only about 1 minute. The colour and flavour are excellent.

Drying frames

By spreading herbs out loosely in a single layer on a drying tray, you will ensure quick, even drying. A tray can be simply made by stretching a piece of muslin or cloth netting over a wooden frame; it is possible to use perforated zinc or wire netting but contact between herbs and metal is best avoided. Stand trays in a suitable place or make a tall structure like an open-sided chest of drawers on legs, with runners for sliding drying trays in and out and room for a small greenhouse heater beneath. This compact drying cupboard set in a dark well-ventilated position will prove very efficient.

Suitability for drying

Check your herb in the encyclopedia before attempting to dry it as some species, especially among the umbellifers, are not worth the effort. The leaves of fennel, dill, sweet cicely, chervil and chives will not dry satisfactorily.

Opposite : *Herbs collected for sorting and drying in a garden shed include sage, garlic, Hamburg parsley and mint on the table; rosemary and wormwood hanging from the beam; bay, yellow tansy flowers, dill and ploughman's spikenard against the wall; and a bucket filled with garden thyme.*

Leaves and flowers

Seedheads

Herbal oil and bundles of dried medicinal herbs spread out for sale in a street market in Portugal.

Among the culinary herbs sweet marjoram, summer savory, mint, lovage and thyme are particularly useful and easy to dry.

Preparing and drying the herbs

Directly the herbs are harvested, spread them out on a table indoors and pick out any weeds and old or discoloured herb leaves. Handle them carefully and do not wash them as some of their goodness will wash away. If they are very muddy, dip them quickly in tepid water and lightly shake them dry. It is best to dry most leaves on their stalks to retain their goodness, to prevent bruising and for easy handling, though the large leaves of lovage and borage, for example, should be gently stripped from their stalks. Cut off the heads of marigolds, elderflowers and mullein and lay them carefully on the drying tray or on perforated paper. Herb leaves are properly dried when they do not bend but break immediately between the fingers. The leaves of some herbs are likely to be ready before their stems, in which case they should be stripped off and stored and the stems discarded. Flower petals should rustle like paper.

Dry seeds without artificial heat in an airy place. Hang the almost-ripe seedheads in a loose bunch, upside down over a cloth or a basket lined with paper. As the seeds ripen some will fall and the rest can be stripped from their stalks. Leave them exposed to the air for a further week or two before storing. Pods of seeds such as mustard should be hung until thoroughly brittle and dry, and the seeds then separated by threshing or picking them

over by hand. Dry heads of sunflowers whole and then separate the seeds when they are quite loose and ready to fall.

Roots

Wipe the earth from herb roots and pull off all fibrous parts. Cut marsh mallow roots and the narrow rhizomes of couch grass into sections about 4cm/1½in long, the small roots of valerian and wood avens into halves or quarters and the larger roots of angelica, sea holly and dandelion into slices. Roots need some artificial heat and may take a week or two to dry properly. They are ready when they can be snapped cleanly between the fingers.

Storing herbs

Store herbs as soon as they are thoroughly dried, especially in humid weather when moisture may be re-absorbed. It is usually convenient to strip leaves from their stems, but do not crumble them as this will lessen their aromatic properties. Put aside some complete twigs of those herbs commonly used for flavouring stews and soups, such as thyme, marjoram, tarragon and bay leaves, and store them for tying into bundles for *bouquet garni*, or to use as an aromatic bed for roasting meat or baking fish. Carefully detach marigold petals to store but leave chamomile, mullein and other flowers complete. Get rid of the little stalks and other rubbish that will be mixed with dried herb seeds by blowing them away or sieving.

Containers

Airtight glass jars are ideal for storage as the quantity and quality of the contents can be seen at a glance and, at the first sign of any condensing moisture inside, the herbs can quickly be removed and dried for a few more days. Imperfectly dried herbs will soon rot and become musty. The drawback to glass jars is that they must be kept in a dark cupboard, as the flavours and properties of herbs will deteriorate in bright light. Earthenware pots with well-fitting corks or other opaque, airtight containers will do very well away from the steams and smells of cooking. Plastic bags, tied tightly at the neck are particularly useful for large quantities of herbs, for herbs dried on the branch and for fennel stalks. Hang them in a shady place. Clearly label and date all containers and as soon as next year's harvest is in, throw the remaining contents onto the compost heap or sprinkle them around indoor pot plants.

Freezing

Most culinary herbs can be frozen satisfactorily. Pick them fresh, lightly rinse if necessary, dry thoroughly and pack in polythene bags; it is not necessary to blanch them. To avoid confusion, freeze *one* herb species at a time, putting only a few sprigs into each bag, then arranging the bags together in a clearly labelled plastic box. It is well worth freezing your favourite herb mixtures in small bags – tarragon, chervil, chives and parsley for egg or fish dishes perhaps, and marjoram, thyme and lovage for a beef casserole. Dill, parsley and chives make a good basic mixture for vegetable sauces. Chop the frozen herbs as soon as they come out of the freezer and do not attempt to use them for garnishes. The large leaves of herbs such as sweet basil can be stored singly by painting them gently all over with olive oil and freezing them between sheets of waxed paper.

'Conceits'

An alternative method is to chop single or mixed herbs and freeze them into ice cubes with water, then, as soon as they are frozen, tip the cubes into labelled plastic bags. Stir these cubes into their appropriate dishes as they cook. To make what a 17th-century writer would have described as a 'conceit', put a cordial herb such as a borage flower or salad burnet leaf into each compartment of an ice tray, fill up with water, freeze and add the decorative ice cubes to drinks.

Cooking with herbs and spices

Although countless traditions and customs surround the use of herbs and spices with certain foods there are no real rules, nor can exact quantities be given. So much depends on individual preferences. Garlic is an obvious example of a herb that some people find offensive in the smallest amounts, while others will greedily eat whole bulbs simmered in an eel sauce or pounded in aïoli. Basil is another herb that arouses strong passions. To be free to follow one's own ideas, to experiment with an unusual herb or to add a whole bundle of fennel to roasting pork rather than the recommended sprig, it is helpful to look at the ways herbs and spices are used in other countries and at other periods. The following recipes are all given their essential character by herbs and spices and suggest and demonstrate some of the infinite variations on the theme.

They begin with basic seasonings, dressings and marinades and some regional flavourings. Uncooked sauces, soups and salad dishes with their emphasis on fresh herbs are given plenty of space. There are instructions for grilling fish in the Indian fashion, in a spicy aniseed paste, for baking herrings in the Scandinavian way with cabbage, mustard, caraway and lemon thyme, and for steaming fish over bundles of sweet herbs. Meat recipes include spiced beef, pork cheese and an unusual combination of lamb, oranges and saffron that is based on a medieval English recipe but tastes like something from the Arabian Nights. Simple savoury puddings using wild herbs contrast with powerfully hot couscous and a *kitcheri* from the Middle East. Look for main-course vegetarian recipes in the sections on rice, pasta, grains and eggs. There are sweet recipes using scented herbs and flowers; flavoured butters, sugars, oils and vinegars, and traditional breads including the poppyseed Challah, dark rye bread and enriched breads flavoured with saffron and spices. For the store cupboard there are sweets, candied herbs, jellies and pickles and quantities of drinks ranging from flower syrups to herb beers, metheglin and spiced punch.

Although countless traditions surround the use of herbs and spices there are no real rules. But to be free to follow one's own ideas it is helpful to look at the ways herbs and spices are used in other countries and at other periods.

Most recipes are for *four people* unless the quantities are obviously enormous; the pit-roasted sucking pig for instance will feed at least 20 people, depending on its size. Sometimes the helpings vary according to the dish. For example there are large helpings of the pesto soup, which might be eaten in large bowls and can be a meal on its own, whereas the helpings of the fish soup with aniseed are rather smaller, as it is rich and thickly creamy. Remember to work from either metric *or* avoirdupois measures as the slight difference between them will alter the balance of the dish.

The emphasis throughout is on fresh herbs. When these are unavailable use aromatic seeds such as dill, lovage and cumin, home-dried herbs or good-quality, bought ones, such as those dried in Provence and sold on the twig. Avoid the dust-flavoured, commercially dried herbs that are sold in fancy, clear-glass bottles and may have been exposed to the light for months. Another obvious tip to remember is that any dried herbs bought in the early summer will be nine months old, so buy only small quantities and get in new supplies after harvest time. Buy spices whole when possible and grind them just before using. Those that cannot easily be ground at home, such as cloves and fenugreek, should be bought powdered.

There are no recipes here that rely for their results upon complicated kitchen gadgets. I have sometimes suggested using an electric liquidizer but have always included an alternative. I have often mentioned using a mouli-légumes – a vegetable mill – but a sieve will do instead. Good, sharp knives are the most important tools. Use a wide, straight chopper and wooden board or a semi-circular chopper in a wooden bowl for chopping herbs, and a pestle and mortar or strong bowl and the end of a rolling pin for pounding them. Most spices can be ground at home in a pepper mill, a coffee grinder or a pestle and mortar. An ordinary liquidizer will do the job well. If the blades stick, lubricate by adding either a little oil if the spices are to be fried, or cooking liquor if they are to be stewed.

Seasonings

Salts

No cook would be without salt – or a salt substitute – in the kitchen. It is a mineral rather than a spice but its flavour is one of the most important ones in cookery. Combined with herbs and spices it makes a valuable addition to the store cupboard.

There are several different types of salt: sea salt, which has the finest flavour; pure rock salt, which is sold in blocks and has a good flavour; and table salt, which runs freely because of the addition of magnesium carbonate but being overrefined, lacks flavour. Bay salt, a coarse impure salt made by evaporating sea water in the sun, is only used for preserving and as an ingredient in moist pot pourri and some herbal medicines.

Flavoured salts

You can use flavoured salts for rubbing into meat or fish before roasting or grilling, or for seasoning vegetables and sauces. Pound rock or sea salt in a mortar with aromatic seeds such as celery, fennel, lovage or cumin or mix salt with dried ground cloves of garlic.

Spiced salt

This mixture is a good basic recipe but vary the spices to suit your own taste. Mix together 500g/1lb of rock or sea salt with 30g/1oz each of ground black peppercorns and ground coriander seeds and 7g/¼oz each of ground bay leaves, ground cloves and dried basil. Store in an airtight jar.

Herbs with a salty flavour

If for some reason you are not allowed to include salt in your diet, there are some herbs with a definite salty flavour that you could try using instead. Summer savory, lovage and celery all fall into this category. They are easiest to use if dried and powdered.

Peppers

The most common of all spices. Black pepper is more pungent and aromatic than white pepper, but is less powerful and has a less acrid taste. Always grind peppercorns just before you use them as they quickly lose their strength when broken. Grind them in a mill or crush them roughly in a mortar. When black and white peppercorns are ground together in equal quantities the result is *mignonette pepper*, a speckled mixture that combines fire and pungency.

Mignonette pepper

Spiced pepper

Spiced pepper should be made up in small quantities to preserve its freshness. Use it in soups and stews or to spice a sweet batter or fruitcake. Fruit tart, especially pear tart, can be seasoned with this mixture. Combine 15g/½oz each of ground white pepper, grated nutmeg and ground mace with 7g/¼oz cayenne and store in an airtight jar.

Herb pepper

Herb pepper is a subtle seasoning with many uses. Mix together 60g/2oz mignonette pepper, 7g/¼oz each of dried and powdered garden thyme, summer or winter savory and marjoram, and a pinch of dried, powdered rosemary.

Herbs with a peppery flavour

Nasturtium, watercress and black and white mustard leaves all have a distinct peppery taste.

Spice mixtures

To draw the full flavour from spice mixtures, heat the ingredients very gently in a dry, heavy frying pan for a few minutes, stirring all the time. Then pound or grind the ingredients and store when cold in an airtight container in a dark place. Ideally, spice mixtures should be prepared just before using, but it is useful to keep some favourite mixtures stored. Make up small quantities to make sure that they do not become stale.

French spice mixture

Garam masala
Five spice powder

Chili powder

Barbecue spice mixture

Spice mixtures often characterize regional and national cooking, flavouring all types of dishes. This French recipe for instance is used in tarts and stews. Combine 45g/1½oz each of ground black and white pepper with 30g/1oz each of ground cloves, grated nutmeg, ground bay leaf and a pinch of ground ginger and mace.

Other important regional spice mixtures are *garam masala* from India, which combines cardamom, cumin, cinnamon, nutmeg and cloves; *five spice powder* from China, which is a mixture of star anise, pepper, fennel seed, cloves and cinnamon; and Mexican *chili powder*, made up of powdered chili and red pepper – cayenne and paprika – cumin, cloves, marjoram and garlic. With added sugar this becomes a *barbecue spice mixture*.

Sweet spices

The sweet spices include nutmeg, cinnamon, cloves, ginger, cardamom, aniseed, vanilla and allspice. This basic mixture is delicious used in cakes, biscuits, puddings and pies. Combine 30g/1oz grated nutmeg with 15g/½oz each of ground cloves, ground ginger, ground allspice, ground cinnamon and a pinch of black pepper.

Fresh or dried herbs can be combined in many different ways.

Fines herbes

Fines herbes are generally used in egg dishes, especially omelettes, and are also good with white fish. Mix 30g/1oz each of chopped parsley and chervil, 15g/½oz chopped chives and a few chopped tarragon leaves.

Herb mixtures

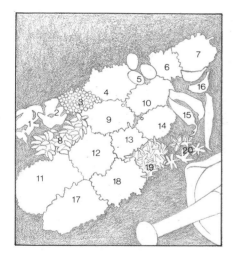

Although sharing some ingredients these regional spice mixtures have very different flavours. French spice mixture: 1 mace 2 ginger 3 white pepper 4 black pepper 5 nutmeg 6 dried bay 7 cloves. Garam masala: 8 green cardamom pods 9 ground cloves and nutmeg 10 ground cumin and cinnamon. Chili powder: 11 dried marjoram 12 ground cumin 13 cloves 14 paprika 15 chilies 16 garlic. Five spice powder: 17 ground cloves and cinnamon 18 black pepper 19 fennel seed 20 star anise.

Mustards

English mustard

Dijon mustard

Bordeaux and German mustards

Moutarde de Meaux

Brown and white mustard seeds are grown separately and the pods reaped and dried before the seeds are mixed and ground to make commercial mustard.

Opposite: *On the left is a bag containing brown mustard seed for sowing, with a field of brown mustard in full bloom behind, the bags on the right contain mixed brown and white seeds and finely ground mustard flour.*

Bouquet garni

There are endless variations of *bouquet garni*. A good basic mixture is a bunch of parsley stalks, 2 sprigs of thyme, 2 sprigs of marjoram and 1 bay leaf. For fish you can add a dry fennel stalk, a twist of finely pared lemon peel and a sprig of lemon thyme. Add a bruised garlic clove and twist of orange peel if you are cooking beef, a sprig of juniper for pork, and a stalk of melilot for rabbit.

The 3 types of mustard seed, black, brown and white, are usually blended in bought mustard. Black mustard seed has the hottest, richest, most pungent flavour and contains more oil than white mustard seed. It is often replaced today by the brown mustard seed, *Brassica juncea*, which is slightly less pungent but easier to harvest. White mustard seed has a more bitter, acrid taste and strong preservative qualities. It is often included in mixtures of pickling spices.

The powerfully hot and penetrating mustard oil is only formed when the seeds are moistened, which explains why dry mustard can be ground to a flour and stored for a long time without losing its strength. The way to reduce mustard seed to fine flour was only discovered in the mid-18th century; before that the seed was pounded as needed in a mustard quern, or the pounded seed was mixed with honey, vinegar and spices and formed into balls that could be stored until needed. John Evelyn's instructions in the *Discourse of Sallets*, written in 1699, are: 'Take the mustard seed, and grind one and a half pints of it with honey and Spanish oil and make it into a liquid sauce with vinegar.'

Dry English mustard is a combination of ground black and white mustard seed and a little wheat flour coloured with turmeric. Mix it to a paste with cold water or vinegar 5 minutes before it is needed. This is often served with roast and cold meat. Among the many French mustards, pale Dijon mustard, made of predominantly black mustard seed with the dark husk removed, white wine and spices, is useful for sauces and dressings and does not discolour them. Bordeaux and German mustards are darker as the seed retains its husk, and they are usually mixed with vinegar, sugar, spices and herbs, especially tarragon. Serve with hot meats and sausages, herring and mackerel. Nowadays it is also possible to get aromatic table mustards, such as the French *Moutarde de Meaux*, which are made of very coarsely ground seed mixed with vinegar and spices. These can be used with a variety of dishes.

Herb mustards

To make herb mustard, pound 30g/1oz black mustard seeds, 30g/1oz white mustard seeds, $\frac{1}{4}$ teaspoon herb pepper (page 160), $\frac{1}{4}$ teaspoon salt and $\frac{1}{4}$ teaspoon dried orange and lemon peel together in a mortar. Mix to a thick consistency with 1 teaspoon honey and herb vinegar (page 165) or crabapple juice. Add a pinch of turmeric and store in corked jars.

An interesting flavoured mustard can easily be made by adding finely chopped tarragon or other herbs to mustard powder and herb vinegar. This should be eaten within a few hours of preparation.

Marinades

Aromatic herbs and spices are an important part of any marinade, as they both flavour and preserve the food. But the principal ingredient is a sharp, acidic liquid – such as wine, vinegar, lemon or lime juice or yoghurt – which tenderizes and breaks down the fibres of meat and fish. Oil is often added to carry the flavourings and to provide lubrication. A large fish or joint of meat can be marinated for as long as 5 days. Leave smaller fish or chopped meat overnight, and minced meat for only an hour or two. Marinating will help to preserve the meat or fish in hot weather.

Once the meat or fish has been removed, strain the marinade and use it later for basting the roast or grilled meat or fish, as a basis for a sauce, or as a cooking liquor or stock for pot roasts and stews. The quantities given here are sufficient to marinate enough fish or meat for 4 people.

A cooked marinade need not be so highly spiced as an uncooked one because cooking will draw out the full flavour.

An uncooked marinade can consist of very simple ingredients. A tablespoon of vinegar with salt, garlic and a few sprigs of thyme, for example, will improve tough or tasteless meat.

In the following recipes the ingredients are simply mixed together and the meat or fish thoroughly steeped in the liquid.

Marinating times

Cooked marinades

Uncooked marinades

Basic cooked marinade

300ml/½ pint red wine
2 sliced carrots
2 sliced shallots
3 bruised garlic cloves
10 black peppercorns
1 teaspoon salt

Simmer all the ingredients for 15 minutes and allow to cool before using. For lamb, bruised rosemary leaves can be added. For game, substitute port for the wine and add a few crushed juniper berries. For fish, add bruised fennel or celery seeds and use white wine. A few leaves of dried melilot give a slightly bitter, hay-scented flavour to pork.

Basic uncooked marinade

150ml/¼ pint red wine
75ml/⅛ pint oil
1 small chopped onion
a small bunch of parsley stalks and fresh
 sprigs of thyme
1 bay leaf
7 crushed coriander seeds
3 crushed allspice berries
1 crushed garlic clove
½ teaspoon salt

This marinade is good with all types of meat.

Marinade for fish

75ml/⅛ pint lemon or lime juice
a handful of pounded fresh coriander
 leaves
1 crushed garlic clove
½ teaspoon cumin seeds
½ teaspoon paprika
salt to taste

This Moroccan recipe is good with most types of fish, particularly if you want to grill or barbecue them.

Marinade for chicken

300ml/½ pint plain yoghurt
1 crushed garlic clove
1 teaspoon crushed aniseed
6 crushed black peppercorns
1 crushed cardamom pod
salt to taste

This is an Indian marinade and gives a delicious flavour to what is all too often a bland and tasteless meat.

Marinade for kebabs

150ml/¼ pint olive oil
juice of 1 lemon
1 thinly sliced onion
black pepper and salt to taste

You can steep both meat and vegetables in this Greek marinade.

Marinade for beef

300ml/½ pint buttermilk
2 thinly sliced shallots
5 crushed black peppercorns
1 bay leaf
1 fresh sprig of thyme
2 cloves
a pinch of grated nutmeg

A German marinade that adds a rich flavour to stews.

Chinese marinade

4 tablespoons soy sauce
1 chopped, crushed garlic clove
1 teaspoon sugar

Steep very thin slices of beef in the marinade for an hour then toss quickly in hot oil.

Mexican marinade

2 seeded chilies
2 peeled garlic cloves
4 peppercorns
¼ teaspoon thyme
¼ teaspoon cumin seed
a pinch of ground cloves
1 teaspoon salt
75ml/⅛ pint white-wine vinegar

Pound the dry ingredients together then mix in the vinegar, or liquidize all together. Most suitable for pork.

Oils, vinegars and dressings

Herb oils

The oil to be flavoured should not have a very pronounced taste. Mild olive oils or good quality sunflower or safflower oils are most suitable.

Lightly bruise a bunch of aromatic herbs and loosely fill a glass jar. Cover the herbs with oil. Tie perforated paper or muslin over the mouth of the jar and set it on a sunny windowsill or by a warm stove. Avoid too hot a position or the herbs will turn musty and begin to cook. Shake the jar or stir the contents with a wooden spoon at least once a day. Within a fortnight the rich oils will have been drawn out of the herbs by the heat and into the surrounding mild oil. Strain the oil, pressing the herbs to extract all liquid. Taste the oil: if the flavour is not strong enough, repeat the process with fresh herbs. When the oil is well flavoured, pour it into clean dry bottles, stopper well and label.

Use the aromatic oil in dressings and marinades and for basting grilled and roasted meat and fish. It will add subtle, rich flavours to the food.

Culinary herbs that are suitable for flavouring oils are thyme, marjoram, rosemary, fennel, tarragon, savory and, especially, basil, whose flavour is lessened by drying but preserved well in oil.

Herb vinegars

The flavours of herbs are absorbed by vinegar in 2 or 3 weeks. Use good-quality wine or cider vinegar and immerse the herbs in it, in a tightly stoppered glass jar or bottle. Strain off the herbs when the vinegar is well flavoured, pressing all their juices through the sieve, and pour the vinegar into clean dry bottles, which should be clearly labelled. Do not use a bottle with a metal cap, as the vinegar will react against it and turn black.

Use the vinegar in dressings, mayonnaise, marinades, stews, soups and gravies. Lemon thyme vinegar adds a subtle flavour to mayonnaise, dill vinegar sharpens a dish of fresh red or white cabbage, tarragon vinegar heightens cold chicken salads or hot gravy.

Suitable herbs are thyme, marjoram, basil, chervil, mint, savory, tarragon, dill (using unripe seed heads with the leaves), fennel, salad burnet, nasturtium (buds, flowers and unripe seeds), shredded horseradish, garlic (bruised) and shallots (chopped). Purple-basil vinegar is particularly delicious.

Flower vinegars

Flower vinegars are occasionally used in cookery as light-scented flavourings for fruit or cream dishes. The flowers can be left in the vinegar and used for garnishing winter salads. These include violets, clove carnations, rose petals and elderflowers.

Spiced vinegar

1 litre/1¾ pints wine or good malt vinegar
10 cloves
1 cinnamon stick
24 peppercorns
1 bay leaf
1 tablespoon white mustard seeds
a small piece of root ginger, bruised
2 mace blades
1 tablespoon dried chili
15 allspice berries

Steep the spices in the vinegar in a stoppered glass jar or bottle for 1 to 2 months, shaking occasionally. Strain and re-bottle the spiced vinegar.

If the vinegar is needed quickly put it in a covered bowl with the spices and put the bowl over a saucepan of cold water. Slowly bring the water to the boil, then remove the bowl to a warm place and leave it, still covered, for several hours. Strain and bottle when cold.

The spices given in this recipe are a good basic blend but can be altered to suit requirements. Use the vinegar to pickle eggs, red cabbage, onions and gherkins or in chutneys.

Spiced lemon vinegar

6 quartered lemons
2.4 litres/4 pints wine vinegar
50g/2oz allspice berries
50g/2oz white mustard seeds
50g/2oz black peppercorns
50g/2oz grated horseradish
1 mace blade
6 cloves
75g/3oz natural salt

Pour the vinegar over the spices in a pan and bring slowly to the boil. Rub the lemons with the salt and put them into a stone jar or deep bowl. Pour the boiling vinegar and spices over them, cover with a cloth and leave for 4 days. Strain into a clean dry bottle, pressing the juice from the lemons, and stopper lightly.

Use as a marinade ingredient or mixed with oil as a dressing for pork and potato salad.

Vinaigrette dressings

Mayonnaises

Avocado mayonnaise

Apple mayonnaise

Sweet elderberry vinegar

1.5kg/3lb elderberries
1.5 litres/3 pints wine vinegar
soft brown sugar

Crush the elderberries in a stone jar or deep bowl. Pour the vinegar over them, cover with a cloth and leave for 5 to 10 days, stirring occasionally with a wooden spoon. Strain off the liquid and discard the fruit. Add 350g/12oz sugar to each 600ml/1 pint of vinegar and stir to dissolve over a low heat. Boil rapidly for 10 minutes, removing any scum. Pour into hot bottles and seal.

Fruit vinegars can be made with other soft fruits such as blackcurrants or raspberries, following the above recipe. Diluted with hot water and sweetened with honey they are an excellent remedy for coughs and colds or a warming winter drink. A spoonful will flavour the fruit filling for steamed puddings or sweet pies.

The simplest cold sauce is a vinaigrette, usually made with a base of 5 parts of oil to 1 of vinegar, seasoned with lemon juice, salt and pepper. Herb flavours can be added by using herb oils and vinegars (page 165), such as green basil oil, which will transform a tomato and onion salad, or tarragon vinegar for a light chicken and potato salad, or use fresh herbs pulped or finely chopped. There are any number of variations – add mustard and a pinch of sugar, a teaspoonful of yoghurt, soured cream or crumbled blue cheese, or steep a bruised garlic clove or slice of onion in the dressing.

Flavour a thick, richly yellow mayonnaise with fresh herbs or spices just before serving – chives or dill for potato salad, grated horseradish and chopped walnuts for smoked or salted meat or fish, paprika or finely ground curry spices for hard-boiled eggs, or a few crushed green peppercorns for beef. Avocado mayonnaise – made by mashing a ripe avocado pear with salt, pepper, paprika and lemon juice before stirring in the mayonnaise – is delicious with crabs, prawns, lobster or mixed with rice as a bed for shell fish. In Sweden a stiff, unsweetened apple purée is stirred into mayonnaise and eaten with duck, goose or pork. To thin down mayonnaise add a little milk; to lighten it fold in a stiffly beaten egg white at the last moment or make the mayonnaise in a liquidizer using whole eggs instead of the yolks alone. If the mayonnaise is to keep for several days, stir a few spoonfuls of very hot water into the finished sauce and store in a cool larder rather than in the refrigerator.

Mustard and dill dressing

1 teaspoon French mustard
1 tablespoon finely chopped, fresh dill leaves
5 tablespoons olive oil
1 tablespoon wine vinegar
a pinch of sugar
salt and pepper

Put all the ingredients in a screwtop jar and shake well. Use to dress herrings or beetroot salad.

Ravigote dressing

5 tablespoons olive oil
1 tablespoon wine vinegar
1 tablespoon capers
½ teaspoon mustard
1 tablespoon finely chopped parsley
1 tablespoon finely chopped chives
salt and pepper

Mix thoroughly together. Use to dress boiled beef or fish or salads of dried pulses – lentils, chick peas or haricot beans.

Mayonnaise

3 egg yolks
salt
300-450ml/½-¾ pint olive oil or other good quality oil
lemon juice or vinegar

Beat the egg yolks and a pinch of salt for several minutes with a wooden spoon. Add the oil, drop by drop, beating constantly. When a quarter of the oil has been added, the rest can be poured in in a thin stream. When the mixture is thick, smooth and shining add lemon juice or vinegar and any other seasoning to taste.

Aïoli (garlic mayonnaise)

8 garlic cloves
3 egg yolks
salt
300ml/½ pint oil
squeeze of lemon juice

Pound the garlic well before adding egg yolks and salt and continue as for mayonnaise. Aïoli can be served with Mediterranean fish soup (page 173).

Sauce rémoulade

1 hard-boiled egg yolk
4 tablespoons light olive or sunflower oil
1 teaspoon white-wine vinegar
1 teaspoon lemon juice
1 minced shallot
1 large bunch of equal quantities of watercress, parsley and fresh chervil, finely chopped
1 small bunch of fresh chives and tarragon, finely chopped
1 crushed garlic clove
a pinch of sugar
salt and pepper

Sieve the egg yolk and beat in the oil gradually. Add the vinegar and lemon juice and continue beating until smooth. Stir in the remaining ingredients and season to taste.

This is not such a substantial mayonnaise and is a good accompaniment to fried fish and cold meat.

Tartare sauce

2 hard-boiled eggs
salt and pepper
mayonnaise made with 300ml/½ pint oil
1 teaspoon grated lemon peel
1 tablespoon finely chopped parsley
1 tablespoon mixed finely chopped fennel, tarragon and chives
1 small, finely chopped shallot
1 tablespoon capers
1 tablespoon finely chopped pickled gherkins
lemon juice

Beat the boiled egg yolks, salt and pepper to a paste with a wooden spoon, then mix in the chopped egg whites, mayonnaise and all remaining ingredients. Season with a little lemon juice if necessary.

One of the best sauces for fried fish, this can also be made with a vinaigrette base.

Green mayonnaise

1 bunch of parsley
1 bunch of watercress
6 large spinach leaves
4 large sorrel leaves
3 fresh sprigs of tarragon
mayonnaise made with 300ml/½ pint oil

Blanch the herbs for 2 minutes in boiling water. (A wire salad basket or chip basket can be used for this.) Plunge the herbs immediately into cold water, shake well and pat dry in a clean cloth. Pound them in a mortar, then put through a sieve or mouli-légumes. Stir into the mayonnaise just before serving and taste for seasoning.

Add finely chopped gherkins, capers, shallots and fennel to a basic mayonnaise and flavour with mustard, to make an excellent sauce for fish.

Sauces

None of the fresh flavour of herbs is lost in an uncooked sauce. All of these will keep for a week in the refrigerator. They can be stirred into pasta or rice, into cooked vegetable salads, or served as an accompaniment to hard-boiled eggs, cold fish or meat.

Uncooked sauces

Pesto (basil) sauce

75g/3oz fresh basil leaves
2 garlic cloves
salt
75g/3oz grated Parmesan cheese
about 4 tablespoons olive oil
25g/1oz pine nuts or grated walnuts (optional)

Pound the basil, garlic and salt to a pulp. Stir in the cheese. Add the oil drop by drop, stirring all the time with a wooden spoon. If using the nuts, pound them with the basil. Stir into pasta or minestrone soup just before serving.

A green sauce for vegetables

25g/1oz crustless bread
1 tablespoon wine vinegar
3 sticks of celery
1 small bunch of parsley
1 garlic clove
4 tablespoons olive oil
salt and pepper

Soak the bread for 5 minutes in the vinegar. Pound the stems and leaves of the celery to a pulp with the parsley and garlic. Stir in the soaked bread, then gradually add the oil, beating with a wooden spoon. Season to taste.

This sauce is particularly good with hot or cold root vegetables.

A green sauce for freshwater fish

1 bunch of fresh mint (Bowles, apple or spearmint)
1 small bunch of fresh chervil
1 grated shallot
1 teaspoon capers
2 anchovy fillets
25g/1oz crustless bread
1 tablespoon vinegar (from capers)

Pound the herbs to a pulp. Add the shallot, capers and anchovies and pound again. Soak the bread for a few minutes in the vinegar and stir into the mixture.

Red chili sauce

1 fresh red chili
2 tomatoes
1 small red pepper
4 unpeeled garlic cloves
$\frac{1}{4}$ teaspoon paprika
4 tablespoons olive oil
2 teaspoons wine vinegar
salt

Put the tomatoes, pepper, chili and garlic into the oven or under the grill for a few minutes to soften. Peel the garlic and discard the seeds of the pepper and chili. Chop and pound them all together in a mortar. Add paprika (and cayenne if a hotter sauce is needed). Stir in the oil, vinegar and add salt to taste. Put through a coarse sieve and serve with hard-boiled eggs, pork, mackerel fillets or other fish.

Cooked sauces

Parsley sauce

Mint and fennel sauce

Dill sauce

Herbs and white sauce

Chopped herbs can be added to a basic white sauce made with 25g/1oz butter, 1 heaped tablespoon flour and 300ml/$\frac{1}{2}$ pint milk. For *parsley sauce*, a traditional accompaniment to boiled ham or fish, add 50g/2oz finely chopped parsley during the last few minutes of cooking; for *mint and fennel sauce*, to go with fish, chicken or vegetables, add 25g/1oz each of fresh mint and fennel; and for *dill sauce*, delicious with cabbage or potatoes, add 50g/2oz finely chopped leaves or, in winter, 1 teaspoon of crushed seeds. Substitute 2 tablespoons of soured cream for some of the milk, and stir into dill sauce off the heat just before serving.

Bearnaise sauce

75ml/$\frac{1}{8}$ pint mixed white wine and wine vinegar – tarragon vinegar if possible (page 165)
1 tablespoon chopped shallot
1 tablespoon chopped chervil
1 teaspoon chopped tarragon
salt and pepper
175g/6oz softened butter
3 egg yolks, thoroughly beaten

a few whole tarragon leaves
lemon juice
a pinch of cayenne pepper

Boil together rapidly the wine and vinegar, shallot, chopped herbs, salt and pepper until reduced by two thirds, then allow to cool to lukewarm and strain. The sauce is now thickened with egg yolks so the remainder of the cooking must be done over a very low heat or, to be safe, over a pan of barely simmering water. Gradually drop small pieces of the softened butter into the strained liquor, and when these have melted, add the egg yolks slowly, stirring constantly until the sauce thickens. Remove from the heat, stir in the tarragon leaves and season with lemon juice and cayenne.

Butter sauce

This is the simplest fresh herb sauce.

100g/4oz butter

50g/2oz finely chopped or pounded fresh herbs

1 tablespoon thick cream

salt and pepper

Melt the butter until it foams. Remove from the heat before it changes colour. Stir in the herbs and cream and season lightly. Serve this light sauce with summer vegetables or fish.

Tomato and basil sauce

500g/1lb roughly chopped tomatoes

3 fresh sprigs of basil, torn in pieces

salt

a pinch of sugar

Heat the tomatoes with a little salt in a covered pan over a low heat for about 5 minutes, to soften. Put through a sieve or mouli-légumes and return to the pan to warm through with the basil and sugar. This is a summer sauce suitable for pasta or rice.

Chervil sauce

1 bunch of chopped fresh chervil

50g/2oz butter

15g/½oz flour

1 chopped spring onion

½ teaspoon grated lemon peel

300ml/½ pint cream

lemon juice

salt and pepper

Cream the butter with the flour in a heatproof bowl over a pan of hot water or in the top of a double saucepan. Stir in the chervil, onion, peel and cream and keep stirring over the heat for 15 minutes or until smooth and slightly thickened. Season to taste with lemon juice and a little salt and pepper.

Chervil is an ingredient in many traditional Lenten dishes, used as a tonic to cleanse the blood. This sauce is a good accompaniment to poached fish or lightly boiled chicken.

Herb sauce

4 fresh sprigs of marjoram

4 fresh sprigs of thyme

1 bunch of fresh chervil

2 fresh sprigs of tarragon

2 peeled shallots

4 white peppercorns

300ml/½ pint light chicken stock

25g/1oz butter

15g/½oz flour

lemon juice

salt

Pound the marjoram, thyme, the stalks from the chervil and tarragon (reserving the leaves), the shallots and peppercorns in a mortar. Bring the chicken stock to the boil, add the pounded herbs and simmer for 15 minutes. In another pan melt the butter, then stir in the flour until it forms a smooth paste. Gradually strain in the stock, stirring constantly, and simmer, still stirring, until smooth and slightly thickened. Simmer for 10 minutes. Remove from the heat and add the chopped chervil and tarragon leaves, then lemon juice and salt to taste. Serve with grilled chicken or veal.

Garlic sauce

6 garlic cloves

50g/2oz butter

150ml/¼ pint light stock

salt

Pound the garlic to a smooth pulp. Beat in the butter with a wooden spoon. Bring the stock to the boil and whisk in the garlic butter. Add salt to taste and serve immediately with grilled lamb chops or steak.

Mushroom sauce

100g/4oz chopped mushrooms

300ml/½ pint milk

a pinch of grated nutmeg

salt and pepper

40g/1½oz butter

½ bruised and chopped garlic clove

1 tablespoon flour

2 teaspoons finely chopped parsley

Simmer the mushrooms in the milk with a little nutmeg and seasoning for about 10 minutes, keeping the pan covered. Melt the butter in another pan, add the garlic and stew for a minute, then stir in the flour and cook for a few minutes longer. Strain in the milk from the mushroom pan little by little, stirring all the time. When the sauce is cooked through, tip in the mushrooms and parsley and check the seasoning. Serve with strips of ham, large-grain Italian rice and a crisp salad.

By doubling the quantities of mushrooms, the sauce can be eaten as a light supper dish, spread on toast and browned under the grill. For a richer sauce, use less milk and stir in cream before serving.

Cumberland sauce

½ an orange (Seville or blood orange if possible)

½ a lemon

1 teaspoon finely chopped shallot

3 tablespoons redcurrant jelly

75ml/⅛ pint port

1 scant teaspoon French mustard (Dijon is good)

a pinch of cayenne pepper

a pinch of ground ginger

salt and pepper

Peel the orange and lemon halves thinly, discarding all white pith, and slice the peel into very fine strips. Put into a small pan of cold water with the shallot, bring to the boil for a minute to blanch then drain well. Slowly melt the jelly in a heavy pan and stir in all the ingredients and the juice from the orange and lemon. Simmer for a few minutes until slightly reduced and season with salt and pepper.

This is traditionally served with venison and goes well with other game and with smoked ham.

Hors d'oeuvre

The flavours of an hors d'oeuvre should be distinct – fresh, spicy, salty or sharp – to stimulate the appetite. The scent and appearance of the dish are important too. In Classical times bundles of mint would be rubbed over tables before a banquet so that the scent would 'stir up . . . a greedy desire of meat'. Cumin seed, warmed in a dry pan to draw out scent and flavour, is a favourite appetizer and digestive in the Middle East.

The following recipes all make a good beginning to a meal but here are some other ideas based on recipes given in other sections: a bowl of green mayonnaise (page 167) with fresh, raw vegetables; hard-boiled eggs with cumin (page 180); chili sauce (page 168) with chilled mackerel; potted meats and pickled mushrooms (page 212). Simply presented, with fresh flavours and contrasting colours, one or two of these dishes are preferable to an array of elaborate concoctions.

Hard-boiled eggs and sorrel

4 chopped hard-boiled eggs
12 large sorrel leaves
100g/4oz butter
salt and pepper

Melt the butter, add the sorrel leaves and simmer gently until tender, without allowing the butter to brown. Take off the heat and mix in the eggs and seasoning. The mixture can either be roughly mashed with a wooden spoon, liquidized or sieved if a smoother paste is wanted. Press into 4 individual pots and chill for 1 to 2 hours. Serve with hot thin toast.

Tapenade

20 stoned black olives
6 anchovy fillets
2 tablespoons capers
2 hard-boiled egg yolks
1 small tin of tuna fish
a pinch of ground bay leaf
1 teaspoon thyme leaves
5 tablespoons olive oil
lemon juice
rum (optional)
pepper

Pound the olives, anchovies, capers, egg yolks, tuna, bay leaf and thyme thoroughly in a mortar. Pour in the oil gradually, beating with a wooden spoon. Season with lemon juice, rum, if available, and pepper. Press into little pots and leave for at least 1 hour in a cool place. Serve with coarse brown bread.

Garlic salted nuts

225g/8oz cashews, almonds or hazelnuts
1 large, bruised garlic clove
3 tablespoons olive oil
1 heaped teaspoon sea salt

Steep the garlic in the oil for 1 hour. Remove the garlic and mix the oil with the nuts and salt until the nuts are glistening. Roast in a slow oven, 150°C/300°F/Mark 2, until the nuts are golden and crisp.

Spiced scallops

4 scallops
6 tablespoons dry white wine or water
1 teaspoon lemon juice
¼ teaspoon ground allspice
¼ teaspoon ground ginger
white pepper and salt
75g/3oz breadcrumbs
25g/1oz butter

Poach the white flesh from the scallops for 5 minutes in the wine or water and lemon juice. Drain, reserving the cooking liquor. Slice the scallops and dust each piece with allspice, ginger, pepper and salt. Butter the scrubbed scallop shells or little ovenproof dishes, sprinkle with half the breadcrumbs and put in the scallop slices. Chop the corals over the slices, dot with the butter and remaining breadcrumbs and add 1 tablespoon of the cooking liquor to each shell or dish. Bake for about 10 minutes in a moderately hot oven, 200°C/400°F/Mark 6.

Hummus and mint

225g/8oz cooked chick peas
225ml/8fl oz plain yoghurt
2 tablespoons olive oil
2 tablespoons chopped mint
¼ teaspoon ground cumin
a squeeze of lemon juice
salt and pepper

Either purée the ingredients through a sieve or mouli-légumes or blend in a liquidizer. Serve cold, garnished with a sprig of mint, with warm Greek bread and olives.

Green olives with coriander

100g/4oz stoned green olives
12 coriander seeds
olive oil
1 bay leaf
3 sprigs of garden thyme
pepper

Crush the coriander seeds in a mortar. Add the olives and lightly crush. Moisten with olive oil, stir in the herbs and season with ground black pepper. Leave in a cool place for about 1 hour for the flavours to amalgamate.

Soups

Soup is the most basic of foods and can vary infinitely, from light, pale and pretty summer soups flavoured and garnished with fresh herbs, to the thick, rich and spicy soups of winter, scattered with cheese or swimming with herb dumplings (page 199) and accompanied by hot, aromatic seed bread (page 200). Try adding juniper berries to onion soup, thyme and orange juice to carrot soup and thin slivers of fresh ginger to Danish apple soup.

Chilled cucumber and dill soup

1 peeled, coarsely chopped cucumber
2 tablespoons chopped dill leaves
8 chopped spring onions
2 tablespoons lemon juice
150ml/¼ pint single cream
salt and pepper
iced water
3 or 4 small pickled gherkins

Liquidize together the cucumber, spring onions and lemon juice, reserving 1 tablespoon of the onions for garnishing. If you do not possess a liquidizer, grate the peeled cucumber and mix with the lemon and spring onions. Stir in the cream and dill leaves, season to taste and add iced water as necessary to reach a pouring consistency. Chill and serve garnished with thinly sliced gherkins and spring onions.

Chilled yoghurt and fennel soup

600ml/1 pint plain yoghurt
75g/3oz grated fennel bulb or 1 bunch of finely chopped fresh fennel leaves
3 skinned, sieved tomatoes
salt and pepper to taste
chopped hard-boiled egg or chopped shelled prawns

Mix together all the ingredients and dilute to the right consistency, if necessary, with a little iced water. Garnish with the egg and prawns and serve chilled.

Green gazpacho

225g/8oz skinned, chopped tomatoes
1 seeded, diced cucumber
1 seeded, chopped green pepper
4 sliced spring onions
2 chopped, crushed garlic cloves
2 tablespoons olive oil
1 tablespoon wine vinegar
12 stoned, chopped green olives
1 heaped tablespoon chopped parsley
1 tablespoon chopped fresh mint
2 chopped fresh sprigs of lemon thyme
1 tablespoon chopped walnuts (optional)
salt and pepper to taste

Mix together all the ingredients and chill. Dilute just before serving with 600ml/1 pint iced water and stir in a few pieces of crushed ice. Serve with coarse brown bread.

Iced borsch

4 beetroots
1 litre/1¾ pints beef stock
1 unpeeled onion, stuck with 1 clove
1 chopped carrot
1 chopped stick of celery
1 small bunch of parsley and fresh dill
1 teaspoon caraway seeds
lemon juice
salt and pepper
2 tablespoons finely chopped fresh dill, chives and tarragon
4 tablespoons soured cream

Roughly chop 3 of the beetroots and simmer in the stock with the onion, carrot, celery, bunch of herbs and caraway seeds for 1 hour. Strain, pressing the vegetables to extract all the juices. Bring the liquid to the boil again and add the fourth beetroot, peeled and finely grated. Simmer for 10 minutes, then allow to cool. Season with lemon juice, salt and pepper. Serve very cold, scattered with the chopped herbs and with the soured cream served separately.

Beef and pepper soup

250g/½lb beef, chopped small
1 sliced red pepper
1 sliced onion
1 tablespoon of oil or dripping
2 tablespoons tomato purée
1½ tablespoons paprika
1 tablespoon caraway seeds
25g/1oz flour
salt and pepper
1.5 litres/2¾ pints hot beef stock or water mixed with red wine
2 tablespoons chopped parsley or caraway leaves
grated rind of 1 lemon
2 crushed garlic cloves
4 tablespoons soured cream

Soften the pepper and onion in the oil or dripping for 5 minutes. Add the beef and stir for a few minutes until lightly browned. Mix in the tomato purée, paprika, caraway seeds, flour and a light seasoning. Cook, stirring, for 10 minutes. Add the hot stock or water and wine, bring to the boil. Cover and simmer for an hour or until the meat is tender. Add the caraway or parsley, lemon rind and garlic just before serving, and stir the soured cream into each bowl at the table.

Sorrel soup

2 handfuls of finely chopped sorrel leaves
50g/2oz butter
1.5 litres/2¾ pints light stock
2 egg yolks
salt and pepper

Melt the butter in a pan and stew the sorrel gently over a low heat for 5 minutes. Do not allow the butter to brown. Add the stock and bring to the boil, clearing any scum from the surface. Season. Beat the egg yolks thoroughly in a serving bowl then pour the boiling soup over them, whisking with a fork. Serve immediately with hot crusty bread and a bland cheese.

Pesto soup

4 tablespoons of pesto sauce (page 168)
oil or dripping
4 finely sliced leeks
1 sliced onion
4 skinned, chopped tomatoes
1 crushed garlic clove
1 handful of chopped green herbs such as
  parsley or caraway leaves
salt and pepper
225g/½lb sliced French beans
4 sliced courgettes
a few shredded cabbage leaves or chopped
  cauliflower pieces
1.75 litres/3 pints light stock or water
75g/3oz pasta – noodles or vermicelli
75g/3oz cooked haricot beans
100g/4oz grated Parmesan cheese

Warm a little oil or dripping in a heavy pan. Add the leeks, onion, tomatoes, garlic, herbs and seasoning. Stew gently for 15 minutes. Stir in the French beans, courgettes, cauliflower or cabbage and cover with boiling water or stock. After a few minutes add the pasta and haricot beans. When the pasta is cooked take the soup off the heat and stir in the pesto sauce. Serve the Parmesan separately.

Without the addition of pesto sauce with its powerful basil flavour, this recipe makes a good minestrone soup. Serve thickly scattered with chopped fresh herbs such as mint, chervil, tarragon and summer savory and liberally sprinkled with Parmesan cheese.

Summer garden soup

1.75 litres/3 pints light stock or water
1 sliced head of chicory
5 large torn sorrel leaves
1 sliced lettuce heart
100g/4oz sliced mushrooms (purple
  wood blewits if available)
100g/4oz shelled peas
1 teaspoon fresh or dried lemon thyme
  leaves
lemon juice
salt and pepper
chopped fresh chervil to garnish

Bring the stock to a rolling boil in a large pan. Add all the remaining ingredients, a light seasoning and a squeeze or two of lemon juice. Cook until the peas are tender – about 5 minutes. Garnish with chervil and serve immediately.

Lovage soup

1 bunch of chopped fresh lovage leaves
  and stems
75g/3oz butter
1 chopped garlic clove
1 handful roughly chopped parsley
2 chopped sticks of celery
grated nutmeg
salt and pepper
50g/2oz brown bread
1.5 litres/2¾ pints of meat or vegetable
  stock
150ml/¼ pint of double cream

Melt the butter in a pan and gently stew the garlic, parsley, celery and a pinch each of nutmeg, salt and pepper. After a few minutes add the chopped lovage. Soak the bread in a little stock for 2 minutes then squeeze it out and add it to the other ingredients in the pan, stirring well. Bring the stock to the boil, pour in gradually and simmer for 10 minutes. Liquidize or put through a coarse sieve or mouli-légumes. Return to the pan and reheat. Stir in the cream off the heat just before serving and adjust the seasoning – add pepper cautiously as lovage has a peppery flavour of its own.

Nettle soup

100g/4oz young nettle tops
25g/1oz butter
350g/12oz peeled, diced potatoes
2 sliced leeks
1 tablespoon each of chopped fresh
  marjoram and thyme
grated nutmeg
salt and pepper
600ml/1 pint hot milk
3 chopped rashers of streaky bacon,
  crisply fried

Melt the butter in a saucepan, add the nettle tops, potatoes, leeks and herbs and cook gently, without browning, for 15 minutes with the lid on. Season lightly with nutmeg, salt and pepper. Pour in 600ml/1 pint of water, bring to the boil and simmer until the potatoes are cooked. Sieve, liquidize or put through a mouli-légumes. Return to the pan and add the milk very hot. Heat through and taste for seasoning. Add the fried bacon pieces at the last minute.

Mediterranean fish soup with saffron

300ml/½ pint cooked prawns
600ml/1 pint scrubbed mussels
1 pinch of powdered saffron
1 cod's head
2 chopped leeks
1 chopped shallot
a bunch of thyme, fennel and parsley
1 bayleaf
finely pared peel of an orange and lemon
salt and pepper
1 glass white wine or vermouth
50g/2oz pasta or rice
fresh basil to garnish
150ml/¼ pint aïoli (page 166)

Shell the prawns and simmer the shells for an hour with the cod's head, leeks, shallot, herbs, peel and seasoning in 1.25 litres/2¼ pints of water and a glass of wine. Strain this stock into a large pan. Drop the mussels into 600ml/1 pint of boiling water. They will open after a few minutes. Lift out and shell those that have opened; discard those that remain closed. Add the mussel liquor to the stock with the saffron. Bring to the boil, drop in the rice or pasta and cook until tender. Stir in the mussels, prawns and a few roughly torn basil leaves. Serve with aïoli, the strong garlicky mayonnaise.

Mulligatawny soup

½ a chicken
225g/8oz red lentils
2 finely sliced onions
1 bay leaf
10 peppercorns, ground
1 teaspoon ground cumin seed
1 teaspoon ground coriander seed
ground seeds from 1 cardamom pod
½ teaspoon turmeric
3 cloves
100g/4oz long-grain rice
100g/4oz butter (or ghee)
2 garlic cloves, bruised and chopped
1 teaspoon paprika
1 scant tablespoon flour
1 tablespoon lemon juice
1 tablespoon orange juice
salt
150ml/¼ pint single cream or coconut milk (made with 25g/1oz creamed coconut and 150ml/¼ pint hot water or by soaking 50g/2oz unsweetened desiccated coconut in the water for 30 minutes then squeezing the milky liquid through a cloth)

Put the chicken and lentils into a pan of 1.5 litres/2¾ pints water, together with half the sliced onion and the bay leaf. Add the ground spices, turmeric and cloves. Cover, bring slowly to simmering point and cook gently until the chicken and lentils are tender. Meanwhile cook the rice very slowly in a separate pan. Melt the butter or ghee and cook the remaining onion and the garlic until golden, then stir in the paprika and flour. Add this paste to the spiced chicken broth, stirring well. Season with lemon and orange juice and salt to taste. Finally stir in the coconut milk or cream. Serve piping hot with separate bowls of cooked rice.

Watercress and orange soup

2 bunches of watercress
grated rind and juice from ½ orange
½ sliced onion
½ clove of garlic
75g/3oz butter
1 bunch of parsley
2 cooked potatoes
600ml/1 pint milk
600ml/1 pint light stock
salt and pepper
cream

Gently cook the onion and garlic in the butter until soft, then add the watercress and parsley and continue cooking over a low heat for 5 minutes. Stir in the potatoes, milk, stock and ½ teaspoon of rind, then cover and simmer for 10 minutes. Liquidize or sieve and carefully add salt, pepper and about 2 teaspoonfuls of orange juice. Too much pepper or orange juice will overpower the delicate flavour of the soup. Thicken and enrich with cream if you wish and float a teaspoonful of whipped cream in each bowl.

Cream of fish soup with aniseed

350g/¾lb filleted white fish such as cod, whiting, sole or plaice
2 teaspoons of bruised aniseed
1 sliced shallot
salt and white peppercorns
100g/4oz almonds, blanched or ground
300ml/½ pint cream
1 heaped tablespoon of finely chopped anise leaves or parsley to garnish

Gently poach the fish with 1 teaspoon of aniseed, the shallot, a pinch of salt and a few crushed peppercorns in 1 litre/1¾ pints of water for 10 minutes or until tender. Strain off the stock and either liquidize the fish with the blanched almonds or put the fish through a coarse sieve and add ground almonds to the resulting purée. Mix the purée back into the stock and heat through. Remove from the heat and stir in the cream, the remaining aniseed and the chopped anise or parsley leaves. Serve this delicate broth with dark rye bread (page 202) and unsalted butter.

Salads

Raw wild herbs and vegetables have been collected and eaten by man since the earliest times, although the earliest surviving salad recipes include quantities of plants that are seldom eaten today. These mixtures were often nutritious, each leaf, bud, flower and seed providing different minerals and vitamins and none of the goodness being lost by cooking. Most housewives had some knowledge of the medicinal values of herbs and would make up their salads according to the needs of the household, attempting to balance cool plants such as purslane, chicory and lettuce with warming, aromatic herbs such as tarragon, chives and rocket (a popular salad plant related to mustard). Winter salads were made from dressed, boiled vegetables and evergreen, dried or pickled herbs.

Spring salads

We tend to forget the importance of fresh salad in the early spring now that green herbs and salads can be imported or deep frozen for consumption at any time of the year. In the days when the winter diet consisted of stored root vegetables and heavily salted fat meat and fish, the first spring greens were vitally important.

Salad and flavouring herbs

Many of the salad herbs must be eaten early in the year, while they are young and before they become bitter and harsh. Some, like dandelion leaves, need to be blanched in the dark or dropped in boiling water for a minute or two to reduce their bitterness. It is often necessary to chop herb leaves finely to make them palatable and to begin by using only small quantities of the more unusual, strong-tasting wild herbs.

Spring salad herbs include the leaves of bistort, borage, salad burnet, watercress, yarrow, sorrel, dandelion, lime and the leaves and buds of alexanders. For flavouring spring salads use sweet cicely, fennel, lovage, coriander, caraway and chervil.

Dandelion salad with bacon

blanched leaves from 2 dandelion plants
50g/2oz diced fat bacon
1 tablespoon chopped chives
1 tablespoon chopped parsley
Fry the bacon in its own fat until it is crisp and dry. Wash and thoroughly dry the dandelion leaves. Mix all the ingredients just before serving. In France this is called *pissenlit au lard*.

An early spring salad

50g/2oz bulgur wheat
25g/1oz sprouted wheat
6 salad burnet leaves
3 yarrow leaves
5 large sorrel leaves
blanched leaves from 2 dandelion plants
2 tablespoons young hawthorn leaves
2 tablespoons finely chopped sweet cicely leaves
vinaigrette dressing
1 tablespoon plain yoghurt
Soak the bulgur wheat in water for 15 minutes, then squeeze dry. Roughly tear the salad burnet, yarrow, sorrel and dandelion leaves. Mix all the ingredients together and toss in a vinaigrette dressing to which a tablespoon of plain yoghurt has been added.

Summer salads

Herb flowers can be used to decorate and flavour summer salads. Use whole flowers of sage, marjoram, rosemary, lavender, borage, chicory, violets and nasturtiums and the petals of marigold, bergamot, rose and clove carnation.

Cooling early summer salad

1 large lettuce
1 bunch of beetroot leaves
8 young borage leaves
3 lime leaves
2 salad burnet leaves
4 chopped lemon balm leaves
a handful of purslane leaves
1 thinly sliced cucumber
vinaigrette dressing
Wash and thoroughly dry all the ingredients, tear the leaves if necessary and toss in a light vinaigrette dressing.

Opposite: *Cooling early summer salad on the left, winter chicory and walnut salad in the centre, potato salad with horseradish and dill in the foreground, and, behind left, a bowl of spring salad herbs – sorrel, watercress and lovage leaves.*

Provençal salad sandwich

1 long French loaf or a flat, round white
* loaf or 4 flat, white rolls*
1 garlic clove
2 tablespoons strong olive oil
8 large lettuce leaves
1 seeded, sliced red pepper
6 skinned, chopped tomatoes
a few black olives or capers
8 fresh basil leaves
lemon juice, salt and pepper

Split open the French loaf, round loaf or rolls. Rub the cut surfaces with garlic and sprinkle with olive oil. Lay on the lettuce leaves, red pepper, tomatoes and olives or capers. Sprinkle with basil, more oil, lemon juice and seasoning. Press the loaves or rolls together again and leave under a weight for 1 hour in a cool place – the refrigerator if necessary.

Summer vegetable salad

100g/4oz shelled young peas
100g/4oz shelled young broad beans
4 sliced carrots
4 sliced radishes
3 sliced spring onions
1 teaspoon chopped summer savory
1 tablespoon chopped apple mint
2 chopped nasturtium leaves
1 tablespoon parsley piert (optional)
1 tablespoon chopped celery leaves
6 chopped unripe seed pods of sweet
* cicely*
vinaigrette dressing

Toss all the ingredients together in a vinaigrette dressing made with tarragon vinegar (page 165).

Winter salads

As fresh herbs are generally unavailable in the winter, use dried leaves and seeds to flavour winter salads. The few hardy herbs that can be gathered are Welsh onions, salad burnet and wild chickweed, but grains, pulses and the seeds of herbs such as fenugreek can be made more nourishing if they are kept damp for a few days and allowed to sprout. Use pickled capers, nasturtium seeds and purslane stalks to add flavour, and old-fashioned garnishes such as pickled clove carnations and dried marigold petals.

Chicory and walnut salad

3 sliced heads of chicory
leaves from 2 corn salad plants
1 bunch of mustard seedlings
25g/1oz sprouted fenugreek seeds
1 chopped head of celery
3 chopped Welsh onions
a handful of chickweed leaves
50g/2oz chopped walnuts
1 teaspoon lovage seeds
vinaigrette dressing

Mix all the ingredients and toss in a vinaigrette dressing.

Spiced rice salad

225g/8oz long-grain rice
a small piece of root ginger
1 finely chopped shallot
5 coriander seeds
5 roughly crushed black peppercorns
2 tablespoons olive oil
1 teaspoon lemon juice
a pinch of grated nutmeg
salt and pepper

Cook the rice very slowly with the piece of ginger until tender. Drain and dry thoroughly, discard the ginger and mix with the remaining ingredients. Leave to cool, covered with a cloth.

Potato salad with horseradish and dill

1kg/2lb potatoes
mayonnaise flavoured with horseradish
* (page 166)*
1 teaspoon dill seeds
1 tablespoon milk

Boil the potatoes in their skins, drain and peel them and slice them thickly while they are still warm. Thin the mayonnaise with the milk, mix in the dill seeds and turn the potato slices in the mayonnaise until each slice is coated, being careful not to break them.

Red cabbage and caraway salad

1 finely shredded red cabbage
1 teaspoon caraway seeds
salt and pepper
75g/3oz pork fat
1 tablespoon vinegar

Mix the caraway seeds, salt and pepper with the cabbage in a warm bowl. Cut the fat into thin strips and fry until brown in a frying pan. Pour the hot, liquid fat over the cabbage and mix in the crisp strips. Heat the vinegar in the frying pan and mix into the cabbage. Leave in a warm place for a minute or two for the flavours to be absorbed.

Serve this unusual salad with a hot cheese, pork or bacon dish.

Celeriac and mustard salad

1 peeled, grated celeriac
1 generous teaspoon Dijon mustard
1 teaspoon lemon juice
mayonnaise made with 3 egg yolks (page
* 166)*
1 tablespoon chopped parsley

Blanch the celeriac in boiling water for 2 minutes to prevent it turning brown, then drain and dry thoroughly in a cloth. Mix the mustard and lemon juice with the mayonnaise. Stir in the celeriac and garnish with parsley.

Beetroot and caper salad

3 large beetroots
1 tablespoon capers
vinaigrette dressing (page 166)
1 teaspoon honey

Boil or bake the beetroots in their skins until tender. Peel, slice and mix while warm with the capers and dressing, sweetened with honey.

Vegetables

Spring vegetables

Spring, before the earliest vegetables have matured, is the time to eat wild herbs; later, in the summer, they become coarse and tough. Young tops and leaves of nettles, ground elder and goosegrass and the leaves and stems of chickweed can all be treated in the same way. Goosegrass and chickweed have only a faint flavour of their own, nettles have a rather fluffy texture and ground elder has an interesting, aromatic taste. All are rich in vitamins and minerals.

Cooking wild herbs

You will need 2 good handfuls of fresh leaves for each person as the leaves shrink in the same way as spinach. Rinse the wild plants – enough for 4 people – in fresh water and put the dripping bundle into a large pan. Add no further liquid but simmer, covered, until nearly tender. Stir in 50g/2oz butter, lemon juice and seasoning to taste and 1 tablespoon of chopped chives, thyme, mint or other flavouring herbs. Serve hot.

Braised alexanders or burdock stems

500g/1lb young alexander or burdock
  leaf stems
50g/2oz butter
150ml/¼ pint stock
1 teaspoon wine vinegar or lemon juice
salt and pepper

Remove the fine outer skin from the fleshy stems as this is bitter. Chop them into 5cm/2in lengths. Melt the butter in a shallow pan, add the stems and stew gently for a few minutes. Pour in 150ml/¼ pint of stock or water, the vinegar or lemon juice and a pinch of salt. Cover the pan and simmer for about 8 minutes until tender. Season to taste.

Leeks steamed with elderflower wine

1kg/2lb leeks
150ml/¼ pint elderflower wine
salt

Wash the leeks and slice into 3cm/1in lengths. Bring the wine to the boil in a saucepan or bottom of a steamer, put the leeks above in a colander or steamer top, cover and cook until the leeks are just tender. The delicate sweetly flowery taste of the wine penetrates the leeks and provides the only seasoning necessary, apart from a little salt.

Other vegetables can be steamed in this way. Sweet parsnips are particularly good.

Spring sformato

1kg/2lb spring vegetables, which might
  include chopped potatoes, carrots,
  turnips, spinach beet and peas and
  beans
a bouquet of fresh sweet herbs such as
  marjoram, lemon or garden thyme and
  mint
a small bay leaf
150ml/¼ pint double cream
3 eggs, separated
25g/1oz grated Parmesan cheese
salt and pepper

Bring 150ml/¼ pint water to the boil and simmer the vegetables until tender, with the bouquet and bay leaf. Drain the vegetables, remove the herbs and mix in the cream and seasoning. Allow to cool a little, then beat in the egg yolks and cheese. Whisk the egg whites stiffly and fold in. Pour into a buttered soufflé dish and steam, or bake gently in a moderate oven, 180°C/350°F/Mark 4, for about 45 minutes.

Steamed hop shoots

500g/1lb of young hop shoots
50g/2oz crisply fried cubes of fat bacon

Steam the shoots like asparagus and toss with the crisp bacon cubes. The shoots are known as *jets de houblon* in France. There they are boiled in salted water with lemon juice and served with creamy sauce or poached eggs.

Braised broad beans with savory

1kg/2lb very young broad beans
1 teaspoon chopped summer savory
1 thinly sliced small shallot
50g/2oz butter
50g/2oz diced cooked ham
salt and pepper

Soften the shallot in the melted butter. Add the ham, savory and the small, whole broad beans in their pods. After a few minutes add 2 tablespoons of water. Cover and stew gently until the pods are tender. Remove the lid and boil for 2 minutes until the liquid is reduced. Correct the seasoning carefully, remembering the saltiness of the ham.

Herbs to garnish spring vegetables

Mix chopped fresh herbs with butter and add to young spring vegetables before serving. Try chervil with baby carrots; lemon thyme with turnips; lemon balm with new potatoes; caraway leaves with spring cabbage.

Summer vegetables

Use the enormous variety of wild and cultivated summer herbs as garnishes, dressings, sauces and stuffings for ripe vegetables. Now that fresh coriander leaves are available, use them lavishly with vegetable curries.

Vegetables poached in a spiced marinade

1kg/2lb young summer vegetables, for example sliced leeks, courgettes sliced lengthways, whole carrots, French or runner beans, broccoli or cauliflower florets

MARINADE

6 tablespoons olive oil

juice of 1 lemon or 1 small glass of white wine

1 tablespoon chopped parsley or fresh coriander leaves

1 bay leaf

salt

6 peppercorns

12 coriander seeds

1 garlic clove

To make the marinade warm the olive oil in a large, shallow pan. Add the lemon juice or wine, herbs and a pinch of salt. Crush together in a mortar the peppercorns, coriander seeds and garlic, add to the pan and stew in the liquor for a few minutes.

Arrange the vegetables carefully in a single layer in the pan and poach them gently in the marinade until *just* tender. Lift the vegetables out with a slotted spoon onto a serving dish. Moisten with a few spoonfuls of the liquor and leave to cool.

Steamed spinach and ginger

750g/1¼lb spinach

1 tablespoon grated root ginger

3 tablespoons oil

1 finely chopped shallot or mild onion

2 crushed garlic cloves

1 tablespoon sherry

salt

Warm the oil and gently simmer the shallot, garlic cloves and ginger until soft. Raise the heat, add the spinach and cook fast for 1 minute, stirring all the time. Add the sherry and a pinch of salt, cover the pan and steam for a few minutes until tender.

Bean sprouts with coriander

225g/8oz bean sprouts

1 tablespoon chopped fresh coriander leaves

4 crushed coriander seeds

2 tablespoons oil

1 tablespoon chopped parsley or fresh caraway leaves

1 tablespoon chopped fresh chives

salt and pepper

juice of ½ lemon

Heat the oil until just warm. Stir in the herbs and season lightly. After a minute or two add the bean sprouts and raise the heat, stirring constantly. Squeeze in the lemon juice, cover tightly and cook for 3 minutes. Serve immediately.

Peas with mint and lettuce

500g/1lb shelled peas

1 bunch of chopped fresh mint and parsley

1 shredded small lettuce

50g/2oz butter

6 chopped spring onions

salt and pepper

Melt the butter and toss the peas in it for 2 minutes. Stir in the remaining ingredients, reserving a little of the mint. Add 150ml/¼ pint of water and simmer for 10 minutes, until the peas are tender. Drain, sprinkle with the remaining mint and serve hot.

A stuffed, savoury green pepper, seasoned with herbs and ready to bake.

Stuffed peppers or tomatoes

2 halved, seeded peppers or 6 halved,
  hollowed large continental tomatoes
100g/4oz long-grain or Italian rice
1 tablespoon chopped parsley
1 teaspoon lemon thyme
1 teaspoon chopped lovage
1 tablespoon chopped chives

Winter vegetables

Spiced baked onions

8 peeled onions
4 halved, bruised garlic cloves
1 torn bay leaf
1 teaspoon fennel seeds
1 teaspoon paprika
1 tablespoon oil
1 teaspoon lemon juice or vinegar
¼ teaspoon salt (spiced if possible, page 160)

Put the onions into a shallow baking dish and sprinkle the spices and other ingredients among them. Cover and bake in a warm oven, 160°C/325°F/Mark 3 for about 1½ hours or until tender. Uncover the dish for the last 10 minutes to allow the onions to brown.

Onion green champ

1 large bunch of chopped green tops of Welsh or spring onions
1kg/2lb potatoes
300ml/½ pint milk
salt and pepper
50g/2oz butter

Boil the potatoes until tender. Meanwhile, simmer the onion greens for 5 minutes in the milk with salt and pepper to taste. Drain the potatoes and shake over a low heat until thoroughly dry and fluffy. Mash well. Add the milk and greens to the mashed potatoes and beat until smooth. Pile into 4 individual hot bowls, make a well in the centre of each and put in a knob of butter. Eat from the outside towards the mid-

salt and pepper
2 tablespoons oil
1 tablespoon lemon juice

Cook the rice until tender and dry (page 196). While it is still warm mix in the herbs and seasoning. Put the peppers or tomatoes into a well-oiled baking dish and fill with the

dle, dipping each forkful of potato mixture into the melted butter.

Young stinging nettle tops, parsley or kale can be substituted for onion greens.

Stuffed cabbage leaves

8 large cabbage leaves
25g/1oz butter
1 finely chopped small onion
1 chopped stick of celery
100g/4oz chopped mushrooms
100g/4oz fresh breadcrumbs
1 egg
1 egg yolk
1 teaspoon dill seeds
2 tablespoons chopped parsley
salt and pepper
spiced salt (page 160)
1 teaspoon vinegar

First make the stuffing. Melt the butter, add the onion, celery and mushrooms and cook gently for 10 minutes. Take off the heat and stir in the breadcrumbs, egg and egg yolk, dill, parsley and seasoning to taste.

Blanch the cabbage leaves in boiling water for 1 to 2 minutes to soften. Drain well. Lay each leaf flat, pile a little stuffing in the centre of each one and roll up, tucking in the ends. Pack closely together in a single layer in a greased baking dish. Sprinkle with spiced salt, a few spoonfuls of water and the vinegar. Cover and bake in a warm oven, 160°C/325°F/Mark 3, for about 1 hour, adding water if necessary.

rice mixture. Pour over the oil and lemon juice, cover with buttered paper or foil, then a lid and bake in a warm oven, 160°C/325°F/Mark 3. The peppers will take an hour, the tomatoes 20 minutes.

Green peppercorns give a hot, fresh spice to winter dishes. Crush 1 tablespoon of green peppercorns lightly and stir into a dish of hot root vegetables, such as parsnips or artichokes, or into a purée of dried haricot beans or green split peas.

Purée of Brussels sprouts with nutmeg

1kg/2lb Brussels sprouts
a pinch of grated nutmeg
75ml/⅛ pint double cream
lemon juice
salt and pepper

Cook the Brussels sprouts in boiling water until you can cut them with a fork. Drain and dry them thoroughly. Put them through a sieve or mouli-légumes or liquidize them. Beat in the cream and nutmeg and season carefully with lemon juice and salt and pepper. Serve hot with boiled ham or sausages.

Purée of celeriac with marjoram

1 peeled large celeriac
1 tablespoon dried marjoram or thyme
500g/1lb peeled potatoes
150ml/¼ pint hot milk
50g/2oz butter
salt and pepper

Cut the celeriac and potatoes into large chunks. Cook them together in boiling water until tender. Drain and shake over a low heat until thoroughly dry and fluffy. Mash well, gradually adding the milk and butter. Beat in the marjoram or thyme, season with salt and plenty of black pepper and serve very hot.

Eggs

Flavouring eggs simmered in their shells

Whole eggs that are left to simmer in liquid for several hours in a low oven develop a soft, creamy texture. If you add herbs to the liquid they also absorb a subtle flavour through their shells. Try leaving eggs for several hours or overnight in a cool oven in a tightly covered pot with water and quantities of onion skins to colour and flavour them, or pack them round with bundles of trimmings from the herb garden such as thyme, marjoram or mint. Well-scrubbed eggs can also be added to slow-cooking stews and pulse dishes.

Hard-boiled eggs

Serve freshly hard-boiled eggs as an hors d'oeuvre with a dish of ground cumin mixed with sesame salt to dip them into, or with one of the uncooked sauces on page 168. Hard-boiled eggs on a bed of watercress or sorrel purée make a light dish for a summer lunch.

Spiced hard-boiled eggs

8 shelled, hard-boiled eggs
1 tablespoon oil
1 teaspoon ground cumin
seeds from 4 cardamom pods
¼ teaspoon paprika
a pinch of turmeric
150ml/¼ pint plain yoghurt
1 teaspoon lemon juice
1 tablespoon chopped fresh coriander or parsley leaves
salt and pepper

Warm the oil in a heavy frying pan. Add the cumin, cardamom, paprika and turmeric and simmer for 2 minutes. Remove from the heat and stir in the yoghurt, lemon juice and herbs. Correct the seasoning. Pour over the hard-boiled eggs and cool.

Simmered eggs

8 shelled, hard-boiled eggs
2 chopped shallots
4 chopped garlic cloves
25g/1oz almonds
¼ teaspoon turmeric
salt and pepper
1 tablespoon oil
150ml/¼ pint water

Pound together in a mortar the shallots, garlic and almonds and mix in the turmeric, salt and pepper. Heat the oil and gently fry the spicy mixture until it is a soft pulp. Mix in the water and add the eggs. Simmer uncovered for about 15 minutes, stirring occasionally, until the water has evaporated.

Serve with rice or hot bread rolls.

Stuffed hard-boiled eggs

Halve the eggs and mash butter or mayonnaise into the yolks. Then into this rich paste beat a mixture of pounded anchovies, shallot and pepper, or capers or green peppercorns, or well-chopped or pounded fresh green herbs. Pile the mixture back into the egg whites and serve on a bed of crisp lettuce.

Baked eggs with tarragon

4 eggs
1 tablespoon chopped fresh tarragon
25g/1oz butter
4 tablespoons cream
salt and pepper

Melt a little butter in 4 individual baking dishes or cocottes. Break an egg into each one. Mix the cream with the tarragon, season lightly and pour over each egg. Bake for 4 to 5 minutes in a moderate oven, 180°C/350°F/Mark 4, until just set.

Tarragon is also the traditional garnish used for *oeufs en gelée* (eggs in aspic).

Panperdy

4 slices of bread
4 eggs
5 tablespoons chopped fresh herbs such as chervil, tarragon and parsley
salt and pepper
50g/2oz butter

Beat the eggs with the herbs and seasonings. Heat the butter in a frying pan until it foams and fry the slices of bread on one side. Turn the slices in the pan and pour half the egg mixture over them. As soon as the bread has taken colour turn it again and pour over the remaining mixture. Turn once more so that the bread slices are enclosed in a light omelette. Slide onto a hot plate and eat immediately.

Recipes for panperdy have been included in European cookery books since medieval times. The early recipes contain cloves, mace and other spices. The name derives from the French *pain perdu*.

Fines herbes omelette

6 eggs
salt and pepper
4 tablespoons finely chopped, mixed fresh chervil, parsley, tarragon and chives
40g/1½oz butter

Mix the eggs lightly in a bowl, season with a little salt and pepper and stir in half the *fines herbes* mixture. Melt the butter in an omelette pan or heavy frying pan until it begins to foam. Before it turns colour pour in the eggs. Sprinkle the remaining herbs over them. Lift the mixture round the edge of the pan with a palette knife as it begins to set and tip the pan to allow the liquid egg to run to the edge. In a few moments the egg will be set but still moist in the centre. Quickly flip over the omelette so that it is folded in half. Slip it onto a warm plate and eat it immediately.

Sorrel omelette

Make an omelette as above, but instead of the herbs add 4 table-spoons of sorrel purée to the eggs in the pan. Sorrel is a natural companion to eggs; its sharpness is offset by the bland, soft texture of the egg.

Fresh green baked omelette

6 eggs
2 thinly sliced leeks
4 thinly sliced spring onions
2 handfuls of chopped leaves from green garden vegetables such as spinach, sprouting broccoli, cauliflower or cabbage
1 bunch of fresh green herbs such as parsley, tarragon and coriander, caraway or dill leaves, chopped
salt and pepper

Beat the eggs and mix in the rest of the ingredients. Pour into a well-buttered 25cm/10in cake tin, cover with a plate and cook in a warm oven, 160°C/325°F/Mark 3, for about 40 minutes. Uncover for the last 10 minutes to brown the top. Unmould onto a dish and serve lukewarm or cold with plain yoghurt and brown bread.

Hot chili omelette

6 eggs, separated
1 seeded, chopped green chili
1 tablespoon oil
1 finely chopped small onion
4 pounded coriander seeds
a pinch of ground ginger
a pinch of turmeric
1 tablespoon chopped fresh coriander leaves or parsley
salt

Warm half the oil and add the chili, onion, coriander, ginger, turmeric, herbs and a pinch of salt. Simmer gently for 5 minutes. Beat the egg yolks with 5 tablespoons of cold water until pale and thick. Mix in the softened herbs and spices. Whisk the egg whites until stiff and fold them into the mixture. Heat the remaining oil in a heavy pan. Pour in the egg mixture and cook as for the *fines herbes* omelette. It will puff up and become golden brown. Lower the heat and cook gently until just set but moist in the centre. To brown the top, turn the omelette gently in the pan or set it under the grill for 1 to 2 minutes. Use more chili if you like 'hot' dishes.

Flavour fresh eggs by slowly simmering in water and herbs, or wrap them in onion skins first to produce a decorative, marbled effect.

Butters and cheeses

Herb butter

Herb butter is made by beating finely chopped herbs such as chervil, parsley and lemon thyme into creamed butter, together with seasonings such as lemon, onion or garlic juice, mashed green peppercorns and salt and pepper. Shape the butter and store in a cool place or the refrigerator. Use it as a garnish for grilled meat or fish, for tossing with fresh young vegetables or spread it on thin brown bread. Cut slices across, but not right through, a long French loaf, spread herb butter into each incision, sprinkle the loaf with cold water and bake it for 7 minutes in a hot oven, 220°C/425°F/Mark 7. This will crisp the crust and melt the flavoured butter into the bread. Alternatively, wrap the buttered loaf in foil and leave it in the oven for 15 minutes at a slightly lower temperature.

Green butter

225g/8oz butter
1 bunch of watercress
1 bunch of chervil
1 bunch of parsley
5 salad burnet leaves
1 garlic clove
1 chopped shallot
salt

Blanch the watercress, chervil, parsley and burnet in boiling water, for 30 seconds. Drain and dry thoroughly, then pound in a mortar with the garlic, shallot and a pinch of salt. Then beat in the butter.

Spiced rum butter

225g/8oz unsalted butter
3 tablespoons rum
100g/4oz soft brown sugar
a pinch of grated nutmeg
a pinch of ground cinnamon
¾ teaspoon grated lemon peel

Cream the butter with the sugar. When it is pale and thoroughly amalgamated, beat in the nutmeg, cinnamon and lemon peel. Gradually beat in the rum. Press into stone pots and store in a cool place. Melt over steamed puddings or spread thickly on hot toast.

Rose petal butter

225g/8oz unsalted butter
4 large handfuls of richly scented rose petals

Put a thick layer of rose petals in a pottery jar. Lay the block of butter on this bed and surround and cover it with more rose petals. Cover and leave overnight in a cool place. Discard the petals, spread the butter on thin brown bread then lay over it several fresh rose petals whose bitter white 'heels' have been snipped off.

Thick cream can be flavoured in the same way.

Cheeses

Simple butters and cheeses that can be made at home. **Opposite:** *Herb butters (left), mashed and shaped. In the foreground a seven herb potted cheese sprinkled with caraway seeds, and, draining on the mat, a heart-shaped savoury cheese. Under the dome are two wild garlic and thyme cheeses, rolled in oatmeal.*

Cream for cream cheese drains through the muslin in the draining jug while a muslin bag of yoghurt hangs in the background. In the plain jug, milk is souring for cottage cheese.

Herbs have played an important part in almost every step of the cheesemaking process. They were used to hasten the souring of milk, and this is recorded in the country names of many herbs. Lady's bedstraw has many local names that refer to its use as a milk coagulant. Butterwort or 'thickening grass', *Pinguicula vulgaris*, with its greasy tongue-like leaves, was used in northern countries to curdle milk, especially in Lapland where it was added to reindeer milk. Fresh stinging nettles or their juices have the same effect and were used in the manufacture of nettle cheese and to help drain curds. The whey from milk curdled with scurvy grass, *Cochlearia officinalis*, was a traditional treatment for scurvy. When rennet was made, herbs and spices were often added to the brine soaking in the stomach of the newly killed calf. They were thought to increase the quantity of rennet and also to help preserve and flavour the rennet and so the cheese.

Herbs are still traditionally used to flavour some hard cheeses, sage for sage derby and Vermont sage cheese, and a species of melilot for gruyère, and are particularly useful as flavourings for the soft, bland curd and cottage cheeses that can be made at home or bought ready made. Chopped herbs and pressed herb juices, spices, strong hot seasonings of crushed fresh or dried peppercorns or cayenne, delicate sweet flavourings of cinnamon, sugar and rosewater, give widely different characters to the cheese, and saffron, marigold petals or spinach juice can be used to vary the colours. A sprig of rosemary or thyme pressed into the curd, or a wrapping of bay leaves give fine flavours. The large leaves of plants such as burdock (butter dock), dock

species (butter leaves), and butterbur, *Petasites hybridus*, are still used in many country districts as cool wrappings for butters and cheeses.

Milk cheese

Warm 1 litre/2 pints of milk to blood heat. Take off the heat and stir in 2 teaspoons of rennet. Leave for 1 to 2 hours until the milk has separated. Tip the curd into a clean piece of muslin and hang the muslin to drain overnight. The whey that drains from the curd makes a refreshing drink. If the curd is still too moist, leave it in a colander for 1 hour, lightly weighted with a plate.

Unpasteurized milk gives a better result, but is rarely obtainable.

Cream cheese

Substitute thick cream for milk and follow the same method as for milk cheese.

Cottage cheese

Stir 1 teaspoon of lemon juice into 1 litre/2 pints of milk and leave in a cloth-covered jug until the milk is thick and sour. Add 1 teaspoon of salt and leave to drain in muslin overnight.

Yoghurt

Bring 1 litre/2 pints of milk to the boil to sterilize it. Leave it to cool to blood heat. Stir in 1 teaspoon of plain (bought or home-made) yoghurt and keep at a constant warm temperature for 8 hours. This can be done by pouring the milk into a thermos, or by leaving the milk in a covered jug in an airing cupboard or beside a cooking range or stove. Too hot a temperature will kill off the yoghurt bacillus.

Yoghurt cheese

This is simply plain yoghurt left overnight in muslin to drain off all liquid.

Potted cheese

Any hard cheese or blue-veined cheese can be potted. Sealed with clarified butter, potted cheeses will keep for a long time if stored in a cool larder. If stored in the refrigerator cover with foil as well as butter.

Savoury cheese

175g/6oz yoghurt cheese (see above)
175g/6oz milk cheese (see above)
3 tablespoons olive oil
4 thinly sliced spring onions
juice of ½ lemon
2 tablespoons finely chopped fennel, mint and coriander leaves
salt and pepper
¼ teaspoon paprika
¼ teaspoon crushed cumin seeds

Mix together all the ingredients except the spices. Pile the cheese into a dish and sprinkle with the paprika and cumin.

Seven herb potted cheese

100g/4oz coarsely grated Cheddar or Cheshire cheese
25g/1oz unsalted butter
3 heaped tablespoons finely chopped fresh herbs (see below)

1 tablespoon brown sherry
a pinch of ground mace
pepper
melted clarified butter

Beat the cheese and butter to a paste. Beat in the herbs, which consist of a generous quantity of parsley, chervil, thyme and chives and smaller quantities of summer or winter savory, sage and tarragon. Add the sherry, mace and pepper to taste. Press into small pots and cover with clarified butter and foil.

Wild garlic and thyme cheese

3 finely chopped ramson (wild garlic) leaves
1 tablespoon finely chopped wild thyme
approximately 175g/6oz milk cheese (made with 1 litre/2 pints milk – see above)
150ml/¼ pint double cream

salt and pepper
50g/2oz toasted coarse oatmeal

Beat the ramson leaves and thyme into the cheese. Whisk the cream until it thickens and stir it into the cheese. Season well. Form into two or three small cylinders and roll each in golden toasted oatmeal. Eat within 2 days.

Some flavourings for soft cheeses

Chopped lemon thyme, borage and sweet cicely leaves or seeds, garnished with borage flowers.
Dried melilot.
Juice pounded from marigold petals and strained.
Grated nutmeg, ground cinnamon and a pinch of ground cloves.
Finely chopped angelica leaves.
Bergamot or scented geranium leaves.

Fish

Seaside plants complement sea fish. Try flavouring sea fish with fennel and lovage or serve accompanied by braised alexanders or pickled samphire. Freshwater fish go well with watercress, mint, sorrel and lemon thyme.

Baked fish

Bake fish wrapped in pastry, oiled paper, foil or unglazed earthenware to retain their full flavour and juices. Include a knob of green butter (page 182) or a bundle of sweet herbs to flavour.

Fried fish

Spice the flour or breadcrumbs used to coat the fish for frying with coarsely crushed peppercorns or fennel seed, dill seed or aniseed, then fry in clarified butter or oil.

Another alternative is to sprinkle freshly grated horseradish mixed with melted butter, salt and pepper over fried fish.

Or fry the fish coated in plain breadcrumbs, place on a warm plate and add chopped herbs, cream, mushrooms and lemon juice to the juices in the pan. Heat through and pour over the fish.

Smoked fish pâté

1 or 2 fish carcasses
1 glass white wine
1 teaspoon white peppercorns
1 bay leaf
salt
100g/4oz smoked haddock
100g/4oz smoked salmon
100g/4oz smoked trout
225g/8oz butter
1 tablespoon flour
150ml/¼ pint thin cream or top of the milk
lemon juice
salt and pepper
3 tablespoons chopped fennel

Make a fish stock with the bones, wine, peppercorns, bay leaf, a pinch of salt and a little water to cover. Simmer for 30 minutes and strain. Melt 50g/2oz butter and gently cook the smoked haddock. Make a light fish sauce by melting 50g/2oz butter, stirring in the flour and adding the fish stock and cream or top of the milk, and lemon juice. Mince coarsely or finely chop all the fish and stir into the sauce. Season carefully. Press into a narrow, buttered loaf tin alternating the mixture with layers of fennel, and cover with the remaining melted butter (clarified if the pâté is to be kept). Serve with thin slices of wholemeal toast.

Marinated raw fish

500g/1lb very fresh fillets of white fish such as plaice or sole
4 tablespoons oil
1 thinly sliced shallot
juice of 1 lime or lemon
1 teaspoon lemon thyme
salt and pepper

Mix together the oil, shallot, lime or lemon juice, herbs and seasoning. Slice the fish fillets into thin strips. Turn them in the marinade until thoroughly coated and leave them in it for 1 hour in a cool place. They will become tender and translucent. Serve with thin bread and butter and a green salad as an hors d'oeuvre.

Marinating to preserve fish

Poach, grill or fry fish coated in flour or breadcrumbs. When the fish has cooled to lukewarm, put it in a clean dish and cover with a marinade (page 164). Whole fish such as mackerel or herring, or steaks of cod, whiting or salmon, will absorb the flavours from the marinade and keep for a week in a cold place.

Marinated salmon

4 salmon steaks
6 black peppercorns
1 bay leaf
150ml/¼ pint white-wine vinegar
2 tablespoons light oil
1 sliced shallot
3 crushed garlic cloves
a twist of finely pared lemon peel
6 crushed allspice berries
2 fresh sprigs of dill
¼ teaspoon salt

Poach the salmon gently in 600ml/1 pint of water with the peppercorns and bay leaf until tender. Transfer the salmon to a shallow dish. Add the remaining ingredients to the stock, bring to the boil and simmer for 30 minutes. Cool to lukewarm, pour over the salmon and leave in a cold place overnight. Serve the salmon with a few spoonfuls of the strained marinade.

Steamed whiting with herbs

1 cleaned whole whiting (about 1.5kg/3lb)
1 bunch of fresh or dried herbs that could include mint, lemon balm, coriander, parsley stems, fennel, thyme and a little melilot
lemon juice
sea salt and pepper

Bring water to the boil in the bottom half of a steamer. Spread the herbs in the top half, lay the fish on them and sprinkle with lemon juice, sea salt and a little pepper. Cover tightly and steam for 20 minutes.

Fish steamed with court bouillon

1 cleaned whole fish (about 1.5kg/3lb) or
*   fish steaks*
1 litre/1¾ pints water or 450ml/¾ pint
*   white wine and 600ml/1 pint water*
2 tablespoons wine or cider vinegar
1 sliced mild onion or 2 shallots
12 black peppercorns
6 coriander seeds
1 sliced carrot
a handful of fennel stalks or leaves
½ teaspoon salt

Simmer all the ingredients, except the fish, for 45 minutes in the bottom half of a steamer. Then set the fish in the top half and steam until tender. Use the stock later as a basis for fish soup.

Braised eel with sage

1 large or 2 small eels
7 fresh sage leaves
2 tablespoons oil
25g/1oz butter
1 thinly sliced onion
225g/8oz thinly sliced green gammon
1 bay leaf
6 bruised garlic cloves
pepper
juice of ½ lemon
1 glass of dry white wine

Slice the eels into thick chunks and fry in a mixture of oil and butter in a flameproof casserole for 5 minutes until browned. Remove them to a warm plate. Take the casserole off the heat and put in, in layers, the onion, the gammon, the sage leaves and bay leaf. Lay the eel chunks on this bed and put the garlic among them. Season with pepper and lemon juice. Pour over the wine and water or fish stock just to cover, heat until bubbling, put on a heavy lid and simmer for about 45 minutes or until the eel falls from the bones.

Trout baked with herbs

4 cleaned whole trout (about 1.5kg/3lb)
75g/3oz butter
100g/4oz finely chopped mushrooms
1 chopped garlic clove
2 tablespoons finely chopped fresh
*   fennel, chives, tarragon and chervil*
squeeze of lemon juice
salt and pepper

Melt 25g/1oz butter in a small saucepan and simmer the mushrooms and garlic for 4 minutes. Add half the herbs, the lemon juice and seasoning. Divide the mixture into 4 and stuff into the bellies of the trout. Lay each fish on a separate piece of buttered foil or oiled paper. Sprinkle over the remaining herbs, dot with the remaining butter, season lightly and wrap up into parcels. Lay in a baking tin and cook in a moderate oven, 180°C/350°F/Mark 4, for about 30 minutes. The fish can also be baked in unglazed earthenware but the outside of the fish must not be seasoned or the flavour will be drawn out with the salt into the clay.

Herrings baked with cabbage and lemon thyme

4 boned herrings
1 shredded small cabbage
2 tablespoons lemon thyme
1 sliced large mild onion
1 sliced large cooking apple
25g/1oz butter
1 teaspoon caraway seeds
½ teaspoon salt
pepper
1 tablespoon cider vinegar
4 teaspoons Dijon mustard

Simmer the onion and apple for 5 minutes in butter in a flameproof casserole or pan. Stir in the cabbage, caraway seeds, half the lemon thyme and seasoning and simmer for a further 5 minutes. Pour in 150ml/¼ pint water and the vinegar and bring to the boil. Open the fish, spread each with mustard and a sprinkling of lemon thyme and close into shape. Bury them deep in the bubbling cabbage mixture. Cover tightly and cook in a moderate oven, 180°C/350°F/Mark 4, for about 45 minutes. Serve very hot with baked potatoes and soured cream.

Grilled cod with aniseed and yoghurt

1 cleaned, small whole cod (1.5kg/3lb)
2 tablespoons aniseed
150ml/¼ pint plain yoghurt
3 tablespoons coriander seeds
4 black peppercorns
1 teaspoon paprika
seeds from 6 cardamom pods
2 garlic cloves
2 shallots
1 tablespoon mint
1 tablespoon fresh coriander leaves
salt
50g/2oz butter

Prick the fish all over with a fork. Heat a dry heavy frying pan and warm the coriander seeds, peppercorns and paprika. Tip these into a mortar and pound with the cardamom seeds, aniseed, garlic, shallots, mint, coriander leaves and salt. Stir in the yoghurt. Spread this paste over the skin of the fish and leave it for at least an hour to absorb the flavours. Dot the fish with flakes of butter and grill it fast for 15 minutes, turning the fish as the paste dries. Lower the heat and continue cooking for another 15 minutes or so until the fish is cooked, basting all the time with the dripping juices.

Fried fillets of plaice with dill

4 large fillets of plaice
1 tablespoon chopped dill leaves
75g/3oz butter
1 tablespoon chopped mint
1 tablespoon chopped chervil
a few chopped tarragon leaves
50g/2oz fresh breadcrumbs
salt and pepper
2 tablespoons oil or clarified butter

Melt the butter, remove from the heat and add the herbs. Dip the fillets in this mixture, then in the breadcrumbs, mixed with salt and pepper. Fry in oil or clarified butter and serve with a light green salad.

Trout are delicious flavoured with watercress, sorrel, mint or chives.

Meat

Meat, poultry, game and cold meats

Protect and flavour roasting meat with an aromatic paste of herbs and spices or serve it with a savoury sauce.

Roast beef

Serve with a sauce made with freshly grated horseradish, thick cream and a little wine vinegar.

Roast lamb

Make an onion sauce and season with black pepper and nutmeg.

Roast pork

Make a paste or stuffing with minced garlic, chopped dill leaves or seeds, parsley, savory, hyssop, salt and pepper and sufficient olive oil and fresh breadcrumbs to make a stiff mixture. Or for a sauce, spice a sour apple purée with bruised aniseed.

Baked ham or bacon

Mix chopped lemon thyme, caraway leaves, ground allspice, mustard, pepper and fresh breadcrumbs with beaten egg to make an aromatic paste. Press into the fat before baking.

A rich daube of beef

1kg/2lb lean beef
250g/8oz cubed green streaky bacon
2 sliced carrots
1 sliced onion
4 roughly chopped tomatoes
2 tablespoons olive oil
bouquet garni (page 162)
MARINADE
150ml/¼ pint olive oil
2 sliced shallots
2 crushed garlic cloves
1 stick of chopped celery
1 sliced carrot
150ml/¼ pint red wine
8 crushed black peppercorns
4 crushed coriander seeds
bouquet of herbs, especially thyme
a twist of orange peel
1 teaspoon salt
GARNISH
2 tablespoons chopped parsley
12 black olives

First make the marinade. Heat the oil and cook the shallots, garlic, celery and carrot for 10 minutes. Add the remaining marinade ingredients and simmer for 30 minutes. Allow to cool. Slice the beef into large pieces and leave in the marinade for at least 12 hours.

In a deep flameproof casserole put first the olive oil, then the bacon, carrots, onion, tomatoes and meat in

that order. Bury the *bouquet garni* in the centre. Put the casserole over a low heat to cook for 15 minutes. Pour over the strained marinade and cover tightly with buttered paper or foil and a heavy lid. Barely bring to the boil, then transfer to a low oven 140°C/275°F/ Mark 1, for 4 to 5 hours or longer. Remove the *bouquet* and stir in the garnish. Serve with noodles, rice or crusty bread.

Roast lamb with cumin

1 shoulder or leg, or 3 rolled, boned
  breasts of lamb
2 tablespoons crushed cumin seeds
4 slivered garlic cloves
½ minced or finely chopped onion
2 tablespoons olive oil
25g/1oz melted butter
1 tablespoon chopped thyme
a pinch of ground bay leaf
salt and pepper

Push the garlic slivers beneath the skin of the joint with a sharp knife. Prick all over with a fork. Mix the remaining ingredients into a paste and rub it over the meat, then leave in a cool place for 1 hour for the flavours to be absorbed. Roast the lamb in a hot oven, 220°C/425°F/ Mark 7, for 15 minutes, then lower the heat to moderate, 180°C/350°F/ Mark 4, for the remainder of the

cooking time. Sliced potatoes and onions can be cooked in the roasting pan with the lamb, absorbing the juices. This will serve 6 to 8 people.

Saffron lamb stew

1kg/2lb cubed shoulder of lamb
a pinch of powdered saffron
1 unpeeled onion
1 teaspoon crushed coriander seeds
1 teaspoon crushed black peppercorns
¼ teaspoon turmeric
1 teaspoon grated orange peel
juice of ½ orange
1 teaspoon salt

Barely cover the lamb with cold water, add the salt and bring slowly to the boil. Skim and add the saffron, onion (the onion skin adds colour), coriander and peppercorns. Simmer slowly for 2 hours. Remove the lamb to a warm serving dish. Keep hot. Discard the onion. Allow the stock to cool slightly, then skim off the fat. Pour 300ml/½ pint stock into a small saucepan and add the remaining ingredients. Bring to the boil, pour over the lamb and serve with a large bowl of plain rice and chopped spinach.

Braised belly of pork with quince and coriander

1kg/2lb thickly sliced belly of pork
3 peeled, cored and sliced quinces
1 small bunch of fresh coriander leaves, chopped
1 tablespoon oil
25g/1oz well-seasoned flour
1 sliced onion

Poultry

Tarragon stuffing for chicken

1 tablespoon chopped fresh tarragon leaves
50g/2oz butter
1 crushed garlic clove
lemon juice
salt and pepper
Beat all the ingredients together.
These recipes will be sufficient for a 2kg/4lb chicken.

Celery stuffing for chicken

2 chopped celery stalks
1 chopped shallot
25g/1oz butter
chopped liver of the chicken
25g/1oz fresh breadcrumbs
1 teaspoon fresh lemon thyme
1 tablespoon chopped celery leaves
1 tablespoon chopped fresh caraway leaves
1 beaten egg
salt and pepper
Gently stew the celery and shallot in the butter until tender. Add the liver and toss until golden. Remove from the heat and add the remaining ingredients, seasoning to taste.

Fennel stuffing for chicken

2 tablespoons chopped fresh Florentine fennel or fennel leaves
50g/2oz strips of cooked ham
25g/1oz butter
ground black pepper
Mix together and stuff the bird. Put

1 bay leaf
150ml/¼ pint light wine, stock or water
Heat the oil in a flameproof casserole. Roll the pork slices in the seasoned flour and brown in the oil with the sliced onion. Mix in the coriander leaves and bay leaf, add the wine, stock or water and cover tightly. Simmer gently for 30

A tender young chicken, whether for roasting, grilling or casseroling, may need only to be seasoned with garlic, lemon, butter and salt, but an older hen needs long simmering with a bundle of herbs, onions, salt and peppercorns to become thoroughly tender and succulent. The good chicken broth it will produce can be enriched with a pig's trotter and bacon rinds.

a bundle of dried fennel stalks under the chicken before roasting.

Herb stuffing for goose

350g/¾lb fresh breadcrumbs
100g/4oz minced ham
2 eggs
1 minced onion
225g/½lb finely chopped celery
3 tablespoons finely chopped thyme, parsley, marjoram and sage
1 teaspoon chopped mugwort tops
1 teaspoon grated lemon rind
salt and pepper
Beat all together. This is sufficient for a 4kg/8lb goose.

Chicken in chili sauce

1 jointed chicken (about 2kg/4lb)
1 seeded, sliced red chili
3 flattened garlic cloves
250g/8oz cubed smoked streaky bacon
3 tablespoons oil
25g/1oz seasoned flour
2 seeded, sliced red peppers
1 sliced onion
4 roughly chopped tomatoes
½ glass of red wine or water
2 teaspoons paprika
¼ teaspoon cayenne
¼ teaspoon powdered saffron
salt and pepper
Fry the garlic and bacon for a few minutes in the oil in a flameproof casserole. Roll the chicken joints in the flour and add, turning until

minutes. Add the quinces and simmer for a further hour. By this time much of the stock will have reduced and been absorbed by the quinces leaving a fresh, spicy sauce to serve with the pork. Serve with hot baked potatoes in their jackets. If quinces are in short supply, pears can be substituted.

golden. Remove the chicken to a warm plate. Add the chili, red peppers and onion and cook gently until soft. Return the chicken to the pot with the rest of the ingredients and simmer gently for 1½ hours or until tender. Check the seasoning. Serve with rice and a green salad.

Duck dressed with mint

1 duck (about 2.5kg/5lb)
a bunch of fresh apple mint and sweet marjoram
50g/2oz butter
150ml/¼ pint stock, white wine or water
500g/1lb shelled peas
2 quartered lettuces
salt and pepper
a pinch of grated nutmeg
a pinch of ground mace
lemon juice
fresh mint to garnish
Brown the duck in foaming butter until golden. Pour out the fat and add the stock, white wine or water. When it has bubbled for a few minutes add the peas, lettuces, herbs and a light seasoning. Cover tightly and stew slowly for 2 hours. Remove the duck to a warm serving dish. Remove the herbs from the stock and skim off the fat. Season the stock with nutmeg, mace and lemon juice, and more salt if necessary. Pour over the duck and garnish with mint. Serve with new potatoes and carrots.

Game

Marinades are particularly useful with game, breaking down tough, stringy fibres and lubricating dry, fatless meat. Keep the strained marinade to use for stock. Sherry makes a good marinade for rabbit, port for venison and cider for pigeons.

Rabbit with celeriac

1 jointed rabbit
1 peeled, sliced celeriac
300ml/½ pint basic cooked marinade (page 164), stock or water
1 tablespoon dripping
25g/1oz flour
1 bay leaf
1 tablespoon mustard
1 teaspoon lovage seeds
8 sliced leeks
225g/8oz mushrooms
salt and pepper

Marinate the rabbit overnight if possible. Dry the rabbit and fry until golden in hot dripping, then remove to a warm plate. Stir the flour into the dripping and slowly add the strained marinade, stock or water, stirring until it becomes a smooth gravy. Add the bay leaf, mustard and lovage seeds. Cover the bottom of a deep pot with the leeks, then the celeriac and finally the rabbit pieces, adding mushrooms, salt and pepper to each layer. Pour over the gravy, cover tightly and cook slowly, at 150°C/300°F/Mark 2, for 2 to 3 hours.

Stuffed pigeons in cabbage

4 pigeons
4 small cabbages or 12 large cabbage leaves
4 large pieces of fat bacon
25g/1oz flour
25g/1oz butter
MARINADE
150ml/¼ pint wine or draught cider
2 tablespoons oil
a twist of orange peel
bouquet garni (page 162)
salt and peppercorns
STUFFING
75g/3oz pearl barley
2 tablespoons chopped parsley and thyme
½ minced onion
25g/1oz melted butter
salt and pepper

Mix together the marinade ingredients, add the pigeons and leave them overnight.

Make the stuffing. Blanch and drain the barley, then simmer it until tender with the herbs and a little fresh water. Drain again and mix with the onion, butter and seasoning.

Remove the pigeons from the marinade and stuff with the herb and barley mixture.

Wrap a piece of fat bacon round each bird and put each in a hollowed cabbage or wrap in cabbage leaves. Pack tightly into a heavy pot, pour in the strained marinade and simmer very slowly for 3 to 4 hours. Remove the pigeons to a warm serving dish, discarding the cabbage. Bind the stock with the flour and butter mixed to a *beurre manié* and pour it over the birds. Serve with crisp roast parsnips.

Cold meats

Cold meat needs stronger flavouring and seasoning than meat that is to be eaten hot. Aromatic thyme, marjoram, juniper and bay and a good dash of spice will help preserve meat, either incorporated in potted-meat mixtures, pâtés or terrines, or used as a stuffing for rolled meat or as a thick coating for joints of ham, pork or beef. Potted meats and pâtés are among the most useful stored foods. Spice them well and line containers with fat bacon, then press the mixture in, making sure there are no pockets of air left in the corners. Seal the cooked dish with melted butter or, for long storage, with clarified butter, then cover with foil.

The flavour of cold meat often seems especially pronounced and defined and it is worth taking particular trouble over the spicing and marinating. The texture of hams, joints of meat, whole birds or terrines will be greatly improved by weighting overnight (with a plate and weights).

Opposite: *Four dishes for a sumptuous cold table. At the back raised rabbit pie with herbs and prunes, then duck, spiced with juniper berries and allspice, ham in a parsley jelly and small pots of aromatic pork cheese.*

Aromatic pork cheese

1kg/2lb finely minced belly of pork
¼ teaspoon ground mace
¼ teaspoon grated nutmeg
2 tablespoons finely chopped mixed fresh herbs, such as parsley, lemon thyme, basil and a pinch of sage
1 tablespoon brandy (optional)

1 teaspoon salt
pepper
lemon thyme

Pound the pork in a mortar with the spices, chopped herbs, brandy – if you have any – and seasoning. Press this paste into small ovenproof pots and set in a shallow tin of water. Bake in a moderate oven 180°C/350°F/Mark 4, for 45 minutes. Leave to cool, then press a sprig of lemon thyme into the fat on each pot. Cover tightly with foil and store in a cool place or the refrigerator. These will keep for at least a week, or longer if the brandy has been added.

Raised rabbit pie with herbs and prunes

1 rabbit
500g/1lb minced fat belly of pork
50g/2oz minced green bacon
½ minced onion
1 minced garlic clove
1 teaspoon mixed spice
1 teaspoon ground allspice
salt and pepper
3 tablespoons fresh green herbs such as parsley, caraway, chives or thyme
100g/4oz prunes, soaked overnight
MARINADE
6 tablespoons olive oil
1 tablespoon vinegar
1 tablespoon lavender leaves
salt and pepper
STOCK
1 split pig's trotter
1 unpeeled onion stuck with 2 cloves
1 chopped carrot
bouquet garni (page 162)
a twist of orange peel
1 teaspoon peppercorns
PASTRY
175g/6oz lard
450g/1lb sifted flour
1 teaspoon salt

Cut the meat from the rabbit bones. Mix together the ingredients of the marinade, add the rabbit meat and leave overnight. Put the rabbit bones in a large pan with the stock ingredients. Cover with cold water, bring to the boil and simmer slowly for 3 to 4 hours. Strain the stock and leave it to cool.

The following day take the larger pieces of rabbit meat out of the marinade, slice and set aside. Mince the remaining rabbit meat with the pork, bacon, onion and garlic and mix with the spices and seasoning. Into another bowl mince the liver of the rabbit with the green herbs and stoned prunes.

Make a hot water crust pastry. Bring the lard to the boil with 200ml/8fl oz water. Pour it into the flour and salt and mix until smooth. Leave to cool for 10 minutes. Roll out about three-quarters of the dough to about 6mm/¼in thick and line a cake or pie tin with a removable base. Pack in the pork and rabbit mixture, then the liver, herbs and prunes and then the larger rabbit pieces. Roll out the remaining dough and cover. Pinch all the joins together to seal. Brush with beaten egg. Make a slit in the centre of the dough lid and push a rolled tube of cardboard down through it to keep it open. Bake for 30 minutes in a moderately hot oven, 200°C/400°F/ Mark 6, then reduce the heat to warm, 160°C/325°F/Mark 3 and bake for a further 1½ hours. When the pie has cooled to lukewarm, remove the cardboard tube and fill the hole with the jellied stock. Keep refilling with the stock until the meat will absorb no more. Leave the pie to cool and store in a cool place until the following day.

Ham in a parsley jelly

1.5kg/3lb boiled bacon
5 tablespoons chopped parsley
1 veal knuckle
1 split pig's trotter
1 chopped onion
1 chopped carrot
1 chopped tomato
a piece of pork rind
150ml/¼ pint white wine
1 crushed garlic clove
4 juniper berries
bouquet garni (page 162)
½ teaspoon salt
6 black peppercorns

Put all the ingredients except the bacon and parsley in a flameproof casserole. Cover with cold water and bring slowly to simmering point. Transfer to a cool oven, 150°C/ 300°F/Mark 2, and cook for 3 to 4 hours. Strain the stock and leave it in a cool place to set to a jelly.

Chop the boiled bacon into chunks. Skim all fat from the jelly, warm for a few minutes to soften and stir in the bacon and parsley.

Taste for seasoning and pour into a mould that has been rinsed in cold water. Leave in a cool place to set. Unmould and slice to reveal the patterns of pink and green.

Spiced meat to be eaten cold

2kg/4lb meat joint or large duck
1 glass wine
2 split pig's trotters
1 chopped onion
1 chopped carrot
2 bay leaves
2 crushed garlic cloves
bouquet garni (page 162)
SPICE MIXTURE
1 tablespoon coarse salt
10 black peppercorns
10 juniper berries
6 allspice berries
½ teaspoon ground cloves

Remove the skin from the joint – you can use beef, pork or mutton – and prick the meat all over with a fork. Leave the skin on the duck and prick with a fork. Combine the ingredients for the spice mixture and rub into the meat or duck. Leave overnight to absorb the flavours. Put the meat or duck into a large pot with cold water to cover and add the remaining ingredients. Simmer gently until tender. Leave the meat or duck to cool in the liquid, then lift into a bowl. Moisten with a few spoonfuls of the stock, cover with greaseproof paper or foil, and leave overnight under a weight of about 2kg/4lb. Strain the stock and leave overnight for the fat to solidify. Remove the fat from the stock and reduce the stock to half by rapid boiling. Leave it to set into a jelly which can then be served with the meat. Meat or duck spiced in this way will keep for at least a week in a cold place.

Outdoor cooking

Barbecues

Herb flavourings are an essential part of outdoor cookery, whether it is a few wild herbs cooked with freshly caught fish or game on a camping holiday or pungent, spicy sauces with a garden barbecue. The flavour of woodsmoke permeates the food and it is worth saving all the prunings and trimmings from the herb garden to throw on the fire during the last few minutes of cooking time to make a strongly aromatic smoke. Bundles of thyme, rosemary, marjoram and fennel, whether fresh or dried, and branches of juniper, myrtle and bay all give a rich scent and flavour to the food. The classic French dish *grillade au fenouil* developed from this simple idea, as it depends upon flaming a large grilled fish over brandy-soaked, dried fennel stalks just before serving.

'Robber cooking'

Cooking over an open fire tends to dry and char the surfaces of large pieces of meat or fish while leaving the inside tough and raw. One delicious and successful way of slow cooking out of doors is by 'robber cooking': whole animals or birds are wrapped in aromatic herbs and leaves for protection and flavouring, then buried in a shallow hole and sprinkled with a thin layer of earth. A fire is lit above and left to smoulder for several hours until the meat is cooked – an ideal method for robbers as there is no trace or smell of the meat as it cooks.

Pit roasting

Polynesians pit roast by lighting a fire in a hole lined with stones. These act as fire bricks when the fire is raked out and the food put in to cook. Chicken and pigs are wrapped in banana leaves and whole fish in seaweed. Other basic methods of outdoor cooking include spit-roasting and grilling and 'gypsy cooking', when small birds or animals are rolled in clay and baked in the ashes of a smouldering fire.

Charcoal grilling

Charcoal, with its glowing, steady heat, is the ideal fuel for outdoor cooking, though wood that is dry and therefore comparatively smokeless will do. Light the fire well in advance and wait until it has settled down to smoulder. Make sure the metal grill or grid is well oiled.

Chicken baked in clay

chicken (about 2kg/4lb)
100g/4oz butter
juice of ½ lemon
1 crushed garlic clove
1 tablespoon lemon thyme
2 teaspoons spiced salt (page 160)

Cream the butter with the lemon juice, garlic, thyme and salt and stuff into the chicken. Do not salt the outside of the bird or the juices will be drawn out with the salt and be absorbed by the clay. Wrap the chicken in buttered paper and roll it in an airtight parcel of wet clay. An unglazed earthenware pot or chicken brick will serve the same purpose as the clay. Bury it in the ashes of a hot fire and cook for 2½ to 3 hours. The natural juices of the bird provide the moisture and steam during cooking. Break open the brittle clay over a bowl to catch the juices and serve with sweet peppers that have been grilled over the fire.

Other birds and animals can be cooked in the same way, but fatty birds such as duck or goose should be roasted over the fire for 10 minutes and their skins pricked all over to drain off some of the fat before wrapping in the clay.

Indonesian barbecued chicken

1 tender chicken
3 sliced shallots
3 sliced garlic cloves
1 teaspoon crushed, fresh ginger
1 teaspoon ground black pepper
1 teaspoon cumin seed
½ teaspoon turmeric
1 teaspoon lemon juice
100g/4oz desiccated coconut
450ml/¾ pint water
1 sprig of basil
salt

Split the chicken in half, down the breastbone. In Indonesia it would be left whole, trussed out flat and skewered. Pound together the shallots, garlic and ginger, then mix in the pepper, cumin, turmeric and lemon juice. Roll the chicken in this mixture and leave to marinate. Put the coconut in a jug, pour over the water and leave to stand for 30 minutes, then strain and squeeze through a cloth. (Or use 50g/2oz packaged creamed coconut mixed with 450ml/¾ pint hot water.) Add the basil, salt and chicken to the coconut milk, bring slowly to simmering point and cook until tender but before the flesh begins to loosen from the bones. Carefully lift out the chicken and grill until richly brown over a charcoal fire, basting occasionally with the coconut milk.

This has a most succulent and subtle flavour with none of the dryness so often associated with barbecued poultry.

To pit-roast a sucking pig

1 sucking pig
10 garlic cloves
100g/4oz fresh root ginger
juice of 5 lemons
150ml/¼ pint soy sauce
salt and pepper
bundles and branches of aromatic herbs

Pound the garlic and ginger and mix with the lemon juice, soy sauce and plenty of coarse salt and black pepper. Rub the pig inside and outside with this and leave it to marinate overnight. Dig a pit a little larger than the pig and line it with rocks and stones. Light a fire in it. After 4 or 5 hours, when there are plenty of ashes and the stones are hissing hot, rake out the ashes and line the pit with aromatic herbs such as rosemary, myrtle, fennel and bay. Put in the pig with a few hot stones inside it and cover it with more bundles and branches of herbs, then the hot ashes and finally a layer of earth or a piece of corrugated iron. Leave it to cook for about 5 hours. Serve with large bowls of spiced rice and red pepper salad or with potatoes that have been baked with the pig. This could feed up to 20 people, depending on the size of the pig.

Clams can be baked in the same way but the cooking time will be shorter, about 1 to 2 hours, and the pit should be lined with seaweed if possible.

Opposite: *On the spit is a rolled topside of beef, rubbed with tomato and cumin sauce, and, grilling, a grey mullet, soon to be flamed over fennel stalks. The chicken, stuffed with a garlic mixture and seasoned with spiced salt, has been baked in the clay brick.*

Roast spare ribs of pork

2kg/4lb spare ribs of pork
2 chopped onions
2 chopped garlic cloves
2 tablespoons olive oil
6 tablespoons tomato paste
3 tablespoons red wine vinegar
150ml/¼ pint red wine, stock or water
1 tablespoon brown sugar
1 teaspoon made or dry mustard
2 tablespoons chopped thyme
1 tablespoon chopped basil
salt and pepper

Soften the onions and garlic in the olive oil for 10 minutes. Stir in the tomato paste and vinegar and cook for 2 minutes. Stir in the red wine, stock or water and add the remaining sauce ingredients. Cover and cook gently for 15 minutes. Pour over the spare ribs and leave for 1 hour before roasting to absorb the flavours.

Tomato and cumin basting sauce for spit-roasted meat

1kg/2lb roughly chopped tomatoes
1 sliced onion
2 sliced garlic cloves
a pinch of salt
2 tablespoons olive oil
1 teaspoon crushed cumin seeds
1 teaspoon coarsely ground black pepper
1 teaspoon sea salt

Put the tomatoes, onion and garlic in a pan with a pinch of salt and simmer slowly, covered, for 15 minutes. Put through a sieve or mouli-légumes, return to the pan and boil for a few minutes until reduced to a thick purée. Stir in the olive oil, cumin and seasoning. Rub into the meat that is to be cooked. As the meat roasts, catch all the drippings and juices to re-use for basting.

This sauce is particularly good with beef or lamb.

Kebabs

Marinate chunks of lamb, pork, beef or fish in the Greek marinade (page 164). Thread onto skewers interspersed with pieces of red pepper, onions, mushrooms and bay leaves. Grill over the fire, basting with the marinade. Serve on beds of parsley or chervil, with flat Greek bread, bowls of plain yoghurt and black olives.

Grilled vegetables

Grill whole sweet peppers, aubergines and tomatoes until their skins are blackened. Peel and slice them and dress while warm with strong green olive oil, lemon juice and salt.

Grilled fish with garlic

1 cleaned whole fish (about 1.5kg/3lb)
2 chopped garlic cloves
3 tablespoons olive oil
sea salt
25g/1oz butter

Brush the fish all over with oil and rub with sea salt. Heat and oil a metal grill. Put the fish on the grill and cook over the ashes of a hot fire, turning several times and basting with oil if it becomes too dry. Fry the garlic in foaming butter until golden. Squeeze the lemon juice into the butter and pour this sauce over the cooked fish on a hot plate.

Prawn satay

12 king prawns (or langoustes or crayfish)
1 crushed garlic clove
3 tablespoons soy sauce
1 teaspoon brown sugar
1 tablespoon sherry
1 sliced, seeded red chili
oil
¼ teaspoon salt

Thoroughly mix together all the ingredients excepting the prawns and oil, then add the prawns and marinate for several hours. Lift out a few chili slices and reserve. Thread the prawns onto skewers, brush with oil and grill, basting with the marinade. Serve on a bed of freshly boiled vermicelli, garnished with the remaining chili.

Grains and pulses

One of the simplest and most delicious ways of cooking grains such as rice, whole wheat, bulgar wheat, barley or millet is as a pilaf. Cook the grain in butter or oil for a few minutes over a medium heat, then cover with stock or water and cook very slowly indeed, in a tightly lidded pan, until the liquid is absorbed. Serve with crisply fried onion and garlic, toasted almonds and fine strips of fresh ginger, or with chopped parsley, coriander or mint leaves and sprinkled with grated Parmesan cheese. Or add spices and onion to the rice before cooking.

Many of the following recipes make substantial vegetarian dishes.

Couscous

225g/8oz couscous
75g/3oz chick peas
1 tablespoon olive oil
1 sliced onion
1 chopped garlic clove
2 sliced carrots
1kg/2lb cubed shoulder of lamb
1 seeded, chopped red pepper
1 tablespoon tomato paste
1 teaspoon paprika
¼ teaspoon chili pepper
salt and pepper
100g/4oz vegetables such as sliced courgettes, tomatoes, runner beans or peas
50g/2oz raisins
1 tablespoon chopped parsley
2 teaspoons Harissa sauce (optional)

Soak the chick peas overnight, then drain and simmer in fresh water for 1 hour. Heat the oil in a saucepan or bottom of a *couscousier*, if you have one. Add the onion and garlic, then a layer of carrots, then the chick peas, lamb and red pepper. Stir in the tomato paste, paprika and chili. Season. Add water to cover, put on a tight-fitting lid and simmer for 1 hour. Rub a few tablespoons of cold water into the couscous to moisten the grains, then put the couscous in a sieve or colander lined with muslin or into the top of the *couscousier*. Set this above the stew, cover with a lid and steam for 1 hour, lifting and stirring the grains occasionally to separate them as they swell, and sprinkling them with water if they become too dry. Add the vegetables and raisins to the stew 15 minutes

before the couscous is ready. To serve, heap the couscous into a large dish and stir in a few spoonfuls of stock from the stew. Lift out the meat and vegetables with a slotted spoon and pile round the couscous. Sprinkle with parsley.

A fiercely hot, spicy sauce called 'Harissa' is often served in a separate bowl or mixed with a little stock and poured over each helping. It can be bought in tins from delicatessens but should be used with care, remembering its potency.

Saffron rice with nuts

225g/8oz basmati or long-grain rice
¼ teaspoon powdered saffron
25g/1oz blanched, roughly chopped almonds
25g/1oz chopped pistachios or hazelnuts
25g/1oz pine nuts
2 tablespoons oil
salt
25g/1oz currants
a pinch of ground cinnamon

Gently fry the rice in 1 tablespoon of the oil, stirring, for 5 minutes. Mix in the saffron, a pinch of salt and cold water to cover the rice. Simmer, covered tightly, until tender. Meanwhile, fry the nuts in the remaining oil until lightly coloured, stirring all the time. Mix in the currants and cinnamon. Pile the yellow rice in a warm, shallow dish and top with the nut mixture.

To make a more substantial dish, cook the rice in chicken stock and add chopped white chicken meat to the nut mixture.

Rice with fresh herbs

225g/8oz long-grain rice
1 large bunch of fresh herbs such as parsley, caraway leaves, lovage, chives, tarragon and mint, chopped
¼ teaspoon salt
3 tablespoons olive oil

Put the rice in a pan. Pour in enough cold water to cover by 6mm/¼in. Add salt, cover tightly and cook over a very low heat until the water is absorbed and the rice is *nearly* cooked. In another pan heat the oil, then stir in the rice until all the grains are well coated. Stir in the herbs. Cover the pan with a clean, folded tea towel and the lid, then leave over a low heat to steam for a further 10 to 20 minutes. Serve in a warm dish together with the golden crust that will have formed at the bottom of the pan.

Brown winter rice

225g/8oz brown rice
salt and black pepper
1 sliced onion
1 tablespoon oil
50g/2oz sunflower seed kernels
1 teaspoon lovage seeds
4 thinly sliced carrots
4 chopped hard-boiled eggs
150ml/¼ pint plain yoghurt

Cover the rice with cold water and leave it to soak for 45 minutes. (This makes the rice less stodgy and shortens the cooking time.) Add 1 teaspoon salt and put the rice over a low heat, in the same water. Simmer gently for about 30 minutes or until tender. Stew the onion in the oil for

5 minutes, then raise the heat and add the sunflower and lovage seeds, carrots, salt and pepper. Stir in the rice and hard-boiled eggs. Serve with a bowl of plain yoghurt.

Spiced haricot beans

500g/1lb dried haricot beans
1 onion
1 sliced small onion
3 cloves
3 flattened garlic cloves
a twist of orange peel
1 tablespoon coriander seeds
1 tablespoon black peppercorns
1 bay leaf
1 faggot of thyme or a handful of thyme
 leaves
1 tablespoon oil
2 tablespoons tomato paste
1 tablespoon wine vinegar or red wine
1 teaspoon paprika
1 teaspoon ground cumin
salt and pepper
75g/3oz fresh breadcrumbs
100g/4oz cubed cooked ham or streaky
 bacon (optional)

Soak the beans overnight. Drain and put in a flameproof casserole with the whole onion stuck with the cloves, the garlic, orange peel, coriander crushed with the peppercorns, the bay leaf and thyme. Cover with water and simmer for about 1½ hours or until the beans are nearly cooked. Drain and reserve the strained cooking liquor. Melt the oil in the cleaned-out casserole and stew the sliced onion for a few minutes. Stir in the tomato paste and vinegar or wine and let it bubble for 1 minute. Pour in 300ml/½ pint of the reserved liquor, season with paprika, cumin, salt and plenty of black pepper and add the beans. Cover with the breadcrumbs and cook without a lid at 150°C/300°F/Mark 2, for about 1 hour. A golden crust will form over the moist, creamy beans.

To make a more substantial dish, add the ham or bacon when stewing the onion.

Paella with peppers

225g/8oz round-grain Italian or Spanish
 rice (not pudding rice)
2 seeded, sliced red peppers
2 chopped garlic cloves
1 skinned chopped tomato
1 tablespoon olive oil
100g/4oz vegetables, such as thinly
 sliced courgettes, runner beans, broad
 beans or peas
about 150ml/¼ pint stock
a pinch of powdered, soaked saffron
1 teaspoon paprika
salt

Fry the garlic, tomato and red peppers in the oil for 5 minutes. Stir in the vegetables and rice. Add boiling stock to cover and the saffron, paprika and salt. Bring to the boil, cover tightly and simmer over a low heat until the rice is tender. Serve very hot in the cooking pan.

Kitcheri (spiced lentils and rice)

100g/4oz small lentils
100g/4oz basmati rice
100g/4oz clarified butter
6 crushed allspice berries
1 tablespoon thinly sliced root ginger
seeds from 4 cardamom pods
1 bay leaf
¼ teaspoon mignonette pepper (page 160)
salt
1 tablespoon wine vinegar or tamarind
 water (made by infusing tamarind)
1 thinly sliced onion
¼ teaspoon sugar

Soak the lentils and rice in water to cover for 1 hour. Drain and cook gently in half the butter, stirring, for 10 minutes. Add the spices, bay leaf, pepper and salt. Cover with cold water and the vinegar or tamarind water. Stir, bring to the boil, cover and simmer very gently for about 20 minutes or until tender. Melt the remaining butter and fry the onion, sprinkled with the sugar, until it is dark brown and caramelized. Mix this into the lentils and rice and serve with quarters of lemon.

Variations on this dish are com-mon throughout the Middle East and India. The English dish kedgeree is derived from kitcheri.

Lentils with cumin

225g/8oz large green lentils
2 teaspoons crushed cumin seeds
2 chopped garlic cloves
1 sliced onion
1 tablespoon oil
1 teaspoon crushed coriander seeds
squeeze of lemon juice
salt and pepper

Fry the lentils, garlic and onion in the oil in a flameproof casserole for 5 minutes. Stir in the remaining ingredients, cover with water and cook in a warm oven, 160°C/325°F/Mark 3, for 2 hours until tender.

A cooked vegetable such as spinach or carrots can be stirred in for the final few minutes of the cooking time.

Spiced corn bread

225g/8oz coarse yellow cornmeal or
 maize flour
85g/3oz white flour
2 teaspoons baking powder
2 teaspoons roughly crushed cumin,
 lovage or caraway seeds or 2 tablespoons chopped green herbs
salt
2 eggs
175g/6oz melted butter
300ml/½ pint milk (approx.)

Mix together the cornmeal or maize flour, white flour, baking powder, spices or herbs and salt, then beat in the eggs and butter. Finally add the milk until the mixture is of a heavy dropping consistency. Pour into a well-greased baking dish measuring about 25cm/10in by 36cm/14in and bake immediately in a fairly hot oven, 200°C/400°F/Mark 6 for about 20 minutes until risen and golden. Cut into thick slices and serve steaming hot with eggs and bacon, sausages or ham.

These quantities will provide enough crunchy bread for 8 people.

Pasta

Several of the herb sauces given in other sections go well with pasta. Pesto sauce is one of the best (page 168), or the tomato and basil sauce (page 169) while the milk cheese with herbs (page 184) melts to become a delicious savoury cream sauce. Stir the sauce into the freshly cooked pasta just before serving in a hot dish.

Spaghetti with a simple herb sauce

500g/1lb spaghetti
2 chopped garlic cloves
1 tablespoon olive oil
2 handfuls of chopped green herbs such
  as parsley, marjoram, chervil and basil.
salt and pepper
4 tablespoons double cream

Cook the spaghetti in fast-boiling salted water until tender but not sticky. Drain well. Meanwhile, soften the garlic in the oil for 3 minutes, then add the herbs and seasoning. Stir the cream into the sauce and pour immediately over the spaghetti.

Serve with a slightly bitter green salad made with a fresh lettuce, salad burnet and curly endive or chicory, tossed in a vinaigrette dressing.

Cannelloni with endive and borage stuffing

500g/1lb cannelloni (squares of pasta)
1 endive
1 large bunch of fresh borage leaves
50g/2oz bread
2 tablespoons milk
100g/4oz grated Parmesan cheese
50g/2oz butter
1 egg
1 egg yolk
1 sliced small shallot
a pinch of grated nutmeg
salt and pepper
6 tablespoons stock

Blanch the endive and borage for 30 seconds in boiling water, then drain and dry thoroughly. Soak the bread

Pasta is a staple, simple food but the variety of its shapes and sizes makes it endlessly fascinating to cook. They all taste good with fresh herb sauces.

in the milk. Pound the endive and borage in a mortar with the soaked bread, 50g/2oz of the Parmesan, 25g/1oz of the butter, the egg, egg yolk, shallot, nutmeg and seasoning. (Minced chicken or other light meat can be added, if wished.) Cook the cannelloni in boiling salted water until tender, then drain carefully. Spread each square flat and put a little mound of stuffing in the middle. Roll up, tucking in the ends neatly. Lay the rolls close together in a shallow baking dish, join side down. Dot with the remaining butter, sprinkle with the remaining Parmesan and the stock and bake for about 20 minutes in a moderate oven, 180°C/350°F/Mark 4.

Noodles with poppy seeds

350g/¾lb thick noodles
2 tablespoons poppy seeds
75g/3oz butter
3 tablespoons fresh breadcrumbs
salt

Cook the noodles in salted boiling water until tender, drain and stir in half the butter. Tip into a warmed serving dish and cover with a cloth. Melt the remaining butter and fry the breadcrumbs until golden then stir in the poppy seeds and fry a few more minutes until crunchy. Scatter these over the noodles and serve this typically German dish as an accompaniment to goulash or roast meat, or on its own with crisply fried cubes of bacon or ham.

Savoury puddings and dumplings

Steamed and boiled puddings have formed the basic diet of country people in northern Europe for centuries. Early puddings consisted of the scoured stomach of a sheep or pig, stuffed with its own suet and offal, which had been thickened with oatmeal, and boiled in water or baked in the ashes of a fire. By the 17th century the suet crust began to be used. Herbs and spices have always been an essential ingredient in these puddings and in sausages, offsetting the fattiness with their hot, sharp flavours, helping the digestion of the heavy ingredients and acting as preservatives. Medieval dumplings resembled puddings, sparrows or other small birds being rolled in paste and dropped in boiling broth. Today dumplings are especially popular in Germany and Scandinavian countries, both sweet, savoury and highly spiced. They make filling, warming additions to broths and casseroles.

Cheese dumplings

2 tablespoons grated cheese
50g/2oz butter
50g/2oz flour
120ml/4fl oz warmed milk (approx.)
2 eggs, separated
seeds scraped from 1 cardamom pod
salt and pepper

Melt the butter and mix in the flour over a low heat. Add the warmed milk, a little at a time, stirring constantly, then simmer the thickened sauce for 10 minutes. Remove from the heat and stir in the egg yolks, cheese, cardamom seeds and seasoning to taste. The mixture can be left now until cooking time or used immediately. Whisk the egg whites until stiff and fold into the mixture. Drop into boiling beef or chicken *bouillon* or salted water, a teaspoonful at a time, and simmer until the dumplings are cooked through and rise to the surface – about 5 minutes.

Herb dumplings

115/4oz shredded suet or dripping
225g/8oz flour, sifted
2 teaspoons baking powder
3 tablespoons chopped mixed herbs such as chives, onion greens, parsley, thyme, lovage leaves or seeds
salt and pepper

Rub the suet or dripping into the flour and baking powder. Stir in the herbs and seasoning and mix with enough cold water to make a firm dough. Roll into small balls (they will swell as they cook). Some pieces of chopped bacon can be pushed into each dumpling if you like. Poach for about 20 minutes in a covered pan of stew, soup or stock. The dumplings will crisp on top if you put the pan under a grill or leave it uncovered in a hot oven for the final 5 minutes of cooking time.

Traditional savoury pudding

350g/12oz sifted flour
3 teaspoons baking powder
salt and pepper
175g/6oz shredded suet
175g/6oz chopped bacon rashers
1 chopped onion or 3 chopped shallots
100g/4oz chopped mushrooms
4 tablespoons mixed, chopped sweet herbs

Mix the flour, baking powder, $\frac{1}{4}$ teaspoon salt and the suet with sufficient cold water to make a stiff dough. Roll it out to an oblong. Mix together the remaining ingredients, season them well and spread over the dough. Roll up into a sausage shape, tucking in the ends. Moisten the joins with cold water and press to seal. Dip a large square of pudding cloth in boiling water, then sprinkle it generously with flour. (This protects the pudding and prevents it becoming saturated as it cooks.) Roll up the pudding in the cloth, leaving space for it to expand, and secure with a safety pin, making sure that all the ends are tucked in. Lower into a large pan of boiling water – a fish kettle is a suitable shape; the pudding can be made round but then it doesn't cook so evenly. Boil for $1\frac{1}{2}$ to 3 hours. Root vegetables and cabbages can be added to the water towards the end of the cooking time. Roll the pudding out of the cloth onto a hot plate and serve surrounded by steaming vegetables, moistened with the cooking liquor if necessary.

Easter ledge or herb pudding

115g/4oz pearl barley
115g/4oz coarse oatmeal
350g/12oz chopped young bistort leaves (known as Easter ledges)
225g/8oz chopped young nettle tops
a handful of chopped blackcurrant leaves
a handful of chopped young dandelion leaves
2 sliced leeks
1 sliced onion
salt and pepper

Soak the barley and oatmeal together in water to cover for about 1 hour, to swell. Drain and mix with the remaining ingredients and season with plenty of salt and pepper. Pack into a greased pudding basin, cover and steam for $1\frac{1}{2}$ hours to 2 hours. Turn out and serve with crisply fried bacon or with roast meat.

This is a traditional spring pudding in northern England, where bistort grows in mountain meadows.

Bread

Herbs have not only been used as flavourings for bread but also as an integral part of the loaf. Fat hen, orache, flax and buckwheat were encouraged to grow among the corn in northern Europe until the 18th century, their ground seeds adding nourishment and variety. During lean years the fleshy roots of angelica, lovage and bistort, among many others, were ground and used as flour for bread.

Today dill and caraway seeds are characteristic flavours in Scandinavian and German bread, fennel and aniseed in Italian and French bread, poppy seed in Jewish and mid-European bread, and coriander, cumin and sesame seed in the bread of the Middle East. The seeds are sprinkled on the tops of loaves or incorporated in the dough. Other ways of flavouring bread include baking loaves on branches of aromatic herbs such as fennel and thyme; brushing bread tins and loaf tops with herb oils; and adding chopped, fresh or dried herbs to the dough before baking.

It is impossible to give precise instructions for making bread as flours are so variable; some absorbing far less liquid. The rising time varies too, according to the warmth of the room and type of flour. In the following recipes the minimum quantity of liquid is given, leaving you to add more if necessary. The ideal dough is soft but firm in texture and you should be able to knead it easily. The rising or proving times given are also the minimum needed if you are proving dough in a warm airing cupboard or plate warming compartment. Dough can be left much longer in a cooler place or even overnight in the refrigerator in a roomy plastic bag.

Newly baked breads, cakes and biscuits: 1 spiced wigs, split into wedges 2 slices of saffron cake 3 Armenian bread 4 plaited Challah bread 5 wholemeal herb and onion loaves 6 Easter biscuits 7 oregano salt sticks.

Oregano salt sticks

Yield: approximately 20 sticks
450g/1lb flour
a handful of chopped fresh oregano or marjoram
salt
15g/½oz fresh yeast
¼ teaspoon brown sugar
1 egg
3 tablespoons cooking oil
150ml/¼ pint warm milk
3 tablespoons grated Parmesan cheese
40g/1½oz coarse sea salt

Put the flour and a pinch of salt to warm for a few minutes in a low oven. Crumble the yeast into a bowl, add the sugar and a few spoonfuls of warm water and mix well. Leave in a warm place until frothy. Make a well in the flour and tip into it the yeast mixture, egg, oil and sufficient milk to make a pliable dough. Knead for a few minutes, then leave to rise in a warm place for 30 minutes. Knead in the oregano or marjoram and Parmesan. Divide the dough into about 20 pieces and roll into

long sticks the thickness of a pencil. Lay them on a greased baking sheet, brush with milk, sprinkle thickly with the sea salt and leave to rise again in a warm place for 10 minutes. Bake in a moderate oven, 180°C/350°F/Mark 4, for 10 to 15 minutes until lightly browned and crisp. Serve warm with soup, hors d'oeuvre, salads or celery sticks.

Challah

Yield: 1 monumental loaf or 2 large loaves
25g/1oz fresh yeast
1 teaspoon brown sugar
675g/1½lb sifted strong white flour
2 teaspoons salt
100g/4oz butter
1 beaten egg yolk
1 egg
2 tablespoons poppy seeds

Crumble the yeast, add the sugar and a few spoonfuls of warm water and leave in a warm place until frothy. Rub the butter into the flour and salt, make a well in the centre and break

in the egg. Add the yeast mixture and sufficient warm water to make a stiff dough (about 300ml/½ pint) and knead until smooth and elastic. Return to the warm bowl and leave to rise for about 45 minutes or until doubled in size. Knead again and divide the dough into three pieces, one large, one medium and one small. Divide each piece into three, roll them into long sausages and plait them up. Lay the largest plait on a greased baking sheet, press the medium plait onto it and the smallest plait onto that, then brush the whole edifice with beaten egg yolk. Scatter thickly with poppy seeds and bake in a hot oven, 220°C/425°F/Mark 7, for 15 minutes. Reduce the heat to warm, 160°C/325°F/Mark 3, and bake for a further 45 minutes or until the loaf sounds hollow when knocked on the bottom. Cool on a wire rack.

If 2 loaves are made then the cooking time may be slightly reduced.

Dark rye bread

Yield: 2 loaves

350g/12oz rye flour
300ml/½ pint milk
75g/3oz butter
2 tablespoons dark treacle or molasses
20g/¾oz fresh yeast
1 teaspoon brown sugar
175g/6oz wholemeal flour
50g/2oz white flour
50g/2oz wheat germ
3 tablespoons plain yoghurt
1 tablespoon grated lemon peel
1 tablespoon caraway seeds
1 teaspoon salt

Scald the milk and stir in the butter and treacle or molasses. Allow to cool to blood heat. Crumble the yeast, stir in the sugar and a little warm water and leave in a warm place until frothy. Mix together the remaining ingredients, add the yeast and milk mixtures and mix well. Knead until the dough is smooth and pliable, then return it to the bowl and leave it to rise for about 45 minutes in a warm place. Knead again, form into 2 loaves and press into loaf tins. Let the dough rise again for 30 minutes, then brush the tops with water and bake in a hot oven, 220°C/425°F/Mark 7, for 15 minutes. Reduce the heat to warm, 160°C/325°F/Mark 3, and bake for a further 30 minutes. Tip out of the tins and cool on a rack.

This dense, dark bread resembles Pumpernickel and keeps well. Slice thinly and spread with cream cheese or unsalted butter and watercress.

Armenian bread

Yield: 3 large flat loaves

1.35kg/3lb sifted strong white flour
300ml/½ pint milk
50g/2oz margarine or butter
25g/1oz lard
25g/1oz fresh yeast
1 teaspoon brown sugar
2 tablespoons sesame seeds
2 tablespoons toasted sunflower seed kernels
1½ teaspoons salt
2 eggs
50g/2oz grated Parmesan cheese
1 tablespoon cumin seeds
1 tablespoon chopped walnuts
1 tablespoon coarsely ground black pepper
a few chopped rue leaves

Scald the milk and stir in the margarine and lard. Allow to cool to blood heat. Crumble the yeast, add the sugar and a few spoonfuls of warm water and leave in a warm place until frothy. Mix together the flour, sesame seeds, sunflower kernels and salt. Stir the yeast and milk mixtures into the flour together with 600ml/1 pint lukewarm water. Beat well and knead until smooth and silky. Leave to rise for about 45 minutes. Knead again and form into 3 large flat loaves. Lay these on greased baking sheets and leave to rise again for 30 minutes. Mix together the eggs, cheese, cumin, walnuts, pepper and rue and spread this thick paste over the loaves. Bake in a hot oven, 220°C/425°F/Mark 7, for 15 minutes, then lower the heat to moderate, 180°C/350°F/Mark 4, and bake for a further 30 minutes or until the loaves are firm and golden and sound hollow when tapped.

Wholemeal herb and onion bread

Yield: 3 loaves

1.35kg/3lb wholemeal flour
100g/4oz chopped fresh green herbs, which could include parsley, chervil, lovage, caraway, thyme, marjoram, chives etc
1 teaspoon lovage seeds
1 finely chopped small onion
1 teaspoon salt
40g/1½oz fresh yeast
½ teaspoon brown sugar
900ml/1½ pints warm water
25g/1oz butter

Put the flour and salt to warm for a few minutes in a low oven. Crumble the yeast into a bowl, add the sugar and a few spoonfuls of the warm water and mix well. Leave in a warm place until frothy. Add the yeast mixture and remaining water to the warmed flour and mix well with a wooden spoon. Mix in the onion, lovage seeds and herbs. Take the dough from the bowl and knead for 5 minutes on a wooden board, pressing and turning the dough to distribute the herbs and yeast evenly. Grease 3 bread tins with the butter. Divide the dough in 3 and press into the tins. Cover the tins with a cloth and leave them in a warm place for about 45 minutes while the dough rises. It will not rise as dramatically as dough made with white flour. Bake for 15 minutes in a hot oven, 220°C/425°F/Mark 7, then reduce the heat to moderate, 180°C/350°F/Mark 4, and bake for a further 30 to 45 minutes. Tip the loaves from their tins and return to the oven for a few minutes to crisp the crust.

The onion and lovage seeds can be omitted and walnuts, hazelnuts or chopped celery added instead.

Soft chervil rolls

Yield: about 10 rolls

450g/1lb strong white flour
15g/½oz fresh yeast
½ teaspoon sugar
300ml/½ pint lukewarm water
salt
2 tablespoons chopped fresh chervil

Crumble the yeast, stir in sugar and a little warm water and leave until frothy. Mix with the flour, salt, and remaining water and knead well. Leave in a warm place for 30 minutes to rise, covered with a cloth. Knead again briefly, mixing in the chervil, and form into small rolls. Lay these on a cloth sprinkled with flour, and cover with another floury cloth and leave to rise for 15 minutes. Slip the rolls onto a very hot, oiled baking sheet, sprinkle with cold water and bake in a hot oven, 240°C/475°F/Mark 8–9 for 8 to 9 minutes.

Cakes and biscuits

There are traditional Christmas recipes for heavily spiced and enriched yeast breads and cakes in most northern countries, especially in Germany and Scandinavia, where the bread is twisted, plaited and coloured with saffron.

Spiced wigs

Wigs or wygges were eaten as a Lenten cake in the 15th century but later became popular as a spiced breakfast cake, eaten with coffee. There are countless recipes for wigs. This one is adapted from an 18th-century cookery book.

Yield: 16 wigs
600g/1lb 5oz sifted strong white flour
¼ teaspoon grated nutmeg
1 teaspoon ground ginger
1 teaspoon mixed sweet spice
75g/3oz white sugar
½ teaspoon salt
150g/5oz butter
15g/½oz fresh yeast
½ teaspoon brown sugar
3 tablespoons sweet sherry
2 beaten eggs

Mix the flour with the nutmeg, ginger, spice, white sugar and salt. Rub in the butter and put in a warm place. Crumble the yeast, add the brown sugar and a few spoonfuls of warm water and leave in a warm place until frothy. Make a well in the centre of the flour and pour in the yeast mixture, sherry and eggs, reserving a spoonful of egg for later. Knead well until heavy and smooth, then leave to rise in a warm place for 1 hour. Knead again and divide the dough in two. Form into 2 round shapes, 2.5cm/1in thick, and put on a greased baking sheet. Cut each round into 8 wedges with a sharp knife and leave to rise for 45 minutes under a cloth. Brush the tops with the reserved egg and bake in a hot oven, 220°C/425°F/Mark 7, for 10 minutes. Reduce the heat to moderate, 180°C/350°F/Mark 4, and bake for a further 30 minutes or until cooked. Break the loaves into wedges, split each in half and eat while warm, with plenty of butter.

Easter biscuits

Yield: 12 very large biscuits
225g/8oz sifted flour
½ teaspoon mixed sweet spice
1½ teaspoons ground cinnamon
a pinch of salt
100g/4oz butter
50g/2oz white sugar
50g/2oz chopped candied peel
50g/2oz currants
1 beaten egg
1 tablespoon milk
25g/1oz vanilla castor sugar (page 204)

Mix the flour, sweet spice, ½ teaspoon of the cinnamon and the salt and rub in the butter. Stir in the white sugar, candied peel, currants, egg and sufficient milk to make a stiff dough. Roll out, cut into 12 large rounds and lay on a greased baking sheet. Sprinkle thickly with the vanilla sugar and remaining cinnamon. Bake in a moderate oven, 180°C/350°F/Mark 4, for about 20 minutes, until pale gold and crisped. Cool on a wire tray.

Saffron cake

¼ teaspoon saffron threads
120ml/4 fl oz warm milk
7g/¼oz fresh yeast
½ teaspoon brown sugar
225g/8oz sifted strong white flour
50g/2oz white sugar
½ teaspoon mixed sweet spice
¼ teaspoon salt
75g/3oz butter
1 egg
50g/2oz stoned raisins or sultanas

Soak the saffron in half the warm milk for 10 minutes. Crumble the yeast, add the brown sugar and remaining milk and leave in a warm place until frothy. Mix the flour with the white sugar, spice and salt and rub in the butter. Make a well in the flour and break in the egg. Add the saffron milk and the yeast mixture. Mix well, adding more milk if necessary to make a stiff dough, then knead until smooth. Knead in the raisins or sultanas. Put the dough in a large, warm bowl and leave to rise, covered with a cloth, for about 1 hour. Knead again briefly and press into a well-buttered 500g/1lb loaf or cake tin. Leave to rise for about 45 minutes. Bake in a fairly hot oven, 200°C/400°F/Mark 6, for 10 minutes, then reduce the heat to warm, 160°C/325°F/Mark 3, and bake for another 20 minutes. Cool on a rack.

Cinnamon crumble cake

100g/4oz self-raising flour
75g/3oz butter
100g/4oz white sugar
100g/4oz semolina
1 heaped teaspoon mixed spice
salt
2 eggs
a little milk
CRUMBLE MIXTURE
75g/3oz butter
50g/2oz plain flour
50g/2oz semolina
75g/3oz demerara sugar
75g/3oz chopped walnuts
1½ tablespoons ground cinnamon

First make the cake mixture by rubbing the butter into the flour, then mixing in the remaining dry ingredients and binding with eggs and milk to a soft, dropping consistency. Now make the crumble by melting the butter and stirring in the remaining crumble ingredients. Grease a 20cm/8in cake tin and smooth in the cake and crumble mixtures in 4 alternating layers with a final topping of crumble. Bake for about 30 minutes in a fairly hot oven, 200°C/400°F/Mark 6. Leave to cool in the tin and serve warm or cold.

Sweet herbs and spices

Desserts

Spices, herbs and honey were used for sweetening food in western Europe until the Middle Ages, when returning crusaders brought home pieces of sugarcane from the Mediterranean. Later, the Venetian galleys that carried spices to northern Europe often included sugar with their cargo and it began to be used in small quantities in well-to-do households – stored with the spices in a locked box or cupboard. The Romans had regarded sugar as a medicine and its reputation as a cure for colds and consumption lasted well into the 17th century.

As sugar became increasingly available, spices became less important since food could so easily be made more palatable and appetizing by adding a few spoonfuls of sugar. But now that the consumption of sugar has reached such unhealthy proportions in the western world it would seem sensible to return to the old methods of sweetening and spicing when possible. The sweet spices include nutmeg, ginger, cardamom, cloves, cinnamon, aniseed and vanilla. Sweet herbs are angelica, sweet cicely, rosemary, lemon balm and bergamot, of which sweet cicely has the most pronounced sweet flavour and is the most useful sugar substitute.

Some sweet flavourings

Try adding chopped sweet cicely leaves or pods or sweet spices to thickly whipped cream. Sweeten batter with finely chopped lemon thyme or lemon balm leaves or with whole bergamot or scented geranium leaves, which are removed before using. Or flavour egg custard with a bay leaf or rosemary.

Flavoured sugar can be made by keeping a sprig of rosemary or a vanilla pod buried in a tightly stoppered jar of castor sugar.

Flavoured sugar

Elderflower pancakes

1 stripped head of elderflowers
100g/4oz sifted flour
a pinch of salt
1 teaspoon castor sugar
½ teaspoon grated orange peel
2 eggs
300ml/½ pint milk
2 tablespoons melted butter
juice of 1 orange
melted honey

Mix together the flour, salt, elderflowers, sugar and orange peel. Add the eggs, beat well, then gradually add the milk, beating all the time. Leave to stand for at least 30 minutes. Stir in the melted butter. Grease a heavy pan and heat until it is very hot. Using a tablespoonful of batter for each, cook the pancakes, tipping the pan, until the pancake is thin, lacey and patterned with gold. Turn over and cook the other side. Pile on a hot plate above the oven (pancakes become soggy if kept warm in the oven). Roll up each pancake and sprinkle them with orange juice and melted honey.

Whole elderflower heads or leaves of borage or clary can be dipped in batter and fried as fritters.

Scented blackberry pancakes

225g/8oz blackberries
2 scented geranium (pelargonium) leaves
1 tablespoon honey
3 tablespoons clotted cream or fresh
* cream cheese (page 184)*
100g/4oz flour
a pinch of salt
1 teaspoon castor sugar
2 eggs
300ml/½ pint milk
2 tablespoons melted butter

Make a syrup by simmering the honey in 150ml/¼ pint water for 10 minutes. Drop in the blackberries and poach until tender with the geranium leaves. Cool, then remove the leaves. Lift the blackberries from the syrup and mix them with the cream or cream cheese. Make a

Scented herb flowers and leaves and the warm flavour of spices make light and delicious fritters and pancakes or unusual waffles: 1 scented blackberry pancakes with clotted cream 2 saffron apple fritters 3 borage leaf fritters 4 elderflower fritters, best served with sugar and thin cream 5 cardamom waffles coated with honey.

batter as for elderflower pancakes, using the flour, salt, sugar, eggs, milk and melted butter and fry the pancakes in a heavy greased pan. Spread blackberries and cream on each pancake, roll them up and pour over a few spoonfuls of the scented syrup. Serve warm.

Soured cream and cardamom waffles

150ml/¼ pint soured cream
seeds from 3 cardamom pods
100g/4oz flour
50g/2oz sugar
1 teaspoon baking powder
a pinch of salt
2 eggs, separated
50g/2oz melted butter
150ml/¼ pint milk
melted honey
lemon juice

Mix together the flour, sugar, baking powder, salt and cardamom. Beat in the egg yolks, melted butter, milk and soured cream and continue beating until smooth. Fold in the stiffly whisked egg whites. Cook until crisp in a well-greased waffle iron and serve hot with melted honey and lemon juice.

Saffron apple fritters

6 medium cooking apples
a pinch of saffron threads
3 tablespoons sunflower oil
100g/4oz sifted flour
a pinch of salt
1 stiffly whisked egg white
oil for frying
3 tablespoons castor sugar

Steep the saffron for 10 minutes in 150ml/¼ pint water. Beat the sunflower oil into the flour with the salt, then mix in the saffron water and beat again. Leave to stand for at least 30 minutes. Just before using the batter, fold in the egg white. Peel and core the apples and slice into rings. Dip each ring in batter and fry in 1cm/½in hot oil until puffed up and golden. Test that the apples are

tender with a skewer. Drain on absorbent kitchen paper, sprinkle liberally with castor sugar and serve immediately, while crisp and hot, with thin pouring cream.

Fresh fruit salad with cardamom

3 unpeeled, cubed apples
2 peeled, thinly sliced oranges
20 peeled, seeded black grapes
2 skinned, sliced peaches
crushed seeds from 2 cardamom pods
juice of ½ lemon
2 tablespoons honey

Make a syrup by simmering the lemon juice and honey with 300ml/½ pint water for 10 minutes. Cool and add the cardamom. Arrange the fruit in a bowl, pour over the syrup and chill for 1 hour. Serve with cream.

Fresh fruit purée with rosemary conserve

600ml/1 pint puréed raspberries, straw-
* berries, redcurrants or blackcurrants*
2 tablespoons fresh rosemary flowers
1 tablespoon castor sugar
150ml/¼ pint thick cream

Pound the rosemary flowers in a mortar and gradually add the sugar until well combined. Mix with the cream and purée and serve cold with thin biscuits.

The flavour, scent and goodness of herb flowers were often preserved by pounding with sugar, the resulting powder being stored in jars and keeping, so it was said, for 7 years. Violet and lavender flowers, rose petals, the leaves of mint and bergamot and the flowers of bergamot and betony can all be preserved in this way. The proportions are 575g/1¼lb castor sugar to each 225g/8oz of flowers.

Rhubarb fool with aniseed

500g/1lb sliced rhubarb
1 teaspoon crushed aniseed
1 tablespoon honey
175ml/6fl oz thick cream

Simmer the honey in 4 tablespoons

water for 5 minutes. Poach the rhubarb gently in this syrup until tender. Sieve and stir in the cream and aniseed.

Syllabub with lemon balm

1 tablespoon finely chopped lemon balm
* leaves*
600ml/1 pint double cream
150ml/¼ pint sweet white wine
juice and zest of 2 lemons
1 teaspoon castor sugar
nutmeg
sprigs of lemon balm to garnish

Whisk together all the ingredients, except the nutmeg and sprigs of lemon balm, until they thicken to the consistency of thick custard. Taste and add more sugar if necessary. Leave for a few hours or overnight to chill. Spoon into tall, frosted glasses, grate a little nutmeg over the top and garnish each with a sprig of lemon balm.

Gooseberry and elderflower soufflé

500g/1lb gooseberries
1 stripped head of elderflowers
4 tablespoons vanilla sugar (page 204)
4 eggs, separated
150ml/¼ pint lightly whipped cream
15g/½oz gelatine

Gently poach the gooseberries with the elderflowers and 3 tablespoons of vanilla sugar in 150ml/¼ pint water. Strain off the juice and sieve the fruit. Dissolve the gelatine in a few spoonfuls of the warm gooseberry juice. Whisk the egg yolks with the remaining sugar until thick and pale, then mix them into the fruit purée with the cream and gelatine. Leave it for 10 minutes for the mixture to thicken. Fold in the stiffly whisked egg whites, pour into a soufflé dish and leave to set in a cool place. Serve with thin almond biscuits.

The elderflowers give a delicious muscatel flavour to the gooseberries. Use them also to flavour gooseberry jam and jelly.

Bilberry tart

1kg/2lb bilberries or blackcurrants
100g/4oz butter
150g/6oz sifted flour
25g/1oz sifted icing sugar
1 egg, separated
lemon juice
2 tablespoons melted honey
1 tablespoon chopped mint
25g/1oz vanilla sugar

Make a rich pastry by crumbling the butter into the flour and icing sugar and binding with the yolk of the egg, a squeeze of lemon juice and cold water. Chill for 30 minutes if possible, then roll out and line a 30cm/12in buttered flan tin. Reserve the trimmings. Arrange the fruit on the pastry and pour the melted honey mixed with mint leaves over it. Cover with a lattice of pastry strips, made from the trimmings, and brush with the lightly beaten egg white mixed with the vanilla sugar. Bake in a hot oven, 220°C/ 425°F/Mark 7, for 10 minutes, then reduce the heat to moderate, 180°C/ 350°F/Mark 4, for a further 20 minutes or until golden and cooked through. Serve warm with softly whipped cream or vanilla ice cream.

Angelica cheesecake

1 tablespoon chopped young angelica
  leaves or sweet cicely leaves
150g/6oz sifted flour
100g/4oz butter
25g/1oz sifted icing sugar
1 egg yolk
3 eggs
225g/8oz milk cheese or cream cheese
  (page 184)
75g/3oz vanilla sugar
50g/2oz sultanas
1 tablespoon lemon juice
1 teaspoon grated lemon peel

Make a rich pastry with the flour, butter, icing sugar and egg yolk, following the directions for the bilberry tart pastry. Use it to line a 30cm/12in flan tin. Beat together the remaining ingredients and pile them into the pastry case. Bake at 180°C/ 350°F/Mark 4, for about 30 minutes or until set. Serve cold.

Baked spiced fruit

4 large, unpeeled, cored apples or 4 large, peeled, uncored pears or 500g/ 1lb apricots or plums, lightly scored with a sharp knife
4 cloves
1 vanilla pod broken into 4 pieces
2 twists of lemon peel
50g/2oz demerara sugar
150ml/¼ pint red wine or water

Arrange the fruit in a single layer in an ovenproof dish. Put the cloves, vanilla and lemon peel among them, sprinkle with the sugar and pour over the wine. Cover tightly and bake in a slow oven, 150°C/300°F/ Mark 2, until tender. Pears will take at least 2 hours, apples 1 hour, and plums and apricots 45 minutes. Serve with home-made cream cheese (page 184) and thin pouring cream.

Apple and cinnamon dumplings

250g/½lb apples, peeled and grated
40g/1½oz melted butter
2 eggs
100g/4oz fresh brown breadcrumbs
50g/2oz flour
50g/2oz sugar
1 tablespoon ground almonds
½ teaspoon grated lemon rind
150ml/¼ pint milk (approx.)
SAUCE
25g/1oz melted butter
1 teaspoon ground cinnamon
1 tablespoon demerara sugar
1 tablespoon lemon juice

To make the dumplings, whisk the melted butter and eggs together lightly with a fork then mix in all the other dumpling ingredients. The mixture should be stiff enough to form into small balls; if it is too soft add more flour. Drop the little dumplings into fast-boiling water and cook for about 10 minutes or until light and puffy right through. Lift them carefully with a perforated spoon onto a hot, shallow dish and pour over the sauce made by heating the butter until it foams and stirring in the remaining sauce ingredients. Either eat immediately or put beneath a hot grill for a few minutes to brown and crisp. Serve with yoghurt or softly whipped cream.

Scented rice with saffron

50g/2oz round-grain pudding rice
¼ teaspoon saffron threads
50g/2oz butter
1 teaspoon lemon juice
1 tablespoon sugar
a pinch of ground ginger
½ teaspoon crushed aniseed
a piece of cinnamon stick
½ teaspoon ground cinnamon

Melt the butter and gently simmer the rice in it until all the grains are glistening. Make a syrup with the lemon juice, sugar and 450ml/¾ pint of water, simmered together for 10 minutes. Pour this over the rice. Soak the saffron in a spoonful of water for a few minutes and add it to the rice with the ginger, aniseed and cinnamon stick. Simmer very gently until the rice is tender and the syrup absorbed. Sprinkle with cinnamon and serve warm with thick cream.

Chocolate and vanilla roll

100g/4oz vanilla sugar
4 eggs
4 tablespoons sieved cocoa
150ml/¼ pint whipped cream
seeds from ½ vanilla pod
icing sugar

Beat the sugar and eggs together until the mixture is thick and pale. Fold in the cocoa and pour into a well-greased, swiss-roll tin measuring about 18cm/7in by 30cm/12in. Bake in a fairly hot pre-heated oven at 200°C/400°F/Mark 6 for 10 to 15 minutes, then turn out onto a cloth on a wire rack. Cool, spread with cream whipped with vanilla seeds and roll up. Sprinkle with icing sugar and serve with raspberries.

Sweets and candies

Candied orange and lemon peel from Spain and North Africa were included in the earliest cargoes of spices to reach northern Europe. In the late Middle Ages, when sugar became more common, other plants began to be candied too, usually to preserve them for medicinal purposes. The candied stems of angelica that we use to decorate cakes and puddings today were sucked as a cure for colds and coughs and for indigestion; the candied roots of borage and bugloss were eaten to 'engender good blood'; the roots of sea holly (eryngo) were considered an aphrodisiac; and the stems of alexanders, burdock and lettuce and the roots of elecampane, parsley and fennel were all candied and stored for winter illnesses. Herbs stored in their own syrup were known as 'wet suckets', but more usually they were kept between papers in boxes and called 'dry suckets'.

The basic principles of candying are the same as those used 400 years ago: the stems or roots are softened and their juices gradually replaced with sugar by repeated immersion in a thick syrup, then they are slowly dried out.

Flowers, leaves and whole branches of sweet herbs such as rosemary can be crystallized and used as sweets, garnishes and decorations. Suitable flowers include violet, borage, bergamot, rosemary, lavender, clove carnation, sage, alkanet, marigold petals and rose petals (with the bitter white heel removed). Leaves include mint, bergamot, violet and lemon balm. There are innumerable recipes in old books on cookery and domestic lore for conserving flowers. The recipe given here for crystallizing mint leaves can be used for any other edible plants.

Candied angelica stems

angelica stems and leaf ribs
sugar

Cut angelica in early summer, using young, tender stems and thick leaf ribs. Slice them into 5cm/2in lengths, put them in a pan with water to cover and simmer until tender. Lift them out and peel off the bitter outer skin with a sharp knife. Return them to the pan and simmer for a few more minutes until they become bright green. Lift them out and drain them thoroughly. Weigh the stems and lay them out in a single layer in a shallow tin or tray. Weigh out an equal quantity of sugar and put it in a heavy pan. Measure 150ml/$\frac{1}{4}$ pint water to each 500g/1lb sugar into the pan, stir them together until the sugar is dissolved, then boil to a thick syrup. Pour this over the stems and leave them overnight. Pour the syrup back into the pan the following day. It will be watery, diluted with juices from the angelica. Boil it up again until thick, then pour

it over the stems. Repeat this 4 times over 4 days, until the liquid is all absorbed. Sprinkle the stems with more sugar until thoroughly coated, then leave in an airy place to dry, on a rack if possible, covered if necessary with muslin as a protection from flies and dust. It is important to leave the stems until they are *thoroughly* dry as otherwise they will grow mould later. Store in an airtight tin or jar, between layers of greaseproof paper. If the stems become at all soggy open the jar and expose them to the air for an hour or two to dry out again.

Candied sweet cicely roots

sweet cicely roots
sugar
lemon juice

Peel and slice sweet cicely roots and simmer until tender in water to cover. Make a syrup as for candied angelica, with the addition of a little lemon juice, and follow exactly the same procedure.

Apart from sea holly roots, which are too rare now to dig in the wild, sweet cicely have the best-flavoured roots for candying, tasting strongly of aniseed and liquorice. In the past the roots had a great reputation as an invigorating medicine for old people: 'it rejoiceth and comforteth the heart and increaseth their lust and strength'.

Crystallized mint leaves

mint leaves
egg white
castor sugar

Gather mint leaves on a sunny morning after the dew has dried. It is important that each leaf be completely fresh and dry. Whisk an egg white with a fork until it is opaque but not foaming. Hold each leaf by its stalk and dip into the egg white, turning until it is completely coated, or paint it all over with a fine paint brush. Next dip the leaf in castor sugar, again making sure that it is thoroughly coated. If a strong mint flavour is wanted, sprinkle a few drops of oil of peppermint over the coated leaves, or submerge a bundle of mint leaves in the sugar for several hours before using it, discarding the bundle later. Lay the coated leaves in a single layer on greaseproof paper on a wire rack and cover with another sheet as a protection from dust. Dry the leaves slowly in a very low oven with the door left ajar or in a warm airing cupboard. When completely dry and brittle, store between layers of greaseproof paper in an airtight tin or jar.

Aniseed brittle

1 tablespoon crushed aniseed
4 heaped tablespoons honey
Bring the honey slowly to the boil in a heavy pan and simmer steadily for about 30 minutes, or until a drop in cold water becomes immediately hard. Stir in the aniseed. Pour onto an oiled marble slab or baking sheet, mark into squares and store, when cool, in an airtight tin.

Horehound toffee

3 sprigs of horehound
100g/4oz soft brown sugar
2 tablespoons dark treacle
juice of $\frac{1}{2}$ orange
$\frac{1}{2}$ teaspoon cream of tartar
Pour 300ml/$\frac{1}{2}$ pint boiling water over the horehound and leave to infuse for 30 minutes. Strain through a sieve, pressing to extract the juice. Pour the liquid into a heavy pan and add the remaining ingredients. Stir to dissolve, bring to the boil and boil fast until a drop hardens in cold water. Pour the liquid onto an oiled marble slab or baking sheet; it will spread out thinly. Mark it in squares with the point of a sharp knife. When it is cool and brittle, break it and store in an airtight jar.

Horehound has been used for hundreds of years as a remedy for coughs and colds.

Butterscotch flavoured with coriander

1 tablespoon crushed coriander seeds
225g/8oz butter
450g/1lb demerara sugar
juice of half a lemon
Melt the butter in a heavy pan. Add the sugar and lemon juice and stir over a low heat to dissolve. Boil fast until a drop becomes brittle in cold water. Stir in the coriander seeds, pour onto an oiled marble slab or baking sheet and mark into squares. When cooled, store in an airtight tin.

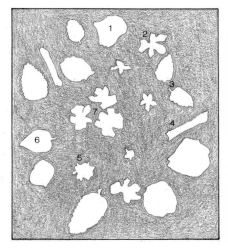

Crystallized fresh herb leaves or flowers and candied stems make attractive decorations for cakes and puddings and can be stored in an airtight tin or jar between layers of greaseproof paper:
1 crystallized rose petal 2 and
7 crystallized white viola flowers
3 crystallized lemon balm leaves
4 candied angelica stem 5 crystallized blue borage flower 6 crystallized violet leaf.

Jellies and jams

Spice country preserves of apple and plum with thyme, savory or mint to accompany meat or cheese, or give them an extra scented sweetness with the leaves of balm, bergamot or pineapple sage.

Bergamot jelly

1 bunch of bergamot leaves
2kg/4lb crab or cooking apples
white sugar

Put the apples in a large pan and add water to cover and the bergamot. Simmer until soft and pulpy, then pour into a clean jelly bag. Leave the apple juice to drip through overnight. Measure the juice and to each 600ml/1 pint, add 350g/12oz sugar. Stir over a low heat to dissolve the sugar, then boil until setting point is reached. Test this by putting a teaspoonful of juice on a cold plate. If a skin forms quickly the jelly is ready. Pour into warm, clean jars, float a fresh bergamot leaf in each jar, seal and cover.

The highly scented bergamot can be replaced by geranium or lemon balm leaves or by spicy flavourings such as bruised caraway seeds, ginger root, cinnamon sticks or cloves.

Spiced sloe jelly

1.5kg/3lb sloes
500g/1lb crabapples
1 cinnamon stick
1 mace blade
10 cloves
6 allspice berries
equal quantities of brown and white sugar

Simmer the sloes, crabapples and spices in water to cover. A few spoonfuls of sherry or port wine added to the liquid will improve the flavour of the jelly. When thoroughly cooked and soft, strain overnight through a clean jelly bag. Stir in 350g/12oz sugar to each 600ml/1 pint of juice and boil to setting point. Pour into warm jars, seal and cover.

Use to flavour gravies, stews and fruit puddings. Rowan or elderberries can be substituted for sloes.

Tomato and cinnamon jelly

1.5kg/3lb tomatoes
10cm/4in cinnamon stick
lemon juice
white sugar

Simmer the tomatoes in 450ml/¾ pint of water with the cinnamon. When thoroughly soft, strain overnight through a jelly bag. To each 600ml/1 pint juice, add the juice of a lemon and 400g/14oz sugar. Stir to dissolve, then boil to setting point. Pour into clean, warm jars and seal.

Mint jelly

1 large bunch of fresh mint
3 tablespoons finely chopped mint
2kg/4lb cooking apples
wine vinegar
equal quantities of brown and white sugar

Put the apples in a large pan and cover with a 50/50 mixture of water and vinegar. Bury the bunch of mint among the apples and simmer until the apples are soft. Strain through a jelly bag overnight. Add 350g/12oz sugar to each 600ml/1 pint of juice and boil to setting point. Leave for 10 minutes in a cool place until the jelly begins to set, then stir in the chopped mint. Pour into warm, clean jars, seal and cover.

The harsh taste of traditional mint sauce often overwhelms meat; wine vinegar and brown sugar provide a more subtle flavour. Thyme, sage or rosemary can be substituted.

Greengage and marigold jelly

2kg/4lb greengages or yellow plums
75g/3oz marigold petals
white sugar

Simmer the greengages until soft in water to cover. Strain through a jelly bag. Next day, add 350g/12oz sugar to each 600ml/1 pint juice. Stir over a low heat until the sugar has dissolved, then boil until setting point is reached. Leave in the pan for 10 minutes off the heat, then stir in the marigold petals. This allows the jelly to set slightly so that the petals are distributed evenly instead of floating in a mass to the top. Pour into warm clean jars, seal and cover.

Rose hip jelly

1.5kg/3lb rose hips
lemon juice
sugar

Simmer the hips in water to cover. Mash with a wooden spoon and strain through a fine jelly bag overnight. To each 600ml/1 pint juice, add the juice of a lemon and 400g/14oz sugar. Stir to dissolve, then boil to setting point. Pour into warm, clean jars, seal and cover.

Rose hips contain far more Vitamin C than any other fruit or vegetable. When cooked as a jelly the irritating little hairs around the fruit are thoroughly strained out.

Morello cherry and vanilla jam

1.5kg/3lb morello cherries
875g/1¾lb vanilla sugar (page 204)
1 vanilla pod
juice of 2 lemons or 300ml/½ pint red or white currant juice

Dissolve the sugar in 300ml/½ pint water over a low heat, then bring to the boil. Add the vanilla pod and the cherries. (If you have time, stone the cherries and add the bruised stones to the mixture in a muslin bag.) Boil for 15 minutes, then leave to cool overnight. The following day add the lemon or currant juice and boil until setting point is reached. Remove the bag of stones and vanilla pod, pour the jam into warm jars, seal and cover.

Hedgerow jam

500g/1lb crabapples
500g/1lb elderberries
500g/1lb blackberries
100g/4oz haws
225g/8oz sloes
1.5kg/3lb sugar
225g/8oz honey
100g/4oz shelled, chopped hazelnuts

Simmer the fruit in 1.5 litres/3 pints water until soft. Stir in the sugar, honey and nuts. Simmer, stirring, until the sugar dissolves, then boil to setting point. Pour into warm jars and cover.

Rose petal jam

500g/1lb red rose petals
225g/8oz white sugar
225g/8oz honey
juice of 2 lemons

Collect the petals from unsprayed, scented roses and snip off the bitter white heels. They can be collected over several days and stored in a covered jar, sprinkled with lemon juice. Simmer the petals in a little water until tender, then stir in the sugar, honey and lemon juice and cook until the syrup is thick. Pour into warmed jars and seal.

Rhubarb and orange cheese

1.5kg/3lb unforced rhubarb (forced rhubarb is too watery)
4 oranges
brown sugar

Peel the oranges thinly and squeeze the juice. Put peel, juice and rhubarb into a pan with sufficient water to cover, then simmer until the rhubarb is tender. Remove the peel and rub the rhubarb through a sieve. To each 450g/1lb of purée add an equal weight of sugar. Stir to dissolve then cook steadily, stirring well, until the purée is thick. Pour into warm jars and seal.

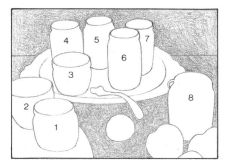

Savoury and sweet jellies can be served with roast meat or spread thickly on bread: 1 and 6 mint jelly 2 and 7 greengage and marigold jelly 3 spiced sloe jelly 4 bergamot jelly 5 sage and apple jelly, made from the mint jelly recipe 8 tomato and cinnamon jelly.

Pickles and ketchup

Herbs and spices add their flavours and preservative qualities to bottled pickles and sauces and help to counteract the strength and acidity of the necessary vinegar and salt. Curry spices such as cumin, coriander and turmeric are common ingredients in Indian recipes for piccalilli and catsup, and chilies can be used to flavour fruit and vegetable chutneys.

The spiced vinegar on page 165 can be used to pickle eggs, vegetables or fish, either chopped up or whole. It is usual to salt fish and vegetables first in order to draw out some of their water content.

Spiced lime pickle in oil

10 limes
600ml/1 pint olive oil
2 tablespoons black peppercorns
1 tablespoon chopped dried chili
1 tablespoon cumin seeds
3 tablespoons salt
4 crushed garlic cloves
1 teaspoon grated fresh root ginger or
ground ginger
1 tablespoon white mustard seeds
3 bay leaves

Heat the oil in a shallow pan until it is very hot, then lower the heat and leave it to cook gently for 10 minutes. Set it aside to cool. Cut the limes into wedges with a stainless steel knife and put them into a large shallow bowl. Crush the peppercorns, chili and cumin seeds roughly in a mortar and sprinkle over the limes. Add the remaining ingredients, stir and leave for 30 minutes. Fill a glass jar with the limes and spices and pour over the cooled oil. Cover with perforated paper or a cloth and set the jar on a sunny windowsill or near a warm stove. Leave for 6 days, shaking or stirring the mixture each day, then cover tightly and store in a cupboard. After 2 or 3 weeks the rinds will have softened and absorbed the aromatic oil and the pickle will be ready to eat. It will keep for at least 6 months.

Slivers of the limes together with a little vinegar can be served with curries or pilafs, used to garnish fish or chicken dishes, or added to salads of spring onions, mint and yoghurt.

Pickled mushrooms

1.5kg/3lb mushrooms
2 tablespoons rock or sea salt
600ml/1 pint good red-wine vinegar
300ml/¼ pint red wine or port
a piece of bruised root ginger
6 cloves

Wipe the mushrooms clean with a cloth and put them in a deep bowl or pot. Sprinkle them with the salt and leave overnight, covered with a cloth. The next day simmer them gently over a low heat in their own liquor until it is all absorbed. Stir in the vinegar, wine and spices. Bring to the boil and cook steadily for 5 minutes. Leave to cool, bottle and tie down securely. Pickled mushrooms make a good hors d'oeuvre.

Preserved tomato sauce

This is one of the most useful and basic preserves for the store cup-board. Use it with rice and pasta dishes, with vegetables and pulses or as a basis for soups.

4.5kg/10lb chopped ripe tomatoes
120ml/4 fl oz olive oil
225g/8oz chopped onions
225g/8oz bruised garlic cloves
1 clove
1 bunch of thyme
1 bunch of parsley stalks
1 bunch of basil
2 bay leaves
salt and pepper

Heat the oil and gently cook the onions and garlic until softened. Stir in the tomatoes, clove and herbs. Cover the pan and simmer gently for 45 minutes. Press the pulp through a sieve or mouli-légumes and heat through again to boiling point. The sauce can either be bottled now or boiled further until it has reduced to a thick purée. Adjust the seasoning and pour into sterilized bottles with a little olive oil at the top. Cover in the usual way with screw tops, clips or Porosan skin.

Mushroom ketchup

Ripe, open mushrooms
black peppercorns and salt
mace
brandy or port (optional)

Layer mushrooms with any broken pieces and stalks in an earthenware jar or deep casserole, with sprinklings of salt between each layer. This can be done over a period of weeks as you pick the mushrooms or all at once with a basketful of bought mushrooms. Press each layer down as you add a new layer. Keep the pot covered and in a warm place – an airing cupboard or beside the kit-chen stove. When the pot is full and the fungi surrounded by their dark liquid, set the pot in the oven and simmer, covered, for an hour. Strain through a muslin or fine sieve, measure the liquid, and to each 1 litre/1¾ pints add 10 bruised black peppercorns and 4 blades of mace. Simmer for a further 20 minutes together with a tablespoon or two of the alcohol, which is not absolutely necessary but will enrich and help preserve the ketchup. Strain into small, hot, sterilized bottles and cover tightly.

Use to flavour soups, gravies and stews and keep in the refrigerator once open.

Pontac ketchup

350g/¾lb elderberries
450ml/¾ pint wine vinegar (mixed with wine or port dregs if possible)
25 black peppercorns
12 cloves
a piece of bruised root ginger
1 mace blade
2 chopped shallots
¼ teaspoon salt

Bake the elderberries and vinegar overnight in a very low oven, in a covered pot. Strain the liquid, stir in the spices and flavourings and bring slowly to the boil. Boil for 5 min-utes, then bottle in sterilized bottles. Use to flavour soups and gravies.

Aromatic oils and vinegars (page 165), pickles and ketchups. From the left: fennel oil, Pontac ketchup, preserved tomato sauce, mixed vegetables and eggs in spiced vinegar, chili oil, preserved tomato sauce, pickled mushrooms, tarragon vinegar and basil oil.

Drinks

Syrups and cool summer drinks

Flavoured syrups are easy to make and have endless uses. Dilute them with iced water for a summer drink or with boiling water during the winter, or add them to cold milk, stirring briskly to avoid curdling. Use as a base for sorbets, ice creams and jellies. As a sauce for puddings, they will give a delicious flavour of summer flowers and fruit.

Bottling

Syrups can either be stored in a deep freeze or in sterilized bottles. To sterilize, submerge the bottle to the level of the cork in boiling water for 15 minutes, or bake in a hot oven, 220°C/425°F/Mark 7, for 30 minutes. After the bottles have been filled with hot syrup they must be sealed immediately with corks, waxed lids or Porosan skin. The high concentration of sugar should keep out bacteria, but if the syrup begins to ferment either throw it away or pour it into a jar with an air lock, as the bottle may explode.

Spiced blackberry syrup

3kg/6lb blackberries
sugar
10 cloves
10 crushed coriander seeds
1 cinnamon stick
1 mace blade
peel of 1 orange
peel of 1 lemon

Simmer the blackberries until soft in 300ml/½ pint of water. Strain through muslin or a jelly bag, pressing out all the juice. Measure the liquid and add 500g/1lb sugar to each 600ml/1 pint. Tie the spices and peel in a piece of muslin and immerse them in the syrup. Bring slowly to the boil and simmer for 30 minutes. Remove the bag. Bottle or freeze.

Elderflower syrup

1 litre/1¾ pints elderflowers
white sugar

Cover the elderflowers with water and simmer gently for 30 minutes. Squeeze the liquid through muslin or a jelly bag. Add 350g/12oz sugar to each 600ml/1 pint of liquid and simmer for a further 15 minutes. Bottle or freeze.

Yoghurt drink

600ml/1 pint plain yoghurt
300ml/½ pint cold water
1 fresh sprig of mint

Whisk the yoghurt and water together. Leave to chill with a sprig of mint to flavour.

Chilled spiced buttermilk

1 litre/1¾ pints buttermilk
1 tablespoon vanilla sugar (page 204)
½ teaspoon ground cinnamon
¼ teaspoon grated nutmeg
a pinch of ground cloves

Put all the ingredients into a bowl and whisk until frothy. Chill for at least 1 hour.

Hop lemonade

15g/½oz fresh hops or 7g/¼oz dried hops
a small piece of bruised root ginger
1 bunch of fresh apple or other mint
1 thinly sliced lemon
100g/4oz demerara sugar

Fill a large pan with 2 litres/3½ pints of cold water and add the hops, ginger, mint and lemon. Bring to the boil and simmer fast for 30 minutes. The liquid will have reduced by about half. Strain and stir in the sugar. Stir to dissolve and boil for 5 minutes. Pour into a jug and cool.

Iced mint

100g/4oz fresh mint leaves
75g/3oz sugar
juice of 3 lemons

Pound the mint leaves to a pulp in a mortar. Add 25g/1oz sugar and pound again. Make a syrup by boiling 1 litre/1¾ pints of water with the remaining sugar for 5 minutes. Take the pan off the heat, allow to cool, then add the lemon juice and mint pulp. Stir well together, then chill for several hours before serving.

Tamarind water

50g/2oz tamarind
3 tablespoons of sugar
3 slices of lemon

Soak the tamarind overnight in 1.75 litres/3 pints water. Strain and add the sugar and slices of lemon. Bring to the boil and simmer for 5 minutes. Cover, take off the heat and leave to cool. Strain off the lemon.

Herb wines, fruit cordials, and refreshing summer drinks: 1 a tumbler of chilled yoghurt 2 Maywine served with orange, wild strawberries and woodruff 3 and 5 spiced blackberry syrup 4 hop lemonade 6 dandelion wine 7 metheglin 8 lavender flowers steeped in Aspi 9 a jug of iced tamarind water 10 iced mint syrup.

Alcoholic drinks

Mead and metheglin

Honey mixed with water ferments naturally and the resulting drink – mead – was the first alcoholic drink made in northern Europe. Traces of mead are found with many early burials such as the Bronze Age burial in Denmark where the mead, in a bucket of birch bark, had been flavoured with bog myrtle and cranberries. Later, mead was the drink of warriors in the mead halls of Saxons and Celts. Quantities of flowers, herbs and berries were used to flavour and preserve both mead and metheglin, a similar drink. Some early recipes use at least 20 different plants.

Ale and beer

Ale, made from fermented grain, was another early drink that was heavily flavoured with herbs. Bitter, aromatic ground ivy and bog myrtle, rosemary, yarrow and betony were added as preservatives and flavourings and for their medicinal properties. Hops have been used in Europe as a powerful preservative and bitter for beer since about 900 A D. They were introduced to Britain by Flemish brewers, but met with much opposition as the traditional herb flavourings were considered far more wholesome. However, Flemish settlers began cultivating hops in Kent in the 16th century and gradually they became accepted. Hops were carried to North America by early settlers, and eventually beer became more popular than ale.

Both ale and beer were used as vehicles for medicines. Purging ales were made by adding senna and wormwood; ales against scurvy included the juice of scurvy grass, sage and cresses; and a common cure for consumption in the late 18th century was an ale in which a parboiled cockerel, spices and dried fruit had been steeped. Ales thickened and enriched with eggs, butter, sugar and spices were popular in the Middle Ages, but began to go out of fashion in the 18th century, though spiced, mulled ale is still a popular winter drink in Scandinavia and Germany.

Wine

The Celtic aristocracy in Germany and France, and later in Britain, traded goods for wine from Greek merchants, and during the days of the Roman Empire vines from the Mediterranean were planted in northern climates. The wine made from these grapes was often thin and vinegary, and herbs such as sage, myrtle and juniper and spices such as nutmeg, cinnamon and cloves were added in an attempt to preserve it and to mask the deteriorating flavour. Other herbs were added for medicinal purposes and the wines were often sweetened with honey, rose or violet petals and dried fruit. As sugar became more plentiful, so home wine-making became popular, using soft fruits from the garden, elderberries and blackberries from the hedges, and flowers and herbs such as cowslips, balm and clary.

Spirits

Apothecaries and monks had distilled juices from medicinal herbs or added their essential oils to fortified wine since the 12th century. By the 16th century, crude spirits began to be distilled by laymen in Europe and these needed heavy flavourings. They were often regarded as medicines because of their stimulating and warming effect and were flavoured with angelica, rosemary, lavender or spices and given names like 'hysterical water' or 'surfeit water'. Bitter herbs such as gentian were infused in alcohol as digestives and stomachics. Juniper berries were used to flavour a new Dutch drink – gin; and fortified wines were flavoured with wormwood, mint and hyssop to make absinthe and vermouth. There are still many regional herb flavourings for alcoholic drinks such as the pastis and ratafias of France, the akvavit of Denmark, Italian vermouths, and vodka, which was first recorded in a Polish herbal in 1534.

The mass production of our modern wines and beers, and the chemical additives used in them, have aroused a new interest in home-made brews.

Steeping herbs in wine

The simplest way to flavour wine with herbs is by steeping. The following herbs are suitable: borage, clary, clove carnation, elderflowers, lavender, lemon balm, lemon verbena, mint, rosemary, woodruff and the scrubbed root of wood avens, which has a dry, aromatic taste.

Maywine

1 bottle of dry white wine or hock
5 thin orange slices
12 sprigs of woodruff
1 teaspoon white sugar
Put all the ingredients in a jug and leave for 1 hour. Strain and serve chilled, with the jug surrounded by crushed ice. Wild strawberries can be added instead of the orange.

Aspi

1 bottle of medium white wine
3 tablespoons lavender flowers
1 tablespoon white sugar
½ glass of brandy
Steep the flowers in the wine for 24 hours. Make a syrup by simmering the sugar with 75ml/3fl oz of water for 10 minutes. When it is cool add to the strained wine with the brandy. Serve cold.

Wine, beer and metheglin

Do not use iron, copper, zinc or brass utensils to make these drinks as they will contaminate the wine or beer. Aluminium, glass, enamel, ceramics and polythene are suitable.

Dandelion wine

2.4 litres/4 pints dandelion flowers
1 tablespoon bruised root ginger
peel of 1 orange, thinly pared
peel of 1 lemon, thinly pared
700g/1½lb demerara sugar
juice of 1 lemon
1 teaspoon wine yeast
Bring 2.4 litres/4 pints of water to the boil, then leave to cool. Remove the bitter stalk and calyx from each dandelion flower and put the flowers in a large bowl. Pour the cooled water over the flowers, cover with a cloth and leave for a day, stirring occasionally. Pour into a large pan, add the ginger and orange and lemon peel and boil for 30 minutes. Strain the liquid and pour it back into the rinsed bowl. Stir in the sugar and lemon juice. Allow to cool. Cream the wine yeast with some of the liquid and add to the bowl. Cover with a cloth and leave to ferment for 2 days, keeping a dish under the bowl to catch any liquid which may froth over the brim. Pour into a cask and bung it with cotton wool to allow any gas to escape, *or* pour it into a jar and fix on an air lock. Leave until all fermentation has finished – when gas bubbles no longer form. Bung or cork tightly for about 2 months, then siphon off and bottle. Leave it for at least 6 months before drinking.

Meadowsweet beer

25g/1oz meadowsweet leaves
25g/1oz betony leaves
25g/1oz agrimony leaves
500g/1lb sugar
Simmer the leaves in 4.8 litres/1 gallon of water for 20 minutes. Strain and stir in the sugar. Cool to lukewarm, then bottle. This beer ferments with natural yeasts. Drink after a week.

Metheglin

2.5kg/5lb honey (lime blossom is especially good)
1 bunch of lemon thyme
1 branch of lemon balm
1 branch of rosemary
10 cloves
6 crushed allspice berries
1 cinnamon stick
a piece of bruised root ginger
1 mace blade
mead yeast or wine yeast (quantity indicated on packet)
Put 4.8 litres/1 gallon of water into a large pan and simmer the herbs and spices in it for 1 hour. Strain warm onto the honey and stir. Allow to cool, then add the mead or wine yeast. Pour into a clean jar and keep surplus liquid in a bottle for topping up later. Leave to ferment in a warm room over a dish to catch the overflowing liquid. Add the reserved liquid when necessary. When the frothing has stopped, insert an air lock. When bubbles no longer appear, remove to a cold place for 2 weeks, keeping it well corked. Siphon off into a clean jar, cork tightly and seal with wax. Store for 6 months. Siphon off again and pour into bottles which should be well corked and wired down. Store the bottles on their sides for at least 2 years as otherwise the metheglin will be excessively sweet.

Avoid Australian honey as bitter eucalyptus spoils the drink.

Mulled wine or port

4 cloves
3cm/1in cinnamon stick
¼ teaspoon grated nutmeg
a twist of finely pared lemon peel
1 bottle of red wine or port
1 glass of sherry
sugar
Put the spices and peel into a pan and just cover with water. Simmer for 30 minutes. Strain and add the sherry and wine or port. Sweeten and heat to just under boiling point.

Hot spiced punch

1 bottle of claret
peel of 1 orange, thinly pared
6 cloves
1 cinnamon stick
3 crushed cardamom pods
3 crushed coriander seeds
1 tablespoon bruised root ginger
50g/2oz stoned raisins
Put all the ingredients, except the raisins, into a large bowl and leave for about 8 hours. Strain and add the raisins. Heat until the wine begins to shake but do not allow it to boil.

Lamb's wool

1 litre/1¾ pints strong ale
6 cooking apples
1 teaspoon ground ginger
¼ teaspoon grated nutmeg
brown sugar

Roast the apples in a hot oven, 220°C/425°F/Mark 7, until they are soft and pulpy. Remove their skins and cores and stir the pulp into the hot ale. Stir in the spices and sugar to taste and serve very hot.

Wassail bowl

2.4 litres/2 quarts good beer
4 glasses of sherry
500g/1lb dark brown sugar
3 lemon slices
1 teaspoon ground ginger
6 small slices of toast

Heat the beer and stir in the sherry, sugar, lemon and ginger. Float the toast on the surface and serve immediately. This recipe allows 300ml/½ pint a person.

Irish ginger

1 litre/1¾ pints whisky
25g/1oz bruised ginger root
pared peel and juice of 1 lemon
350g/12oz sugar
225g/8oz stoned raisins
1 tablespoon caraway seeds

Put all the ingredients into a wide-mouthed bottle, cork and keep for 2 weeks, shaking daily. Strain and bottle. This can be drunk immediately and will keep indefinitely.

Coffee substitutes

Spiced sloe gin

1kg/2lb sloes
1 bottle of gin
50g/2oz crushed barley sugar
1 thinly sliced orange
1 thinly sliced lemon
a piece of bruised root ginger
3cm/1in cinnamon stick
8 cloves

Prick each sloe with a darning needle. Layer in a wide-mouthed bottle with the barley sugar, fruit and spices. Fill up with gin to cover it all. Cork and leave for 6 months in a fairly warm dark place such as a cupboard under the stairs. Strain and re-bottle.

Ratafias

Ratafia is made by steeping fruit or herbs in colourless brandy. Soak the fruit and any other spices and flavourings in the brandy for a month on a sunny windowsill where it will be warmed by day and cooled by night, or keep in a warm place such as an airing cupboard or near the kitchen range. Strain, add sugar syrup if necessary and re-bottle.

Raspberry ratafia

1kg/2lb raspberries
600ml/1 pint brandy
1 vanilla pod
6 coriander seeds

Steep the fruit and spices in the brandy for 1 month. Strain and re-bottle. This can be drunk at once.

Orange ratafia

peel and juice of 6 oranges
600ml/1 pint brandy
500g/1lb granulated sugar
6 bruised sweet cicely seeds
1 mace blade
3cm/1in cinnamon stick

Stir the orange peel and juice, sugar and spices together until the sugar has dissolved. Stir in the brandy, pour into a wide-mouthed bottle and cork tightly. Leave in a warm place for 1 month. Strain and re-bottle. It can be drunk immediately.

Spiced drinks for festive occasions: 1 a decanter of sloe gin 2 frothing lamb's wool 3 orange ratafia 4 and 5 raspberry ratafia 6 brandy bitters (page 271) 7 wassail 8 spiced punch.

Dandelion and chicory roots are the most common coffee substitutes. Grow both plants in moist, rich soil and harvest the roots in the autumn when they are plumped full of food reserves. Dig chicory in the autumn of its first year and leave the dandelion roots until they are 2 years old. Scrub the roots thoroughly; slice the chicory root but leave dandelion roots whole and dry slowly in a low oven with the door left ajar or on a rack above the stove. Store the dried and brittle roots in an airtight tin or jar and roast lightly in a hot oven for 10 minutes before grinding. The roots are more bitter and less aromatic than coffee beans. When mixed with genuine ground coffee these substitutes are said to counteract the stimulating effect of caffeine.

The seeds of goosegrass have also been used as a coffee substitute. Collect these in summer when they have ripened and dried on the plants, roast for 5 minutes in a dry frying pan and grind them before use.

Household herbs and spices

Collected together in this chapter are some of the household herbs and spices that have played such an important part in basic day-to-day living from the time of the first settled agricultural communities until the early years of this century. In every country, from India and Egypt to Scandinavia and America, the wealthy have spent lavishly on imported aromatics for domestic use while country men and women have gathered their ingredients from woods and hedgerows and from their gardens.

As well as flavouring and preserving food, many herbs make good domestic cleansers, insecticides, fumigants or air fresheners, and can be used for the homely jobs of polishing and cleaning floors and furniture and washing and scenting linen, or for more creative pursuits such as candle making or dyeing. Some of the recipes that follow are adapted from printed books on 'huswifery' and from the handwritten 'receipt' books that are passed down within families. All work well and, although they may not be such absolute necessities today when the squirt of an aerosol spray can instantly kill '99 per cent of germs', electric light can be turned on by a switch and clothes can be fast-dyed in a washing machine, they still have real practical use and relevance and some advantages over their modern counterparts.

The first pages are especially concerned with scent. From the earliest times men have been aware of the effects of scent upon the emotions and upon bodily health. An early Greek physician, Marestheus, who wrote several books on the subject, instructed that invigorating herbs such as marjoram should be used for the garlands of guests, never the lily for instance, whose scent has a languorous effect. Pestilential airs were combated with sharp herb vinegars and smouldering aromatic roots. Romans set bowls of mint in their bedrooms to refresh the senses and later herbalists stress the cheering effect of such herbs as rosemary, meadowsweet and basil, and the alerting effect of bunches of southernwood and lemon balm when sniffed during long

Perhaps the most famous scented flower is the rose, whose petals form the base for countless recipes for pot pourri, sweet sachets, powders and perfumes.

sermons. Rooms were scented with pot pourri, sweet bags and burning spicy pastes, and pomanders were warmed in the hand to give their scent or else strung around the waist. By the 18th century, candles and even writing paper and ink were scented, and as Court ladies offered their hands to be kissed they would press their hollow rings to spray rose or violet water over their admirers. Powdered herbs were puffed about Court apartments and sickrooms with bellows (Cardinal Richelieu's favourite method of fumigation), and over the elaborate hair styles of women of fashion.

Perhaps the most famous scented flower is the rose, whose petals form the base for countless recipes for pot pourri, sweet sachets, powders and perfumes and whose scent strengthens as it dries, lasting for several years. The rich, red, single *Rosa gallica*, sometimes known as the 'Provins Rose' or the 'Apothecary's Rose', is one of the oldest known species. It is native to Persia and the eastern Mediterranean and was cultivated on an enormous scale in Persia and Egypt and then by the Romans who introduced it to Europe. The damask rose, *R. damascena*, and the musk rose, *R. moschata*, are other old and valued species. One story of the creation of the rose is that it sprang from a drop of sweat falling from the brow of the prophet Mohammed who said, 'Whosoever would smell my scent would smell the rose.' The very astringent essential oil or 'attar' from its petals has an antiseptic strength that is seven times greater than that of carbolic acid.

It is generally the leaves of herbs that contain the most antiseptic essential oils. Oil of thyme is one of the most powerful herbal germicides, with 12 times the strength of carbolic acid, and many other herbs are strongly antiseptic, especially aromatic labiates such as hyssop, lavender and rosemary, bay and juniper trees and the fleshy roots of elecampane and angelica. Among the many antiseptic spices, cloves, cinnamon and cassia are particularly potent. The essential oils of cloves and cinnamon have been proved to destroy the typhoid bacillus in less than half an hour.

Herbs against insects

Herbalists of every period and nationality have recommended various plants as efficient insecticides and often describe strewing and hanging summer herbs about the house as cooling and refreshing – it is true that the temperature in a room can be reduced by quantities of scented plants whose oxidizing oils form an aromatic ozone.

Strewing

Herb strewing is particularly associated with northern Europe and Britain, where from medieval times until the late 18th century, a thick layer of rushes covered stone or earth floors in even the humblest cottage, keeping rooms warm in winter and cool in the summer, like a thatched roof. When possible, flea-repellent, antiseptic and strongly scented herbs such as wormwood, rue, hyssop, savory and santolina would be mixed among them, or the fresh scents of costmary, germander, lavender and meadowsweet added to help overpower musty and insanitary smells. The long leaved sweet flag was a prized strewing herb.

Strewing herbs on the floor is hardly necessary today, but it is practical to lay dried sprigs of southernwood and costmary beneath carpets against moths and other insects. Bunches of fresh, sweet-smelling and fly-repellent herbs placed in large pots or vases or hung in doorways and windows are cooling and pleasant in the summer. If aromatic garden herbs are in short supply, branches of elder leaves deter flies efficiently and bundles of meadowsweet, which often grows prolifically in roadside ditches, will give a lingering almond scent. A pot of basil on the windowsill is a traditional fly deterrent on the Continent.

Herbs in the larder

In the larder, herbs can be used with real effect against pests. It is well worth putting a few bay leaves in corn and flour bins and among dried pulses to prevent weevils. A bunch of fresh or dried tansy will discourage flies, and before the use of refrigerators was rubbed on meat to keep off bluebottles. Scatter dried pennyroyal and other mints, wild marjoram or rue on larder shelves against ants. Dried stinging nettles are the best packing material there is for storing fruit and root vegetables or moist cheeses. They are usually stingless when dried and have strong preservative qualities that will keep fruit skins smooth and flesh moist for many weeks.

Herbs in the linen cupboard

Dried herbs were commonly hung in closets or laid in presses between sheets, clothes or furs to act as perfumes and moth repellents. Lavender is still popular today, especially in England; in France southernwood, which has an almost sickly sweet scent, is called *garde robe*. Rue, santolina, costmary and camphor plant, tansy, rosemary and woodruff all have insecticide qualities, but the dried roots of orris, elecampane, wood avens and sweet flag have more lasting scents and do not have the disadvantage of dropping their leaves among the linen.

Moth bags and sachets

Crushed or powdered herbs can be sown into muslin bags or sachets to be stored among clothes, with spices added to help balance the scent. These herb insect repellents are infinitely preferable to moth balls and just as efficient. An electric grinder or liquidizer will reduce dried herbs to a powder or they can be crushed with a pestle and mortar. Quantities of recipes for these sweet powders were recorded, many at the royal Courts of Europe where they were handed down by successive royal perfumers. Powdered orris from the rhizome of the Florentine iris was one of the most popular ingredients. It has a strong violet scent that lasts for many years, increasing as it matures, and has the additional advantage of being one of the most easily obtainable scent fixatives.

A sachet powder used by Queen Isabella of Spain

4 parts dried, crushed, red rose petals
3 parts dried clove carnation petals
2 parts powdered orris
2 parts powdered coriander seeds
1 part powdered calamus root (sweet flag)
½ part powdered gum benzoin
(Based on a 17th-century recipe.)

A strong-scented moth bag

4 parts dried, crushed mint
4 parts dried, crushed rue
2 parts dried, crushed southernwood
2 parts dried, crushed rosemary
1 part powdered cloves

An insect-repellent mixture

3 parts dried, crushed tansy
3 parts dried, crushed wormwood
3 parts dried, crushed costmary

'An agreeable sweet-scented composition' for sachets

24 parts powdered orris
8 parts powdered calamus root (sweet flag)
6 parts powdered rhodium (rosewood)
5 parts powdered gum benzoin
1 part powdered cinnamon
½ part powdered cloves
(From *The Toilet of Flora*, 1775.)

A spicy sachet mixture

6 parts dried, red rose petals
4 parts dried, crushed thyme
2 parts dried lavender
2 parts crushed coriander seed
2 parts powdered calamus root (sweet flag)
1 part powdered cinnamon
1 part powdered cloves
1 part powdered mace

An aromatic sachet powder

4 parts dried, crushed sweet marjoram
2 parts dried thyme
2 parts dried, crushed basil
1 part caraway seeds
1 part dried lemon peel
1 part grated nutmeg

A sharp lemon sachet mixture

4 parts dried, crushed lemon verbena
4 parts dried lavender
4 parts dried, crushed pelargonium (scented geranium) leaves
1 part dried, crushed peppermint

Herbs to use in the house: sweet flag, left, for its lasting scent, basil as a fly deterrent, santolina, southernwood, rosemary and tansy for the linen cupboard, marjoram, centre foreground, and bay in the larder.

Herbs for washing and polishing

Sweet water for linen

Besides storing clothes and linen with scented herbs and sachets or in coffers of fragrant wood, such as cypress, juniper or sandalwood, sweet herbs were commonly used in the rinsing water during laundering, or else the newly washed sheets were sprinkled with herb waters and spread to dry over bushes of lavender and rosemary. The simplest way to make a sweet rinsing water is to brew a strong infusion of the herbs in a large teapot or lidded saucepan and then to strain this into the washing machine or bowl. The most suitable herbs are sweet marjoram, costmary, rosemary, mint (apple mint and eau-de-Cologne mint are good), hyssop, wall germander, lemon balm, bay and angelica. To make rosewater, gillyflower (clove carnation) or violet water, fill a pan with fresh, scented petals, just cover them with water and bring to simmering point for a few minutes. Leave to cool slightly then strain. These waters will keep for a few days in a cool place or in a refrigerator.

Distilled waters (page 248) can be kept for a long time. Most old recipes for sweet waters require some distillation and, although a still is no longer an essential piece of household equipment, one of these interesting recipes for perfuming heavy homespun linen is included here.

'Three poundes of Rose water, Cloves, Cinamon, Saunders [sandalwood], two handfull of the flowers of Lavender, lette it stand a moneth to still in the Sonne, well closed in a Glasse; then destill it in Balneo Mariae [glass still]. It is marvellous pleasant in savour, a water of a wondrous swetenes, for the perfumyng the shetes of a bedde, whereby the whole place shall have a most pleasaunt scent.' (1562)

Soap herbs

It is easy to understand how necessary heavy perfuming of clothes and household linen was when reading old recipes for soap using wood ash, bran, fat, pigeon dung and urine and looking at the old diagrams of 'buck tubs', 'tenter hooks' and 'box mangles'. An enormous amount of work was involved in washing, starching and goffering the innumerable lacy ruffs and frills. The cleaning of the jewel-studded outfit of a courtier at the Court of Elizabeth I or Louis XIV would not be undertaken lightly or often.

There are many plant species that contain saponins and will produce an appreciable amount of cleansing lather when boiled. Soapwort, *Saponaria officinalis*, is the herb that has been most commonly used in Europe – among its many names are fuller's herb, latherwort, crow soap, soap root, and, in France, *herbe à foulon*. Early herbals describe the 'great scouring qualities that the leaves have; for they yeald out of themselves a certaine juyce when they are bruised, which scoureth almost as well as Sope.' But with the increased use of animal fats for soap it became less popular and from the early 17th century is seldom mentioned in British herbals except as a medicine for the 'French Pox'. However, in France and other European countries it continued to have some household use until the late 19th century. The double-flowered variety is sometimes grown as an old-fashioned garden plant and the pink single flowers bloom along the banks of streams near old fulling mills, where it was used for cleansing cloth. Soapwort was introduced to North America by early settlers. It is still known to dyers and to those who restore old fabrics and tapestries as a gentle and thorough washing agent.

The leaves or roots can be used, though leaves are most likely to be available. Bruise the leaves in a mortar and put them in a saucepan with spring or rainwater to cover. Tap water will not work so well because of the chemical additives. Bring to the boil, simmer for 30 minutes, strain and use the soapy liquid for your wash. An alternative method is to chop the leaves, knot them up in squares of muslin, bruise them with a rolling pin and simmer them with the material in a big pan.

Other members of the soapwort family (the Caryophyllaceae) also produce appreciable amounts of lather, for example ragged robin, *Lychnis flos-cuculi*, the campions, clove pinks and carnations. Some American soap herbs include *Chenopodium californicum* (roots), soap plant, *Chlorogalum pomeridianum* (bulb), and the sweet-pepper bush, *Clethra alnifolia* (flowers).

Wooden floors and furniture

The scents of beeswax, roses and lavender have strong associations with dark oak floors and gleaming furniture in cool parlours. In the 16th century, rosewater and the distilled water from violets, rosemary and gillyflowers (clove carnations) were sprinkled over the floor to scent and cool a room, and strong herb vinegars (page 165) used in the sick room against infection. Floors were scrubbed with bundles of fresh rosemary and lavender for special occasions. In northern Europe the large, oily seed pods of sweet cicely were gathered until this century and used crushed as a polish for wooden furniture, giving it a sweet aniseed scent, and the leaves of lemon balm, myrtle and sweet marjoram have been used in a similar way. In Shakespeare's play, *The Merry Wives of Windsor*, the chairs are scoured 'with juice of balm and every precious flower'. Early European and North American housewifery books recommend scores of recipes for scented polishes. Rich linseed oil is a common ingredient, often combined with beeswax (odd candle ends usually being melted down for the purpose), turpentine and vinegar. A red dye made from the root of alkanet might be included to bring out the depth of colour in mahogany furniture.

Making furniture cream : *Melt the beeswax in the turpentine in the top of a double saucepan, above gently simmering water. Bring 1 litre/1¾ pints water to the boil in another saucepan and then stir in the soft soap. Leave both mixtures to cool before mixing the liquid soap gradually into the soft beeswax until it reaches the consistency of thick cream. Add lavender oil drop by drop until the scent is noticeable but not overwhelming.*

Lavender furniture cream
350g/12oz beeswax
1.75 litres/3 pints turpentine
1 litre/1¾ pints water
50g/2oz soft soap
oil of lavender
Follow the method set out above, taking the utmost care as turpentine is highly inflammable. Oil of rosemary can be substituted for the lavender oil.

Linseed furniture oil to deter woodworm
150ml/¼ pint raw linseed oil
150ml/¼ pint turpentine
50ml/2fl oz vinegar
50ml/2fl oz methylated spirits
Measure the ingredients into a bottle for storage and label clearly. Shake well before using. Apply with a soft cloth and polish to a shine with a clean duster.

Polish to soften and preserve hard leather upholstery
450ml/¾ pint raw linseed oil
200ml/7fl oz vinegar
Bring the oil to the boil, boil for 1 minute then cool. Mix with the vinegar when nearly cold. Shake vigorously before using. Rub into leather with a soft cloth, leave for a few minutes then polish with a clean duster.

Pot pourri, pomanders and herb pillows

Pot pourri

There are two methods of making pot pourri, the dry and the moist methods. The first is the simplest to make, and the prettiest, but the second will last much longer and has a richer, fuller scent. Moist pot pourri is also called 'sweet jar' and is the oldest method. The petals are left to rot down into an aromatic cake, which explains the rather unromantic translation of the French name *pot pourri*, which means 'rotten pot'.

These dry or moist aromatic mixtures of flowers, herbs and spices should be kept in covered pots or bowls, which can be warmed and opened to release their scent when required. During the height of their popularity in Europe, in the 17th and 18th centuries, fine china pot-pourri jars were the vogue, often elaborately encrusted with china flowers and with an inner

perforated pot from which the scent was wafted and a stand in which it was set after being warmed by the fire. But any pretty, opaque pot with a lid, such as a ginger jar, will work well.

The scent of a well-made pot pourri can last for as long as 50 years, so it is well worth taking some trouble over its preparation. Rose petals usually form the base of the mixture; these should be from the strongly scented, old-fashioned species, the 'Provins Rose' (*Rosa gallica*) and the damask and cabbage varieties. Red or pink roses are generally preferred. Lavender is another common ingredient, and is the only other flower that keeps its scent well when dried without needing a fixative. Any other scented flowers and leaves can be added and spices, essential oils and fixatives mixed in to help hold and preserve their scent. Listed below is a selection of possible ingredients that shows the enormous range of scents available.

Ingredients for pot pourri

To a base of rose petals a dry, spicy mixture might include bay leaves, eucalyptus leaves and flowers, ground ivy, walnut leaves, myrtle, lovage, thyme, sage and broken pods of tonquin bean. For a light, summery mixture add melilot, lemon thyme, costmary and eau-de-Cologne mint, and for a sweet mixture add bergamot, violet and rose-scented geranium.

Freshly grind or crush the spices just before using, as you would for cooking. Roughly chop ginger, cinnamon stick and vanilla pod and freshly grate orris root if possible, thus giving an interesting texture and longer life to a dry pot pourri. When the scent begins to fade, revitalize the mixture with a few drops of brandy or flower oil.

To make pot pourri, add dried, fragrant flowers and leaves to a base of red rose petals, then mix in flower oils, freshly ground spices and powdered orris root to fix the scent.

Flowers for colour
(dry pot pourri)
Alkanet, borage, cornflower, delphinium, feverfew, marigold, mullein, pansy, primrose, tansy.

Spices
Allspice, aniseed, caraway, cardamom, cassia buds, cinnamon, cloves, coriander, ginger, mace, nutmeg, pepper and vanilla pod.

Scented flowers
Bergamot, chamomile, clove carnation, eucalyptus, honeysuckle, hyssop, jasmine, lavender, lily-of-the-valley, mignonette, myrtle, peony petals, phlox, rose petals and buds, rosemary, sweet marjoram, syringa, violet, wallflower.

Scented leaves
Angelica, basil, bay, bergamot, costmary, eucalyptus, ground ivy, hyssop, lemon balm, lemon thyme, lemon verbena, lovage, melilot, mints (eau-de-Cologne, peppermint), myrtle, pelargonium, rosemary, sage, sweet marjoram, tarragon, thyme, violet, wall germander, walnut, woodruff.

Other ingredients
Angelica root, cedar wood, juniper berries, orange, lemon, lime and tangerine peel.

Essential oils
These can usually be obtained at herb shops and chemists and should only be added with restraint and discretion, a drop at a time, or you will drown all the subtle scents that make a home-made pot pourri so different from a bought mixture. Bergamot (from the citrus fruit, no relation to the herb), bitter almond, clove, eucalyptus, peppermint, rose (usually called 'attar'), sandalwood, tonquin bean.

Fixatives
Fixatives can be bought at a herb shop, craft shop or chemist and

include the following: grated or powdered root of calamus (sweet flag), orris or vetiver; dried pods of tonquin bean (*Dipteryx odorata*), which contain coumarin; dried oakmoss (*Evernia pranastri*); sandalwood raspings or oil; and powered resins such as gum benzoin, storax, frankincense or myrrh.

Animal fixatives – civet, musk, ambergris – though common in old recipes, should not be used today.

Moist pot pourri or sweet jar

Gather on sunny mornings as they bloom throughout the summer

1.5 litres/3 pints rose petals
600ml/1 pint peony petals
600ml/1 pint clove carnation petals
600ml/1 pint sweet marjoram flowers and leaves
300ml/½ pint myrtle leaves
300ml/½ pint lavender flowers
300ml/½ pint lemon verbena leaves

Dry each batch you pick for only 2 days, until they are limp and leathery. Layer them in a large crock, sprinkling each layer with a handful of mixed *bay salt* (if available) and *pure rock salt*, then weighting it down with a heavy plate. Stir the mixture before adding each new layer. A

Pomanders

Citrus pomanders

dark liquid may form. When the crock is nearly full stir the contents, sprinkle once more with salt, weight down and leave for 2 weeks. By this time the ingredients will have become a sort of aromatic cake. Break this up and mix it with:

8 broken bay leaves
the rind of an orange and lemon, dried and powdered
15g/½oz powdered cloves
15g/½oz powdered allspice
15g/½oz powdered orris root
15g/½oz grated nutmeg
2 tablespoons brown sugar
8 tablespoons brandy

Press into the crock again, weight and leave to mature for 6 months.

Dry pot pourri

Gather petals, flowers and leaves on sunny mornings throughout the summer and dry them carefully, away from direct heat, in an airy, shady room. They will shrink down to about a third of the original quantity. Store in separate airtight containers. In the autumn rub a large bowl with oil of cloves and tip in

2.4 litres/4 pints rose petals
600ml/1 pint clove carnation petals
600ml/1 pint lemon verbena leaves

600ml/1 pint lavender flowers
300ml/½ pint rosemary flowers and leaves
300ml/½ pint sweet marjoram flowers and leaves
150ml/¼ pint peppermint-scented pelargonium or peppermint leaves
600ml/1 pint mixed flowers such as rose buds, hyssop, violets etc

Mix these round with your hands then add

50g/2oz chopped orris root
1 tablespoon grated or powdered orris root
1 tablespoon powdered gum benzoin
½ a vanilla pod chopped into 3
25g/1oz broken dried tangerine peel, each piece stuck with a clove
1 teaspoon crushed allspice berries
1 teaspoon crushed coriander
8cm/3in broken cinnamon stick
2 broken bay leaves
1 teaspoon grated nutmeg
2 broken blades of mace
1 tablespoon chopped dried ginger

Mix all well together then add

a few drops of oil of rosemary or basil

Store for 6 weeks in a dark, tightly stoppered jar for the scents to blend and mature, stirring every few days with a wooden spoon. Tip into potpourri jars with well-fitting lids.

Because of the old belief that scents have a direct bearing on health and happiness and that disease results from contact with 'corrupt and contagious airs', there was increasing emphasis on scent in Europe from the late Middle Ages. By the 16th century not only clothes and household linen but leather boots and gloves were scented.

Pomanders were first recorded in France where they were probably carried as a protection against the plague. The name derives from the French *pomme d'ambre*, 'apple of amber' – the first pomanders being small balls of ambergris combined with other scented ingredients that courtiers and those in high office sniffed 'against the pestilent airs' as they walked in public places. Later pomanders were often made of silver, gold or porcelain, perforated to allow the scent to escape and filled with precious spices blended with resins or garden earth. A typical 16th-century recipe begins 'take an ounce of garden mould and steep it in rose water for several days'.

A humbler citrus pomander might be carried by priests, physicians and judges, who were often in close contact with victims of the plague and other infectious illnesses. This is easy to make, has a long-lasting scent and can be kept with clothes in a drawer or cupboard, hung on a ribbon to perfume the air or added to a bowl of dry pot pourri.

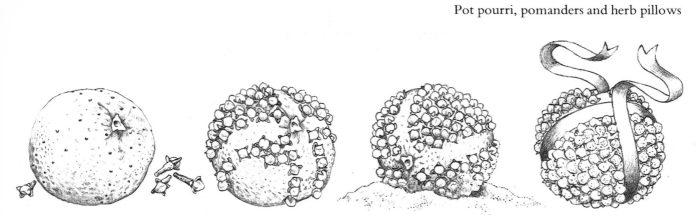

Making a pomander: *Prick an orange all over with a knitting needle, leaving a central 'cross' free for a ribbon.*

Press a clove into each hole until the surface of the fruit is completely covered except for the cross.

Roll the pomander in powdered cinnamon, nutmeg, ginger and orris and tie it round with a length of ribbon.

Choose an unblemished orange, lemon or lime and poke holes all over it with a darning or knitting needle, keeping these as close together as possible. Press a whole clove into each hole, until the orange is completely covered. You will need about 25g/1oz of cloves to each fruit. For an extra-spicy scent, roll the pomander in a mixture of powdered cinnamon, nutmeg and ginger, then rub it all over with orris powder to make sure the scent is well fixed. Leave it in a brown paper bag in an airing cupboard or cooler dark cupboard until it is hard and dry. It will keep its scent for years, becoming increasingly shrunken and wizened.

Necklace pomanders

Small pomanders were often strung together and worn as necklaces or bracelets. Simple versions of these can be made by blending lumps of softened beeswax with spices and aromatics, or by pounding fresh rose petals to a paste, shaping them into beads with rose or rosemary oil and leaving them to dry on a sunny windowsill. Pierce both wax and paste beads through with a hot needle before they harden. Other devices used for carrying strong scents were vinaigrettes, perforated boxes containing sponges soaked in herbal vinegar, and cassolettes, which were filled with an aromatic paste.

Herb pillows

Herbs that retain their scent well when dried were mixed with rough bedding from the earliest times, and as mattresses became more sophisticated herb stuffings were still used for pillows. Favourite herbs were woodruff and agrimony, lavender, rose petals and hops. Hops are the best pillow stuffing for insomniacs as they have a soporific and slightly narcotic effect. (Another old recipe for sleeplessness advises hanging muslin bags filled with rosemary seeds about the bedroom.) Some recipes for these soothing pillows are given below. Either sew a small pillow slip for the herbs or make them into a sachet and tuck this in beside an ordinary pillow in a pillow case. These mixtures will need renewing each year but a light pot-pourri mixture could be used, which would last much longer.

A Provençal pillow
4 parts dried mignonette
2 parts dried rose petals
1 part dried rosemary

A pillow for love
4 parts dried violet flowers
3 parts dried rose petals
1 part tonquin bean
1 part dried orris root

A country pillow
3 parts dried meadowsweet
3 parts dried agrimony
2 parts dried honeysuckle

A pillow against headaches
6 parts dried lemon verbena
2 parts dried lavender
1 part dried sweet marjoram
a few crushed cloves

A pillow to soothe the nerves and quieten the brain
2 parts dried peppermint
2 parts dried chamomile
1 part dried lady's bedstraw or woodruff

For dogs and cats to prevent fleas
1 part dried rue
1 part dried costmary

Incense and candle making

Apart from their delicious and sometimes intoxicating scents, incense and other burning aromatics have a powerful cleansing effect upon the air. This has always been understood and the temples and palaces that were sweetened with incense were well fumigated at the same time. Incense is made from frankincense and myrrh, which are both fragrant gums from small trees growing in southern Arabia and Somaliland. In these countries there are still some desert tribes who clean their bodies by crouching over a smouldering pot of charcoal and aromatic gums and spices, their robes spread like tents around them to keep in the fumes and promote heavy sweating.

In Europe the habit of burning aromatics to scent and purify a room was spread by the Romans, and when spices were unobtainable sweet-smelling herbs were used instead. By the early 16th century, common purifying and cleansing herbs included rosemary, bay, juniper, angelica, lavender and southernwood. During times of plague and pestilence fires would be lit in public places and sulphur, saltpetre, branches of bay and juniper and roots of angelica thrown onto the flames. Several members of the daisy family have antiseptic properties and are traditional fly repellents including ploughman's spikenard, elecampane, fleabane and tansy.

In 16th-century Europe professional perfumers were employed to scent the houses and castles of the wealthy. For this purpose, herbs were either burned slowly over charcoal or in a special perfuming pan that could be carried about the house and placed in cupboards and musty places, or else dried, powdered, mixed into a paste and formed into pastilles that could be stored. There are many old recipes for burning perfumes, often very simple and easily adapted for use today. 'One should be sure night and morning to perfume the house with angelica seeds, burnt in a fire-pan or chafing dish of coales.' (1661) 'Take 3 Spoonfuls of Perfect Rosemary and as much Sugar as half a Walnut beaten into a small powder; all these boyle together in a Perfuming-pan upon hot Embers, with a few Coals.' (1719)

The results are generally fresher and more interesting than the heavy Eastern scent of joss sticks or the chemical smells of sanitary air fresheners. In France 'fumes' have never completely fallen from favour and housewives still carry a pan of heated, smoking cloves, cayenne or mixed spices from room to room to freshen the air. Use a heavy iron frying pan, heat the dry ingredients until they begin to smoke, then remove the pan from the stove.

Lavender incense sticks

Strip long, dried lavender sticks of their flowers and push the bare stalks into a bowl of sand or earth, light the tips and leave them to smoulder like joss sticks.

Incense of roses

50g/2oz scented, red rose petals
25g/1oz dried, powdered lavender
15g/½oz powdered orris
15g/½oz powdered gum benzoin
rosewater

Thoroughly crush the rose petals in a mortar and beat in the lavender, benzoin and orris. Mix in sufficient rosewater to make a thick paste, shape into small lozenges, the size of a nutmeg, and put them to dry on thick paper in the sun for a week. Heat in a hot pan to scent the room.

Strongly scented incense

3 parts powdered frankincense
2 parts powdered orris
1 part powdered cloves
1 part raspings of sandalwood
a few drops of bergamot oil

Mix together the dry ingredients, then add the oil, mixing thoroughly. Store in a cool, dark cupboard for at least 2 months to mature. Sprinkle a teaspoonful into a hot, dry iron pan or over smouldering coal or charcoal.

'An odoriferous parfume for chambers'

150ml/¼ pint rosewater
1 tablespoon powdered cloves

Mix the ingredients well and store for a few days to mature. Sprinkle a few drops in a hot, dry iron pan to scent the room.

(From *A Queen's Delight*, 1662.)

Tansy, ploughman's spikenard and the fleabanes were traditional fly-repellent herbs, while the roots of elecampane, centre, were smouldered as a fumigant.

Candle making with herbs and spices

Many ingenious ideas for lighting were devised in the days when wild and cultivated plants formed the basis of household economy. Fat, oil or wax and some form of wick were the essentials. In northern Europe and North America the pith of rushes or the tall, downy stem of the great mullein were dried and coated in several layers of melted, clarified animal fat (tallow), then left to harden and used as candles. Narrow wicks for either wax or tallow candles were sometimes rolled from the thick, silver down of mullein, coltsfoot or mugwort leaves, and herbs and spices used to scent them. The first North American colonists soon discovered that a slightly brittle, greenish and deliciously resin-scented wax could be collected from the surface of a pan of bayberry fruit boiling in rainwater. A similar but inferior wax is produced by the resinous nutlets of the related sweet gale and there are several South American species that yield high-quality wax. Bayberry wax can still occasionally be bought today but is extremely expensive, double the price of costly beeswax.

Beeswax
Candles made from pure beeswax (obtained in tablets or sheets) are a deep, opaque, tawny-yellow colour with a rich, sweet scent, and burn slowly with a steady light. A proportion of beeswax can be melted with paraffin wax or tallow.

Tallow
Clarify beef, pork or bacon fat to prevent spluttering by melting it in a pan of hot water then leaving this to cool until the hardened fat can be lifted off the top. A little added beeswax will result in a cleaner and slower-burning candle.

Paraffin wax
Odourless paraffin wax is easily obtainable from craft shops; it is cheap, burns slowly and well and can be coloured and scented. Read the accompanying instructions, which may advise combining the wax with stearic acid or stearin.

Herbs

Add dried herbs to the melted wax just before pouring it into the mould. The best of all herbs for this purpose is rosemary, which gives the candle a wonderfully aromatic scent. Stir in as many of the spiky dried leaves as the wax will take. Dried lavender stalks snipped into short lengths with scissors also give a sweet scent. Both these herbs with their refreshing, antiseptic properties are especially suitable for burning in the sickroom. Other good herbs include hyssop, savory, thyme, germander, bergamot and mint. The resulting candles (when made with paraffin wax) will be translucent and a pale grey-green colour, filled with the suspended leaves.

Fresh herbs can be pressed round the outside of the candle to make decorative patterns. This can be done on a plain or a dyed and scented candle. Arrange the herb over the candle and 'iron' it down by pressing it gently into the wax with the back of a hot, dry spoon. This is a fiddly job and may need some practice. The temperature of the spoon is important; if too hot it will blacken the herb, if too cold it will be ineffective. Now heat a tin or pan half filled with clear paraffin wax and dip in the candle once or twice until a thin transparent glaze covers the herbs, then leave to harden.

There are many variations on this theme and the results can be spectacular. Try a tall, cool mint candle coloured pale green, scented with a few drops of peppermint oil and decorated with the largest mint leaves in the garden.

Colours

Buy colour concentrates in powder or tablet form from craft shops, or melt wax crayons with the candle-wax. Powdered dyes are generally very concentrated, so need only be used in tiny quantities. It is easier to judge the final colour with tablet dyes, though less economical.

The use of stearic acid or stearin is often recommended with commercial dyes. It helps to distribute the colour more evenly in paraffin wax. Use 10 per cent stearin to wax, and melt it separately, dissolving the dye in the stearin before adding both to the liquid wax.

Turmeric stirred into melted wax will turn the candle a rich orange-yellow. This is particularly successful with tallow, which can be made to resemble beeswax.

A candle packed with fresh rosemary or a tall, mint candle, decorated with a sprig of peppermint, will scent the air as they are burned.

Scents

Only the very faintest scent is obtained by heating even the strongest-smelling herbs in wax and straining them off, though this method is often recommended. For a scented candle use either whole herbs as recommended above or add a few drops of essential oil to the melted wax before pouring it into the mould. Herb oils and essences can be bought in most chemist, herb or craft shops. Use them with restraint, a drop at a time, or the candle may smell like a bar of cheap soap.

A basic candle recipe

Use old tins or plastic cartons as a mould for the candle, or any container with a small hole in the base will do. Glass candle moulds can be bought from craft or hobby shops or from candle suppliers. Lengths of wick can be bought, or make your own by soaking cotton (not nylon) string in a boracic solution (the crystals are obtainable at a chemist) then leaving it to dry.

Cut the wick 15cm/6in longer than the mould. Tie one end of the wick to a short stick or pencil and thread the other end through the hole in the bottom of the mould, leaving 1cm/½in hanging through. Lay the pencil across the top of the mould, pull the wick taut through the hole and plug round the hole with plasticine or sticking plaster to prevent the wax dripping through. Put lumps of wax in the top of a double saucepan or in an old tin over a saucepan of boiling water and heat slowly until the wax is thoroughly melted and has reached a temperature of about 88°C/190°F. Stir in the dried herbs, spices or oils and colour, and immediately pour the wax into the mould, keeping the wick central.

Leave for a few minutes for the wax to cool. It will shrink and form a depression; fill this with more melted wax until the base is smooth. Now stand the mould in a jug of cold water, making sure that no water enters the mould, and, when the wax is quite cool, put the jug into the refrigerator. The cold water will be sucked up inside the mould and will help to loosen the wax. When thoroughly cold, tip out the candle, trim the wick and burnish the wax, if you wish, with a piece of cotton dipped in vegetable oil.

If the candle sticks in the mould try oiling the mould with vegetable oil before pouring in the melted wax. Mixing the wax with stearin should make unmoulding easier.

Clean utensils with very hot water. Clean wax from fabric by covering it with blotting paper and then ironing to melt the wax.

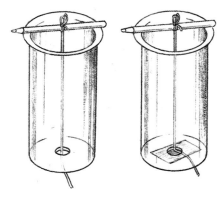  

Candle making: *Tie one end of the wick to a pencil and thread the other through the mould. Pull taut and* block the hole with sticking plaster. Melt the wax and stir in colours, scents and herbs, then pour immediately into the mould. When slightly cooled, carefully fill the depression that will have formed in the base of the candle with more wax. Stand the mould in a jug of cold water to set, then tip out the candle, trim the wick and burnish with a cloth dipped in vegetable oil.

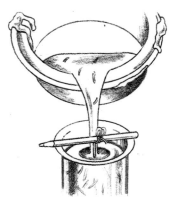 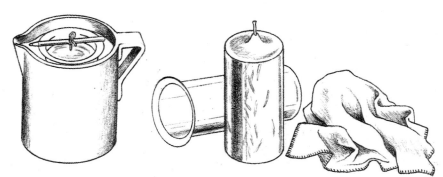

233

Yellow from onion skins and pink from madder – the soft colours of herbal dyes blend together and can be combined with the natural shades of undyed wool.

Herbal dyes

No chemical dye can achieve quite the depth and lustre of many plant dyes. The rich and subtle variations of tone and colour derived from flowers, leaves and roots may mellow and soften with time but will never lose their natural harmony.

Plant dyeing is an ancient traditional skill. It was already an established craft in China by 3000 BC, while madder and indigo were known in India from around 2500 BC. Egyptians of the same period used mordants, and dyed cloth red and yellow with safflower and blue with indigo or woad. In the 1st century AD, Dioscorides, the Greek physician and herbalist, listed the principal dyeing plants as woad, weld and madder, and by the Middle Ages large tracts of agricultural land in Europe and Britain were given over to the cultivation of these herbs. Separately they yield blue, yellow and red dyes, but by blending them and using different mordants a whole spectrum of colours could be obtained. In 1856 a synthetic lavender-coloured dye was developed from a component of coal tar, and soon a wide range of these chemical 'aniline' dyes was produced. They were cheap and easy to use and rapidly supplanted the natural dyes for commercial dyeing. However, in Scotland and Ireland (where some tweeds are still dyed with lichens), in Scandinavia and in rural communities all over the world, there has been no break in the traditions of natural dyeing and recent years have seen a tremendous renewal of interest in their work.

One of the reasons why chemical dyes are suitable for commercial purposes is that the cloth from every dye bath will be almost identical in colour. One of the pleasures of dyeing with herbs is that no two baths will ever give exactly the same results, there will always be an element of surprise, with variations according to the season, the weather, the maturity of the plant, its position in the sun or shade and the quality of the water used for dyeing. It is worth noting these details in case an unexpected colour is obtained that you would like to try and repeat.

All plants will yield some colour as a dye, though with different degrees of brightness and fastness. Greenish yellows, yellow-browns and brownish greys, are the most common colours, then rusty reds, burnt oranges and tawny golds. Blues are rarer; woad and indigo are the best known of these, but have not been included here as the dyeing methods are complex. It is not necessary to pick plants from the countryside – strong dyes can be obtained from such garden weeds as dandelion, dock, stinging nettle and horsetail, from the prolific agrimony, meadowsweet, gorse and elder, and from cultivated plants such as fennel, rue, iris, dyer's chamomile, golden rod, broom, hops and lily-of-the-valley. Herbs that cannot be grown in the garden can be bought dried from a herb shop or dye supplier, though the best results are usually achieved with fresh plants. Use flowers and tender, young leaves immediately and do not overheat, as the colour may be dulled. Berries are best when fresh and overripe, but frozen, dried or canned berries may also be used. Roots and onion skins can be dried.

Wool is the fibre referred to in these recipes as it takes natural dyes so evenly. The tough, tightly woven fibres of cotton and linen are more difficult to dye and synthetic fibres seldom react well.

A mordant is necessary to fix most dyes, to ensure that they are fairly colour fast and thoroughly absorbed by the fibre. The principal chemical mordants are listed on page 238, though other more unusual mordants, such as wood ashes, salt, vinegar, soda, urine and yoghurt, have been used.

Soft, warm colours and aromatic scent from herbal dyes. **Opposite:** *A rusty cauldron gives an instant iron mordant to dull the dye colour. Bowls of alkanet, turmeric and onion dyes stand ready for use, with a basket of fleece behind. Hanging on the line are a selection of herb-dyed yarns, including, from the right, madder, indigo, gorse, onion skins and alkanet.*

Preparation

Wool: *Separate fleece into piles of up to 225g/8oz. Wind yarn into manageable hanks and secure in several places with string. Sew cloth ends together to make a continuous roll.*

Equipment: *Use a stainless steel pan for mordanting and dyeing and a glass rod to stir the wool. Other useful items are buckets, a jam thermometer, a sieve or colander, scales, sharp knife, cup or beaker, pestle and mortar.*

Equipment for dyeing

Pans made from stainless steel are best for mordanting and dyeing, but enamel or galvanized iron will do. Iron or copper (or, to a certain extent, aluminium) will modify the colour of the dye. You will need buckets for rinsing, a large sieve or colander, scales, containers for mordants and powders, a rod for stirring (usually made of glass) and a sharp knife and pestle and mortar for chopping and crushing herbs. A jam thermometer is helpful but not essential. Use soft water for washing and dyeing wool. Either collect rainwater or soften hard tap water with zeolite (Calgon) or vinegar.

Preparing the wool

Whether wool is to be dyed as fleece, yarn or cloth, it must be thoroughly cleaned or 'scoured' before dyeing. Surprisingly, wool will not shrink or become felted during prolonged soaking or simmering if it is always handled gently when hot and wet. Slide the wool into the dye pot, barely stir it when either mordanting or dyeing, never agitate or rub it and never subject it to sudden changes in temperature. Heat very slowly to simmering point and when rinsing use progressively cooler changes of water.

The wool of a fleece is not uniform in quality; some will be fine and some very coarse. Grade the fleece into separate heaps and divide each heap into piles weighing up to about 225g/8oz.

Wind yarn into manageable hanks of not more than 225g/8oz (the following recipes are based on 100g/4oz hanks) using a large piece of cardboard. Tie the two ends of the hank together and secure it in several places with strings tied into figures of eight – loose enough to allow the dye to penetrate all the yarn, but secure enough to prevent it tangling.

Cloth is more difficult to dye evenly and is also more likely to shrink. Sew the ends together to form a continuous roll, then suspend it from a shaped bar (a bent coathanger for instance), resting the ends on the rim of the dye pan. Make sure the cloth is fully immersed in the dye and move it around gently from time to time to ensure even dyeing.

Scouring

Oily fleece, yarn or cloth should be scoured before dyeing. Prepare a bath with up to 45 litres/10 gallons (depending on the amount of wool you are using) of soft water at a temperature of about 60°C/140°F. Add 175ml/6fl oz ammonia and 75g/3oz of soft soap, put the wool in and leave to soak for an hour or longer. Squeeze it to the side of the sink and drain the water away. Lift out the wool and prepare a second sink of soap and water at a temperature of about 49°C/120°F (you are unlikely to need ammonia for this bath unless the wool is very oily). Soak for an hour, drain and rinse several times in warm water. The wool can be spun dry in a washing machine, but put the fleece in a large muslin bag first. Dry away from direct heat.

Wetting

Wool takes a dye much better if thoroughly wetted first. Do this immediately before mordanting and repeat before dyeing if the mordanted wool has been allowed to dry. Wool does not absorb water easily, but common washing soda or a special wetting agent – obtainable from some dye suppliers – added to the water will speed up the process enormously. When ready to mordant the wool for dyeing, weigh it. Prepare a bath of warm water at about 49°C/120°F and add 9g/⅓oz of washing soda for each 450g/1lb of wool used. Enter the wool and soak for an hour, then drain the sink. Alternatively use 1ml of wetting agent per 175g/6oz wool in warm water at about 49°C/120°F and soak for 5 minutes.

Scouring

Wetting

Mordanting

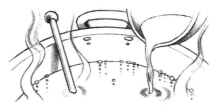

Scouring: *Soak the wool for 1 hour in soft water, ammonia and soft soap at 60°C/140°F. Drain. Repeat at 49°C/120°F. Rinse several times and dry.*

Wetting: *Soak in warm water and washing soda for 1 hour, then drain. Alternatively, add wetting agent to warm water and soak for 5 minutes.*

Mordanting: *Dissolve the mordant before adding to a pan of water. Heat the pan and put in the wetted wool. Follow the appropriate mordant recipe.*

Dyeing 1

Dyeing 2

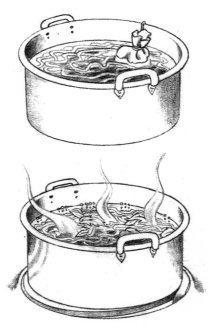

Dyeing 1: *Suitable for tough plants and roots, which may need to be boiled for a long time to extract the dye. Put the herbs in the dye pan, barely cover with water and bring to the boil. Simmer for between 1 and 3 hours, strain and cool the liquor. Throw away the plant material. Enter the well-wetted, mordanted wool into the dye and bring slowly to the boil over 1 hour. Simmer for at least 1 hour.*

Dyeing 2: *Suitable for fresh leaves and flowers that should not be boiled for long. If the herbs are likely to become entangled with the wool, enclose them in a muslin bag, otherwise pack the dye pan with alternate layers of herbs and wool, with plants on the top and bottom. Barely cover the wool with water. Bring slowly to the boil over 1 hour, then simmer for about 1 hour.*

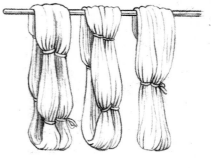

Rinsing: *After simmering for an hour, or when the wool has reached the depth of colour required, remove the skeins gently with a glass rod.*

Squeeze out the excess dye, then rinse the wool thoroughly in a bucket in hot, then warm and finally in cold water, but not under a running tap.

Drying: *Hang the wool up to dry in a warm, shady place, well away from direct heat or light.*

Mordanting

Chemical mordants

The common chemical mordants are alum (potassium aluminium sulphate), cream of tartar (tartaric acid), chrome (potassium dichromate), iron (ferrous sulphate) and tin (stannous chloride). Each mordant affects the colour of the dye with its own particular quality. Alum produces clear, bright colours; chrome gives a mellow and beautiful tone. Tin brightens colours; iron dulls or saddens them and is useful for browns and blacks. Some mordants may be bought at a chemist, but all can be acquired from a chemical or dye supplier.

It is usually convenient to mordant a quantity of wool at a time. If it is not to be used straight away then it should be dried and labelled. Soak it again in water and washing soda before dyeing.

Alum and cream of tartar

100g/4oz wool

25g/1oz alum (potassium aluminium sulphate)

7g/¼oz cream of tartar (tartaric acid)

sufficient soft water to cover the wool (approx. 5 litres/1 gallon)

Dissolve the alum and cream of tartar in a little boiling water and stir into the remaining water. Set over the heat and when warm slide in the thoroughly wetted wool. Take 1 hour to slowly bring the solution to simmering point. Simmer gently for a further hour. Remove the wool and place in dye bath.

Note: too much alum will make the wool sticky.

Chrome

Use with care. IT IS POISONOUS.

100g/4oz wool

4g/⅛oz chrome (potassium dichromate)

sufficient soft water to cover wool

Follow the same method as for alum. Chrome gives a soft 'handle' to wool, but is affected by light before dyeing, so store it in a dark jar or cupboard, cover the pan with a lid as it simmers and keep the mordanted wool in a dark place.

Note: too much chrome will darken the colour.

Iron and cream of tartar

100g/4oz wool
4g/⅛oz iron (ferrous sulphate)
7g/¼oz cream of tartar
sufficient soft water to cover wool
Either follow the same method as for alum or this alternative method. Dissolve the iron and cream of tartar in a little boiling water. Wash and dye the wool and remove it from the dye bath. Add the mordant solution to the dye, stir and slip in the wool

Basic dyeing methods

Fibrous plants and roots need long boiling to extract the dye. From the left are onion skins, roots of dock, yellow flag and, in the foreground, dandelion.

again. Continue simmering for about 30 minutes. Wash the wool thoroughly.
Note: too much iron hardens wool fibres and may cause them to rot eventually. The brown wools in Oriental carpets that have been mordanted with iron tend to disintegrate before the other colours.

Tin

100g/4oz wool

225g/8oz crystals of tin (stannous chloride)
sufficient soft water to cover wool
Follow the same method as for alum, but dissolve the crystals in warm water, not boiling. Enclose them in a muslin bag if they will not dissolve completely. Wash the wool immediately in warm, soapy water, then rinse thoroughly.
Note: too much tin will make wool harsh and brittle.

There are two usual methods of dyeing with plants. The first is to boil the plant in water until all its colour is extracted and then to use the liquor for dyeing. This method is most suitable for tough plants, bark and roots, which may need several hours of boiling to extract all dye. The second method is to simmer the plant and wool together. This is most suitable when using fresh leaves and flowers, which should not be boiled for long. As a rough guide, the plant material should at least equal the wool in weight. In fact it is often necessary to double the plant weight to achieve a strong colour.

When testing a new dye it is interesting to use a selection of natural wools – white, light grey, dark grey – to see the variations in colour (page 243). Divide the wool into 9 small skeins, 3 skeins of each shade.

Method 1

Chop and crush tough dye plants. If they are very fibrous, leave them to soak overnight in tepid water. Put the dye plants in a large pot and barely cover with rainwater or soft water (include the water used for overnight soaking). Bring slowly to the boil and simmer gently for between 1 and 3 hours. Strain, discard the plants and leave the liquor to cool. Slip the wetted, mordanted wool into the dye and bring very slowly to simmering point. This should take about an hour. Simmer gently for a further hour. When testing a dye using 9 small skeins as suggested above, remove 1 skein of each colour after the first 10 minutes' simmering, another 3 skeins 20 minutes later and leave the last 3 for the full hour to compare results. Lift the wool gently from the dye and rinse, first in hot, then lukewarm, then cold water, and hang up to dry.

Method 2

Make alternate layers of the dye plant and wool in the dye pot, the first and last layers being of the dye plant. Just cover with cold rainwater or soft water and heat very slowly, taking at least an hour to reach simmering point. Simmer for about an hour, proceeding as for method 1.

If the dye plants are likely to break up and become entangled with the wool, enclose them in muslin bags and layer these among the wool.

To test for colour fastness

The fastness of plant dyes to both light and the rigours of washing is variable, though mordants will help to hold the colours. Most herbal dyes will fade or mellow with age but are still beautiful, like old Persian carpets. To test for colour fastness, wind a little of the dyed yarn onto a card, shield half with plastic or thick card and expose to direct sunlight for a fortnight. Compare the results. Store plant-dyed clothes in cupboards and try to keep direct sunlight off hangings and rugs.

Recipes for herbal dyes

Dyed fleece can be carded for woollen spinning or combed for worsted spinning and colours can be blended together during these processes. Try blending dyed and natural fleece together or twisting the spun yarns into subtle colour mixtures. 'Locks' of dyed fleece can be woven without being spun at all and the spun yarn can be used for knitting, weaving and embroidery.

The recipes below were tested with 100g/4oz mordanted yarn. Increase the quantities of herbs proportionately if using more wool.

Agrimony

Agrimonia eupatoria
Mordant: chrome
Use 200g/7oz whole, fresh or dried plants – flowers, stems and leaves – and follow dyeing method 1.
Colours: chrome gives fawn, iron gives brownish grey.

Bloodroot

Sanguinaria canadensis
Mordant: alum and cream of tartar
Use 100g/4oz fresh or dried chopped roots. Soak these overnight in tepid water and include the water in the dye bath. Follow dyeing method 2.
Colours: alum gives red–orange, tin gives orange.

Comfrey

Symphytum officinale
Mordant: tin
Use 450g/1lb fresh leaves, stalks and flowers. Follow dyeing method 2.
Colours: tin gives an acid yellow and chrome a bright, greenish orange.

Dandelion

Taraxacum officinale
Mordant: alum and cream of tartar
Use 200g/7oz scrubbed, chopped dandelion plants, root and leaves. Follow dyeing method 1.
Colours: alum gives fawn, iron gives grey, tin a yellowish fawn.

Some dried dye plants: moving clockwise, juniper berries, chamomile, agrimony, marigold, St John's wort, turmeric, and madder in the centre.

Dock

Rumex obtusifolius
Mordant: iron and cream of tartar
Use 675g/1½lb fresh, scrubbed and chopped dock roots, boil for 2 hours, strain and follow dyeing method 1.
Colours: iron gives a good grey, chrome an orange-brown.

Dyer's chamomile

Anthemis tinctoria
Mordant: chrome
Use 200g/7oz fresh or dried flowers (more for a concentrated colour). Put the flowerheads in a loose muslin bag and follow dyeing method 2, simmering the wool for 30 minutes.
Colours: chrome gives a rich, tawny orange, iron a greenish brown.

Horsetail

Equisetum arvense
Mordant: chrome
Use 675g/1½lb fresh horsetail plants (but not the fertile stems). Layer them in the dye pot following dyeing method 2.
Colours: chrome gives a light yellow ochre, alum a pale yellow.

Juniper

Juniperus communis
Mordant: alum and cream of tartar
Use 100g/4oz fresh or dried crushed berries, boil for 3 hours and follow dyeing method 1.
Colours: alum gives a pale cream or fawn, chrome a pale khaki.

Madder

Rubia tinctorum
Mordant: alum and cream of tartar
Use 50g/2oz powdered root from a dye supplier. Mix this to a paste with *hard* water (add lime or chalk if your water is soft) and gradually dilute with sufficient water to barely cover the wool. Chopped root can also be used; soak it for several hours in the dyeing water. Add a small handful of bran in a muslin bag to brighten the colour. Heat very slowly adding the wool when the liquid is lukewarm. Take from 1 to 2 hours to reach simmering point, simmer for 10 minutes then leave the wool in the dye until it cools. Rinse the wool, wash it in soapy water, rinse again and hang to dry.
Colours: variable, depending on the quality of the root. Alum gives carrot red, chrome a reddish brown, tin gives pinkish orange.

Other members of the bedstraw family can be treated in the same way. Most give a rusty colour.

Marigold

Calendula officinalis
Mordant: alum and cream of tartar
Use 100g/4oz dried petals or at least 300g/11oz fresh flowerheads. Enclose dry petals in muslin bags and follow dyeing method 2.
Colours: alum gives a pale, creamy yellow, chrome a yellow-fawn.

Onion

Allium cepa
Mordant: alum and cream of tartar
Use 100g/4oz dried onion skins, boil for 2 hours and follow dyeing method 1.
Colours: alum gives a clear, rich yellow, chrome a warm brown, iron a dark brown and tin a strong orange.

Parsley

Petroselinum crispum
Mordant: chrome
Use 225g/8oz fresh stalks and leaves, follow dyeing method 2.
Colours: chrome gives a greenish yellow, alum a pale, creamy yellow.

St John's wort

Hypericum perforatum
Mordant: chrome
Use at least 250g/9oz chopped flowering tops in muslin bags and follow dyeing method 2.
Colours: chrome gives a strong yellow-brown, alum a pale brown.

Sorrel

Rumex acetosa
Mordant: chrome
Use 225g/8oz fresh, chopped stalks, leaves and flowers of wild or garden sorrel. Follow dyeing method 1.
Colours: chrome gives a yellowish fawn, tin a pale, yellowish green.

Stinging nettle

Urtica dioica
Mordant: alum and cream of tartar
Use at least 225g/8oz fresh nettle tops, layering with the wool and following dyeing method 2. Wear protective gloves.
Colours: alum gives dull yellow-fawn, chrome a strong orange-brown, iron a smoky grey and tin a dark yellow ochre.

Tansy

Tanacetum vulgare
Mordant: tin
Use 100g/4oz fresh tansy leaves, follow dyeing method 2.
Colours: tin gives a sharp lemon yellow, chrome a dull mustard yellow.

Turmeric

Curcuma domestica
Mordant: chrome
Use 100g/4oz powdered turmeric dissolved in a little boiling water. Strain through a piece of muslin; tie up any undissolved dye in the muslin and add to the dye pot. Follow dyeing method 2.
Colours: Chrome gives a deep orangey yellow or brown, tin a hot orange.

Weld

Reseda luteola
Mordant: alum and cream of tartar
Use 100g/4oz whole flowering or seeding plants. Follow dyeing method 1, simmering the plants for 2 hours.
Colours: alum gives a strong, soft yellow, tin a clear yellow.

Herb-dyed wools

The wools on the opposite page have been dyed using the herbal recipes on pages 240–1. The skeins at the top are undyed wools – white and 2 shades of grey that were blended before being spun from white and dark fleeces. Each plant dye was tested on a knotted skein of these 3 natural shades. Details of the plants and mordants used and of the length of time the wools were simmered (after being brought up to simmering point) are listed below. The skeins are numbered down the page from 1 to 43, starting with the undyed wool.

1 **Undyed wool:** white, light grey, dark grey.

2 **Onion:** iron mordant, simmered for 30 minutes.

3 **Dyer's chamomile:** iron mordant, simmered for 30 minutes.

4 **Onion:** iron mordant, simmered for only 2 minutes.

5 **Agrimony:** iron mordant, simmered for 1 hour.

6 **Dock:** iron mordant, simmered for 1½ hours.

7 **Stinging nettle:** iron mordant, simmered for 1 hour.

8 **Dandelion:** iron mordant, simmered for 1 hour.

9 **Dandelion:** alum mordant, simmered for 1 hour.

10 **Agrimony:** chrome mordant, simmered for 1 hour.

11 **Juniper:** chrome mordant, simmered for 10 minutes.

12 **St John's wort:** alum mordant, simmered for 2 hours.

13 **Juniper:** alum mordant, simmered for 1½ hours.

14 **Stinging nettle:** alum mordant, simmered for 1 hour.

15 **Juniper:** chrome mordant, simmered for 1½ hours.

16 **Dandelion:** tin mordant, simmered for 1 hour.

17 **Parsley:** alum mordant, simmered for 1 hour.

18 **Marigold:** alum mordant, simmered for 1 hour.

19 **Weld:** alum mordant, simmered for 1 hour.

20 **Horsetail:** alum mordant, simmered for 30 minutes.

21 **Parsley:** chrome mordant, simmered for 1 hour.

22 **Onion:** alum mordant, simmered for 10 minutes.

23 **Tansy:** tin mordant, simmered for 1 hour.

24 **Comfrey:** tin mordant, simmered for 1 hour.

25 **Weld:** tin mordant, simmered for 1 hour.

26 **Marigold:** chrome mordant, simmered for 1 hour.

27 **Stinging nettle:** tin mordant, simmered for 2 hours.

28 **Horsetail:** chrome mordant, simmered for 2 hours.

29 **Onion:** alum mordant, simmered for 1 hour.

30 **Onion:** tin mordant, simmered for 10 minutes.

31 **Turmeric:** chrome mordant, simmered for only 2 minutes.

32 **Tansy:** chrome mordant, simmered for 1 hour.

33 **Comfrey:** chrome mordant, simmered for 1 hour.

34 **Onion:** chrome mordant, simmered for 1 hour.

35 **Stinging nettle:** chrome mordant, simmered for 1 hour.

36 **St John's wort:** chrome mordant, simmered for 2 hours.

37 **Dyer's chamomile:** chrome mordant, simmered for 30 minutes.

38 **Turmeric:** chrome mordant, simmered for 30 minutes.

39 **Bloodroot:** alum mordant, simmered for 1 hour.

40 **Bloodroot:** tin mordant, simmered for 1 hour.

41 **Turmeric:** tin mordant, simmered for 30 minutes.

42 **Madder:** alum mordant, brought up to simmer during 1 hour, then simmered for 10 minutes.

43 **Madder:** tin mordant, brought up to simmer during 1 hour, then simmered for 1 hour.

Cosmetic herbs

In most museums, among temple carvings and massive sculptures, there will be found a small glass case of ancient cosmetic implements that bring the past immediately alive. The shapes of these cosmetic tools and jars are still universal thousands of years later. Some of their contents would not be considered safe to use today, but the basic methods for making cosmetics at home also remain the same, and the natural ingredients – oils and essences from plants, honey, beeswax, eggs and lanolin – are unchanged.

From excavated perfume laboratories in Egypt we have a good idea of the ancient Egyptians' preoccupation with scent and their advanced techniques. Egyptian ladies washed in scented waters, outlined their eyes with kohl, used an eye shadow of powdered lazuli and a rouge of henna leaves, and all Egyptians kept their skins supple with oil rubs; the rich using precious perfumed oil, the poor a crude palm oil. All lasting perfumes were based on oil or wine, as distillation was unknown.

Face packs used by Roman ladies are recorded by Ovid in a fragment from a larger book he wrote on perfumes. To whiten the skin a mixture of barley, bean flour, eggs, hartshorn, pulped narcissi bulbs, honey and aromatic gums was used, and he assures us that 'every woman who spreads this on to her face will render it smoother and more brilliant than her mirror'. At the Roman baths the water was often scented with lavender and other aromatic herbs, and afterwards the bathers were rubbed with olive oil and pumice stone or massaged with scented oils such as saffron oil.

Indian women also used (and still use today) kohl and henna, kohl around their eyes and henna on hands and feet, and their baths were scented with heavier perfumes, jasmine, patchouli, and sandalwood. Aristocratic Chinese ladies slept in face packs of rice flour pounded with oil and used a white rice-based face powder during the day. Like most Eastern women, they oiled their hair and bound into it strong-scented flowers such as jasmine and frangipani, which, by a process of *enfleurage*, scented the hair long after the

The enormous variety of wild and cultivated herbs with beneficial properties can be used either as central ingredients for cosmetics, or as subtle additives.

flowers had died. Men and women of all nationalities used vegetable hair dyes, henna to give a whole range of red tints, saffron for yellow shades and walnut rind to darken the hair.

An Arabian doctor, Avicenna, discovered the secret of distilling the essential or volatile oil from flowers and herbs in the 10th century, and by the early 16th century most large houses in Europe possessed a stillroom, and a corner of every herb garden was set aside for 'herbes to stylle'.

Some of the cosmetics employed by courtiers in the 17th and 18th centuries sound extremely dangerous. The skin was whitened with powdered lead or ground alabaster mixed with sulphur and borax, and a rouge of red mercuric sulphide and coloured lead was applied to the cheeks, which were then glazed and glued with white of egg. Finally, the pupils of the eyes were dilated and made to sparkle with drops of poisonous deadly nightshade. However, the French Revolution dramatically reversed the fashion for elaborate make-up and throughout the 19th century the emphasis was on simple flower waters, safe herb oils and a natural, unstudied look. The few, lightly scented cosmetics that were used were made at home.

In the twentieth century came the cinema with new ideas of feminine beauty, and the mass production of cosmetics became big business.

There are great advantages in making cosmetics at home, foremost among them being the choice of pure and natural ingredients and the freedom to make up preparations that suit different types of skin and hair and have their own special scent. Skin, hair, teeth and nails all benefit from a balanced and varied diet of soothing emollient creams, invigorating astringents and toners and nutritious oils, and to achieve that balance it is necessary to recognize your own type of skin and to adjust the ingredients accordingly. As in cookery, the enormous variety of wild and cultivated herbs with beneficial properties can be used either as central ingredients or as subtle additives and perfumes.

Ingredients and basic preparations

Many of these recipes for simple cosmetics, particularly those that include such ingredients as egg, milk and unpurified water, will not keep for long. Make them up in small quantities and store in the refrigerator. Those based on preservatives such as vinegar, oil and especially alcohol will keep for months or even years. Store these in opaque glass or pottery jars in a dark cupboard. Proportions and ingredients are flexible and this is another good reason for making only small quantities at a time. Experiment with the preparations as you would with culinary recipes and you will soon find the ingredients that suit your skin and the scents that you are happiest with.

Skin types

Different skin types are often referred to in the recipes. Oily skin needs regular cleansing to prevent blocked pores that develop into spots and blackheads or infected areas. Horsetail, yarrow, nettle and houseleek are among the astringent, cleansing herbs that will contract and dry oily skin. Dry skin feels stretched and tight, becomes easily chapped in cold weather, flaky in hot sun and is prone to wrinkles. Rich moisturizing creams and lotions will help replace the missing natural oils; use the emollient herbs – chamomile, comfrey, marsh mallow and marigold. Sensitive skin is often soft textured, will rapidly change colour and may react violently to insect bites and stings. Use a gentle cleanser and light herbal infusions of parsley, chervil or elderflower. Watch carefully for allergic reactions to preparations containing essential herb oils as these can sometimes irritate delicate skins.

Herbs for the skin

Borage: leaves are softening and cleansing

Burdock: roots and leaves are soothing and demulcent

Chamomile: flowers are soothing, cleansing and gently astringent

Chervil: leaves are gently astringent

Coltsfoot: leaves are soothing and help to prevent thread veins

Comfrey: leaves and root are emollient and healing

Dandelion: leaves and root are tonic and cleansing

Elder: flowers are softening, soothing and cleansing

Eucalyptus: leaves are invigorating

Fennel: leaves are cleansing and gently astringent

Goosegrass: leaves are healing and deodorant

Horsetail: non-fertile stems and branches are astringent, strengthen nails and close skin pores

Houseleek: leaves are healing and nourishing

Lady's mantle: leaves are healing, astringent and reduce inflammation

Lavender: antiseptic and stimulant

Lemon balm: leaves are soothing and astringent

Lime: flowers are soothing, cleansing and bleaching

Lovage: leaves and root are cleansing and deodorant

Marigold: leaves and flowers are healing and soothing

Marsh mallow: root and leaves are emollient and healing

Mint: leaves are healing, stimulating and antiseptic

Parsley: leaves are gently astringent and help to prevent thread veins

Plantain: leaves are astringent and cleansing

Rosemary: leaves are invigorating and astringent

Sage: leaves are deodorant, strongly astringent, close pores and revitalize tissues

Stinging nettle: leaves, seeds and roots are cleansing, toning, improve circulation.

Thyme: leaves are deodorant and antiseptic

Witch hazel: astringent, antiseptic

Yarrow: leaves and flowers are strongly astringent

Other ingredients

These can be bought from most chemist shops.

Alcohol: colourless, flavourless pure spirit, used as a preservative. As the unlicensed sale of pure alcohol is illegal in many countries, vodka can be used as a substitute and in some recipes, surgical spirit.

Alum: an astringent mineral salt, bought as a coarse, white powder.

Arrowroot: a nutritious powdered starch obtained from the dried rhizomes of a West Indian plant and used as a thickening agent for cosmetics.

Beeswax: used in cosmetics as a nourishing and emollient binding agent for creams, and generally sold in pressed cakes.

Benzoin or gum benjamin: an aromatic resin that is both astringent and strongly preservative. It can be bought as a powder or tincture.

Borax: an emulsifying salt that is slightly acidic and antiseptic, often used to emulsify beeswax.

Cocoa butter: a thick, creamy oil used as an emollient to lubricate the skin.

Fuller's earth: a clay-like substance, rich in minerals and often used as a binding agent for cosmetics. Bought as a fine grey powder.

Glycerine: a thick, colourless liquid derived from vegetable oils; used as a moisturizer and softener.

Honey: a wonderful skin food, rich in minerals and vitamins, which heals, moisturizes and softens the skin. It is also used to bind cosmetic preparations.

Kaolin: a fine white clay used as a binding agent.

Lanolin: a rich, sticky, fatty matter extracted from sheep's wool; invalu-

able for creams and lotions as it is so easily absorbed by the skin. Use anhydrous lanolin, which is prepared without water.

Lemon juice: an acid, cleansing treatment for oily skin.

Oil: used as a preservative and to soften the skin. Wheatgerm oil is healing and contains Vitamin E; olive oil is rich and emollient, but occasionally strong smelling; almond oil is a valuable skin food, but expensive, use safflower or sunflower oil when large quantities are required. Castor oil is a strengthening hair oil; a specially treated

castor oil, often called 'Turkey red', disperses in water and so can be used in the bath.

Vinegar: an important cosmetic ingredient that invigorates, softens and cleanses the skin and restores lost acidity. Cider vinegar has the added benefit of malic acid from apples and is generally considered the best vinegar for cosmetic use.

Water: an essential ingredient in many preparations. Cosmetics will keep longer if distilled or purified water are used; spring or rainwater or softened tap water are good for the complexion and hair.

Infusion

Decoction

Maceration

Basic preparations

Infusion: a tea made by pouring boiling water over herb leaves and/or flowers, which is then left to infuse in a covered pot or pan before straining. The minimum infusion time is 15 minutes; leave for 2 to 3 hours to extract all the properties of the herb. Most cosmetic infusions are strong, 2 tablespoons or 50g/2oz dried herb or 100g/4oz fresh herb to 600ml/1 pint boiling water. Halve the herbs for a weak infusion. Use stainless steel, ceramic, glass or enamel pans for infusions; aluminium pans will taint the preparation.

For a *milk infusion*, put 1 tablespoon or 25g/1oz dried herb or 50g/2oz fresh herbs in a cup, fill to the brim with cold milk, cover with a saucer and leave to infuse for 1 to 4 hours before straining.

Decoction: a brew made from the tougher parts of herbs – the roots,

bark, wood chips or seeds. Use the same type of container as above and the same proportions of plant material and water. Boil the herb gently in a covered pan for a minimum of 20 minutes or ideally for 2 to 3 hours. The liquid should reduce to about 450ml/¾ pint. Strain.

Herbal vinegar: properties of a herb preserved in vinegar. Fill a glass bottle or jar with herbs and either white-wine vinegar or cider vinegar. Cover and leave to *macerate* for 2 to 3 weeks. Repeat with fresh herbs if necessary. Strain and bottle.

Herbal oils: properties of a herb preserved in oil. Bruise or crush the herbs and loosely pack a glass bottle or jar. Fill the jar with olive oil or other mild oil such as sunflower, corn or peanut. Stir well and cover with a piece of muslin or perforated paper. Leave on a sunny windowsill or in a warm place for 2 to 3 weeks,

stirring or shaking daily. Strain off the oil and repeat with fresh herbs until the oil smells strongly herbal; 2 lots of herbs are usually enough.

Essential or volatile oils: herb oils cannot be extracted satisfactorily without special equipment. Buy these from a chemist or herb shop.

Herbal extract or tincture: properties of a herb preserved in alcohol. Loosely fill a glass jar with crushed, fresh herbs, cover with pure alcohol or vodka. Stopper and leave for 1 week. Strain and repeat the process with fresh herbs. Strain again. The alcohol should now smell strongly of the herb. If the extract is to be stored for long add a few drops of tincture of benzoin as an added preservative.

Herb essence: essential oil preserved in alcohol. *Never* take internally. Stir 1 tablespoon of essential oil into 600ml/1 pint pure alcohol, vodka or surgical spirit.

Distillation techniques and herb scents

Methods of scent extraction

Distillation

Distillation is the most common method used to extract the essential oil from plants, though the heat involved is too fierce for the more delicate flowers. Leaves, bark, roots, seeds and tough flowers such as roses and lavender are suitable. The basic apparatus consists of a still or retort in which the liquid and material are heated, a condenser to cool and condense the resulting vapour, and a receiver to collect the distilled liquids.

The simplest type of distillation involves boiling the plant material, lavender flowers for example, in water in the still until the steam, laden with minute particles of essential oil is passed into the condenser. There the vapour cools and condenses and the resulting liquid drips into the receiver. As the essential oil is insoluble in water it soon separates and can be collected. Distillation by steam is slightly more complicated but quicker and is generally preferred. In this case the plant material is spread on an open tray and steam is forced through it under pressure, carrying the particles of essential oil into the condenser.

Extraction

The strong scents of flowers such as lavender can be preserved in oil or pure alcohol, which are the bases for home-made perfumes.

The essential oils of plants are soluble in alcohol and volatile solvents, such as petroleum ether, and these substances are used in a method called, simply, extraction, which is used to separate the essential oils from delicate flowers. Petroleum ether is allowed to run from a tank slowly through the plant material, washing out the essential oils and carrying them into a vacuum still. There the solvent is distilled and returned to the tank leaving a solid

substance, a mixture of essential oils and plant waxes, in the retort. This substance is shaken with alcohol into which the oil dissolves and then distilled until a pure 'floral absolute' is extracted.

Enfleurage

The method known as *enfleurage* uses no heat and is suitable for the most delicate flowers such as violet, lily-of-the-valley and mignonette. It is based on the principle that essential oils are absorbed by fats and oils, a principle that has been used since ancient times in the manufacture of herbal oils and ointments. Shallow trays are greased on both sides with purified fat and fresh blossoms are spread thickly between them. Every few days the spent flowers are removed and replaced with fresh ones until, in about 4 weeks, the fat is saturated with the flower oil. This fat is called a 'pomade'. The oil is then extracted from the fat with an alcoholic solvent. Sometimes cloths soaked in olive oil are used instead of trays, the blossoms being replaced as necessary until the olive oil is fully charged with the perfume. Then the oil is squeezed from the cloths and the essential oils separated with alcohol as before. Macer-

Maceration

ation is a similar and quicker method used for less fragile flowers, in which successive batches of fresh flowers are left to soak in warm fat for several days until the fat is strongly impregnated. Again the oils are washed out of the fat with alcohol. A simple example of maceration is the scented fat that can be poured from the roasting pan after pork has been cooked in rosemary.

Attar of roses is one of the oldest and most famous perfumes. One story of its discovery is that a Persian princess and her bridegroom were rowing on a lake covered thickly with ceremonial rose petals. A hot sun was shining and the princess, after idly dabbling her fingers in the water, found that her hands were covered with a yellowish, richly rose-scented oil.

Herb scents

Alcohol perfumes were first distilled in the 14th century and two of these are still famous today. Hungary water is said to have been invented by a hermit, who gave the recipe to the Queen of Hungary to preserve her beauty (or, according to another story, to restore the use of paralysed limbs). This was based on oil of rosemary with additions of mint, rose, orange flower and lemon peel, distilled in grape spirit. Soon afterwards the nuns in a French Carmelite abbey made Carmelite water from lemon balm, angelica, lemon peel, coriander and other spices distilled in orange-flower water and alcohol. Eau-de-Cologne is perhaps the most famous herbal water. It was invented in the early 18th century and contains bergamot oil (from the rind of the bergamot orange), neroli oil (from orange flowers) and rosemary, distilled in a grape spirit. Although the art of perfumery is extremely complex, it is possible to make perfumes at home, without a still and, though the essential oils and spirit are expensive, the results will be cheaper and often more subtle and original than bought perfumes. They can be based on oil or on pure alcohol, which is the only solvent that can safely be used at home to dissolve the herb or flower oils. Unlike those based on oil, alcohol perfumes can be diluted with distilled water bought from the chemist. As pure alcohol is often impossible to buy, vodka or brandy can be substituted, although the resulting perfume may look slightly cloudy or lumpy and the scent can be somewhat unpredictable.

Try making up the recipes on the next page using fresh herbs, floral waters or oils and experiment to find the combination you prefer. The perfume must be stored in an airtight bottle away from the light, and the space between the surface of the liquid and the stopper should be as small as possible, to reduce the harmful effects of the air. As the perfume is used, drop glass marbles into the bottle to keep the liquid at the same high level.

Hungary water

4 tablespoons fresh, crushed rosemary
3 tablespoons fresh, crushed mint
3 tablespoons crushed rose petals
1 tablespoon grated lemon peel
150ml/¼ pint orange-flower water
150ml/¼ pint alcohol or vodka

Steep all the ingredients together in a glass jar for 2 weeks. Strain through a muslin, squeezing all the juices through. Bottle and store for a further 2 weeks to mature.

Perfumes can be made from any scented flowers using this method. Simply steep the flowers in alcohol then strain off. If the scent is not sufficiently strong repeat with several successive batches of fresh flowers. Try using the leaves of pelargonium (scented geranium), basil, bergamot, bay, different species of mint, walnut and the flowers of violets, lavender, jasmine and wall-flower. Add spices such as cloves and cinnamon.

Cologne oil

150ml/¼ pint begamot oil
100ml/3½ fl oz neroli oil
100ml/3½ fl oz sweet orange oil
100ml/3½ fl oz lemon oil
50ml/2fl oz lavender oil
50ml/2fl oz rosemary oil
15ml/½ fl oz petit grain oil
20ml/¾ fl oz diethyl phthalate

The oils are available from chemists or from specialist perfume suppliers. Mix them together in a bottle, shaking thoroughly, then add the diethyl phthalate. This is a thin, scentless, very refined oil that will dissolve and dilute the essential oils, leaving a clear solution. Store in an airtight bottle in a dark place.

The blend of oils is identical to that of eau-de-Cologne and the scent is very similar, although in this case it is based on oil, not on alcohol. This means it will not evaporate so quickly as true eau-de-Cologne. Add a few drops to the bath water or use it to scent home-made hand or face lotions (page 252).

A simple herb perfume

2 tablespoons essential flower oil
600ml/1 pint alcohol or vodka

Mix 4 tablespoons of the alcohol thoroughly into the oil then add the remaining alcohol slowly, mixing all the time. Bottle, cover tightly and leave for at least a month to mature.

Rosewater is a basic ingredient of many scents and herbal cosmetics.

Bathing with herbs

Bath bags

The simplest and most pleasurable way of using herbs to soften or tone up the skin and relax and scent the body is to include them in the bath. One can just drop them in the water and lie like Ophelia among the floating flowers, but later the sodden herbs cling to the body and block the plug hole. To avoid this problem either add a strong infusion or decoction of herbs to the water or tie them up in a piece of muslin or cheesecloth or in the foot of a clean nylon stocking. Suspend this bag on a string beneath the hot-water tap so that the water runs through it into the bath or, to extract all the properties from the herbs, infuse it in a jug of boiling water for a few minutes then add both liquid and herb bag to the bath water. Rub the bag briskly over the body, squeezing the juices from the herbs like a sponge. Afterwards, put the bag to dry in the airing cupboard and it should last for several baths, although gradually losing its scent.

Try making up your own mixtures using either fresh or dried herbs. For an extra-cleansing effect add a tablespoon of fine oatmeal or bran to each bag. Do not bath in excessively hot water and, to reap the benefit of the herbs, lie quietly and rest for at least 15 minutes.

Bath waters and oils

History records the famous and extravagant baths of past beauties; Cleopatra in asses' milk, Nero's Poppaea in perfumed milk, Mary Queen of Scots in red wine, Catherine the Great and Madame de Pompadour in potent herb baths and Madame Tallien in freshly crushed strawberries. These rather more practical recipes for bathing waters can be made up easily at home and will keep for at least a week in the refrigerator, or for 2 to 3 weeks if made with distilled or purified water. A teaspoon of brandy in each 600ml/1 pint will preserve them for longer. Add a cupful of the scented water to each bath.

Oil- and vinegar-based recipes will keep for as long as you wish and are best stored in a cool, shaded place. Turkey red oil is a specially treated castor oil that will dissolve in the bath water and be absorbed into the skin. Other oils will not mix with the water but float on the surface, so rub them into the skin in the bath and get out slowly so that they coat the body.

Cleansing bath bag

3 parts dandelion leaves
3 parts stinging nettles
2 parts blackcurrant leaves
2 parts pelargonium (scented geranium) leaves

This is a good garden mixture of traditional cleansing herbs with pelargonium added for its scent. Use gloves to stuff the bag if the nettle leaves are fresh; they will be made harmless by the boiling water.

Relaxing bath bag

3 parts chamomile
2 parts meadowsweet
2 parts lime flowers
1 part valerian root

All these herbs have a soothing and faintly sedative effect.

Invigorating bath bag

3 parts marigold
3 parts pennyroyal (or other mints)
2 parts grated lovage root
1 part pine needles

Marigold is included as an astringent, pennyroyal to refresh, lovage as a deodorant and pine needles to stimulate the circulation.

Lemon-scented bath bag

3 parts lemon verbena or lemon balm
2 parts rosemary
2 parts fennel (fresh leaves or bruised seeds)
a twist of lemon peel

Lemon verbena is included for its scent, rosemary for its invigorating and disinfectant action and fennel as a light astringent and cleanser.

Lavender bath water

1 part lavender flowers
2 parts bay leaves
4 parts fine oatmeal
4 parts bran

Simmer together in a large pan of water covered with a tightly fitting lid for 1 hour. Strain.

Healing bath water

4 parts comfrey root
3 parts mint
1 part bruised houseleek leaves

Make a decoction of the comfrey root by boiling for a minimum of 30 minutes in a covered pan. Strain the boiling liquid over the mint and houseleek, cover and leave to infuse for at least another 30 minutes. Strain.

Elderflower milk bath

300ml/½ pint milk

100g/4oz fresh or 50g/2oz dried elderflowers

Infuse the fresh elderflowers in the cold milk for 1 to 4 hours *or* pour 300ml/½ pint boiling water over the dried elderflowers, cover, leave to infuse for at least 30 minutes, strain and add to the milk. This gentle, nourishing bath will help soften the skin. A mixture of powdered milk and dried elderflowers can also be made up into bath bags. Chamomile or lime flowers can be substituted for the elderflowers.

Herbal foot bath

a large handful of fresh or 3 tablespoons dried herbs (sage, thyme, lavender, sweet marjoram or bay)

1 tablespoon of sea salt

Put the herbs and salt in a large bowl with boiling water and use as a foot bath for tired feet when sufficiently cooled. This has a surprisingly re-freshing and restoring effect on the rest of the body.

For a warming mustard foot bath, bruise a tablespoon of black mustard seeds or mix a paste with 2 teaspoons mustard flour and add boiling water.

Rosemary bath oil

4 parts Turkey red oil

1 part essential oil of rosemary

Store in a bottle and shake well before use. If using a glass bottle, add a long sprig of rosemary as a decoration, but be careful that no spiky leaves escape into the bath.

A vinegar bath

600ml/1 pint cider vinegar

a good handful of fresh aromatic herbs (refer to the list of cosmetic herbs for those most suitable for your skin)

Steep the herbs in the vinegar following the procedure for making herb vinegars *or* bring herbs and vinegar slowly to simmering point on the stove, cover tightly, remove from the heat and leave to infuse overnight. Strain and bottle. Use a cupful in each bath or a few spoon-fuls in a wash basin.

A vinegar bath will soften the skin, soothe aching muscles and relieve skin irritation.

Almond bath oil

4 parts almond oil (or a cheaper vegetable oil such as safflower, olive or corn oil)

1 part essential oil of your choice (thyme, cloves, eucalyptus etc)

1 part vodka or brandy

Shake all the ingredients together in a bottle. Add 1 teaspoon to each bath beneath a fast-running hot tap to help it disperse. The alcohol is not essential but counteracts the greasi-ness of the oil.

Herbs in the bathroom: soap scented with lemon balm, a frothing, mild herbal shampoo, and, in a porcelain bowl, rosemary-oil conditioner (page 259).

Soap

The first 'soaps' were made from lye, a strong alkaline solution that often had a base of ash and animal fats, or from the roots and leaves of plants containing saponin, such as soapwort. Later the fine castile soap, with an olive-oil base, was manufactured in Spain and exported all over Europe. In 16th-century Britain 'wash balls' were used in most households for cleansing the face and hands, made from shavings of castile soap, mixed herb oils and distilled waters, spices, aromatics and a wide variety of other ingredients such as pounded almonds, raisins, brown breadcrumbs and honey. Try making a modern version as suggested, or the sweet marjoram complexion soap.

Take great care with the caustic soda, which has a powerfully corrosive action. Wear long sleeves and rubber gloves and, if a drop falls on your skin, wash it off immediately with cold water. Keep children well out of the way. The fumes are also damaging so avoid breathing above the pan. Use an enamel or stainless-steel pan as the soda will badly affect other metals.

Sweet marjoram soap

25g/1oz fresh or 15g/½oz dried sweet
  marjoram
150ml/¼ pint boiling water
3 teaspoons caustic soda
300ml/½ pint almond oil
100g/4oz coconut oil
1 tablespoon glycerine
1 tablespoon fine oatmeal

Line 2 or 3 soap dishes or small, shallow moulds with waxed paper, Cling Film or wet cotton and follow the method set out below. It is safer to use the caustic soda outside in the fresh air so that its fumes are quickly dispersed.

When the soap is set, unmould and wrap in fresh waxed paper and leave in a cool, dry cupboard for at least a fortnight to mature.

Other herbs can be substituted for the sweet marjoram or try using a few drops of essential oil – oil of cloves makes a very good soap scent.

Herbal 'wash ball'

2 bars glycerine or unscented soap, grated
25g/1oz finely chopped herbs
a few drops of essential oil
1 tablespoon fine oatmeal or bran

Melt the ingredients gently over hot water in a double saucepan and pour into moulds lined with waxed paper.

Making soap: Infuse the marjoram in boiling water for 30 minutes. Strain into a glass or china bowl.

When slightly cooled stir in the caustic soda with a wooden spoon until dissolved. Leave until lukewarm.

Put the oils and glycerine in an enamel or stainless-steel pan and gently warm to dissolve.

Carefully pour oils and glycerine into the bowl. Stir until the mixture thickens. This may take 20 minutes.

Stir in the oatmeal (and any other additions such as chopped herbs, essential oils etc).

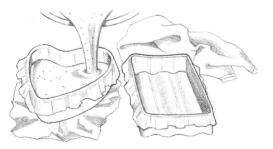

Pour into prepared moulds, cover with a thick cloth and leave in a warm place for 2 days or until set.

Herbal skin care

The first step towards a healthy complexion is to make sure the skin is regularly and thoroughly cleaned. You can use the soaps and herbal infusions suggested for bathing, but the face and hands, so often exposed to city grime and fumes, may need additional deep-cleansing methods and preparations. Apart from refreshing and enlivening the skin, these should help prevent the spots and blemishes that result when the pores are clogged with oil.

Facial steamers

Facial steamers thoroughly soften the skin and open the pores. They should only be used regularly by those with oily or normal skins. Dry skin can benefit from occasional steaming, perhaps once a fortnight, but people with sensitive skin or broken red veins should not try this method, nor should anyone who has breathing difficulties.

Herbal face packs

Only use a face pack when there is plenty of time to relax properly. If you have not just used a steamer, open the pores of the skin by covering your face with a wet, hot (but not uncomfortably hot) flannel or towel for 5 minutes before applying the pack. Spread the mixture over the face (avoiding eyes and lips), lie down, shut your eyes and relax for at least 20 minutes. Rinse off the pack with warm water then close the pores with cold water or an astringent herbal infusion. All face packs are likely to have a drying effect on the skin, so it may be necessary to apply a moisturizing lotion.

Skin tonics

Use an infusion of astringent herbs to rinse the face after washing or after a cleansing steamer or face pack, or simply as a refreshing skin stimulant and toner. Yarrow, lady's mantle and horsetail make fairly strong astringents; dandelion, parsley, fennel, rosemary, elderflowers and chervil have a gentler effect. Coltsfoot, marigold, parsley and chervil are tonic herbs that help combat thread veins. For sensitive or dry skins combine the herb infusions with equal quantities of rosewater or orange-flower water.

A mixture of witch hazel and rosewater is very effective as a skin tonic and can either be made up at home or bought ready-mixed from the chemist. Use in equal quantities for oily skin or 3 parts rosewater to 1 of witch hazel for dry skin.

Fresh herb infusions will not keep for longer than a few days but the following recipes can be stored for a long time. They are best suited to fairly oily skin and will help to cleanse and dry skin that is prone to blemishes and spots. Apply with a soft sponge, clean lint or cotton wool and wipe off the excess with a tissue.

Lotions, creams and moisturizers

One of the first commercial skin lotions was sold by an Englishman, Gervase Markham, in the 17th century and contained rosemary, fennel, feverfew, violets and nettles; it had to be diluted with milk before application. The first recorded recipe for cold cream was written down by the Greek physician, Galen, in the 2nd century AD. It contained beeswax, oil of roses and water and this combination is still used today, though the extremely expensive oil or attar of roses is usually replaced by cheaper vegetable oils.

A straightforward culinary mayonnaise makes a good skin lotion or can be used as a face pack. Use the recipe in the cookery chapter (page 166). To the nutritious egg, stimulating vinegar and softening oil add a tablespoon of moisturizing honey and pulped emollient herbs such as borage, or marsh mallow leaves or root. Add the more astringent herbs for oily skin. The recipes given are suitable for the face, hands and any other part of the body. In order for the oil and water to blend properly, mix them slowly and gradually together; they must both be at about the same temperature.

Opposite: *Astringent herbs, scented flower waters, citrus fruits, spices, herb vinegars and preservatives such as borax, orris and tincture of benzoin are the important ingredients for gentle skin tonics and lotions.*

A herbal steamer

600ml/1 pint boiling water
2 tablespoons dried or 1 handful of fresh herbs such as chamomile, elder or lime flowers, comfrey or houseleek leaves etc. (Refer to the list of cosmetic herbs to find those suitable for your type of skin)
Put the herbs in a pudding basin or jug and pour over the boiling water. Hold your face a comfortable distance above the steam, cover your head with a towel and remain there for 10 minutes. Either pat your face gently with absorbent tissues and rinse in fresh tepid water or with a slightly astringent herbal infusion, or take advantage of your softened skin to apply a cleansing and nourishing face pack. Do not go immediately into a cold room or out of doors.

Herbal ingredients of a face pack

Herbs can be used fresh, either pounded to a paste or simmered with a little milk or water to a thick, sludgy consistency. Or mix a strong infusion or decoction of fresh or dried herbs with the other face-pack ingredients.

Non-herbal ingredients

Many vegetables and fruits are valuable ingredients in face packs – crushed cucumber and green pepper, avocado, melon, carrot and lettuce, apricot and strawberries, for instance. Add a few drops of cider vinegar or lemon juice to restore the skin's natural acidity. Buttermilk, whey and yoghurt are good ingredients for oily skin and creamy milk or soured cream for dry skin. Among the richest oils are almond, avocado and wheatgerm oil; corn, peanut and sunflower oil are less expensive but still effective. Lanolin and glycerine are enriching ingredients and boiled linseed or quince seed provide healing mucilage.

A binding agent is necessary for a firm face pack. Fuller's earth is a nutritious binder or you can use honey, beeswax, brewer's yeast, kaolin or mashed banana. Corn or oatmeal, bran or wheatgerm flour are soothing and cleansing and should be mixed to a paste with a spoonful of milk or herbal infusion. Egg is a good binder – use the yolk for dry skin, the beaten white for oily skin.

A basic face pack

A basic face pack is made by simply mixing pulped complexion herbs to a paste with fuller's earth. A pack for dry skin might include pounded marsh mallow leaves or root simmered in a little milk, combined with honey, almond oil and a few drops of cider vinegar, and mixed to a paste with egg yolk and fine oatmeal. For oily skin use an infusion of nettle and yarrow, lemon juice, beaten egg white and brewer's yeast. It is worth experimenting to find a combination of ingredients that particularly suits your skin.

A deep-cleansing face pack

1 teaspoon beeswax
1 tablespoon lanolin
75ml/⅛ pint strong herb infusion
1 tablespoon (approx.) fuller's earth or kaolin
optional: for dry skin 3 drops wheatgerm oil; for oily skin ¼ teaspoon tincture of benzoin
Melt the beeswax and lanolin in the top of a double saucepan and slowly add the infusion, stirring all the time. Stir in the optional ingredients and then sufficient fuller's earth or kaolin to make an easy-spreading paste.

Herb-vinegar astringent

300ml/½ pint herb vinegar
300ml/½ pint distilled elderflower water
Bottle the ingredients and shake well before using. Vinegar should always be diluted before using directly on the skin; 2 tablespoons to a wash basin of water should be sufficient.

Lavender astringent

3 parts lavender flowers
1 part powdered orris
sufficient cider vinegar to cover
Combine the ingredients and leave to stand for at least 2 weeks. Strain through a muslin or coffee filter and bottle. Dilute before use as above.

Spicy body toner or aftershave lotion

1 tablespoon fresh rosemary
1 tablespoon fresh mint
¼ teaspoon grated orange peel
¼ teaspoon grated lemon peel
¼ teaspoon grated nutmeg
100ml/4fl oz distilled rose or elderflower water
50ml/2fl oz pure alcohol or vodka
Pound the herbs in a pestle and mortar and beat in the remaining ingredients *or* blend all together in a liquidizer. Pour into a glass jar or bottle and leave on a sunny windowsill or in a warm place for at least a week. Strain and bottle.

A basic moisturizer

3 parts rosewater
4 parts glycerine
Mix together and store in a bottle. Either use on its own or with 3 parts of a strong herb liquor such as a decoction of mallow or comfrey root or an infusion of their leaves. After diluting the mixture in this way, it must be used within a week, so only make up a small quantity.

A simple lotion

a handful of fresh chamomile, meadowsweet, elder or lime flowers
75ml/⅛ pint warm milk, cream, buttermilk or whey
honey
Soak the flowers in the liquid in a covered pan for 3 hours. Strain, reheat and dissolve a little honey in the liquor. A spoonful of oatmeal, bran or wheatgerm will thicken the lotion. Keep refrigerated and use within a week.

Comfrey cream cleanser

*150ml/¼ pint strong infusion of comfrey
  leaves*
150ml/¼ pint almond or olive oil
2 tablespoons melted beeswax
2 tablespoons cocoa butter
1 teaspoon borax
2 teaspoons honey

Melt the oil, beeswax and cocoa
butter in the top of a double
saucepan. Warm the infusion in
another pan, stir in the borax and
honey and thoroughly dissolve.
Remove both pans from the heat and
gradually combine the mixtures,
then beat steadily with a wooden
spoon or electric mixer and the
mixture will thicken to a creamy
consistency as it cools. Pot up and
label the jar.

This cleanser is gentle, soothing
and healing and is suitable for use as a
baby cream.

Elderflower cleansing lotion

75ml/⅛ pint distilled elderflower water
1 teaspoon grated unscented soap
175ml/6fl oz sesame-seed oil
3 tablespoons cocoa butter
1½ tablespoons melted beeswax

Soften the soap in the top of a double
saucepan, then mix in and warm the
oil, cocoa butter and beeswax.
Warm the elderflower water in a
separate pan then beat gradually into
the oil mixture. Pour into a bottle or
jar, allow to cool, cover tightly and
label.

Chamomile and cucumber lotion

75ml/⅛ pint strong chamomile infusion
350g/12oz cucumber
6 teaspoons glycerine

Chop the cucumber finely and
squeeze out the juice. Slightly warm
the infusion and stir in the glycerine
then, when thoroughly amalgamated, stir in the cucumber juice.
Cool and bottle. Refrigerate. This
lotion will help smooth and soften
rough skin.

Elderflower cream

*2 level tablespoons dried elderflowers or
  sufficient fresh flowers to be just covered
  by the oil*
150ml/¼ pint almond oil (or other oil)
4 teaspoons lanolin
1 teaspoon honey

Warm the oil and lanolin in the top
of a double saucepan. Add the
flowers and simmer for 30 minutes.
Strain and stir in the honey. Cool,
pot up and label this emollient
cream.

Nourishing marigold cream

75ml/⅛ pint strong marigold infusion
6 teaspoons melted beeswax
6 teaspoons lanolin
6 tablespoons almond oil (or other oil)
½ teaspoon borax

optional: 2 capsules wheatgerm oil

Warm the wax, lanolin and oil in the
top of a double saucepan. Warm the
infusion in a separate pan and
thoroughly dissolve the borax in the
infusion. Take both pans from the
heat and gradually combine, then
beat or whisk together until cooled
and thickened. Stir in the wheatgerm oil for extra Vitamin E. Pot up
and label.

*An infusion of marigolds makes a
nourishing skin cream when whisked
into a mixture of melted beeswax,
lanolin and almond oil. A little borax is
necessary to help emulsify the beeswax
and as a preservative, and wheatgerm
oil can be added for its Vitamin E.*

Herbs for the hair

Traditional hair preparations

A complete list of the animal, vegetable and mineral ingredients that have been included in hair preparations would be even longer than a list of face-pack ingredients. Aromatic gums and woods, the ashes of goat's dung and bees and every sort of alcohol have been used to perfume, strengthen and thicken the hair, while scented oils, pomades of apples and puppy dog's fat, bear's grease and macassar oil (which made antimacassars necessary on every Victorian armchair) have been used to smooth and enrich it. There are old recipes for black hair dyes of fried gall nuts, burned copper and cloves from Morocco, golden hair dyes of alum, honey and black sulphur from Venice and an alarming Elizabethan auburn hair dye of pure oil of vitriol. The chemical ingredients listed on the labels of modern shampoos, conditioners, lighteners and brighteners are almost as daunting. They may act quickly but the effect is often short-lived and they can be too harsh for fine, dry hair. Herbal ingredients, together with natural soaps and oils, work slowly but thoroughly, enriching and conditioning all types of hair, helping to eliminate scurf and dandruff and never harming the delicate structure of the hair.

Herbal properties

Burdock: root helps to prevent dandruff

Catmint: leaves encourage hair growth and soothe scalp irritation

Chamomile: flowers gently soften and lighten the hair

Garlic and onions: bulbs stimulate hair growth and help control dandruff, but the smell is a drawback

Goosegrass: the whole herb is tonic and cleansing, and helps to prevent dandruff

Henna: powdered leaves make a healthy red hair dye and conditioner

Horsetail: non-fertile stems and branches strengthen the hair

Lime: flowers soften and cleanse the hair

Marigold: petals lighten hair colour

Mullein: flowers lighten hair colour

Nasturtium: leaves help hair growth

Parsley: leaves and stems enrich hair colour and give lustre

Rosemary: the best all-round hair tonic and conditioner, leaves and flowering tops give lustre and body and slightly darken the hair

Rhubarb: root makes an effective yellow hair dye

Sage: leaves are tonic and conditioning and darken the hair

Soapwort: leaves and roots are cleansing

Southernwood: leaves encourage hair growth and help prevent dandruff

Stinging nettle: leaves help prevent dandruff and are both tonic and conditioning

Witch hazel: leaves and bark are astringent and cleansing

Herbal hair conditioners and shampoos

A warm oil conditioner can be used before shampooing and is especially suitable for dry, brittle, fly-away hair. Make a strong herbal oil as described on page 165 with rosemary, chamomile, southernwood, grated burdock root or other hair herbs and a vegetable oil such as safflower, sunflower, soya bean, peanut or olive oil (the latter may slightly darken the hair). Warm the oil and rub it thoroughly into the scalp and hair. Cover the hair with a plastic bath hat or plastic bag and then wrap it tightly in a thick towel wrung out in very hot water. Reheat the towel when it cools and continue for at least 15 minutes – the longer the better. As an alternative to the herbal oil, use an ordinary vegetable or almond oil with a few added drops of essential oil of rosemary, chamomile etc.

Fly-away hair

To smooth down fly-away hair after shampooing and to give it gloss and shine, simply sprinkle a few drops of oil of rosemary onto a natural bristle hair brush and give the hair a thorough brushing. This stimulates the scalp and helps draw the natural oils along the hair shafts.

Do not expect a shampoo made entirely from herbs to cover your head with rich suds; remember that lather is not a sign of cleansing power. Soapwort, the most common soap herb in northern climates, gives a slight, greenish lather that gently and thoroughly cleanses the hair.

Herbal-oil conditioner

3 tablespoons herbal oil (as above)
1 tablespoon cider vinegar (or fresh lemon juice)
1 egg yolk (or whole egg for oily hair)
1 teaspoon honey

Gently warm all the ingredients, except the oil, in the top of a double saucepan. Beat well with a wooden spoon, then remove from the heat, cool and add the oil gradually, beating all the time. Use within a few days.

For delicate, weak hair try using a drop of oil of rosemary in warmed castor oil. This thick, pale yellow oil, obtained from the seeds of *Ricinus communis*, is particularly strengthening. Alternatively an ordinary mayonnaise (page 166) with an added tablespoon of pulped, fresh hair herbs makes an excellent home-made conditioner.

These oily conditioners really need to be shampooed out; an ordinary rinse cannot cope with the heavy oil.

Rosemary-oil conditioner

2 drops of oil of rosemary
1 tablespoon almond oil
1 tablespoon glycerine
1 tablespoon lanolin
1 egg (yolk only for dry hair)

Combine the oils, glycerine and lanolin in the top of a double saucepan and warm gently. Remove from the heat and beat in the egg. This is a less oily conditioner that can be rubbed into the scalp after shampooing. Leave it in for at least 10 minutes, then rinse thoroughly.

Soapwort shampoo

1 tablespoon grated or powdered soap-wort root
a handful of fresh or 1 tablespoon dried chamomile flowers or other herbs
300ml/½ pint boiling water

Pour the boiling water onto the soapwort and chamomile, cover and leave to infuse until cool. The chamomile will add additional strength and scent to the shampoo. A slightly less lathery and greener infusion can be made with soapwort leaves instead of root.

Soapbark shampoo

1 tablespoon soapbark chips (sometimes obtainable at health shops)
300ml/½ pint water

Make a decoction, simmering the chips for 30 minutes

A mild shampoo

2 tablespoons of a strong infusion of herbs
2 tablespoons of a pure baby shampoo or dissolved, unscented soap

Use an infusion of sage for dark hair, yarrow for oily hair, marigold petals for blonde hair, a mixture of nettle and burdock for dandruff and so on.

An egg beaten into the shampoo and a tablespoon of powdered gelatine dissolved in the warm infusion will give extra body.

Dry shampoo

1 teaspoon powdered orris
2 teaspoons powdered arrowroot

Systematically part the hair over the head, sprinkling some of the absorbent powder along each parting. Leave on for 10 minutes, then brush vigorously until the powder, dirt and excess oils are gone.

Fine cornmeal or fuller's earth can be used in the same way. Mix them with a drop or two of rosemary oil.

A natural shampoo can be made by infusing grated soapwort root (in the large jar) with dried chamomile flowers or other hair herbs.

Herbal rinses and treatments

To prevent scalp itching

Vinegar rinses

Vinegar, especially cider vinegar, is one of the best hair rinses for all types of hair. Either use it straight from the bottle or make up a herb vinegar, as described at the beginning of the chapter, with the herbs most suitable for your hair. Mix 75ml/⅛ pint into a basin of warm water and use it for the final rinse, giving the hair a good soak. This helps restore the natural acid balance of the skin of the scalp, stops scalp itching and controls scurf and dandruff. It also thoroughly cleanses the hair and skin, gets rid of all traces of soap and does not leave an unpleasant smell of its own. Fresh lemon juice can be used as an alternative to vinegar, and is especially suited to fair hair.

Scented rinses

A scented rinse can be made by simply adding lavender water, rosewater, elderflower water or orange-flower water to the final rinse. A strong infusion of herbs is both scented and beneficial, and can be mixed with vinegar or lemon juice or used on its own. Make this with one of the hair herbs listed, or make up a mixture of dried herbs whose scent and properties best suit your hair, and keep this in a tightly stoppered jar in the bathroom cupboard. Pour 600ml/1 pint boiling water over a handful of the dried herbs or 2 handfuls of fresh herbs before washing the hair and leave to infuse in a covered teapot or pan. Strain into the final rinsing water and thoroughly soak the hair in it.

Hair loss

Herbs that are said to strengthen the hair and prevent hair loss are southernwood, mallow roots, parsley seed, rosemary and catmint. Any of these can be simmered in vinegar, wine or oil and used as strengthening hair rubs. The last two herbs may slightly darken fair hair. Garlic and chilies are effective but it is difficult to rinse out their strong smell.

Dandruff

Dandruff and scurf are also common hair problems that are often made worse by repeated applications of strong, commercial dandruff treatments. For all but the worst cases (when a doctor should be consulted), the stinging nettle and vinegar recipes given below work very well.

Scented rinse for blonde hair

4 part dried chamomile flowers
4 parts dried marigold petals
3 parts dried orange-flowers
2 parts dried elderflowers

Scented rinse for dark hair

3 parts dried sage leaves
3 parts dried witch hazel leaves
3 parts dried rosemary
2 parts dried lime flowers

Rinse for out-of-condition hair

3 parts dried thyme leaves
3 parts dried stinging nettle leaves
2 parts dried, grated burdock root
2 parts dried nasturtium leaves
1 part dried southernwood leaves
For all 3 recipes add a strong infusion to the final rinsing water.

Southernwood hair tonic

Southernwood has been used for hundreds of years to encourage the growth of hair and beards – hence its common name 'lad's love'.
75ml/⅛ pint strong infusion of southernwood
75ml/⅛ pint vodka (or mild eau-de-Cologne)
Shake well and bottle. To use, shake and add 1 tablespoon to 1 tablespoon of warm water. Sprinkle evenly over the hair, being careful to avoid the eyes, and massage well into the scalp. Repeat twice a week.

As an alternative tonic, make a tincture of southernwood with pure alcohol or vodka and dilute in the same way.

Treatment for dandruff

fresh nettles
cider vinegar
Either steep fresh nettles in vinegar for a week or two, strain and bottle, or simmer fresh nettles in vinegar for 30 minutes. Rub 2 tablespoons into the scalp twice a week to prevent dandruff. Or make a tonic or tincture with nettles in the same way as the southernwood hair tonic. If at all prone to scurf it is well worth rinsing the hair regularly in nettle infusion and vinegar.

Other herbs that can be used to treat dandruff are burdock, goose-grass, southernwood, witch hazel, and horsetail. Make a strong infusion of any of these herbs and mix with cider vinegar.

Herbal hair colourants and dyes

Highlights

Effective dyes

Testing the colour

With the exception of henna and rhubarb, hair dyes made with herbs have a mild, gentle and cumulative action with none of the harsh, damaging effects of chemical hair dyes.

To slightly lighten or darken the hair or to intensify and highlight its present colour, use a strong infusion of herbs as a rinse (see recipes below). To obtain a more concentrated colour, make a strong infusion using the same quantities of herbs as for the rinses, but with only 75ml/⅛ pint of liquid. Mix this to a paste with powdered kaolin. Make successive partings over the head and apply the paste evenly, from the scalp to the tips of the hair. Leave it on for at least 30 minutes, then rinse off. The change in colour will not be dramatic but will gradually become noticeable after several applications.

Among the most effective vegetable hair dyes are rhubarb, whose powdered root yields a strong yellow colour, and henna, which gives a whole range of reds and can also be used as a vehicle for other dyes. The leaves of henna are sold dried and ground as a dark brown powder and are one of the oldest known hair and body dyes, used in Eastern countries to dye the hands and feet and as a rouge, and by the prophet Mohammed to redden his beard. It is still a common hair colourant in modern hairdressing salons. Both dyes stain hands and nails, so use rubber gloves.

It is important to test your mixture on a small piece of hair before dyeing, especially if using henna. On blonde or grey hair henna may give a bright, brassy-orange colour; it is most suited to brown hair, which it is likely to dye a warm shade of rich chestnut or auburn. The great advantage of dyeing with henna is that the hair is thoroughly conditioned as it is being dyed, the henna coating each hair, giving it strength, body and lustre.

Blonde hair rinse

2 tablespoons fresh or 1 tablespoon dried chamomile flowers
2 tablespoons fresh or 1 tablespoon dried marigold or mullein flowers
2 tablespoons fresh lemon juice
Pour 600ml/1 pint boiling water over the flowers and leave covered to infuse for at least 30 minutes. Stir in the lemon juice and use for the final rinse-and-soak.

Dark hair rinse

2 tablespoons fresh or 1 tablespoon dried sage leaves
2 tablespoons fresh or 1 tablespoon dried rosemary
600ml/1 pint strong household tea
Pour the boiling tea over the herbs and leave to infuse for at least 30 minutes. Strain and use for the final rinse-and-soak after a shampoo, adding sufficient water to cover the hair.

Henna hair dye

4 tablespoons henna powder (obtainable from a chemist or health shop)
hot water
Make a paste with the powder and hot water and leave this to mature for 30 minutes. Test it on a few strands of hair. To increase the red colour add more henna powder, to tone it down add a strong chamomile infusion. For a very dark, rich colour buy black henna powder, which is mixed with indigo.

When the colour is satisfactory, rub systematically through the hair as described in previous recipes, using rubber gloves. Cover the hair with a plastic bath hat or bag and wrap tightly round with a steaming-hot, damp towel. After an hour rinse the paste off a few strands of hair and see how the colour is developing. It may be necessary to leave the dye on overnight for a really strong colour, in which case dispense with the hot towel and sleep with the bath cap on.

Rinse thoroughly, wash hair with a mild shampoo and rub a little oil into the scalp. The dye can last 5 or 6 months.

Rhubarb hair dye

3 tablespoons dried and powdered or freshly crushed and pulped rhubarb root
1 litre/1 pint water
kaolin powder
Make a decoction, simmering for 30 minutes with the lid of the pan off so that the liquor reduces by about half. Thicken this liquor with kaolin powder until it is the consistency of thick paste. Shampoo the hair then follow the procedure for the herb infusion hair dyes, carefully covering the hair. Rinse off a little paste after the first 15 minutes and then after every 5 minutes to check the colour. The rhubarb will have given all its colour after about 1 hour. Rinse the paste off thoroughly and rub a little oil through the hair to counteract the rhubarb's astringent action.

Herbs for health

During the early Middle Ages in northern Europe and Britain all medical practitioners were in Holy Orders, and the hospitals (apart from those for lepers) were attached to religious institutions. Medical treatment was based on herbal remedies accompanied by a curious mixture of pagan and superstitious magic, prayers and appeals to the Christian saints, and offerings of money. The Church ruled that most illnesses were caused by sin, but that, by God's mercy, healing plants were provided to assuage illness and priestly physicians supplied to administer them; the result of this formula was that serious scientific enquiry into the properties of these plants was stifled until the early years of the Renaissance.

An edict passed by Pope Innocent III in the 13th century contributed to a change in the medical structure by ruling that no ecclesiastic should practise medicine for private gain or shed blood in any way. This led many of the monks who worked in the monastic physic gardens to renounce their vows and become apothecaries, either cultivating their own herbs and setting up in apothecary shops, or wandering from village to village as quack doctors, selling their own compounded drugs. The priest-physicians who remained in the Church were forced to hand all surgical work to laymen, who were often local barbers. The result was a steadily widening division between physicians and surgeons, the physicians becoming increasingly concerned with theory and book learning, while the surgeons undertook the practical side. In some cases the physician would have no contact with the patient at all, relying for his diagnosis on studying samples of the patient's urine and casting his horoscope, then sending directions for treatment to the surgeon or apothecary. Some physicians made up their own medicines, but this was generally the job of the apothecary.

The treatment of disease was heavily influenced by the writings of Hippocrates and Galen, Greek physicians, whose theory that man's health depended on the balance maintained within the body between the four

The roots of medicinal herbs are easy to dry, store and transport and often contain the most important principles of the plant.

'humours' was scarcely questioned until the 17th century. This idea bears certain parallels with the traditional medicine of China, which is based on the harmonious balance existing between the two essences, yin and yang, and five elements. The European theory held that the four fluids in the body – blood, phlegm, yellow bile and black bile or spleen – corresponded to the four elements – air, water, fire and earth. A high proportion of blood, which was hot and moist like the air, resulted in a sanguine temperament or humour; of phlegm, which was cold and moist like the water, in a phlegmatic temperament; of yellow bile, which was hot and dry like fire, in a choleric temperament; and of black bile, which was cold and dry like the earth, in a melancholic temperament. Illness resulted when these humours became unbalanced, and to restore harmony the excess humour had to be drawn off – involving the use of violent herbal emetics, purgatives and counter irritants, as well as blood letting, leeching and cupping. The herbs prescribed had to counter the predominant humour, so that borage and marjoram, for instance, would be prescribed to cheer, invigorate, warm and thus reduce a cold, melancholy humour caused by an excess of black bile.

There was also a revival in the 16th century of the ancient 'doctrine of similars' or 'signatures', which was based on the premise that 'like cures like', the appearance of the plant providing the clues for its medical use. A widespread belief that the cure was to be found with the cause was revived much later as the basis for homeopathic medical treatment. Astrology played an integral part in most prescriptions, the herbal ingredients being chosen, collected and administered only at the appropriate moment according to the positions of the moon and planets. Thus the construction of the final medicine might be extremely complex. Many famous 'cure-alls' or 'treacles' had 40 or 50 ingredients, while one celebrated poison antidote, known as 'Venice treacle', included no less than 73 ingredients. The word 'treacle' is derived from the Latin word for a counter poison – *theriaca*.

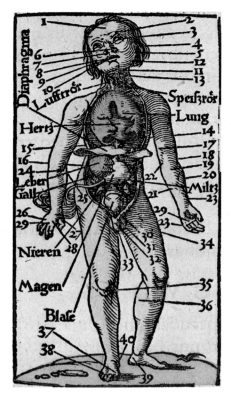

The Classical division of all matter into four elements, air, water, fire and earth, with their corresponding bodily humours, sanguine, phlegmatic, choleric and melancholic, was fundamental to Western medicine until the late 17th century.

The majority of these ingredients would be herbal, often in a vehicle of wine, sugar or honey, but there were also animal ingredients that ranged from the easily obtainable dung of doves and sheep, pulverized earthworms and viper's fat to extremely expensive powdered Egyptian mummy or unicorn's horn. Chemical ingredients increased in popularity after the successful treatment with mercury of the epidemic syphilis that raged across the Continent in the 16th century and also owing to the growing numbers of alchemists who, in their search for the *Elixir vitae*, advanced the knowledge of chemistry and metallurgy.

Some treatments from the 16th century and earlier are still familiar in therapeutic 'fringe' medicines, such as the internal and external use of the essential oils of aromatic herbs in aromatherapy. In this instance the oils are considered the pure and ethereal spirit of the plant and therefore act most effectively, through the mind and emotions, on the physical body. Herb dew was used then, as it is today – the 16th-century writer Sir Hugh Plat describes gathering this in May 'with a large sponge in the morning', and there were special methods of breathing and gymnastics. Music was thought particularly beneficial, the bass, alto, tenor and soprano being used as parallels for the four humours. The importance of preventive medicine was always stressed, especially regarding diet, following the old Hippocratic doctrine, 'Let your food be your medicine and medicine your food.'

Two of the most ancient methods of using medicinal herbs are no longer viable, or at least they have changed emphasis. One was treatment by the smoke of burning herbs, when the patient was held or leaned over a fire of smouldering aromatic plants and breathed in their 'virtues'. In Pliny's day this primitive method had changed to sucking the smoke into the lungs through a hollow reed and later, of course, pipes and cigarettes were introduced. It is still possible to buy herb tobacco for different ailments, but the bad effects of drawing smoke down into the lungs would certainly outweigh any advantage gained from the herbs. The burning of herbs, however, is still a practical and pleasant way of fumigating a sickroom. Another way of drawing the good herb into the body was by taking it, dried and finely powdered, as snuff. Yarrow, sneezewort, betony, ground ivy, thyme and woodruff were among the herbs most commonly used, and these were thought to clear the head and cure headaches and melancholia.

As the Renaissance reached northern Europe and the rigid authority of the church was weakened, medicine began to evolve as a science and doctors gradually became a more organized and responsible body of men. To the modern eye their methods seem crude and violent – blood-letting and strong purgatives still being common treatment for most diseases – but they were questioning the ancient theories of the Classical Greek philosophers and scorning the old superstitions and rituals that had clouded the true value of drugs. The Wise Women or Herb Women who had taken the roles of doctor and midwife in most country villages for so long were regarded with increasing suspicion and some began to be harried and branded as witches.

As the modern system of medicine developed, the active principles in plants were isolated, tested, synthesized, and incorporated into the official pharmacopoeias of each country. Well over 40 per cent of modern medicines have their origins in nature rather than laboratories. At the same time traditional herbal medicine has continued to be practised by those who feel that the whole plant provides a balanced remedy that is most suited to the body, whereas an extracted part, taken out of its true context, may have an unnatural and even toxic effect. In China this herbal medicine coexists with modern methods and on the Continent traditional tisanes and herbal medicines have also remained in use. In Britain and North America, however, the traditions had barely survived during the present century until the renewal of interest shown during recent years. There are professional herbalists and homeopathic doctors of course, but there are now also many enthusiastic amateurs who depend on books (often unreliable ones) for their herbal prescriptions and feel, mistakenly, that all natural remedies must automatically be superior to and safer than a prescription from a qualified doctor. It is dangerous to underestimate the strength of herbal medicines.

For this reason the recipes that follow are all of a simple and domestic nature, being mild remedies for sore throats, 'flu, bowel troubles, indigestion and so on, with some explanation of the action of the herb. They are not written as prescriptions but rather as a source of reference and it is assumed that the reader will approach them with an attitude of commonsense. Many of those listed are tisanes or infusions of herbs, or decoctions, and these, unless otherwise stated, may be taken in a *standard dose of one wineglassful three times a day*. A standard tisane or infusion is made in the same way as tea. Pour 600ml/1 pint boiling water onto 15g/½oz dried or 25g/1oz fresh herb, cover and leave to infuse for ten minutes at least before straining. A standard decoction is made by bringing the same quantities of herb and water slowly to the boil in a covered pan and simmering for five minutes or longer according to the herb used. Do not use an aluminium pan.

The fleshy tap root of the mandrake was used as a powerful narcotic and anesthetic. Many old herbals illustrate it as a human form with a dog attached to pull it from the ground. This was because its shrieks and groans were expected to madden and finally kill the gatherer – one of many superstitions that may have been spread by professional herb gatherers to frighten off amateurs.

Herbs for colds, coughs and fevers

Cold remedies

Herbs to soothe a fever

Coughs and sore throats

At the onset of a cold there are many herbal remedies that will help to reduce the severity of the symptoms. Cayenne tea or a mustard foot bath, for instance, will quickly and thoroughly warm a chilled body and stimulate the circulation (page 40). Once the cold is established try breathing the vapour from a steaming herbal inhalant to clear the head and soothe the respiratory tract, covering the head with a towel to contain the steam.

The borage family are the best known of the cooling, refrigerant herbs, and are especially popular for colds and fevers in France. Infuse the large mucilaginous leaves of borage and use in tisanes or for sponge washes. Lungwort, alkanet and viper's bugloss also work well, as do tisanes made from the succulent acid leaves of sorrel and purslane.

An infusion of elderflowers will help to cure a throat infection, and a hot elderberry drink is one of the best-known remedies for soothing an inflamed throat and quieting a cough. Simmer the raw berries, strain, sweeten with honey and drink a wineglassful, hot, 3 times a day. Ginger and cloves simmered with the berries or syrup add their warming, antiseptic properties. Blackcurrants make a good substitute for or addition to elderberries.

All members of the onion family are helpful for treating colds, coughs and sore throats, but the mild-flavoured leek is most acceptable. Cook 2 sliced leeks in a very little water then squeeze their juice through a coarse cloth or press through a fine sieve to make a purée. Stir in honey to taste and eat a spoonful or two when necessary.

Cayenne tea

¼ teaspoon cayenne pepper
150ml/¼ pint boiling water or hot milk
Stir the cayenne into the liquid and sip slowly. This will warm the whole system and is an old remedy for warding off disease.

If the taste is too strong, take cayenne in pill form, or try ground ginger with honey – a deliciously warming drink.

Peppermint, yarrow and elder-flower drink for a cold

1 teaspoon dried peppermint
1 teaspoon dried yarrow
1 teaspoon dried elderflowers
600ml/1 pint boiling water
1 pinch powdered mixed spice
1 teaspoon lemon juice
Infuse the herbs in the water for at least 5 minutes, then add the remaining ingredients and honey to sweeten if necessary. Take a wineglassful every 2 hours.

This pleasant, soothing mixture will induce a gentle perspiration, thus helping to reduce a fever.

Eucalyptus inhalant

essential oil of eucalyptus
a jug of boiling water
This is one of the most valuable home remedies, as a relief for coughs and catarrh and as an antiseptic treatment for throat infections. Add a few drops of oil to the boiling water, cover the head with a towel to contain the steam and breathe in the vapour. Stay in a warm room after using an inhalant.

A handful of fresh or dried leaves simmered for a few minutes in a pan of water, then poured into a jug, can be used for the same purpose. Or sprinkle a little of the essential oil on a pillow or handkerchief.

Peppermint inhalant

1 teaspoon dried peppermint
1 teaspoon dried lime flowers
1 teaspoon dried chamomile flowers
1 teaspoon dried basil
1 teaspoon dried sage
1 litre/1¾ pints boiling water
Put the herbs in a jug and pour over the boiling water. Breathe in the

vapour as directed above.

Crushed juniper berries and mullein leaves also make effective inhalants when infused in hot water.

Spiced basil tisane to reduce fever

1 teaspoon dried basil
seeds scraped from 1 large cardamom pod
¼ teaspoon ground cinnamon
600ml/1 pint boiling water
¼ teaspoon brown sugar or molasses
Infuse the basil and spices in the water for 10 minutes. Sweeten with sugar and take a small wineglassful every 2 hours to reduce fever and soothe pain in the joints. This is a common country medicine in India.

A mild flower mixture for children

a small piece of liquorice root
¼ teaspoon dried lime flowers
¼ teaspoon dried chamomile flowers
¼ teaspoon dried elderflowers
600ml/1 pint boiling water
Peel and bruise or crush the liquorice and infuse with the flowers in the

water for 10 minutes. Sweeten with honey if necessary. Take a wineglassful every 3 hours, either hot or cold.

There are many other herbs that stimulate a mild perspiration and help control and soothe fevers. The principal herbs for this purpose are angelica, boneset, clove carnation petals, elecampane root, lemon balm, marigold flowers, meadowsweet flowers, wood avens, woodruff, yarrow and many aromatic members of the *Labiatae* – catmint, germander, marjoram, peppermint and thyme.

Electuary of hyssop for coughs

a good handful of bruised hyssop
450g/1lb honey
1 teaspoon powdered liquorice or 1 piece
* of crushed liquorice stick*
1 teaspoon crushed aniseed
¼ teaspoon powdered ginger or crushed
* root ginger*
Bring the honey slowly to the boil and lift off any scum with a spoon. Stir in the remaining ingredients, cover and simmer very slowly for 30 minutes or until the honey has a pronounced hyssop flavour. Strain through a sieve and pour into pots. Cool, cover and store.

Take a spoonful when troubled with a cough or sore throat, or add to a hot tisane or elderberry syrup.

Coltsfoot tisane for coughs

1 teaspoon dried coltsfoot leaves
1 teaspoon dried, ground ivy leaves
1 tablespoon dried marsh mallow root
600ml/1 pint water
Bruise the marsh mallow root and soak in the water for at least 30 minutes or overnight. Bring to the boil and pour over the herbs, cover and infuse for at least 15 minutes. Strain carefully through a fine sieve or muslin to catch the fine hairs from the coltsfoot leaves. Take the standard dose (page 265).

Coltsfoot is one of the oldest known cough medicines.

Sage gargle

1 teaspoon dried sage
1 teaspoon dried plantain
1 teaspoon dried rosemary
1 teaspoon dried honeysuckle flowers
600ml/1 pint boiling water
honey
Make an infusion, sweeten to taste and use as a gargle for sore throats.

Some simple cough remedies

AGRIMONY: use an infusion of leaves or decoction of root and leaves to relieve coughs and fever.

ANISE: infuse 2 teaspoons bruised seeds in 300ml/½ pint boiling water or infuse the leaves. Both liquids will loosen and soothe a cough and relieve catarrh.

BAYBERRY: gargle with a decoction of the bark or infusion of leaves.

BORAGE: use an infusion of the leaves to soothe an inflamed throat or for catarrh.

CHICKWEED: use an infusion to soothe and cool the throat. This is reputed to restore a lost voice.

LOVAGE: infuse seeds or leaves as a gargle for sore throats.

MARSH MALLOW: use the flowers in a tisane as a gargle or drink a decoction

A medieval apothecary often dispensed both medicines and advice.

of the roots in milk. Hollyhock flowers can also be used.

MULLEIN: the large furry leaves or yellow flowers taken as a tisane make a soothing, slightly sedative drink and act as a mild expectorant. Strain the fine hairs carefully through a cloth before drinking.

ROSE: infuse the leaves or petals as a gargle, they are astringent, antiseptic and healing to the throat.

SAGE: use an infusion, either alone or mixed with thyme, as a drink or gargle for throat infection or persistent cough. Red sage is said to be most efficacious.

SEA HOLLY: the candied roots are a soothing cough remedy. Add a few drops of orange-flower water to the syrup for extra flavour.

SUNFLOWER: use a decoction of the seed (25g/1oz to 600ml/1 pint water) mixed with honey as an expectorant.

VIOLET: use the flowers mashed with brown sugar or a tisane of leaves.

WOOD SAGE: use an infusion of the leaves as a bitter and astringent tisane or gargle.

Herbal baths and massages

Sedative herbs

Herbal footbaths will quickly relax the muscles and ease tension.

A tisane to soothe the nerves

1 teaspoon grated valerian root
1 teaspoon dried mint
½ teaspoon dried chamomile flowers
½ teaspoon dried lavender flowers
600ml/1 pint boiling water
Infuse for 15 minutes and take a small glassful 3 times a day. This should not be taken regularly for more than a few days at a time as valerian is slightly narcotic.

Although one of the most effective sedative herbs the taste is rather unpleasant; it is usually disguised by mixing with other, sweeter herbs.

Herbs for relaxation

Herb baths or footbaths will quickly relax the muscles and ease tension. Use one of the bath-bag mixtures described on page 251 or a mixture of crushed juniper berries, lavender and rosemary in a footbath. A strong decoction of the root of sweet flag added to the bath water is a good remedy for insomnia, or a few drops of the essential oil of herbs such as eucalyptus, chamomile, basil or geranium will help. Lie quietly and inhale the steam.

Massaging, when done by a skilled masseur, should both relax and invigorate the whole body. Add a few drops of oil of marjoram, lavender or geranium to the massage oil. Never use essential oils directly on the skin; they must always be diluted.

Pillows stuffed with dried hops are an old treatment for insomnia. If the hops rustle too much, soften them with a few drops of alcohol, vodka or brandy. Add some lavender flowers or lemon verbena leaves for their scent and sedative properties. Recipes for herb pillows are given on page 229.

Petals of the corn poppy, *Papaver rhoeas*, are still made into a sedative syrup in France. They are one of the ingredients in the *Tisane de Sept Fleurs*, prescribed for sleeplessness. This also includes the flowers of mullein, lime, violet, coltsfoot, common mallow and marsh mallow. Poppies have not only been used as the symbol of sleep since early Greek times but have an old reputation for curing headaches. According to a 14th-century herbal poppies will 'slake the peyne and distroye the mygreyn'.

A tisane for insomnia

1 teaspoon dried lemon balm
1 teaspoon dried marjoram
1 teaspoon dried hops or hop leaves
1 teaspoon crushed aniseed or anise leaves
600ml/1 pint boiling water
Make an infusion and take a glassful each evening before going to bed.

Relaxing herb milk infusion

1 tablespoon dried peppermint
300ml/½ pint boiling milk
Pour the milk over the peppermint in a jug, cover and leave to stand in a warm place for 10 minutes before straining. Re-heat before drinking if necessary.

Bergamot leaves or flowers can be substituted – both bergamot and peppermint make delicious, scented, relaxing drinks.

Sedative herbs

Soothing, sleep-inducing tisanes can be made with any of these herbs, either mixed or on their own.

Basil, bergamot, chamomile flowers, elderflower, goosegrass, lemon thyme, lemon verbena, lime flowers, young lime leaves, vervain, violet leaves and flowers, and the seeds of anise, fennel and especially dill – use 1 teaspoon of bruised seeds to each cup of boiling water.

Herbs against headaches

Lavender is the best known of the headache herbs, taken as a weak tisane (1 teaspoon dried flowers to 600ml/1 pint water), the vinegar dabbed on the temples and forehead or the water used as a face rinse.

Other herbs include betony, which has a particularly pleasant taste, ground ivy, lady's bedstraw, melilot, rosemary, which has a similar action to lavender, wild marjoram and wood avens and woodruff.

Pennyroyal once had a reputation for curing headaches. Gerard advises in his herbal that 'A Garland of Pennie Royall made and worne about the head is of great force against the swimming in the head, and the paines and giddiness thereof'.

Winter tonic herbs

Invigorating tonic herbs

A well-balanced diet usually incorporates the minerals, vitamins and trace elements needed to keep the body in good health, but during the winter a lack of fresh green vegetables and salads often results in some debility. Tonic herbs that are available in the winter include salad burnet, watercress and wild chickweed, which is rich in copper and iron and grows fresh and green even through snow. Dried tonic herbs, preserved herb syrups and wines are especially valuable at this time.

A 'tonic' increases or restores the tone or healthy condition of the system and is strengthening, invigorating and bracing. All the herbs described here act in this way. When scurvy was a common disease, many were valuable anti-scorbutics, providing the essential vitamins that were needed when recovering from an illness or to correct malnutrition.

Many of the elements we require, iron and Vitamin C in particular, are to be found in one of the most common herbs – the stinging nettle. Use the young tops fresh, and dry a good quantity in the late spring before they become tough and develop irritating properties. Drink a wineglassful of the tisane twice a day, or take as a syrup, wine or beer, or as a puréed vegetable or in a soup or pudding. Other well-known sources of Vitamin C include rose hips, which can be taken as a tisane, syrup or jelly, and watercress. The more exotic sweet peppers also contain quantities of this vitamin, which is concentrated in ground paprika.

Spring tonic drink

1 tablespoon chopped, fresh nettle tops
1 tablespoon chopped, fresh dandelion
  leaves
1 teaspoon chopped, fresh blackberry or
  blackcurrant leaves
1 teaspoon chopped, fresh borage leaves
600ml/1 pint boiling water
1 teaspoon fresh lemon juice
Infuse the herbs in the boiling water in a covered jug and add lemon juice to taste. Take a wineglassful at a time as a general tonic.

Agrimony in ale

2 tablespoons dried agrimony
600ml/1 pint natural beer or ale
a twist of orange peel
Infuse the herb and peel in the beer for 12 hours. Strain and drink.

Agrimony also makes a good country tonic tisane with a slight, aromatic flavour and is a popular ingredient in herb beers.

Rosemary in wine

6 sprigs fresh rosemary
1 bottle sweet white wine
Steep the rosemary in the wine for 4 days in a covered bottle. Take a wineglassful at a time as a tonic.

Mint cordial

25g/1oz mint leaves
600ml/1 pint boiling water
200g/7oz brown sugar
2 tablespoons brandy
Infuse the mint in the boiling water for 2 hours in a covered jug. Strain into a saucepan then dissolve the sugar in the liquor and boil for 5 minutes. Allow to cool and stir in the brandy. Bottle and take a tablespoon at a time as a strengthening tonic and digestive.

Ginseng tea

1 teaspoon powdered ginseng root
600ml/1 pint boiling water
Simmer for 15 minutes and take standard dose. Ginseng had a reputation in the East for thousands of years as the ultimate tonic medicine, strengthening all parts of the body and prolonging life. The root is bought from health shops or herbal suppliers, either whole, as a powder, or as pills.

Strengthening drink for convalescents

25g/1oz chopped, bruised angelica root
  or 1 tablespoon bruised seeds
600ml/1 pint water
1 tablespoon brandy
juice from ¼ lemon
Bring the water and angelica slowly to simmering point in a covered pan and simmer gently for 15 minutes. Leave to cool, still covered, strain and add brandy and lemon. Take a tablespoon before meals.

Angelica has a stimulating effect so do not take just before going to bed as it may keep you awake.

Tonic herbs

These herbs should be regularly included in the diet, in omelettes and salads or sprinkled over hot vegetables, or they can be infused and drunk as tisanes.

Capers, caraway, celery, chervil, chickweed, chives, garlic, Good King Henry, goosegrass, lady's mantle, mint, parsley, plantain, salad burnet, sorrel, sweet cicely, watercress, yarrow.

Bitter tonic herbs

Herbs for the digestion

Many of the first spring herbs have reputations as blood 'cleansers' or 'purifiers' and are traditionally eaten at Easter or at the Jewish Passover. They are often bitter, which has the effect of increasing the secretion of digestive juices, stimulating a sluggish stomach and restoring the appetite. This was especially valuable after a winter diet of heavily salted and stodgy food. Strong bitters such as gentian and bogbean help to strengthen the whole system and have a cleansing and antiseptic action.

Individual reactions to these bitter tonics may vary, but generally only a very small dose serves to stimulate the appetite – a large dose may have the opposite effect.

Gentian and peppermint
25g/1oz powdered gentian root
1 teaspoon dried peppermint
900ml/1½ pints water
honey
Bring the gentian and water slowly to the boil and simmer for 30 minutes, when the liquid will have reduced to about 600ml/1 pint. Add the peppermint, cover and leave to infuse for a few more minutes, then add honey to taste. The peppermint and honey help to ease the extreme bitterness of the gentian. Take 1 or 2 spoonfuls about 30 minutes before a meal.

The closely related centaury can be taken in the same way, but use the leaves – 25g/1oz infused in 600ml/1 pint boiling water.

Centaury in wine
50g/2oz flowering tops of centaury
1 tablespoon juniper berries
1 tablespoon brown sugar
1 litre/1¾ pints white wine
Macerate the herbs and sugar in the wine in a sunny place for 8 days. Strain into a clean bottle, cover and store. Take a tablespoon or small glassful before meals.

Gill tea
1 tablespoon dried ground ivy
600ml/1 pint boiling water
1 teaspoon fresh orange juice or ½ teaspoon dried orange peel
Infuse the herb in the boiling water for 5 to 10 minutes only (any longer and the taste will become soured).

Strain, and flavour the rather bitter, aromatic drink with the orange.

This old domestic medicine is called after the country name for ground ivy, 'gill-over-the-ground', a name that is still used widely in America.

Most herbs and spices stimulate the appetite and are good for the digestion.

Some bitter tonic herbs that stimulate the appetite
BOGBEAN: take 2 tablespoons of an infusion of the leaves before meals.
BURDOCK: take an infusion of the leaves or decoction of the root (made by simmering 25g/1oz bruised sliced root in 600ml/1 pint water for 30 minutes) or a decoction of the seeds.
CHICORY: eat the blanched leaves in

salads or make an infusion of the leaves or root.

DANDELION: use in the same way as chicory.

FENUGREEK: take an infusion of seeds (1 teaspoon in 600ml/1 pint boiling water) as a good general tonic. Or the seeds can be sprouted and eaten as a bitter addition to salads; they are rich in minerals.

HOREHOUND: take an infusion of the leaves before meals.

MUGWORT: take an infusion of the leaves and/or tops (1 teaspoon to 600ml/1 pint boiling water).

SAGE: infuse the leaves and/or flowers and add lemon rind.

WOOD SAGE: infuse the leaves.

Several other bitter herbs that were formerly used as cleansing and tonic medicines are now no longer con-sidered safe, unless taken under medical supervision. The strongly aromatic tansy is one of the oldest medicinal plants, whose juice used to be mixed with orange juice and honey or included in Easter tansy cakes and puddings. The bitter buds and stems of broom were once a popular medicine, but should not be taken as they contain a dangerous principle.

Aperitifs and digestives

Traditional digestives

Causes of indigestion

The function of aperitifs

Most herbs and spices are good for the digestion simply because their strongly aromatic or bitter scents and flavours make the saliva run and stimulate the secretion of gastric juices, which are needed to digest food. Bitter aperitifs taken before a meal and aromatic seeds and leaves eaten with food, such as the traditional fennel with fish, sage with cheese, horseradish with beef and chilies with beans, all have a stimulating and soothing effect on the intestines and stomach and help digest rich, fatty or heavy foods. The last dish at a Roman supper was often a special cake stuffed full of the seeds of dill, cumin, caraway and fennel; at a medieval banquet there might be a final dish of sage-leaf fritters; today there would very likely be a bowl of peppermint sweets. All these make good digestives. Green herbs, sunflower seeds, green vegetables, wheatgerm and brewer's yeast all supply the Vitamin B that is needed to help digestion and should be included in the diet. Most spices, with their strong, warming, volatile oils, have a beneficial effect on the digestion and an antiseptic, cleansing action on the gut. Pepper is the most famous and popular of all.

There are many causes of indigestion, apart from illness, anaemia or a gastric ulcer. Hurried eating or eating while tense or upset are common causes. A lack of B vitamins or an unbalanced meal of incompatible foods will often result in indigestion. Under these circumstances the digestive action of the saliva is unable to function properly, the gastric juices cannot be freely produced, digestion slows down and the food begins to ferment, producing 'gas' and causing wind. An aperitif 30 minutes before a meal helps relaxation, allays anxiety and stimulates the appetite. It will also act as a digestive if taken after eating. The recipes for herb bitters given opposite can be taken instead of these alcoholic aperitifs.

The digestive syrups described here should be stored in the refrigerator and used within a week.

Brandy bitters
1 litre/1¾ pints brandy
40g/1½oz sliced gentian root
25g/1oz dried orange peel
2 teaspoons cardamom seeds scraped from their pods
¼ teaspoon ground cinnamon
¼ teaspoon cloves
Combine the ingredients, bottle, cover tightly and store. Take 1 or 2 tablespoons before meals.

Nutmeg brandy
40g/1½oz grated nutmeg (about 1½ whole nutmegs)
600ml/1 pint brandy
Steep together for 3 weeks, shaking or stirring occasionally. Strain through fine muslin and bottle. Take 1 tablespoon before meals or stir 1 tablespoon into a glass of hot milk at bedtime. This has a sedative as well as a digestive action.

Seed cordial
1 teaspoon crushed caraway seed
1 teaspoon crushed fennel seed
1 teaspoon crushed aniseed
1 teaspoon crushed lovage seed
50g/2oz sugar
600ml/1 pint brandy
Steep together for a month, shaking or stirring occasionally. Strain and bottle. Take 1 or 2 tablespoons before meals.

Clove carnation brandy

100g/4oz fresh clove carnation petals
a twist of orange peel
600ml/1 pint brandy

Snip the bitter white 'heels' off the petals. Steep the petals and peel in the brandy for a fortnight, strain and bottle. Take 1 or 2 tablespoons before meals.

Lemon balm cordial

4 sprigs lemon balm
2 sprigs hyssop
2 sprigs basil
2 sprigs mint
2 sprigs sage
1 tablespoon chopped, crushed angelica
root
50g/2oz sugar
600ml/1 pint brandy

Steep the herbs and sugar in the brandy for a fortnight, shaking occasionally. Strain and repeat with fresh herbs if the taste is not sufficiently pronounced. Strain and and bottle. Take a tablespoon of this digestive before meals.

Tarragon digestive

4 sprigs French tarragon
quarter of a vanilla pod
600ml/1 pint brandy

Steep together for a fortnight, strain and bottle. Take a tablespoon of this digestive before meals.

Juniper syrup

100g/4oz juniper berries
twist of lemon peel
1 litre/1¾ pints water
2 tablespoons honey

Simmer the berries and peel in the water until soft. Sieve and press some of the pulp through as well. Stir in the honey, bring to the boil again and simmer until slightly thickened. Bottle and store in the refrigerator. Take a tablespoon after meals to settle the stomach. A larger quantity can be made and bottled to keep for many months in sterilized jars with rubber rings.

Herb syrup

15g/½oz chopped, crushed dandelion root
15g/½oz chopped agrimony root and leaves
15g/½oz centaury leaves or tops
15g/½oz sage leaves
1 litre/1¾ pints water
crushed seeds from 2 cardamom pods
2 tablespoons honey

Add the herbs to the cold water, bring slowly to simmering point and simmer gently for 10 minutes. Strain, add the cardamom and honey and simmer for a further 10 minutes until slightly thickened. Take 1 tablespoon before or after meals for the digestion.

Digestive tisane

1 teaspoon bruised fennel seed
1 teaspoon dried or 2 sprigs fresh peppermint
1 teaspoon dried or 5 fresh chamomile flowers
1 teaspoon dried or 2 sprigs fresh lemon balm
600ml/1 pint boiling water

Pour the water over the seed and herbs, cover and leave to infuse for 10 minutes. Take the standard dose of a wineglassful 3 times a day or, for children, add a tablespoon of the infusion to a cup of hot milk.

Spiced slippery elm

1 teaspoon powdered slippery elm bark
½ teaspoon crushed allspice berries
600ml/1 pint boiling water
lemon juice

Pour the water over the allspice berries, cover, leave to infuse for 10 minutes and strain. Mix the slippery elm to a paste with a little cold water then slowly add the allspice infusion, stirring to make a smooth liquid. Add lemon juice to taste. Take a wineglassful 3 times a day. This will soothe and stimulate the digestive organs and is especially suitable for convalescents being nutritious and helpful in restoring a lost appetite.

Marsh mallow syrup

50g/2oz marsh mallow root
2 litres/3½ pints water
175g/6oz sugar
orange-flower water

Steep the root overnight in the water. Add the sugar, stir to dissolve, bring to the boil and simmer at a good pace until the syrup is slightly thickened – for about 15 minutes. Strain, add orange-flower water to taste. Take a tablespoon after meals to prevent indigestion.

Some simple digestive remedies

ANGELICA: chew the fresh stems after meals to prevent flatulence and indigestion or steep the stems for a fortnight in brandy and take before or after meals.

ASAFOETIDA: add a good pinch of powdered asafoetida to a cup of hot water and sweeten with honey. This was a favourite Roman digestive.

CARDAMOM: infuse the crushed seeds from a pod in a cup of boiling water and take a tablespoon after meals.

CINNAMON: add ½ teaspoon of powdered cinnamon to a cup of hot milk and sweeten to taste with honey.

DILL: infuse 1 teaspoon bruised seeds in 300ml/½ pint boiling water and take in tablespoon doses. The seeds of anise, caraway, coriander, cumin, fennel and lovage can be used in the same way. The seeds can also be infused in milk or simply chewed after meals, or the leaves of these herbs used for digestive tisanes.

ELECAMPANE: chew a piece of the root candied or raw after meals.

SWEET FLAG: chew a piece of the root after meals or mix a teaspoon of powdered root to a paste with an equal quantity of bran and a little milk. Take a tablespoon after meals.

Other beneficial digestive herbs include chamomile, garlic, ginger, golden rod, horehound, lemon balm, mugwort, peppermint, ramsons, thyme and yarrow.

Laxative and binding herbs

Many herbs are strongly purgative and have a long history of medicinal use; in the past these have been prescribed far too freely. It is seldom wise to use purgatives regularly as they eventually irritate the intestine and cause it to lose the ability to function properly on its own, which can result in chronic constipation.

The intestine reacts strongly to emotion, and worry about the efficient functioning of the bowels can often actually lead to constipation. Individuals have different patterns of bowel movements, often related to their diet, and some may only evacuate their bowels every 4 or 5 days with no ill effects. Regular exercise and a good mixed diet that includes plenty of roughage such as bran, brown bread, unpeeled vegetables and fruit are usually quite sufficient to keep the bowels in a healthy state. The herbs and spices that are most beneficial are listed here and can be taken as tisanes or simply included in the diet. Prolonged constipation or diarrhoea or obvious changes in the regularity of the bowel should be reported immediately to the doctor or qualified herbal practitioner.

Constipation

A chopped or grated raw apple eaten before breakfast or last thing at night has a most beneficial effect on the intestine and is a good remedy for both constipation and diarrhoea.

Apple and dandelion salad

1 chopped, unpeeled apple
3 dandelion leaves
1 chopped fresh or dried fig
1 torn basil leaf
2 teaspoons olive oil
1 teaspoon lemon juice
salt and pepper

Toss the ingredients together and eat immediately, before the apple has a chance to turn brown.

Violet syrup

2 tablespoons violet flowers
300ml/½ pint boiling water
1 tablespoon brown sugar

Pour the water over the violets, cover and infuse for several hours. Strain, pressing the juice through the sieve. Dissolve the sugar in the liquor and boil for 5 minutes. Take 1 tablespoon before breakfast and between meals. This is suitable for children.

Liquorice and aniseed

25g/1oz liquorice root
4 dried prunes or figs
¼ teaspoon aniseed
1 teaspoon honey

Soak the liquorice root and dried fruit overnight. Simmer gently with the aniseed for 10 minutes, remove the liquorice and sweeten with honey. Eat the fruit for breakfast or last thing at night.

Other laxative herbs

AMERICAN SENNA: infuse the leaves with ginger. Not to be taken regularly.

MARSH MALLOW: flowers, leaves and root all contain valuable mucilage for the intestine. Take an infusion or decoction. Hollyhock or common mallow can also be used.

PELLITORY-OF-THE-WALL: take an infusion of the leaves.

RHUBARB: stew the stems.

SLIPPERY ELM: mix 1 tablespoon of the powdered bark to a paste with water and honey and take a tablespoon before breakfast and at night.

Diarrhoea

Most herbs prescribed for diarrhoea have an astringent action.

Bilberry and allspice

1 tablespoon dried bilberries
1 litre/1¾ pints water
½ teaspoon bruised allspice berries
1 teaspoon fresh lemon juice

Soak the bilberries in the water for several hours or overnight. Add the allspice berries, bring slowly to the boil and simmer gently for 5 minutes. Take off the heat and infuse, covered, for a further 5 minutes. Strain, stir in the lemon juice and take a wineglassful every few hours, either hot or cold.

Spring remedy

2 fresh, young nettle tops
1 tablespoon fresh, chopped blackberry leaves
1 sprig fresh peppermint
1 head of meadowsweet flowers
600ml/1 pint boiling water

Infuse in a covered pot for 10 minutes, strain and take 3 times a day in wineglassful doses.

Other binding herbs

AGRIMONY: infuse the leaves and flowering tops.

BISTORT: take a decoction of root.

MEADOWSWEET: infuse the leaves or flowers.

PLANTAIN: infuse the leaves, or macerate a teaspoon of bruised seeds in a glass of water for an hour, then strain and take a wineglassful at a time.

WOOD AVENS: take an infusion of leaves or decoction of root.

Herbs associated with child bearing

This is an area where magic most often overlaps with herbal medicine. Many of the herbs prescribed for childbirth were considered to have supernatural powers and to be strongly protective, for at the moment of birth both mother and baby were most open to infection and in the terms of the old herbalists that meant open to the devil and wicked spirits.

The herbal teas recommended here are strengthening tonics with some astringent action. Most of the herbs are set under the dominion of Venus in the old herbals, or under the protection of Our Lady. The former generic name for chamomile – *Matricaria*, from *matrix*, 'a womb' – referred to its use for uterine complaints. These herbs can also be used to ease menstrual pains. Tansy and feverfew were the chief herbs for this purpose but are not recommended today. Use them, or southernwood, externally as an infusion in the bath or as a steam treatment.

In North Africa and the Middle East the seeds of fenugreek are commonly taken to stimulate breast milk and are also thought to encourage 'an alluring roundness of the breast' in women generally. In India and some other Eastern countries the spicy seeds of the familiar garden plant love-in-a-mist or fennel flower, *Nigella sativa*, are often used for this purpose, and in northern Europe the milk thistle with its pronounced white veins was thought 'a great breeder of milk and a proper diet for wet nurses'. The perennial goat's rue, popular in the past, is sometimes fed to cows today to increase their milk yield, and borage, watercress and parsley are also said to increase the flow of breast milk.

Sore nipples may occasionally inhibit the flow of milk when the feeding of the baby becomes associated with pain. A soothing compress or ointment may help. If the nipple becomes cracked then seek professional advice.

Strengthening and astringent teas

Herbs to encourage lactation

Compresses and ointments

A tea for pregnancy
1 teaspoon dried lady's mantle
1 teaspoon dried yarrow leaves
1 teaspoon dried raspberry leaves
600ml/1 pint boiling water
Infuse the herbs in the water for at least 10 minutes. Add honey and lemon to taste.

Raspberry has long had a reputation as a herb for fertility and pregnancy.

Motherwort tea
1 teaspoon dried motherwort
1 teaspoon dried ground ivy
1 teaspoon dried lemon balm
600ml/1 pint boiling water
Motherwort, *Leonurus cardiaca*, is a bitter tonic herb formerly much used to speed delivery. Aromatic ground ivy, which is said to act on the uterus, and lemon balm, should improve the very bitter taste of motherwort. Take this tea during the last few weeks of pregnancy.

Other herbs to take during pregnancy
Infusions of chamomile, costmary, rose petals, and a decoction of fenugreek are all good tonics.

Herbs with slightly antiseptic properties and pleasant scents can be infused in the water used for sponging during the early stages of labour. Those most suitable include chamomile, chervil, costmary, lavender and rosemary.

Marsh mallow compress
30g/1oz marsh mallow root
150ml/¼ pint water
15g/½oz chamomile flowers
Steep the root in the water for several hours or overnight. Bring slowly to the boil and simmer for 10 minutes. Put the flowers in a jug, pour the boiling liquid and roots over them, cover and leave to cool until lukewarm. Soak clean lint in the liquid and apply to the breast.

Tisane for a nursing mother
1 teaspoon crushed aniseed
1 teaspoon crushed dill seeds
¼ teaspoon fenugreek seeds
1 teaspoon dried sweet marjoram
600ml/1 pint boiling water
Infuse for 10 minutes, strain and take the standard dose. Honey may be added to cover the bitter taste of fenugreek.

Marigold ointment
2 tablespoons bruised marigold petals
2 tablespoons bruised violet leaves
3 tablespoons lard
Melt the lard over a low heat, add the petals and leaves, cover and bring slowly to simmering point. Remove from the heat but leave covered until quite cold. Warm again until melted then sieve. Pour into a pot, allow to cool and store in the refrigerator. Use on sore nipples as required and wash off before feeding. Bruised violet leaves are also beneficial.

Herbs for the eyes and mouth

Eye herbs

Several herbs with irritant and acrid properties have been used as eye herbs, to clear the eyes and remove filmy coverings and 'slimie things'. The most dangerous and well known of these are greater celandine and rue, which were often made more bearable by tempering them with mothers' milk. They are occasionally recommended even today, but should certainly never be used on such a delicate part of the body. Fennel, eyebright and clary (clear eye) are traditional and safe eye herbs that can be used as soothing lotions and compresses. The lotions can be wiped gently over the closed eyes with a sponge. For compresses soak pieces of clean lint or cotton in the herb juice or infusion and lay them over the eyes for at least 10 minutes while lying down and relaxing. Or make little sachets of eye herbs, like tea bags, soak them in warm water for a few minutes and lay them over the eyes; these can be dried and used several times. All these recipes can be used for soothing, strengthening and cleansing the eyes and for reducing inflammation of the eyelids.

Teeth and gums

Charcoal or the ashes of herbs mixed with salt are the most common ingredients in domestic recipes for toothpowders, the ashes disinfecting and whitening the teeth, the salt strengthening and stimulating the gums. Toast a slice of bread until it is thoroughly charred, then pound it with a pinch of sea salt and a tablespoon of dried peppermint, sage or rosemary leaves or with a few drops of the essential oil of these herbs. Rub this over the teeth and gums and rinse with water or with a herb mouthwash.

Marsh mallow eye lotion

1 teaspoon dried marsh mallow leaves
1 teaspoon dried raspberry leaves
2 fresh or dried witch hazel leaves
300ml/½ pint boiling water
Infuse the leaves in the water and leave covered until cool. Strain and store in the refrigerator. Use as a cold, refreshing eye lotion.

Chickweed eye compress

a handful of fresh chickweed
75ml/⅛ pint milk
Wash the chickweed and shake it dry. Simmer with the milk in a covered pan for 10 minutes. Lift out the herb and crush to a pulp with a pestle or wooden spoon. When it is tepid, lay the pulp over the eyes, lie down and relax for 10 minutes.

Nasturtium seed compress

1 tablespoon crushed nasturtium seed
1 tablespoon grated raw potato
Blend well together and use as an eye compress. This is particularly helpful for styes, the seeds being antiseptic and the potato soothing.

Marigold and apple compress

1 tablespoon marigold petals
75ml/⅛ pint boiling water
1 peeled, chopped apple
Infuse the petals in the water and leave to stand for 10 minutes. Strain, add the apple to the yellow infusion and stew gently until a soft pulp. Allow to cool then use as an eye compress.

Cucumber and clary compress

4 slices of cucumber
1 teaspoon clary seeds or 3 clary leaves
Pound the cucumber to a pulp. Soak the clary seeds in a tablespoon of water until this becomes a thick mucilage or pound the clary leaves to a pulp. Combine the cucumber and clary and use as an eye compress to reduce puffiness around the eyes.

Other herbs for the eyes, used as compresses or lotions

EYEBRIGHT: infuse the whole plant.
FENNEL: infuse the leaves or seeds.
HORSETAIL: use a decoction for swollen eyelids.
LEMON VERBENA: infuse the leaves.
ROSE: infuse the hips or soften the rose petals in cold milk

Infusions of coltsfoot, chervil, borage, chamomile, plantain and elderflower are also beneficial for the eyes.

Eucalyptus mouthwash

15g/½oz eucalyptus leaves
1 litre/1¾ pints water
2 drops oil of cloves
2 drops tincture of myrrh
Bring the leaves and water slowly to the boil, simmer for 5 minutes then leave to cool, covered tightly. Stir in the oil and myrrh and store in the refrigerator.

Myrrh has long had a reputation for strengthening spongy gums and also acts as a preservative.

An infusion of any of the following herbs will make a cleansing and refreshing mouthwash or gargle: aniseed, golden seal, lavender, marigold, marjoram, peppermint, rosemary, sage and thyme.

Herbs for cuts and wounds

First aid herbs

Some of the old treatments for fresh burns and wounds that included the use of thick oils and ointments are not used today as it is thought bacteria may get beneath the ointment and infect the softened skin. Minor cuts and grazes, however, will benefit from a wash with antiseptic herbs and bruised or pulped leaves provide emergency dressings. Gauze dressings soaked with infusions of astringent herbs or diluted antiseptic herbal oils or ointments will soothe and help to clear up cuts that are taking a long time to heal. These should be changed frequently and the wound exposed to the air as soon as possible. If a wound refuses to heal or begins to suppurate then an astringent wash or loose compress of antiseptic herbs should help.

These first recipes are tried and tested domestic remedies with real healing power. They are followed by a list of the most important of the many herbs that have astringent action, 'astringency' meaning the power to draw together or contract the organic tissues.

Herbs for boils

Boils can be soothed and brought quickly to a head by the application of a hot poultice. Antiseptic herbs are used here to discourage the infection from spreading; they will also help to soothe the part. A boil that develops into an abscess should be treated by a doctor.

Mixing a 'cure-all' or 'treacle', a complex potion with many ingredients.

Witch hazel wash

3 tablespoons dried leaves or a handful of fresh leaves
600ml/1 pint water
Simmer for 10 minutes, strain and use as a strongly astringent wash or on a loose compress to soothe abrasions or bruises.

Crushed-houseleek dressing

Wash then pound a handful of the fleshy leaves of houseleek until well pulped. Spread on clean gauze and apply to an infected cut.

Elder-leaf wash

1 large double handful of fresh elder leaves
1 litre/1¾ pints water
Simmer slowly together in a covered pan for about 15 minutes. Leave to cool, still covered. Strain and use to wash infected cuts or grazes, inflammations or boils. This simple remedy is extremely effective.

A strong, healing ointment can be made by simmering elder leaves or unripe berries in lard or linseed oil.

Antiseptic garlic dressing

3 cloves garlic
2 tablespoons water
Pound the garlic to a pulp with pestle and mortar and dilute with the water, or simply liquidize both together. Use on clean gauze as an antiseptic dressing. This dressing, used on sphagnum moss, was applied to the wounds of soldiers during the First World War.

Garlic vinegar also makes a stinging but cleansing wash.

Other wound herbs

These herbs can be used directly as poultices (drop their leaves into boiling water for a second then cool, bruise and apply to the part) or make healing, beneficial washes from infusions or decoctions: agrimony, arnica, betony, bistort, burdock, chamomile, chickweed, coltsfoot, comfrey, golden rod, goosegrass, ground ivy, horsetail, hyssop, lady's mantle, lavender, marigold, marjoram, nasturtium seed, plantain, rosemary, sage, St John's wort, savory, Solomon's seal, thyme, woad, wormwood, yarrow.

Linseed poultice for boils

25g/1oz ground or crushed linseed
1 tablespoon chamomile flowers
75ml/⅛ pint boiling water
Infuse the flowers for a few minutes. Stir in enough linseed to make a paste and apply on a clean cloth.

Other herbs for boils

CHICKWEED: simmer a handful of herb to a pulp in a very little water. Apply hot to the boil.
NASTURTIUM: crush the seeds to a pulp with a little water.
ONION: boil to a pulp.
SLIPPERY ELM: mix powdered bark to a thick paste with warm water and a few drops of eucalyptus oil.
SORREL: cook the leaves to a pulp.

Herbs for aches: massage oils and unguents

Warm compresses and gentle rubs and massage can help ease muscular pains and rheumatic aches. But never massage inflamed or swollen joints or tissues.

Any of these herbs can be simmered in oil or lard for an hour then strained, pressing carefully through the sieve: crushed, fresh leaves of bay, marjoram, rosemary or sage, juniper berries or lavender flowers.

A few drops of oil of thyme or oil of cinnamon added to olive oil can be used as a rub. Synthetic oil of wintergreen is valuable for rheumatic joints (natural wintergreen is too strong). The warmed, pulped leaves can also be used as a soothing poultice.

The leaves and roots of ground elder boiled to a pulp in a little water and applied as a poultice are an old remedy for gout. An infusion of ground elder can be added to the bath water or drunk as a tisane. Tisanes recommended for rheumatism include boneset, dandelion, juniper and stinging nettle.

Herbs for sprains

The painful swelling can be reduced and soothed with cold compresses and supportive bandages. If a sprain occurs on a walk in the country, the leaves of any of the following herbs can be bruised and bound onto the part: agrimony, comfrey, common mallow or marsh mallow, St John's wort, vervain or wintergreen. If the sprain occurs within reach of a stove, it is worth softening the leaves for a moment in a sieve held in the steam over boiling water, then pulping them and applying as a compress. Or soak a piece of lint in the rich, red oil made by macerating the flowering tops of St John's wort in oil and bind on with a bandage to soothe the sprain.

Herbs for insect bites and stings

Be careful to remove the sting of a bee or wasp before using these herbs. To reduce the pain and lessen the swelling, rub on the crushed, fresh leaves of basil, betony, borage, comfrey, dock, lemon balm, marigold, marsh mallow, parsley or any of the mints. Extract of witch hazel or oil of thyme or eucalyptus applied with cotton wool will soothe the part, or use the juice from a freshly sliced onion or leek. Any of these herbs can also be used in a strong infusion as a wash.

Herbs for warts and corns

Warts remain a mystery to the medical profession. They may persist and linger for years or suddenly disappear completely, only to reappear later. The acrid juice from certain herbs will often get rid of warts. Protect the surrounding skin with a piece of card with a hole in the middle, the same size as the wart. Squeeze on a few drops of the yellow juice from the stem of the greater celandine, or the white juice from a dandelion stem, or juice from fresh marigold leaves. Leave this on for as long as is convenient and repeat twice a day.

The horny, dead tissue of a corn is often caused by pressure from badly fitting shoes. Rub with a crushed clove of garlic, a crushed, fresh houseleek leaf, or a slice of lemon or bind these on with a bandage.

Herbs for chilblains

Chilblains usually occur on the fingers and toes when these parts are deprived of blood during the winter. Keep these vulnerable extremities warm and make sure sufficient green vegetables are included in your diet. Drink a daily tisane of rose hips or horsetail. Anoint the itching, swollen chilblains with marigold oil or an ointment made by simmering marigold flowers for 30 minutes in lard or vegetable or nut margarines. Or boil a small onion for 10 minutes, then cut it in half and bind this on as a soothing poultice.

Glossary

Alkaloid: a powerful plant constituent containing nitrogen, which acts on the animal system (e.g. morphine)

Annual: a plant with a life cycle of 1 year

Anther: part of the stamen bearing pollen grains

Antidote: counteracts a poison

Antiscorbutic: remedy for scurvy, a disease caused by lack of Vitamin C

Antiseptic: counteracts infection by destroying or inhibiting the growth of bacteria

Astringent: draws together and contracts organic tissues

Axil: the angle between the stem and leaf stalk of a plant

Biennial: a plant with a life cycle of 2 years, blossoming and fruiting during the second year

Bract: a modified leaf growing at the base of a flower

Bulb: a swollen underground storage organ, made up of fleshy leaves

Bulbil or **bulblet:** a small, bulb-like organ

Calyx: grouped sepals, the outer parts of a flower

Carminative: relieves flatulence by helping to dispel wind

Chlorophyll: green colouring matter in a plant

Composite: member of the daisy family, the *Compositae*

Cordial: a food or drink that comforts, invigorates and cheers

Corm: bulb-like underground stem

Corolla: the petals as a whole

Crucifer: a member of the cabbage family, the *Cruciferae*

Deciduous: shedding leaves annually

Decoction: boiling or simmering the tougher parts of a herb in liquid to extract the active principles of the herb

Demulcent: soothing, relieves irritation

Deodorant: removes or lessens smells

Distillation: separating the volatile from the fixed part of a substance by a process of evaporation and condensation

Diuretic: stimulates the flow of urine

Emetic: causes vomiting

Emollient: softening and relaxing

Evergreen: retaining leaves all year round

Expectorant: helps clear phlegm from the bronchial tubes

Febrifuge: helps reduce fever

Flatulence: a condition caused by gas accumulating in the stomach or bowels

Fruit: seeds and surrounding structure

Habitat: the area where a plant grows naturally

Indigenous: native to an area

Infusion: steeping a herb in water to extract its active principles

Introduced: not native to an area, brought in by man

Labiate: a member of the thyme family, the *Labiatae*

Lanceolate: leaves that are long, narrow, tapering, spear-shaped

Laxative: relaxes and loosens the bowels

Lobed: leaves that are divided but not into separate leaflets

Mucilage: a viscous, gelatinous substance obtained from certain herbs

Narcotic: a substance that, according to dosage, soothes pain or induces stupefaction and death

Nervine: a remedy for nervous disorders

Palmate: a leaf that has more than 3 leaflets radiating from 1 point (like fingers from the palm of a hand)

Panicle: grouped flowers

Perennial: a plant that lives for longer than 2 years

Petiole: leaf stalk

Pinnate: a leaf divided into at least 4 leaflets arranged in 2 rows along a stalk

Principle: active chemical constituent of a plant

Purgative: a powerful laxative given to evacuate the bowels

Rhizome: creeping, usually swollen, underground stem

Runners: horizontal stems that run above ground, rooting at intervals

Sedative: soothing medicine that calms the nerves

Sepals: the outer flower parts that together form the calyx

Stamen: male reproductive organ in a plant

Stigma: the part of the style that receives pollen during fertilization

Stomachic: strengthens and tones the stomach

Style: extension of the ovary in a plant

Tisane: an infusion or tea prepared with 1 or more herbs or spices

Trifoliate: leaf that has 3 leaflets

Tuber: swollen portion of an underground root or stem

Toxic: a poisonous substance

Umbel: a flowerhead with stalks that radiate from 1 point

Umbellifer: a member of the parsley family, the *Umbelliferae*

Vermifuge: helps destroy and expel intestinal worms

Vulnerary: heals wounds

278

Bibliography

The quotation on page 8 was taken from *The Englishman's Flora* by Geoffrey Grigson, 1952

Herbals, flora and medicinal

Arber, Agnes *Herbals, Their Origin and Evolution: A Chapter in the History of Botany, 1470–1670* Cambridge University Press, London 1953; Hafner Press, New York 1970

Banckes, Richard *Herball* ed. by Larkey and Piles. Scholars' Facsimiles, New York 1941

Brownlow, Margaret E *Herbs and the Fragrant Garden* Darton, Longman and Todd, London 1978

Clarkson, Rosetta E *The Golden Age of Herbs and Herbalists* Constable, London 1973; Dover Publications, New York 1972

Copeman, W S C *Doctors and Disease in Tudor Times* Dawson's of Pall Mall, London 1960

Culpeper's Complete Herbal Foulsham, London 1952; Sterling, New York 1959

de Bairacli Levy, Juliette *The Illustrated Herbal Handbook* Faber, London 1960. *Common Herbs for Natural Health* Schocken Books, New York 1974

Fitter, R and Fitter, A *The Wild Flowers of Britain and Northern Europe* Collins, London 1974; Scribner, New York 1974

Grieve, Mrs M *A Modern Herbal* ed. Mrs C F Leyel. Penguin, London 1976; Dover Publications, New York 1971

Grigson, Geoffrey *The Englishman's Flora* Hart-Davis, MacGibbon, London 1975

Grigson, Geoffrey *A Herbal of All Sorts* Phoenix House, London 1959

Hall, Dorothy *The Book of Herbs* Angus and Robertson, London 1972; Scribner, New York 1974

Harrison, S G, Masefield, G B and Wallis, Michael *Oxford Book of Food Plants* Oxford University Press, London and New York 1973

Hatfield, Audrey Wynne *A Herb for Every Ill* Dent, London 1973; St Martin, New York 1974

Hatfield, Audrey Wynne *Pleasures of Herbs* Thorsons, London 1964; St Martin, New York 1964

Law, Donald *The Concise Herbal Encyclopedia* Bartholomew, Edinburgh 1976; St Martin, New York 1974

Leaves from Gerard's Herball ed. M Woodward, Minerva Press, London 1971; Dover Publications, New York 1969

Leyel, Mrs C F *Compassionate Herbs* Faber, London 1946

Leyel Mrs C F *Green Medicine* Faber, London 1952

Leyel, Mrs C F *Herbal Delights* Faber, London 1937

Loewenfield, C and Back, P *The Complete Book of Herbs and Spices* David and Charles, London 1974

Loewenfield, C and Back, P *Herbs for Health and Cookery* Pan Books, London 1977

Lust, John *The Herb Book* Bantam, New York 1974

Macleod, Dawn *A Book of Herbs* Duckworth, London 1968. *Herb Handbook* Wilshire, North Hollywood, CA

Northcote, Lady Rosalind *The Book of Herbs* Bodley Head, London 1912. *Book of Herb Lore* Dover Publications, New York 1971

Palaiseul, Jean *Grandmother's Secrets* Penguin, London 1973; Putnam, New York 1974

The Penguin Medical Encyclopedia ed. Peter Wingate. Penguin, London and New York 1972

Potter's New Cyclopaedia of Botanical Drugs and Preparations ed. R C Wren, F L S. Potter and Clarke Ltd, Health Science Press, Devon 1975; Harper and Row, New York 1972

The Rodale Herb Book ed. William H Hylton. Rodale Press, St Emmaus, PA 1976

Rohde, E Sinclair *The Old World Pleasaunce* Herbert Jenkins, London 1925

Rohde, E Sinclair *The Scented Garden* Gale, Detroit, MI 1972

Sitwell, Edith *A Book of Flowers* Macmillan, London 1952

Thompson, William A R *Herbs that Heal* A and C Black, London 1976

The Wisdom of Andrew Boorde ed. H Edmund Poole. Edgar Backus, Leicester 1936

Gardening

Hatfield, Audrey Wynne *How to Enjoy Your Weeds* Frederick Muller, London 1977; Macmillan, New York 1973

Howes, E N *Plants and Beekeeping* Faber, London 1946

Hyams, Edward *A History of Gardens and Gardening* Dent, London 1971

Leighton, Ann *Early English Gardens in New England* Cassell, London 1970. *Early American Gardens: For "Meate and Medicine"* Houghton Mifflin, Boston and New York 1970

Loewenfeld, Claire *Herb Gardening* Faber, London 1973

Philbrick, H and Gregg, R B *Companion Plants* Watkins, London 1976

Cookery

Acton, Eliza *Modern Cookery for Private Families* Longmans Green, London 1863

Ayrton, E *The Cookery of England* Penguin, London 1977

Boulestin, Marcel X *What Shall We Have Today?* Heinemann, London 1931. *Boulestin's Round-the-Year Cookbook* Dover Publications, New York 1975

Brissenden, Rosemary *South East Asian Food* Penguin, London and New York 1978

Costa, M *Four Seasons Cookery Book* Sphere, London 1972

David, Elizabeth *Spices, Salt and Aromatics* Penguin, London 1973

David, Elizabeth *Summer Cooking* Penguin, London 1965

Farmhouse Fare. The Farmers Weekly Countryside Books, Studio Vista, London 1966

Glasse, Hannah *The Art of Cookery Made Plain and Easy* Wangford 1774; Shoe String Press, Hamden, CT 1971

Grigson, J *Good Things* Penguin, London 1971

Hartley, Dorothy *Food in England* Macdonald, London 1975

Haynes, Oriana *Cooking and Curing* Duckworth, London 1937

Irwin, F *The Cookin' Woman* Oliver and Boyd, Edinburgh 1949

Roberts and Porter *Cups and their Customs* John Van Voorsh, 1864

Roden, C *A Book of Middle Eastern Food* Penguin, London 1968; Knopf, New York 1972

Singh, Dharamjit *Indian Cookery* Penguin, London and New York 1972

Smith, E *The Compleat Housewife* Literary Services, Farncombe, Surrey 1974

Stobart, Tom *Herbs, Spices and Flavourings* Penguin, London 1977

Tannahill, Reay *The Fine Art of Food* Folio Society, London 1968

Wilson, Anne *Food and Drink in Britain* Penguin, London 1973; Barnes and Noble, New York 1974

Household and cosmetic

Buchman, Dian Dincin *An ABC of Natural Beauty* Duckworth, London 1976. *Complete Herbal Guide to Natural Health and Beauty* Doubleday, New York 1973

Buchman, Dian Dincin *Feed Your Face* Duckworth, London 1973

Genders, Roy *A Book of Aromatics* Darton, Longman and Todd, London 1977

Genders, Roy *A History of Scent* Hamish Hamilton, London 1972. *Perfume Through the Ages* Putnam, New York 1972

Hériteau, Jacqueline *Potpourris and Other Fragrant Delights* Penguin, London 1978

Huxley, Alyson *Natural Beauty with Herbs* Darton, Longman and Todd, London 1977

Plat, Sir Hugh *Delightes for Ladies* Crosby Lockwood, London 1948

Sanderson, Liz *Herbal Cosmetics* Latimer New Dimensions Ltd, London 1977

Thomas, Virginia Castleton *Secrets of Natural Beauty* Harrap, London 1973. *My Secrets of Natural Beauty* Keats, New Canaan, CT 1972

Dyeing

Adrosko, Rita J *Natural Dyes and Home Dyeing* Constable, London 1971; Dover Publications, New York 1971

Dye Plants and Dyeing Brooklyn Botanic Garden Record, *Plants and Gardens* Vol. 20, No. 3. New York 1964

Mairet, Ethel *Vegetable Dyes* Faber, London 1952

Robertson, Seonaid *Dyes from Plants* Van Nostrand Reinhold, New York 1973

Index

M

Acknowledgments

The publishers would like to thank the following for their assistance with the photography.

Colman's Mustard, Carrow, King's Street, Norwich, Norfolk, NR1 2BB (163)
Susan Collier for the use of her kitchen (175, 201)
The National Institute of Medical Herbalists Ltd, 50 Sandygate Road, Crosspool, Sheffield, S10 5RY (248–9)
Diane Radford, 4 Watling Street, St Albans, Hertfordshire, for the scent bottles she designed (252)
Molton Brown, 58 South Molton Street, London W1Y 1HH, for their natural herbal hair care products and for the use of their salon (259)
For kitchen props:
Divertimenti, 68 Marylebone Road, London W1 (161, 183)
21 Antiques, 21 Chalk Farm Road, London NW3 (173, 183, 201, 205, 212–13)
Browns for Living, 26 South Molton Street, London W1Y 1HH (178)

Elizabeth David Shop, 46 Bourne Street, London SW1 (183)
Chattels, 53 Chalk Farm Road, London NW3 (183)
Sally Lawford's Country Kitchen, 231 Royal College Street, London NW1 (191)
Strangeways Limited, 502 King's Road, London SW10 (198)
Orchard Antiques, 52 Porchester Road, London W2 (201)
Heal's, 196 Tottenham Court Road, London W1 (215)

Photographs
(l) left (r) (right (t) top (b) bottom (c) centre
Ardea LONDON/Avon and Tilford: 131(l) 134(r)
K A and G Beckett: 135(b)
Bodleian Library, MS Bodley 130, f26: 12(t)
Michael Boys/Susan Griggs Agency: 138(b) 144–5
Pat Brindley: 138(t)
Reproduced by permission of the British Library: 12(b) 15(b) 124(t) 264
Jane Burton/Bruce Coleman Ltd:

132(c)
Eric Crichton: 130(r) 131(c) 132(r)
E Duscher/Bruce Coleman Ltd: 152
Fotomas Index: 10 16(t)
Rolph Gobits: 248–50 252 255 257 259
Christine Hanscomb: 161–2 167 172–3 175 178 181 183 187 191 195 198 201 205 209 211 212–13 215 219
Robert Harding Associates: 18 19(b) 20(tl and c)
The Iris Hardwick Library of Photographs: 124(b) 125(b) 128(t)
Alan Hutchinson Library: 21(tr)
Lucinda Lambton: 125(tl)
The Mansell Collection Ltd: 17(br)
Tania Midgley: 122 125(tr) 128(b) 136
Bildarchiv der Österreichischen Nationalbibliothek: 11 265 267–8 270 276
A P Paterson: 140
Edward Piper: 135(t) 137 146 151
S Prato/Bruce Coleman Ltd: 132(bl)
Alan Randall: 223 226–7 231–2 234–5 238–9 240

Hans Reinhard/Bruce Coleman Ltd: 147
Spectrum Colour Library: 19(t) 20(tr and b) 21(tl) 134(l)
Pamla Toler: 9 23 121 155 159 221 242 245 263
Tessa Traeger: 125(c) 133(r) 156
Victoria and Albert Museum, photos Derrick Witty: 14 15(t) 16(b) 17(l)
Michael Warren AIIP: 129 130(l) 131(r) 132(tl) 133(l) 139 141
Jeremy Whitaker: 123
Zefa: 21(tl)

Artwork
Liz Butler: 24–5 30–2 34–5 38–9 42–3 46–7 50–1 54–5 58–9 62–3 66–7 70–1 74–5 79 82–3 86–7 90–1 94–5 98–9 102–3 106–7 109–11 116–19
Eugene Fleury: 13 20–1
Deborah King: 26–9 33 36–7 40–1 44–5 48–9 52–3 56–7 60–1 64–5 68–9 72–3 76–7 80–1 84–5 88–9 92–3 96–7 100–1 104–5 112–15
Coral Mula: 161 200 204 209 211 214 218 225 229 233 236 237 247 253
Anne Savage: 127 143 148–50